The Best Of
Alex
2016

Charles Peattie & Russell Taylor

Masterley Publishing

The Best Of
Alex
2016

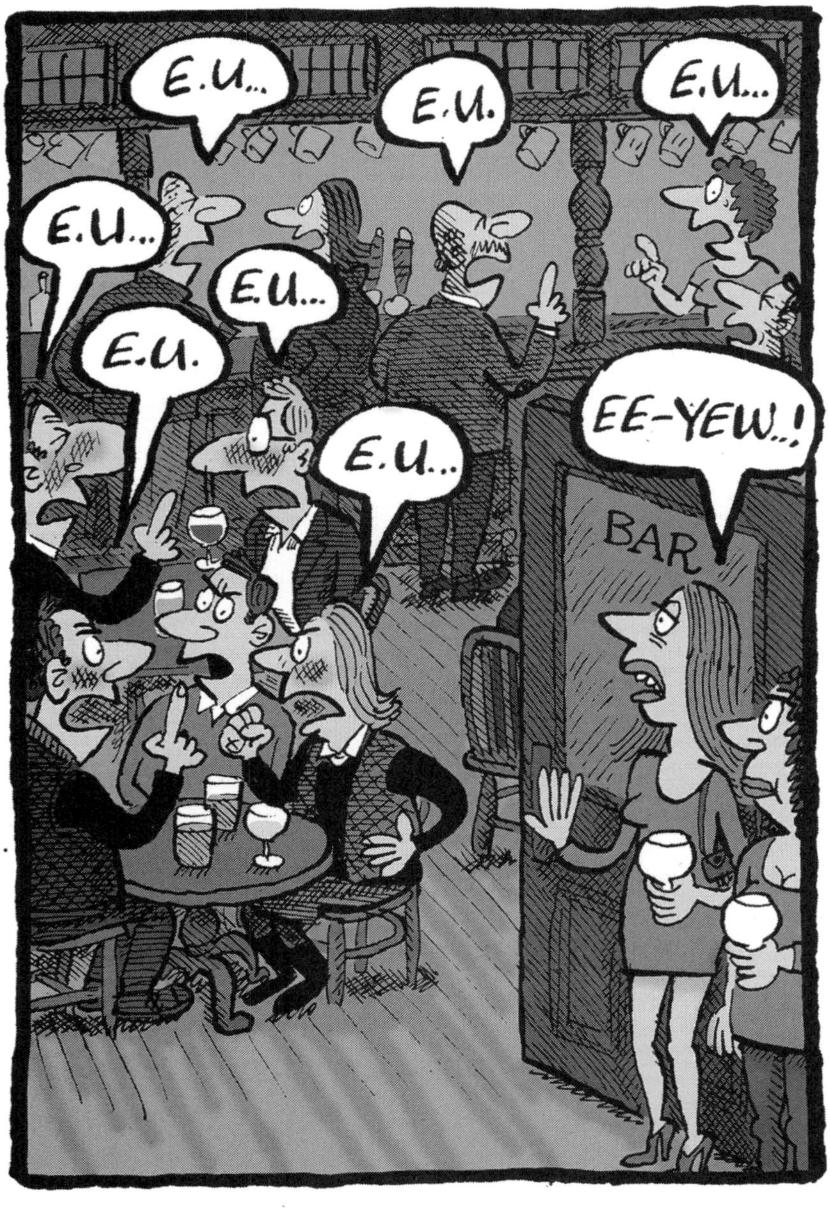
E.U...
E.U.
E.U...
E.U...
E.U...
E.U.
E.U...
EE-YEW..!
BAR

First Published in 2016 by MASTERLEY PUBLISHING

Layout and Design: Suzette Field

Colouring and Artworking: Sofie Dodgson and Miki Lowe

ISBN: 978-1853759666
Printed in the UK by CPI William Clowes Beccles NR34 7TL

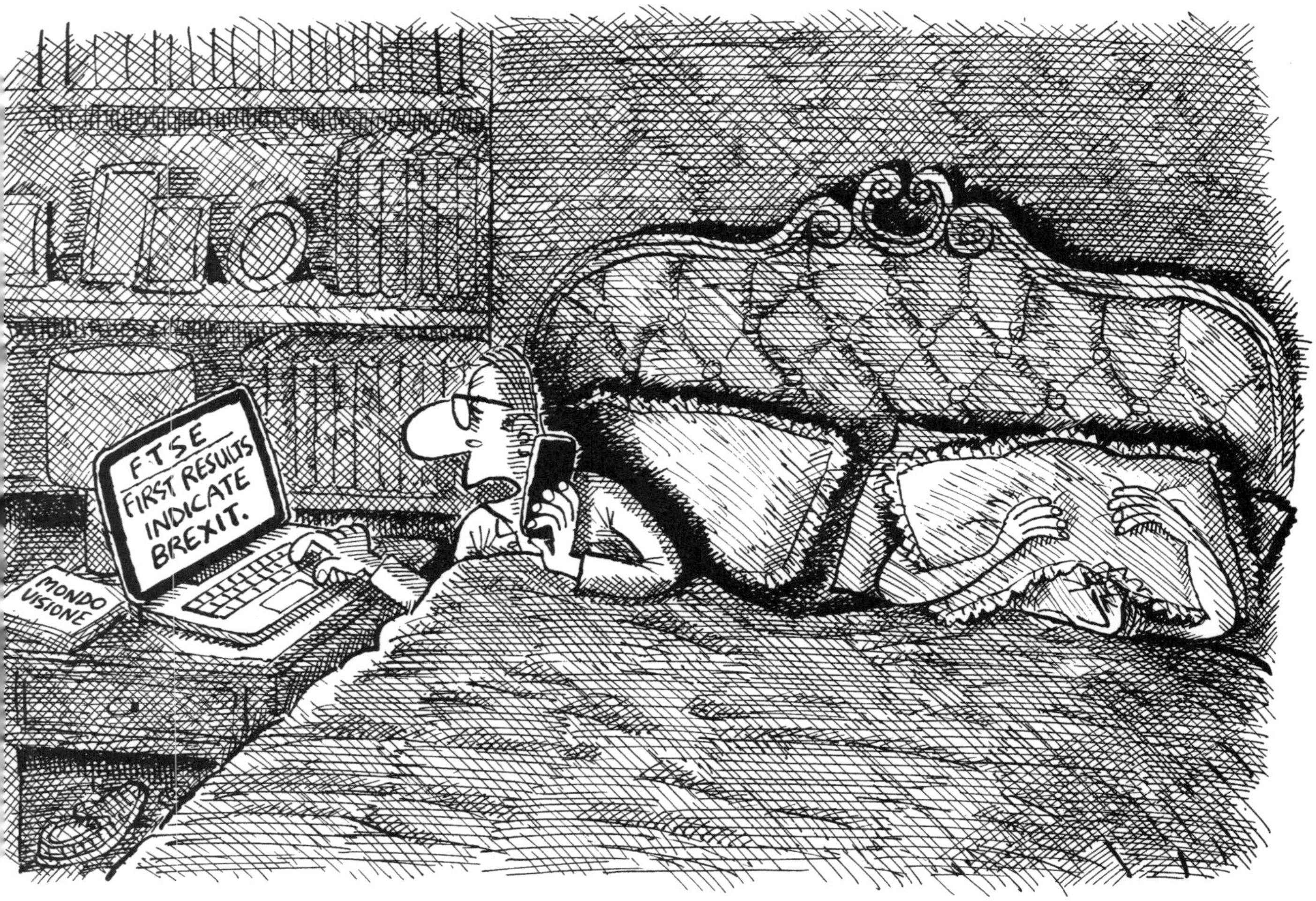
FTSE
FIRST RESULTS INDICATE BREXIT.
MONDO VISIONE

Our usual gratitude goes to our generous sponsors.

FTSE Russell is a leading global provider of benchmarks, analytics and data solutions for investors worldwide.

Mondo Visione is the leading source of insight and knowledge about the world's exchanges and trading venues. As a conference and event organiser it helps to shape the development of markets.

FOREWORD

The day of a General Election or Referendum is a nightmare for cartoonists. We have to think up and draw out a joke on polling day itself (when no one knows what result will be) which will appear in the next day's paper (by which time everyone will know what it was). There is no way we can shirk the subject and we have to deliver a gag that is apposite, pithy and works whatever the outcome of the vote, without actually specifying who won. This is why the cartoon you will see in a newspaper on the Friday following a General Election will usually feature a man crawling out of a dog kennel or some such hiding place, saying something along the lines of "is it all over yet?". We may find ourselves kicked out of the cartoonists' equivalent of the Magic Circle for revealing that trade secret.

Back in 1987 when, like Alex, we were full of youthful brashness we took a gamble on the General Election result. We sent in a cartoon to the newspaper about bankers celebrating a Thatcher victory (Chanting "Ere we go! Ere we go! Ere we go!" in reference to the miners' strike). Luckily we called it right or our careers could have been over that day. On Brexit Referendum Day we were a little more wily and hedged our bets, but all the same a vote for Britain to quit the EU seemed so unlikely that we thought up a batch of cartoons for the next week about it having all turned out to be a damp squib. Awakening to the shock result on June 24th we had to bin every single one of those jokes.

Alex was a "reluctant Remainer" in the Brexit vote. Like many others in the City of London he faced a head v heart dilemma. His disdain for Eurotrash bankers is no secret, but he was fearful about the business chaos that Brexit would unleash and the damage it could do to his bonus prospects.

Conversely, business chaos is usually good for us financial cartoonists. It gives us loads of fresh material and we've now replaced that week's worth of lost jokes several times over.

Yes, sometimes we do feel uncomfortable about being so self-centred and short-termist.

We can only hope our banking fraternity readers will respect us for it.

Charles Peattie Russell Taylor

Charles Peattie and Russell Taylor

Alex - investment banker

Penny - Alex's wife

Christopher - their son

Clive - Alex's colleague

Bridget - Clive's wife

Rupert - senior banker

Cyrus - Alex's boss

Vince - trader

Leo - graduate trainee

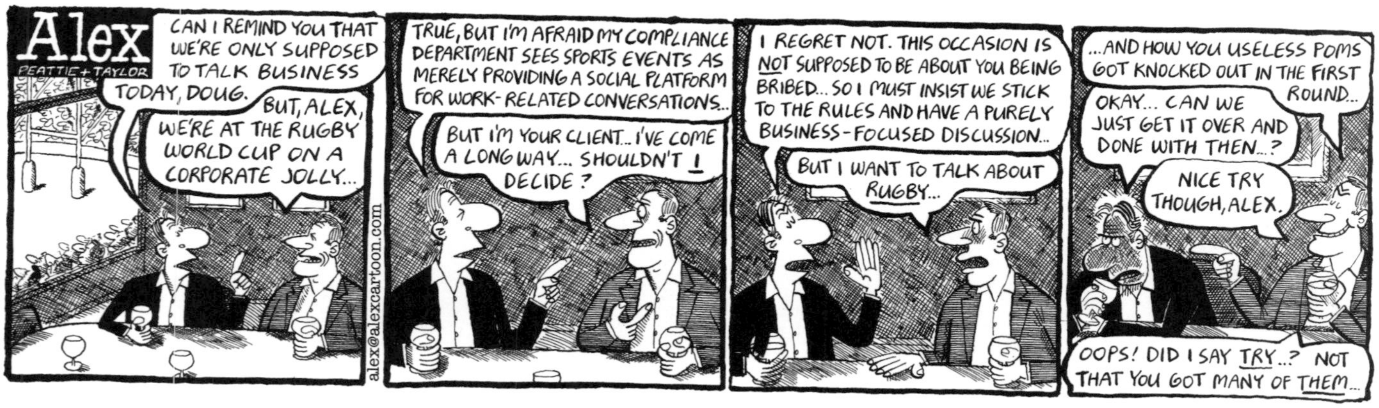
Alex
PEATTIE + TAYLOR
CAN I REMIND YOU THAT WE'RE ONLY SUPPOSED TO TALK BUSINESS TODAY, DOUG.
BUT, ALEX, WE'RE AT THE RUGBY WORLD CUP ON A CORPORATE JOLLY...
TRUE, BUT I'M AFRAID MY COMPLIANCE DEPARTMENT SEES SPORTS EVENTS AS MERELY PROVIDING A SOCIAL PLATFORM FOR WORK-RELATED CONVERSATIONS...
BUT I'M YOUR CLIENT... I'VE COME A LONG WAY... SHOULDN'T I DECIDE ?
alex@alexcartoon.com
I REGRET NOT. THIS OCCASION IS NOT SUPPOSED TO BE ABOUT YOU BEING BRIBED... SO I MUST INSIST WE STICK TO THE RULES AND HAVE A PURELY BUSINESS-FOCUSED DISCUSSION...
BUT I WANT TO TALK ABOUT RUGBY...
...AND HOW YOU USELESS POMS GOT KNOCKED OUT IN THE FIRST ROUND...
OKAY... CAN WE JUST GET IT OVER AND DONE WITH THEN...?
NICE TRY THOUGH, ALEX.
OOPS! DID I SAY TRY..? NOT THAT YOU GOT MANY OF THEM...

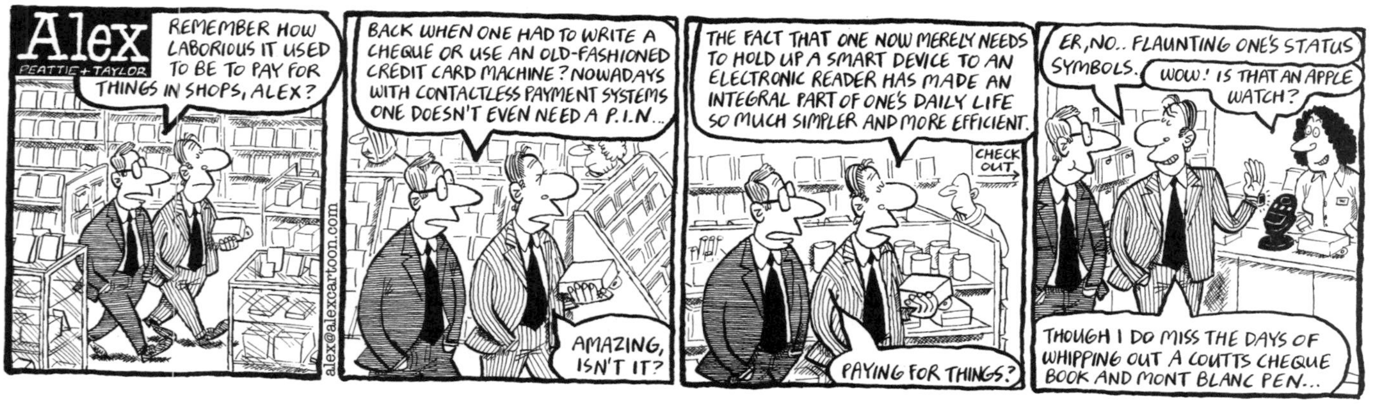
Alex
PEATTIE + TAYLOR
REMEMBER HOW LABORIOUS IT USED TO BE TO PAY FOR THINGS IN SHOPS, ALEX?
BACK WHEN ONE HAD TO WRITE A CHEQUE OR USE AN OLD-FASHIONED CREDIT CARD MACHINE? NOWADAYS WITH CONTACTLESS PAYMENT SYSTEMS ONE DOESN'T EVEN NEED A P.I.N...
AMAZING, ISN'T IT?
alex@alexcartoon.com
THE FACT THAT ONE NOW MERELY NEEDS TO HOLD UP A SMART DEVICE TO AN ELECTRONIC READER HAS MADE AN INTEGRAL PART OF ONE'S DAILY LIFE SO MUCH SIMPLER AND MORE EFFICIENT.
CHECK OUT
PAYING FOR THINGS?
ER, NO.. FLAUNTING ONE'S STATUS SYMBOLS.
WOW! IS THAT AN APPLE WATCH?
THOUGH I DO MISS THE DAYS OF WHIPPING OUT A COUTTS CHEQUE BOOK AND MONT BLANC PEN...

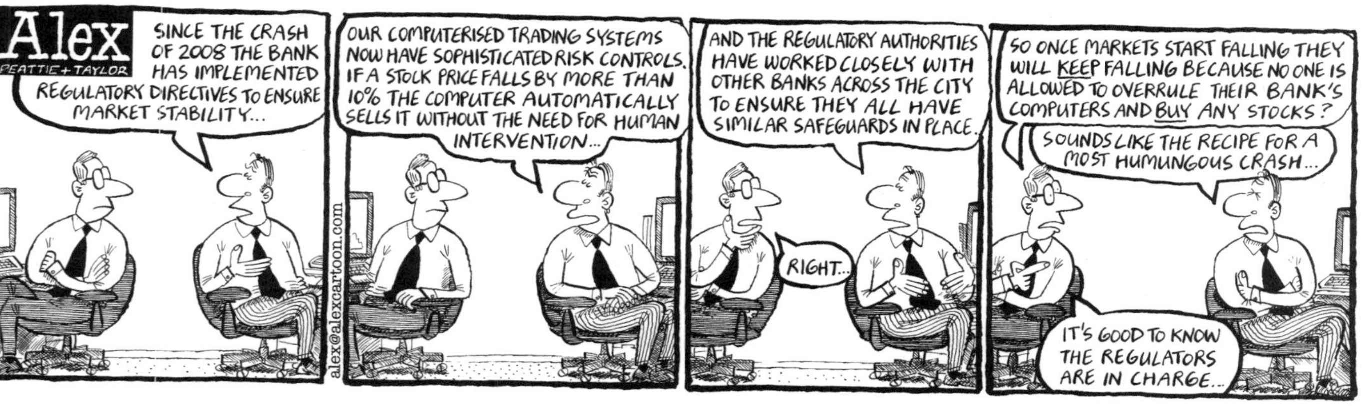
Alex
PEATTIE + TAYLOR
SINCE THE CRASH OF 2008 THE BANK HAS IMPLEMENTED REGULATORY DIRECTIVES TO ENSURE MARKET STABILITY...
OUR COMPUTERISED TRADING SYSTEMS NOW HAVE SOPHISTICATED RISK CONTROLS. IF A STOCK PRICE FALLS BY MORE THAN 10% THE COMPUTER AUTOMATICALLY SELLS IT WITHOUT THE NEED FOR HUMAN INTERVENTION...
alex@alexcartoon.com
AND THE REGULATORY AUTHORITIES HAVE WORKED CLOSELY WITH OTHER BANKS ACROSS THE CITY TO ENSURE THEY ALL HAVE SIMILAR SAFEGUARDS IN PLACE.
RIGHT...
SO ONCE MARKETS START FALLING THEY WILL KEEP FALLING BECAUSE NO ONE IS ALLOWED TO OVERRULE THEIR BANK'S COMPUTERS AND BUY ANY STOCKS?
SOUNDS LIKE THE RECIPE FOR A MOST HUMUNGOUS CRASH...
IT'S GOOD TO KNOW THE REGULATORS ARE IN CHARGE...

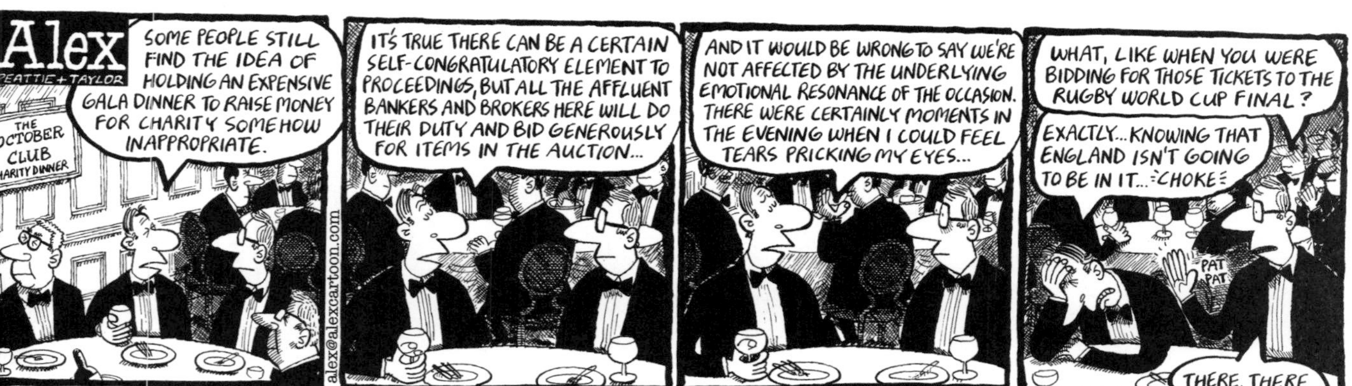
Alex
PEATTIE + TAYLOR
SOME PEOPLE STILL FIND THE IDEA OF HOLDING AN EXPENSIVE GALA DINNER TO RAISE MONEY FOR CHARITY SOMEHOW INAPPROPRIATE.
THE OCTOBER CLUB CHARITY DINNER
IT'S TRUE THERE CAN BE A CERTAIN SELF-CONGRATULATORY ELEMENT TO PROCEEDINGS, BUT ALL THE AFFLUENT BANKERS AND BROKERS HERE WILL DO THEIR DUTY AND BID GENEROUSLY FOR ITEMS IN THE AUCTION...
alex@alexcartoon.com
AND IT WOULD BE WRONG TO SAY WE'RE NOT AFFECTED BY THE UNDERLYING EMOTIONAL RESONANCE OF THE OCCASION. THERE WERE CERTAINLY MOMENTS IN THE EVENING WHEN I COULD FEEL TEARS PRICKING MY EYES...
WHAT, LIKE WHEN YOU WERE BIDDING FOR THOSE TICKETS TO THE RUGBY WORLD CUP FINAL?
EXACTLY... KNOWING THAT ENGLAND ISN'T GOING TO BE IN IT... CHOKE
PAT PAT
THERE, THERE...

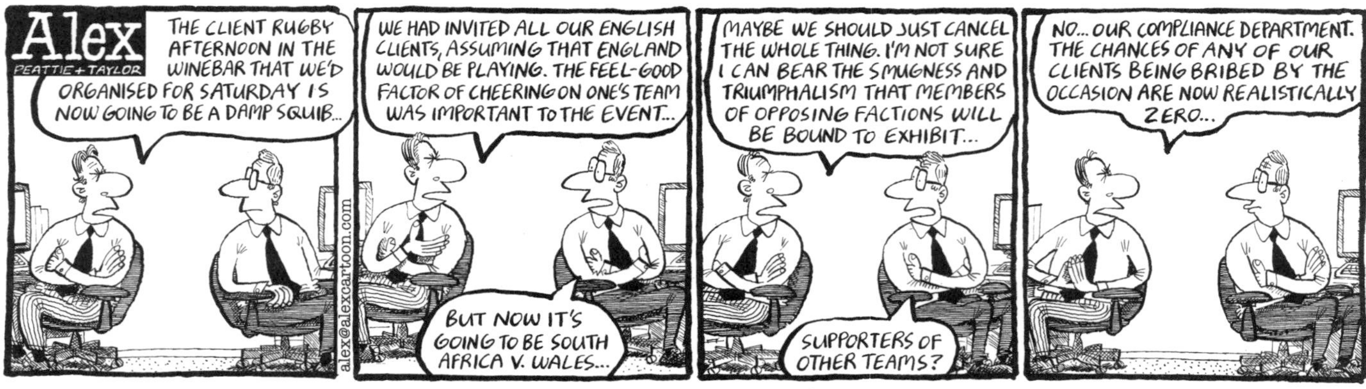
Alex
PEATTIE+TAYLOR
THE CLIENT RUGBY AFTERNOON IN THE WINEBAR THAT WE'D ORGANISED FOR SATURDAY IS NOW GOING TO BE A DAMP SQUIB...
WE HAD INVITED ALL OUR ENGLISH CLIENTS, ASSUMING THAT ENGLAND WOULD BE PLAYING. THE FEEL-GOOD FACTOR OF CHEERING ON ONE'S TEAM WAS IMPORTANT TO THE EVENT...
BUT NOW IT'S GOING TO BE SOUTH AFRICA V. WALES...
alex@alexcartoon.com
MAYBE WE SHOULD JUST CANCEL THE WHOLE THING. I'M NOT SURE I CAN BEAR THE SMUGNESS AND TRIUMPHALISM THAT MEMBERS OF OPPOSING FACTIONS WILL BE BOUND TO EXHIBIT...
SUPPORTERS OF OTHER TEAMS?
NO... OUR COMPLIANCE DEPARTMENT. THE CHANCES OF ANY OF OUR CLIENTS BEING BRIBED BY THE OCCASION ARE NOW REALISTICALLY ZERO...

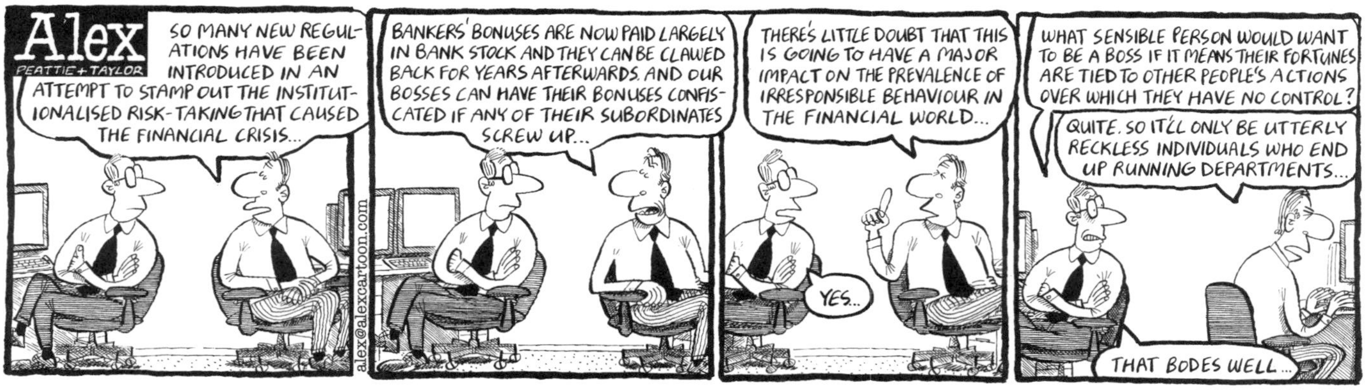
Alex
PEATTIE+TAYLOR
SO MANY NEW REGULATIONS HAVE BEEN INTRODUCED IN AN ATTEMPT TO STAMP OUT THE INSTITUTIONALISED RISK-TAKING THAT CAUSED THE FINANCIAL CRISIS...
BANKERS' BONUSES ARE NOW PAID LARGELY IN BANK STOCK AND THEY CAN BE CLAWED BACK FOR YEARS AFTERWARDS. AND OUR BOSSES CAN HAVE THEIR BONUSES CONFISCATED IF ANY OF THEIR SUBORDINATES SCREW UP...
alex@alexcartoon.com
THERE'S LITTLE DOUBT THAT THIS IS GOING TO HAVE A MAJOR IMPACT ON THE PREVALENCE OF IRRESPONSIBLE BEHAVIOUR IN THE FINANCIAL WORLD...
YES...
WHAT SENSIBLE PERSON WOULD WANT TO BE A BOSS IF IT MEANS THEIR FORTUNES ARE TIED TO OTHER PEOPLE'S ACTIONS OVER WHICH THEY HAVE NO CONTROL?
QUITE. SO IT'LL ONLY BE UTTERLY RECKLESS INDIVIDUALS WHO END UP RUNNING DEPARTMENTS...
THAT BODES WELL...

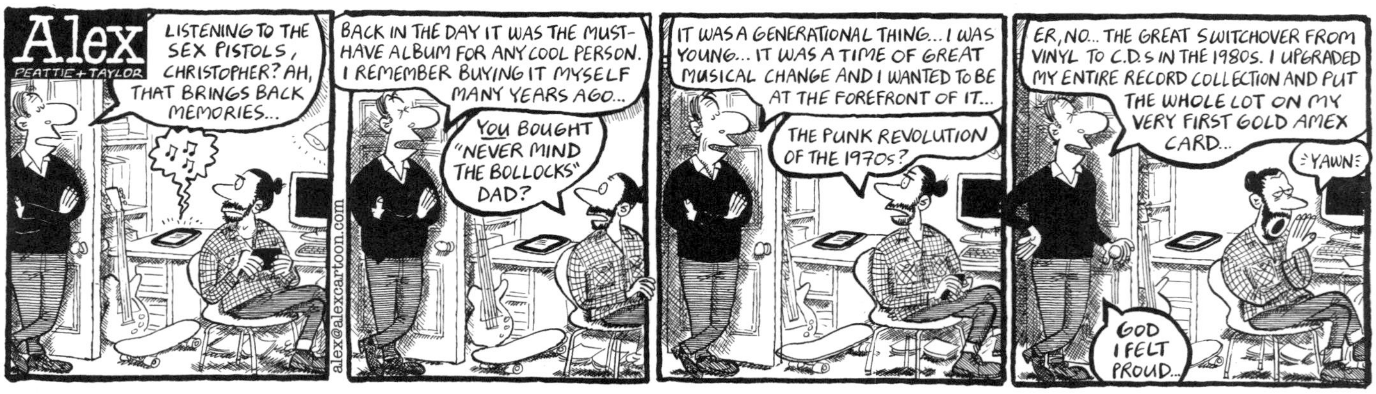
Alex
PEATTIE+TAYLOR
LISTENING TO THE SEX PISTOLS, CHRISTOPHER? AH, THAT BRINGS BACK MEMORIES...
BACK IN THE DAY IT WAS THE MUST-HAVE ALBUM FOR ANY COOL PERSON. I REMEMBER BUYING IT MYSELF MANY YEARS AGO...
YOU BOUGHT "NEVER MIND THE BOLLOCKS" DAD?
alex@alexcartoon.com
IT WAS A GENERATIONAL THING... I WAS YOUNG... IT WAS A TIME OF GREAT MUSICAL CHANGE AND I WANTED TO BE AT THE FOREFRONT OF IT...
THE PUNK REVOLUTION OF THE 1970s?
ER, NO... THE GREAT SWITCHOVER FROM VINYL TO C.D.s IN THE 1980s. I UPGRADED MY ENTIRE RECORD COLLECTION AND PUT THE WHOLE LOT ON MY VERY FIRST GOLD AMEX CARD...
YAWN
GOD I FELT PROUD...

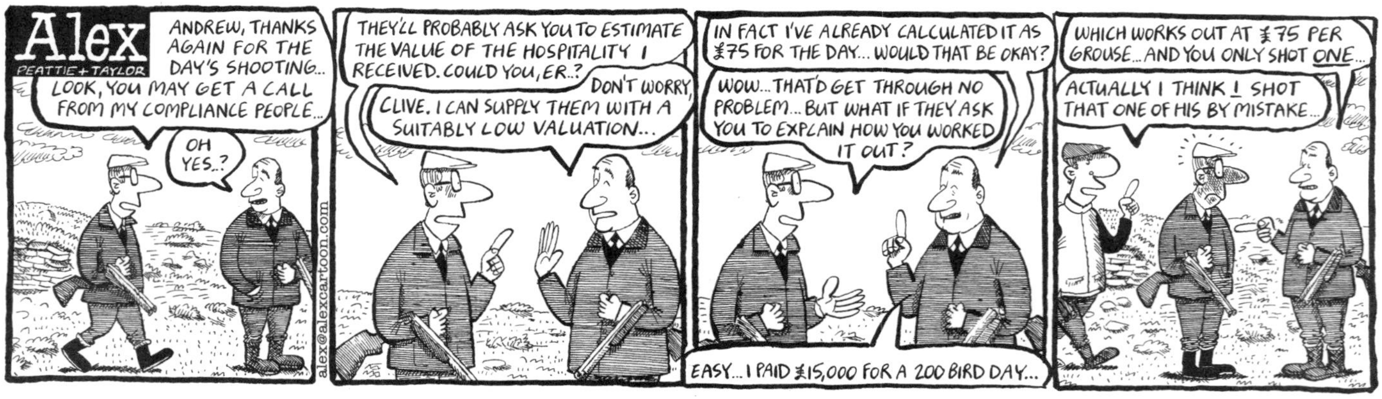
Alex
PEATTIE+TAYLOR
ANDREW, THANKS AGAIN FOR THE DAY'S SHOOTING... LOOK, YOU MAY GET A CALL FROM MY COMPLIANCE PEOPLE...
OH YES..?
alex@alexcartoon.com
THEY'LL PROBABLY ASK YOU TO ESTIMATE THE VALUE OF THE HOSPITALITY I RECEIVED. COULD YOU, ER..?
DON'T WORRY, CLIVE. I CAN SUPPLY THEM WITH A SUITABLY LOW VALUATION...
IN FACT I'VE ALREADY CALCULATED IT AS £75 FOR THE DAY... WOULD THAT BE OKAY?
WOW... THAT'D GET THROUGH NO PROBLEM... BUT WHAT IF THEY ASK YOU TO EXPLAIN HOW YOU WORKED IT OUT?
EASY... I PAID £15,000 FOR A 200 BIRD DAY...
WHICH WORKS OUT AT £75 PER GROUSE... AND YOU ONLY SHOT ONE...
ACTUALLY I THINK I SHOT THAT ONE OF HIS BY MISTAKE...

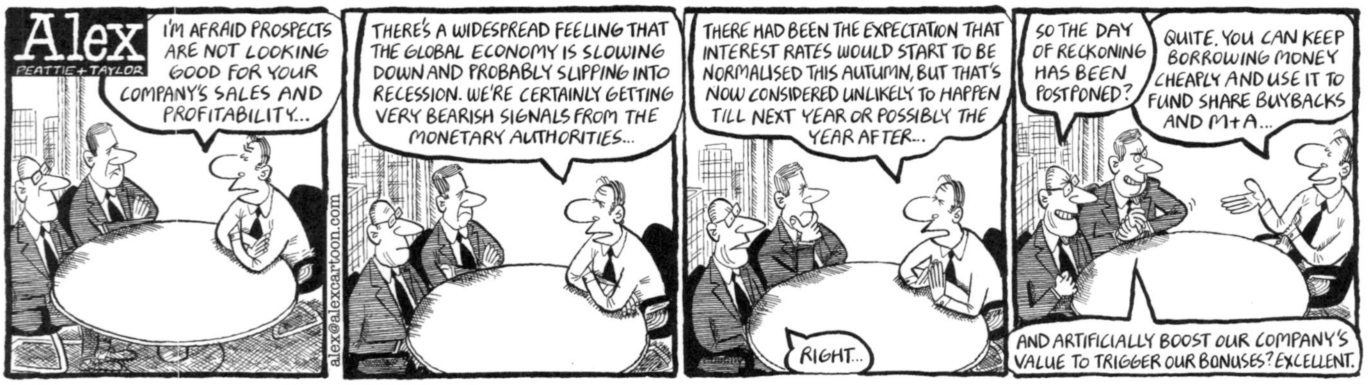
Alex
PEATTIE + TAYLOR
I'M AFRAID PROSPECTS ARE NOT LOOKING GOOD FOR YOUR COMPANY'S SALES AND PROFITABILITY...
alex@alexcartoon.com
THERE'S A WIDESPREAD FEELING THAT THE GLOBAL ECONOMY IS SLOWING DOWN AND PROBABLY SLIPPING INTO RECESSION. WE'RE CERTAINLY GETTING VERY BEARISH SIGNALS FROM THE MONETARY AUTHORITIES...
THERE HAD BEEN THE EXPECTATION THAT INTEREST RATES WOULD START TO BE NORMALISED THIS AUTUMN, BUT THAT'S NOW CONSIDERED UNLIKELY TO HAPPEN TILL NEXT YEAR OR POSSIBLY THE YEAR AFTER...
RIGHT...
SO THE DAY OF RECKONING HAS BEEN POSTPONED?
QUITE. YOU CAN KEEP BORROWING MONEY CHEAPLY AND USE IT TO FUND SHARE BUYBACKS AND M+A...
AND ARTIFICIALLY BOOST OUR COMPANY'S VALUE TO TRIGGER OUR BONUSES? EXCELLENT.

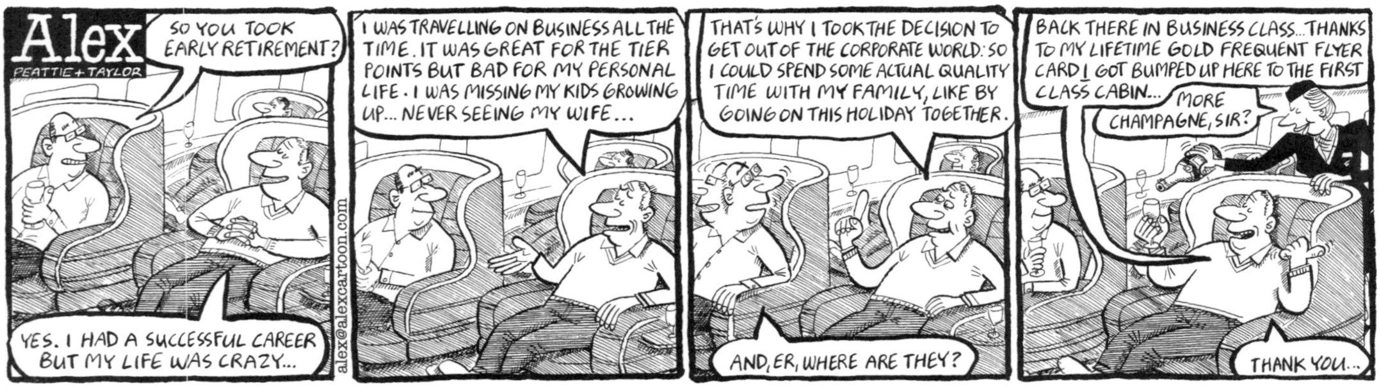
Alex
PEATTIE + TAYLOR
SO YOU TOOK EARLY RETIREMENT?
YES. I HAD A SUCCESSFUL CAREER BUT MY LIFE WAS CRAZY...
alex@alexcartoon.com
I WAS TRAVELLING ON BUSINESS ALL THE TIME. IT WAS GREAT FOR THE TIER POINTS BUT BAD FOR MY PERSONAL LIFE. I WAS MISSING MY KIDS GROWING UP... NEVER SEEING MY WIFE...
THAT'S WHY I TOOK THE DECISION TO GET OUT OF THE CORPORATE WORLD: SO I COULD SPEND SOME ACTUAL QUALITY TIME WITH MY FAMILY, LIKE BY GOING ON THIS HOLIDAY TOGETHER.
AND, ER, WHERE ARE THEY?
BACK THERE IN BUSINESS CLASS... THANKS TO MY LIFETIME GOLD FREQUENT FLYER CARD I GOT BUMPED UP HERE TO THE FIRST CLASS CABIN...
MORE CHAMPAGNE, SIR?
THANK YOU...

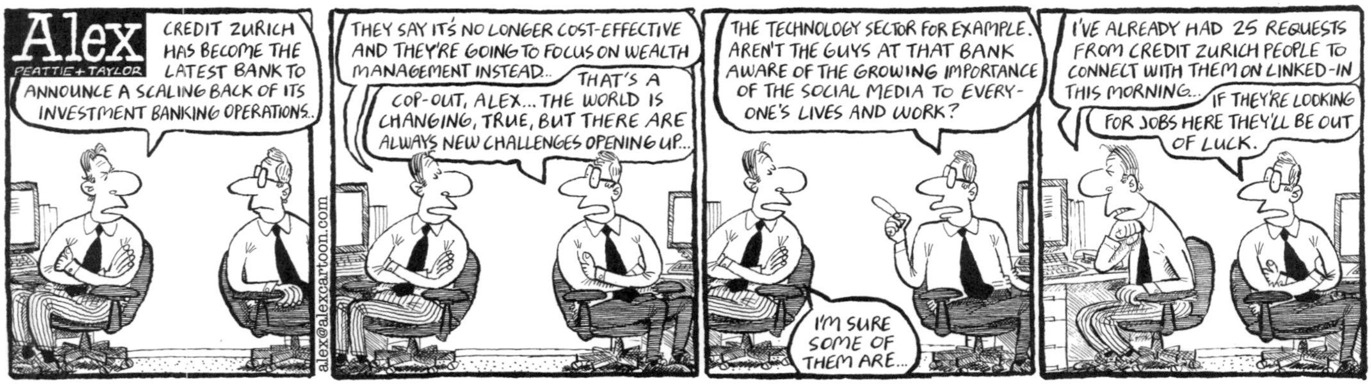
Alex
PEATTIE + TAYLOR
CREDIT ZURICH HAS BECOME THE LATEST BANK TO ANNOUNCE A SCALING BACK OF ITS INVESTMENT BANKING OPERATIONS...
alex@alexcartoon.com
THEY SAY IT'S NO LONGER COST-EFFECTIVE AND THEY'RE GOING TO FOCUS ON WEALTH MANAGEMENT INSTEAD...
THAT'S A COP-OUT, ALEX... THE WORLD IS CHANGING, TRUE, BUT THERE ARE ALWAYS NEW CHALLENGES OPENING UP...
THE TECHNOLOGY SECTOR FOR EXAMPLE. AREN'T THE GUYS AT THAT BANK AWARE OF THE GROWING IMPORTANCE OF THE SOCIAL MEDIA TO EVERY-ONE'S LIVES AND WORK?
I'M SURE SOME OF THEM ARE...
I'VE ALREADY HAD 25 REQUESTS FROM CREDIT ZURICH PEOPLE TO CONNECT WITH THEM ON LINKED-IN THIS MORNING...
IF THEY'RE LOOKING FOR JOBS HERE THEY'LL BE OUT OF LUCK.

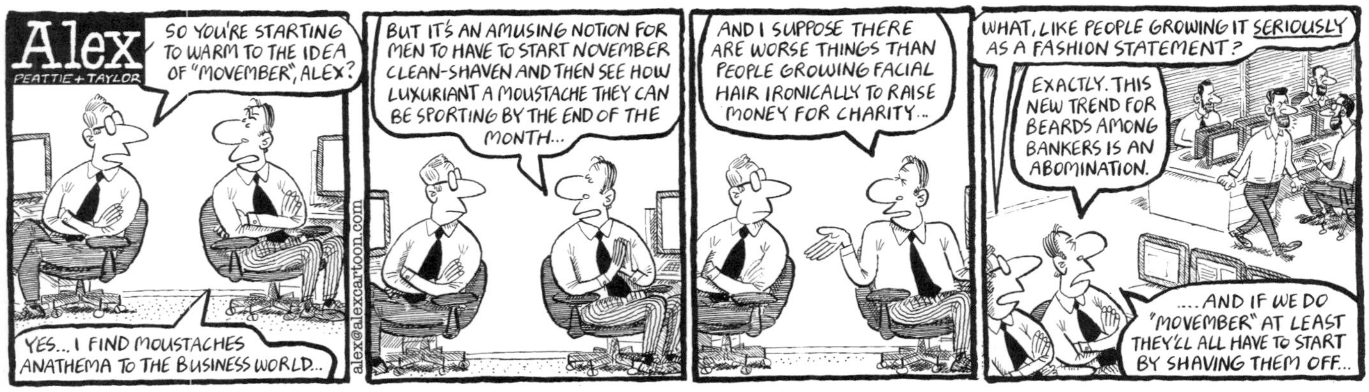
Alex
PEATTIE + TAYLOR
SO YOU'RE STARTING TO WARM TO THE IDEA OF "MOVEMBER", ALEX?
YES... I FIND MOUSTACHES ANATHEMA TO THE BUSINESS WORLD...
alex@alexcartoon.com
BUT IT'S AN AMUSING NOTION FOR MEN TO HAVE TO START NOVEMBER CLEAN-SHAVEN AND THEN SEE HOW LUXURIANT A MOUSTACHE THEY CAN BE SPORTING BY THE END OF THE MONTH...
AND I SUPPOSE THERE ARE WORSE THINGS THAN PEOPLE GROWING FACIAL HAIR IRONICALLY TO RAISE MONEY FOR CHARITY...
WHAT, LIKE PEOPLE GROWING IT SERIOUSLY AS A FASHION STATEMENT?
EXACTLY. THIS NEW TREND FOR BEARDS AMONG BANKERS IS AN ABOMINATION.
....AND IF WE DO "MOVEMBER" AT LEAST THEY'LL ALL HAVE TO START BY SHAVING THEM OFF...

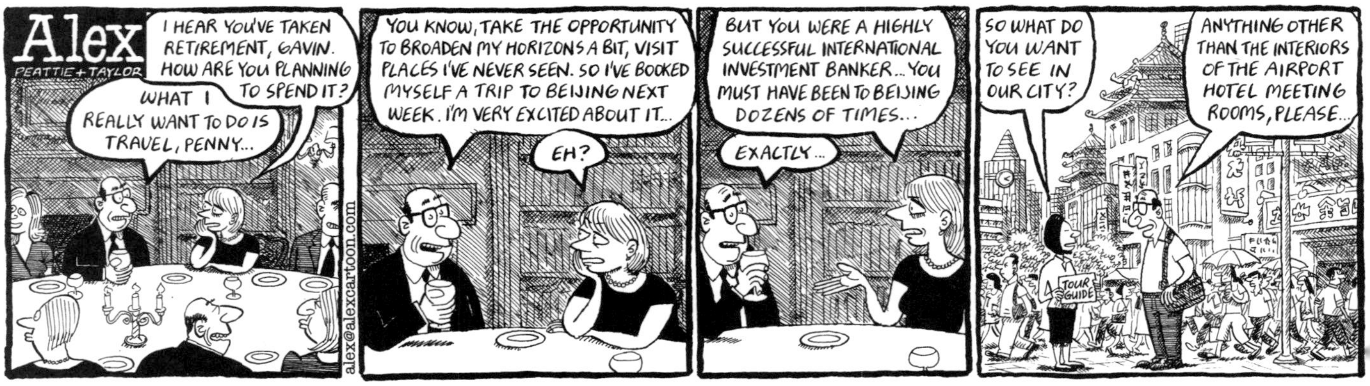
Alex
PEATTIE + TAYLOR
I HEAR YOU'VE TAKEN RETIREMENT, GAVIN. HOW ARE YOU PLANNING TO SPEND IT?
WHAT I REALLY WANT TO DO IS TRAVEL, PENNY...
alex@alexcartoon.com
YOU KNOW, TAKE THE OPPORTUNITY TO BROADEN MY HORIZONS A BIT, VISIT PLACES I'VE NEVER SEEN. SO I'VE BOOKED MYSELF A TRIP TO BEIJING NEXT WEEK. I'M VERY EXCITED ABOUT IT...
EH?
BUT YOU WERE A HIGHLY SUCCESSFUL INTERNATIONAL INVESTMENT BANKER... YOU MUST HAVE BEEN TO BEIJING DOZENS OF TIMES...
EXACTLY...
SO WHAT DO YOU WANT TO SEE IN OUR CITY?
ANYTHING OTHER THAN THE INTERIORS OF THE AIRPORT HOTEL MEETING ROOMS, PLEASE...
TOUR GUIDE

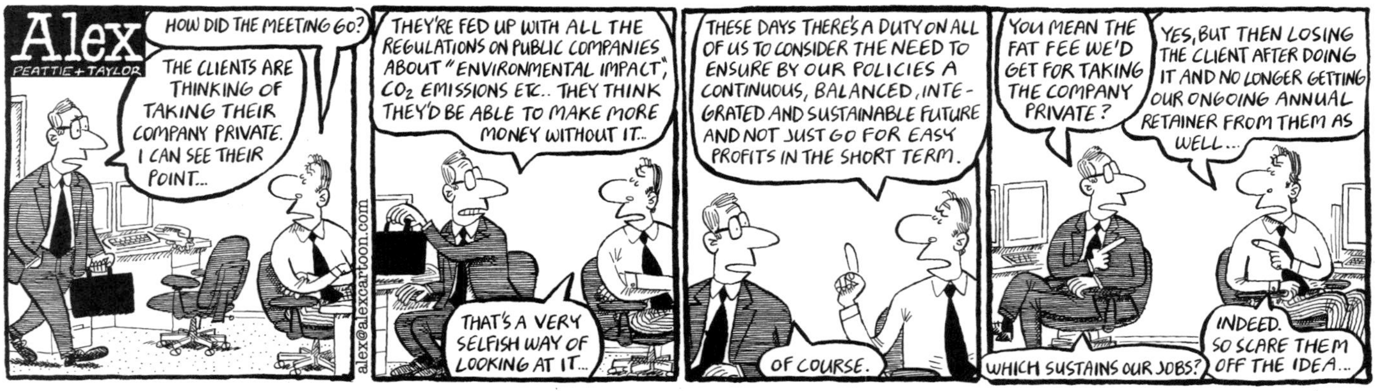
Alex
PEATTIE + TAYLOR
HOW DID THE MEETING GO?
THE CLIENTS ARE THINKING OF TAKING THEIR COMPANY PRIVATE. I CAN SEE THEIR POINT...
alex@alexcartoon.com
THEY'RE FED UP WITH ALL THE REGULATIONS ON PUBLIC COMPANIES ABOUT "ENVIRONMENTAL IMPACT", CO2 EMISSIONS ETC.. THEY THINK THEY'D BE ABLE TO MAKE MORE MONEY WITHOUT IT...
THAT'S A VERY SELFISH WAY OF LOOKING AT IT...
THESE DAYS THERE'S A DUTY ON ALL OF US TO CONSIDER THE NEED TO ENSURE BY OUR POLICIES A CONTINUOUS, BALANCED, INTEGRATED AND SUSTAINABLE FUTURE AND NOT JUST GO FOR EASY PROFITS IN THE SHORT TERM.
OF COURSE.
YOU MEAN THE FAT FEE WE'D GET FOR TAKING THE COMPANY PRIVATE?
YES, BUT THEN LOSING THE CLIENT AFTER DOING IT AND NO LONGER GETTING OUR ONGOING ANNUAL RETAINER FROM THEM AS WELL...
WHICH SUSTAINS OUR JOBS?
INDEED. SO SCARE THEM OFF THE IDEA...

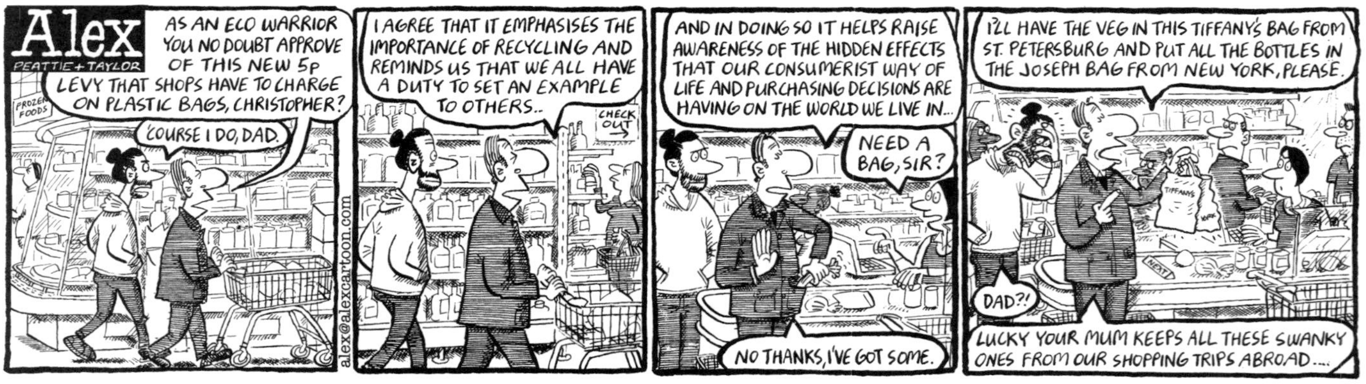
Alex
PEATTIE + TAYLOR
AS AN ECO WARRIOR YOU NO DOUBT APPROVE OF THIS NEW 5P LEVY THAT SHOPS HAVE TO CHARGE ON PLASTIC BAGS, CHRISTOPHER?
FROZEN FOODS
'COURSE I DO, DAD.
alex@alexcartoon.com
I AGREE THAT IT EMPHASISES THE IMPORTANCE OF RECYCLING AND REMINDS US THAT WE ALL HAVE A DUTY TO SET AN EXAMPLE TO OTHERS...
CHECK OUT
AND IN DOING SO IT HELPS RAISE AWARENESS OF THE HIDDEN EFFECTS THAT OUR CONSUMERIST WAY OF LIFE AND PURCHASING DECISIONS ARE HAVING ON THE WORLD WE LIVE IN...
NEED A BAG, SIR?
NO THANKS, I'VE GOT SOME.
I'LL HAVE THE VEG IN THIS TIFFANY'S BAG FROM ST. PETERSBURG AND PUT ALL THE BOTTLES IN THE JOSEPH BAG FROM NEW YORK, PLEASE.
TIFFANY
DAD?!
LUCKY YOUR MUM KEEPS ALL THESE SWANKY ONES FROM OUR SHOPPING TRIPS ABROAD....

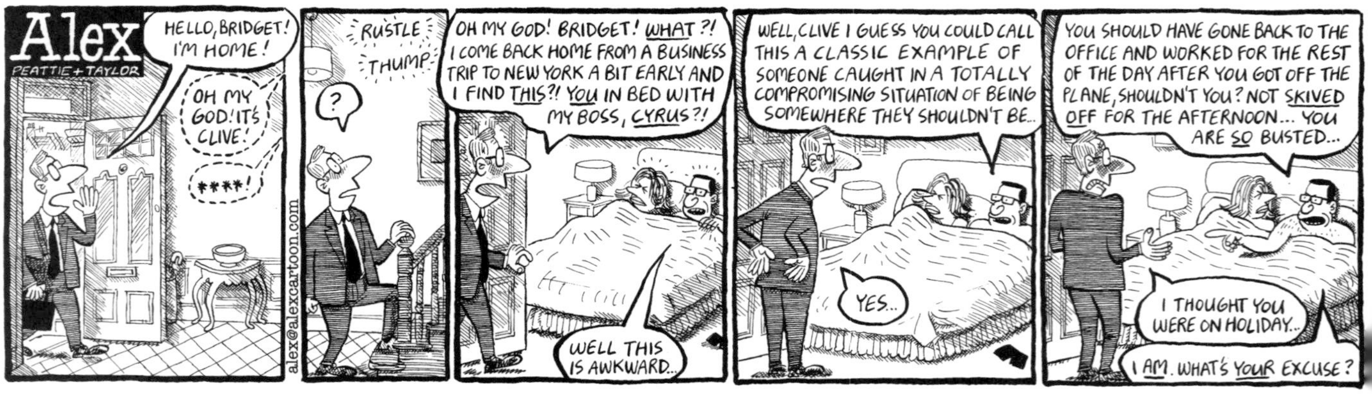
Alex
PEATTIE + TAYLOR
HELLO, BRIDGET! I'M HOME!
OH MY GOD! IT'S CLIVE!
****!
alex@alexcartoon.com
RUSTLE
THUMP
?
OH MY GOD! BRIDGET! WHAT?! I COME BACK HOME FROM A BUSINESS TRIP TO NEW YORK A BIT EARLY AND I FIND THIS?! YOU IN BED WITH MY BOSS, CYRUS?!
WELL THIS IS AWKWARD...
WELL, CLIVE I GUESS YOU COULD CALL THIS A CLASSIC EXAMPLE OF SOMEONE CAUGHT IN A TOTALLY COMPROMISING SITUATION OF BEING SOMEWHERE THEY SHOULDN'T BE...
YES...
YOU SHOULD HAVE GONE BACK TO THE OFFICE AND WORKED FOR THE REST OF THE DAY AFTER YOU GOT OFF THE PLANE, SHOULDN'T YOU? NOT SKIVED OFF FOR THE AFTERNOON... YOU ARE SO BUSTED...
I THOUGHT YOU WERE ON HOLIDAY...
I AM. WHAT'S YOUR EXCUSE?

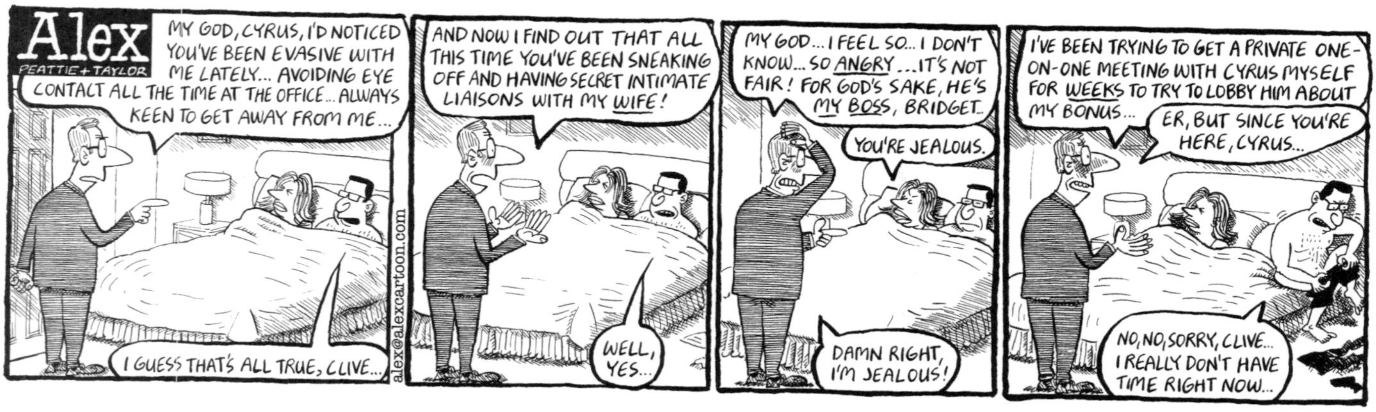
Alex
PEATTIE+TAYLOR
MY GOD, CYRUS, I'D NOTICED YOU'VE BEEN EVASIVE WITH ME LATELY... AVOIDING EYE CONTACT ALL THE TIME AT THE OFFICE... ALWAYS KEEN TO GET AWAY FROM ME...
I GUESS THAT'S ALL TRUE, CLIVE...
alex@alexcartoon.com
AND NOW I FIND OUT THAT ALL THIS TIME YOU'VE BEEN SNEAKING OFF AND HAVING SECRET INTIMATE LIAISONS WITH MY WIFE!
WELL, YES...
MY GOD... I FEEL SO... I DON'T KNOW... SO ANGRY... IT'S NOT FAIR! FOR GOD'S SAKE, HE'S MY BOSS, BRIDGET...
YOU'RE JEALOUS.
DAMN RIGHT, I'M JEALOUS!
I'VE BEEN TRYING TO GET A PRIVATE ONE-ON-ONE MEETING WITH CYRUS MYSELF FOR WEEKS TO TRY TO LOBBY HIM ABOUT MY BONUS...
ER, BUT SINCE YOU'RE HERE, CYRUS...
NO, NO, SORRY, CLIVE... I REALLY DON'T HAVE TIME RIGHT NOW...

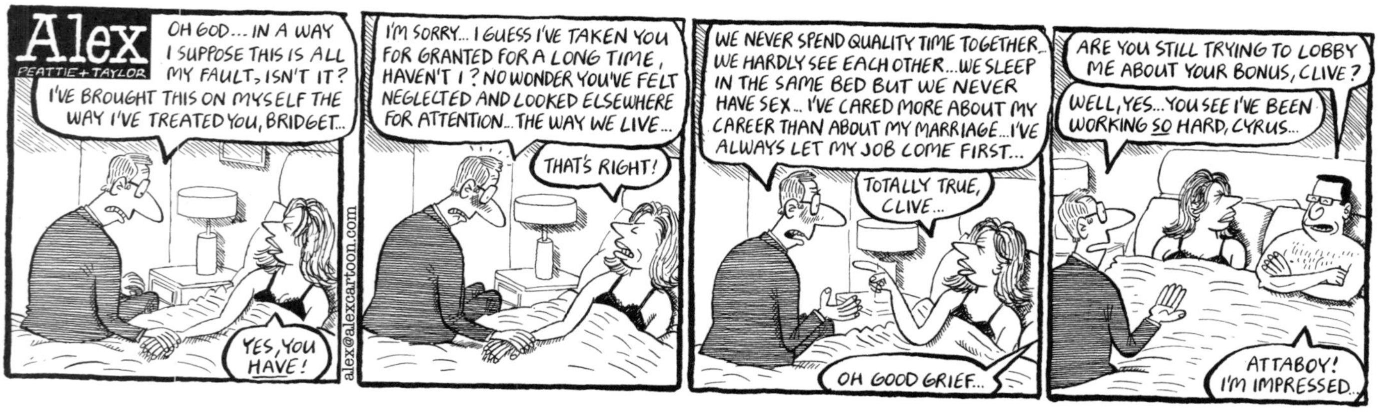
Alex
PEATTIE+TAYLOR
OH GOD... IN A WAY I SUPPOSE THIS IS ALL MY FAULT, ISN'T IT?
I'VE BROUGHT THIS ON MYSELF THE WAY I'VE TREATED YOU, BRIDGET...
YES, YOU HAVE!
alex@alexcartoon.com
I'M SORRY... I GUESS I'VE TAKEN YOU FOR GRANTED FOR A LONG TIME, HAVEN'T I? NO WONDER YOU'VE FELT NEGLECTED AND LOOKED ELSEWHERE FOR ATTENTION... THE WAY WE LIVE...
THAT'S RIGHT!
WE NEVER SPEND QUALITY TIME TOGETHER... WE HARDLY SEE EACH OTHER... WE SLEEP IN THE SAME BED BUT WE NEVER HAVE SEX... I'VE CARED MORE ABOUT MY CAREER THAN ABOUT MY MARRIAGE... I'VE ALWAYS LET MY JOB COME FIRST...
TOTALLY TRUE, CLIVE...
OH GOOD GRIEF...
ARE YOU STILL TRYING TO LOBBY ME ABOUT YOUR BONUS, CLIVE?
WELL, YES... YOU SEE I'VE BEEN WORKING SO HARD, CYRUS...
ATTABOY! I'M IMPRESSED...

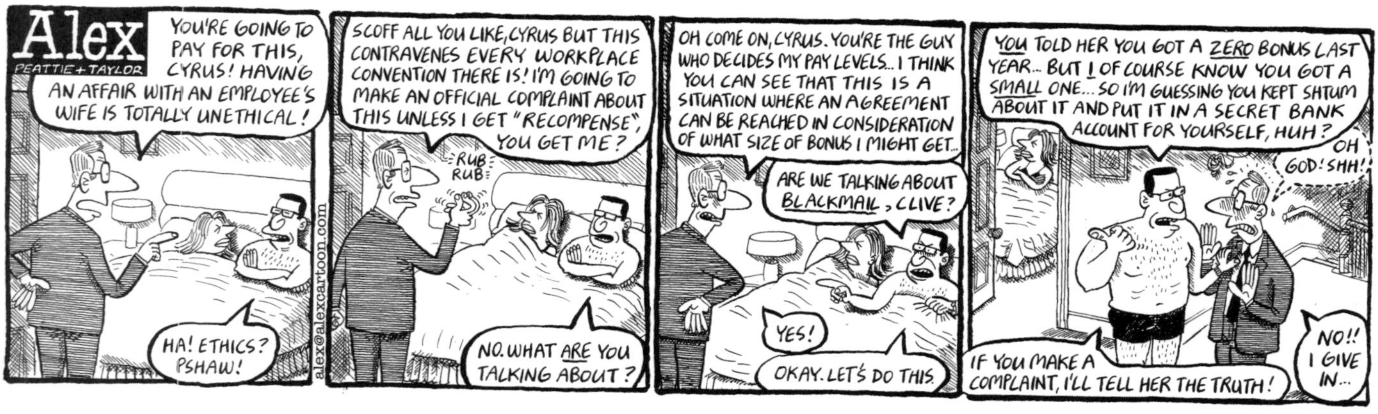
Alex
PEATTIE+TAYLOR
YOU'RE GOING TO PAY FOR THIS, CYRUS! HAVING AN AFFAIR WITH AN EMPLOYEE'S WIFE IS TOTALLY UNETHICAL!
HA! ETHICS? PSHAW!
alex@alexcartoon.com
SCOFF ALL YOU LIKE, CYRUS BUT THIS CONTRAVENES EVERY WORKPLACE CONVENTION THERE IS! I'M GOING TO MAKE AN OFFICIAL COMPLAINT ABOUT THIS UNLESS I GET "RECOMPENSE", YOU GET ME?
RUB RUB
NO. WHAT ARE YOU TALKING ABOUT?
OH COME ON, CYRUS. YOU'RE THE GUY WHO DECIDES MY PAY LEVELS... I THINK YOU CAN SEE THAT THIS IS A SITUATION WHERE AN AGREEMENT CAN BE REACHED IN CONSIDERATION OF WHAT SIZE OF BONUS I MIGHT GET...
ARE WE TALKING ABOUT BLACKMAIL, CLIVE?
YES!
OKAY. LET'S DO THIS.
YOU TOLD HER YOU GOT A ZERO BONUS LAST YEAR... BUT I OF COURSE KNOW YOU GOT A SMALL ONE... SO I'M GUESSING YOU KEPT SHTUM ABOUT IT AND PUT IT IN A SECRET BANK ACCOUNT FOR YOURSELF, HUH?
OH GOD! SHH!
IF YOU MAKE A COMPLAINT, I'LL TELL HER THE TRUTH!
NO!! I GIVE IN...

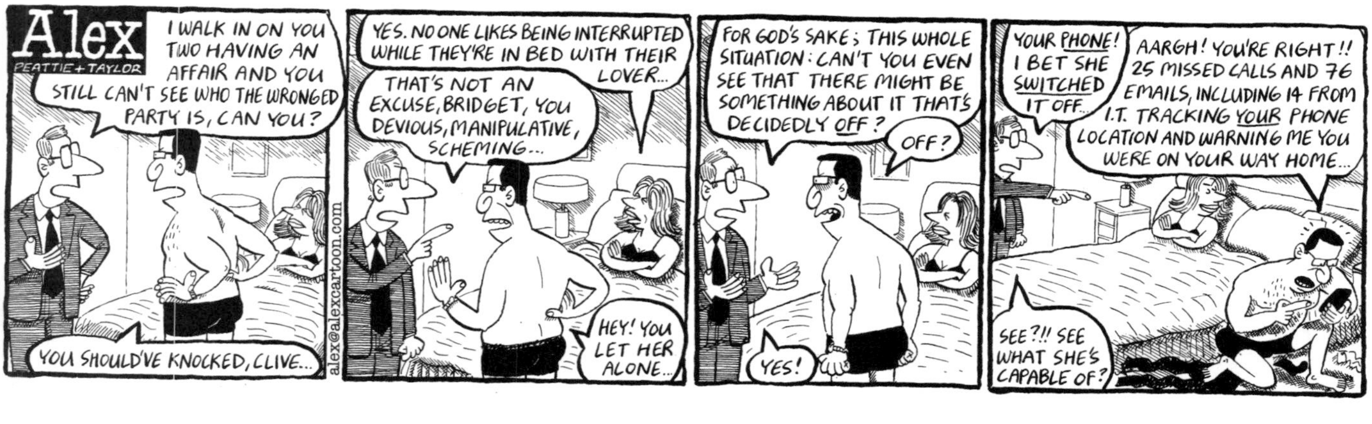
Alex
PEATTIE+TAYLOR
I WALK IN ON YOU TWO HAVING AN AFFAIR AND YOU STILL CAN'T SEE WHO THE WRONGED PARTY IS, CAN YOU?
YOU SHOULD'VE KNOCKED, CLIVE...
alex@alexcartoon.com
YES. NO ONE LIKES BEING INTERRUPTED WHILE THEY'RE IN BED WITH THEIR LOVER...
THAT'S NOT AN EXCUSE, BRIDGET, YOU DEVIOUS, MANIPULATIVE, SCHEMING...
HEY! YOU LET HER ALONE...
FOR GOD'S SAKE; THIS WHOLE SITUATION: CAN'T YOU EVEN SEE THAT THERE MIGHT BE SOMETHING ABOUT IT THAT'S DECIDEDLY OFF?
OFF?
YES!
YOUR PHONE! I BET SHE SWITCHED IT OFF...
AARGH! YOU'RE RIGHT!! 25 MISSED CALLS AND 76 EMAILS, INCLUDING 14 FROM I.T. TRACKING YOUR PHONE LOCATION AND WARNING ME YOU WERE ON YOUR WAY HOME...
SEE?!! SEE WHAT SHE'S CAPABLE OF?

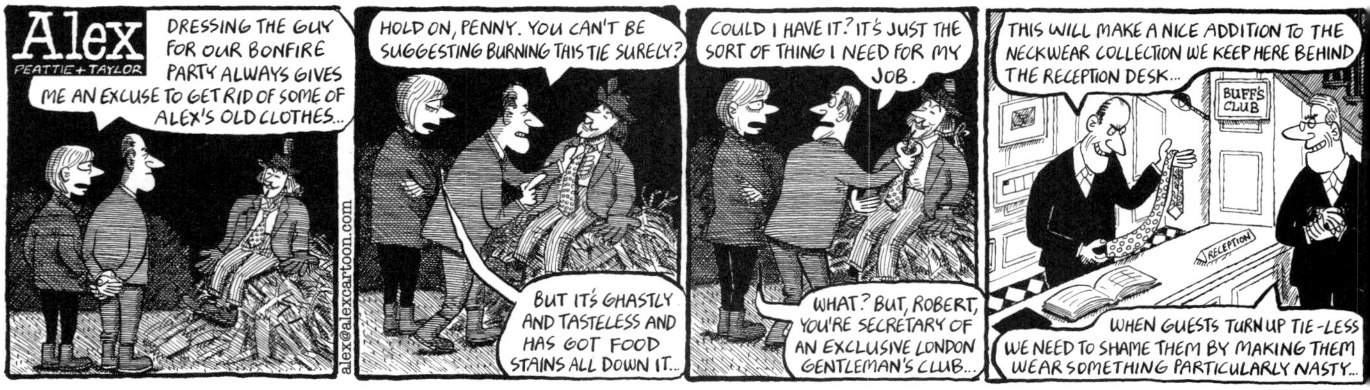
Alex
PEATTIE + TAYLOR
DRESSING THE GUY FOR OUR BONFIRE PARTY ALWAYS GIVES ME AN EXCUSE TO GET RID OF SOME OF ALEX'S OLD CLOTHES...
HOLD ON, PENNY. YOU CAN'T BE SUGGESTING BURNING THIS TIE SURELY?
BUT IT'S GHASTLY AND TASTELESS AND HAS GOT FOOD STAINS ALL DOWN IT...
alex@alexcartoon.com
COULD I HAVE IT? IT'S JUST THE SORT OF THING I NEED FOR MY JOB.
WHAT? BUT, ROBERT, YOU'RE SECRETARY OF AN EXCLUSIVE LONDON GENTLEMAN'S CLUB...
THIS WILL MAKE A NICE ADDITION TO THE NECKWEAR COLLECTION WE KEEP HERE BEHIND THE RECEPTION DESK...
BUFF'S CLUB
RECEPTION
WHEN GUESTS TURN UP TIE-LESS WE NEED TO SHAME THEM BY MAKING THEM WEAR SOMETHING PARTICULARLY NASTY...

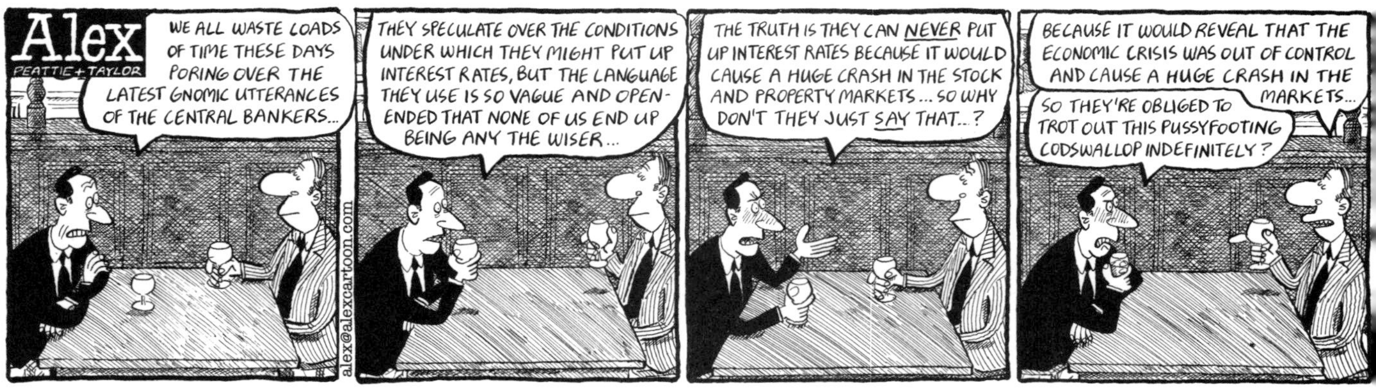
Alex
PEATTIE + TAYLOR
WE ALL WASTE LOADS OF TIME THESE DAYS PORING OVER THE LATEST GNOMIC UTTERANCES OF THE CENTRAL BANKERS...
THEY SPECULATE OVER THE CONDITIONS UNDER WHICH THEY MIGHT PUT UP INTEREST RATES, BUT THE LANGUAGE THEY USE IS SO VAGUE AND OPEN-ENDED THAT NONE OF US END UP BEING ANY THE WISER...
alex@alexcartoon.com
THE TRUTH IS THEY CAN NEVER PUT UP INTEREST RATES BECAUSE IT WOULD CAUSE A HUGE CRASH IN THE STOCK AND PROPERTY MARKETS... SO WHY DON'T THEY JUST SAY THAT...?
BECAUSE IT WOULD REVEAL THAT THE ECONOMIC CRISIS WAS OUT OF CONTROL AND CAUSE A HUGE CRASH IN THE MARKETS...
SO THEY'RE OBLIGED TO TROT OUT THIS PUSSYFOOTING CODSWALLOP INDEFINITELY?

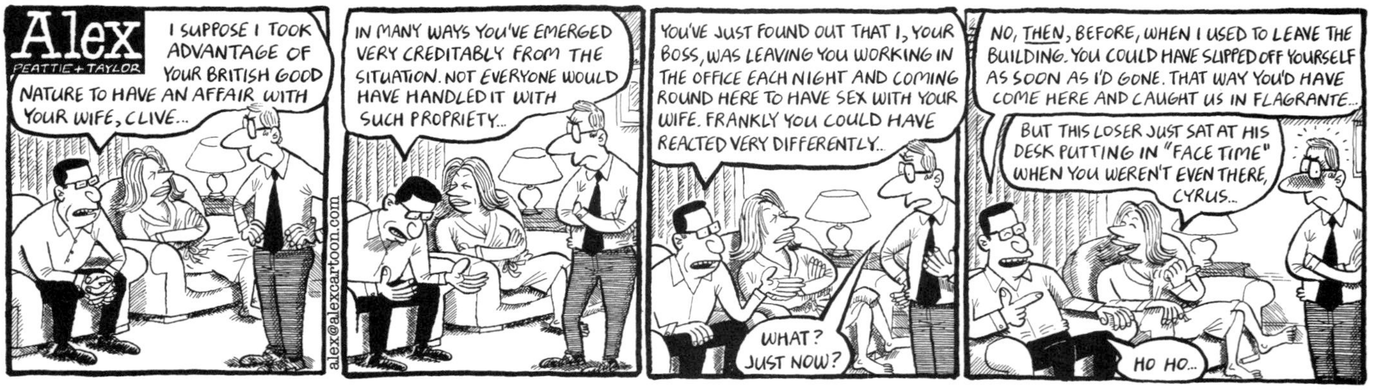
Alex
PEATTIE + TAYLOR
I SUPPOSE I TOOK ADVANTAGE OF YOUR BRITISH GOOD NATURE TO HAVE AN AFFAIR WITH YOUR WIFE, CLIVE...
IN MANY WAYS YOU'VE EMERGED VERY CREDITABLY FROM THE SITUATION. NOT EVERYONE WOULD HAVE HANDLED IT WITH SUCH PROPRIETY...
alex@alexcartoon.com
YOU'VE JUST FOUND OUT THAT I, YOUR BOSS, WAS LEAVING YOU WORKING IN THE OFFICE EACH NIGHT AND COMING ROUND HERE TO HAVE SEX WITH YOUR WIFE. FRANKLY YOU COULD HAVE REACTED VERY DIFFERENTLY...
WHAT? JUST NOW?
NO, THEN, BEFORE, WHEN I USED TO LEAVE THE BUILDING. YOU COULD HAVE SLIPPED OFF YOURSELF AS SOON AS I'D GONE. THAT WAY YOU'D HAVE COME HERE AND CAUGHT US IN FLAGRANTE...
BUT THIS LOSER JUST SAT AT HIS DESK PUTTING IN "FACE TIME" WHEN YOU WEREN'T EVEN THERE, CYRUS...
HO HO...

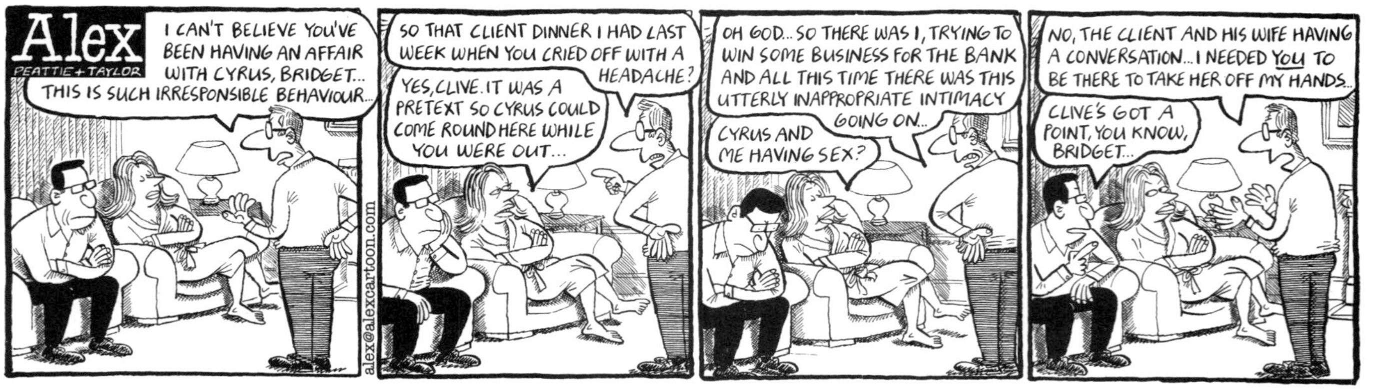
Alex
PEATTIE + TAYLOR
I CAN'T BELIEVE YOU'VE BEEN HAVING AN AFFAIR WITH CYRUS, BRIDGET... THIS IS SUCH IRRESPONSIBLE BEHAVIOUR...
SO THAT CLIENT DINNER I HAD LAST WEEK WHEN YOU CRIED OFF WITH A HEADACHE?
YES, CLIVE. IT WAS A PRETEXT SO CYRUS COULD COME ROUND HERE WHILE YOU WERE OUT...
alex@alexcartoon.com
OH GOD... SO THERE WAS I, TRYING TO WIN SOME BUSINESS FOR THE BANK AND ALL THIS TIME THERE WAS THIS UTTERLY INAPPROPRIATE INTIMACY GOING ON...
CYRUS AND ME HAVING SEX?
NO, THE CLIENT AND HIS WIFE HAVING A CONVERSATION... I NEEDED YOU TO BE THERE TO TAKE HER OFF MY HANDS...
CLIVE'S GOT A POINT, YOU KNOW, BRIDGET...

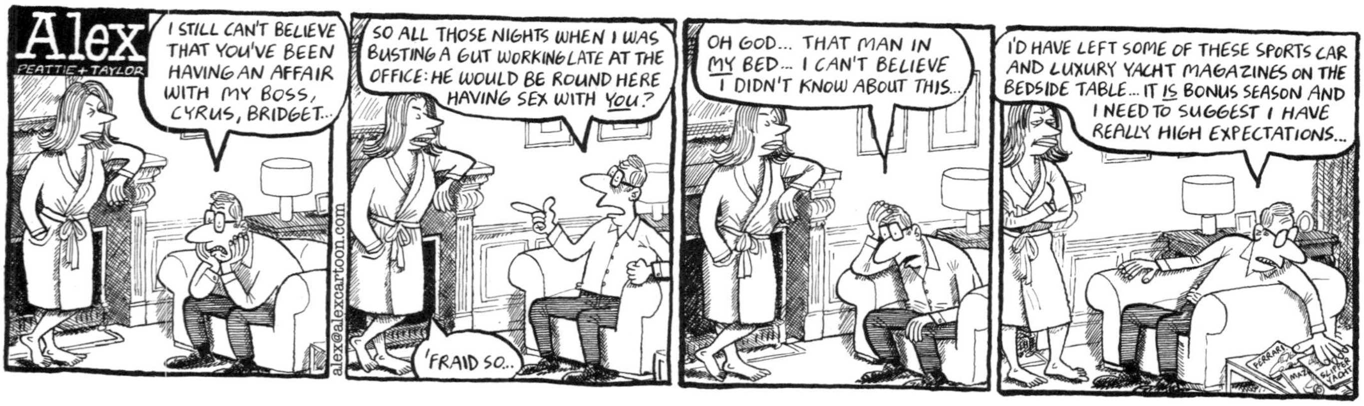
Alex
PEATTIE+TAYLOR
I STILL CAN'T BELIEVE THAT YOU'VE BEEN HAVING AN AFFAIR WITH MY BOSS, CYRUS, BRIDGET...
alex@alexcartoon.com
SO ALL THOSE NIGHTS WHEN I WAS BUSTING A GUT WORKING LATE AT THE OFFICE: HE WOULD BE ROUND HERE HAVING SEX WITH YOU?
'FRAID SO..
OH GOD... THAT MAN IN MY BED... I CAN'T BELIEVE I DIDN'T KNOW ABOUT THIS...
I'D HAVE LEFT SOME OF THESE SPORTS CAR AND LUXURY YACHT MAGAZINES ON THE BEDSIDE TABLE... IT IS BONUS SEASON AND I NEED TO SUGGEST I HAVE REALLY HIGH EXPECTATIONS...
FERRARI

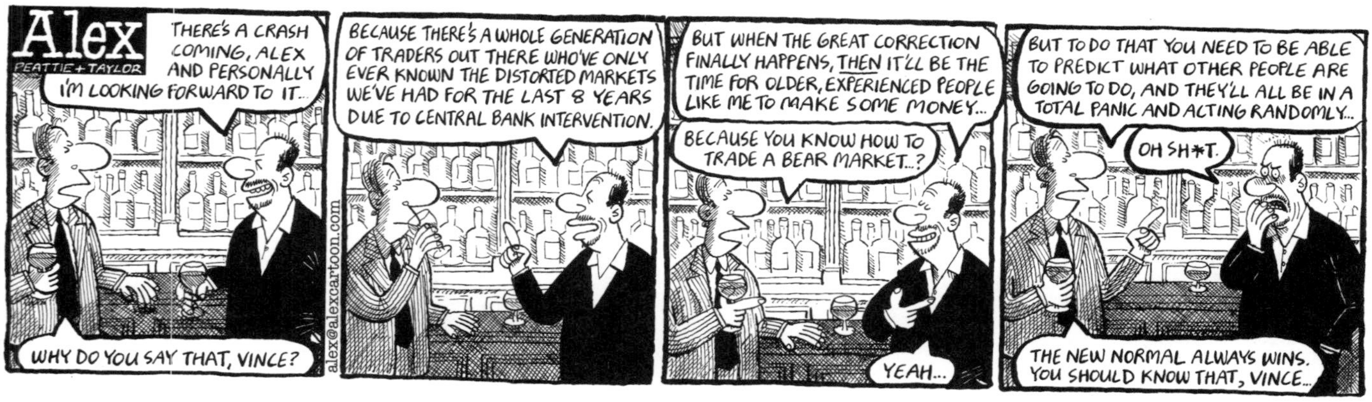
Alex
PEATTIE+TAYLOR
THERE'S A CRASH COMING, ALEX AND PERSONALLY I'M LOOKING FORWARD TO IT...
WHY DO YOU SAY THAT, VINCE?
alex@alexcartoon.com
BECAUSE THERE'S A WHOLE GENERATION OF TRADERS OUT THERE WHO'VE ONLY EVER KNOWN THE DISTORTED MARKETS WE'VE HAD FOR THE LAST 8 YEARS DUE TO CENTRAL BANK INTERVENTION.
BUT WHEN THE GREAT CORRECTION FINALLY HAPPENS, THEN IT'LL BE THE TIME FOR OLDER, EXPERIENCED PEOPLE LIKE ME TO MAKE SOME MONEY...
BECAUSE YOU KNOW HOW TO TRADE A BEAR MARKET..?
YEAH...
BUT TO DO THAT YOU NEED TO BE ABLE TO PREDICT WHAT OTHER PEOPLE ARE GOING TO DO, AND THEY'LL ALL BE IN A TOTAL PANIC AND ACTING RANDOMLY...
OH SH*T.
THE NEW NORMAL ALWAYS WINS. YOU SHOULD KNOW THAT, VINCE...

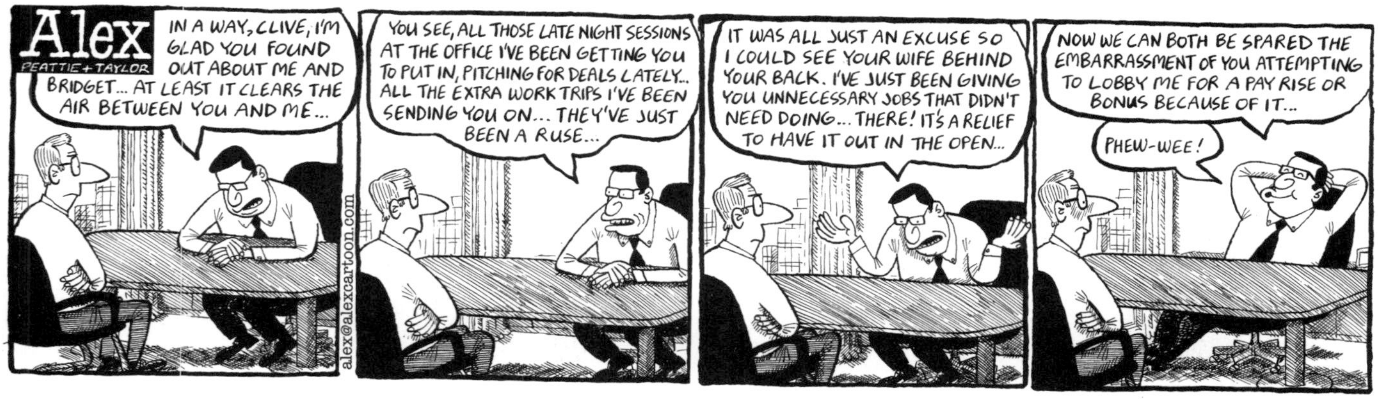
Alex
PEATTIE+TAYLOR
IN A WAY, CLIVE, I'M GLAD YOU FOUND OUT ABOUT ME AND BRIDGET... AT LEAST IT CLEARS THE AIR BETWEEN YOU AND ME...
alex@alexcartoon.com
YOU SEE, ALL THOSE LATE NIGHT SESSIONS AT THE OFFICE I'VE BEEN GETTING YOU TO PUT IN, PITCHING FOR DEALS LATELY... ALL THE EXTRA WORK TRIPS I'VE BEEN SENDING YOU ON... THEY'VE JUST BEEN A RUSE...
IT WAS ALL JUST AN EXCUSE SO I COULD SEE YOUR WIFE BEHIND YOUR BACK. I'VE JUST BEEN GIVING YOU UNNECESSARY JOBS THAT DIDN'T NEED DOING... THERE! IT'S A RELIEF TO HAVE IT OUT IN THE OPEN...
NOW WE CAN BOTH BE SPARED THE EMBARRASSMENT OF YOU ATTEMPTING TO LOBBY ME FOR A PAY RISE OR BONUS BECAUSE OF IT...
PHEW-WEE!

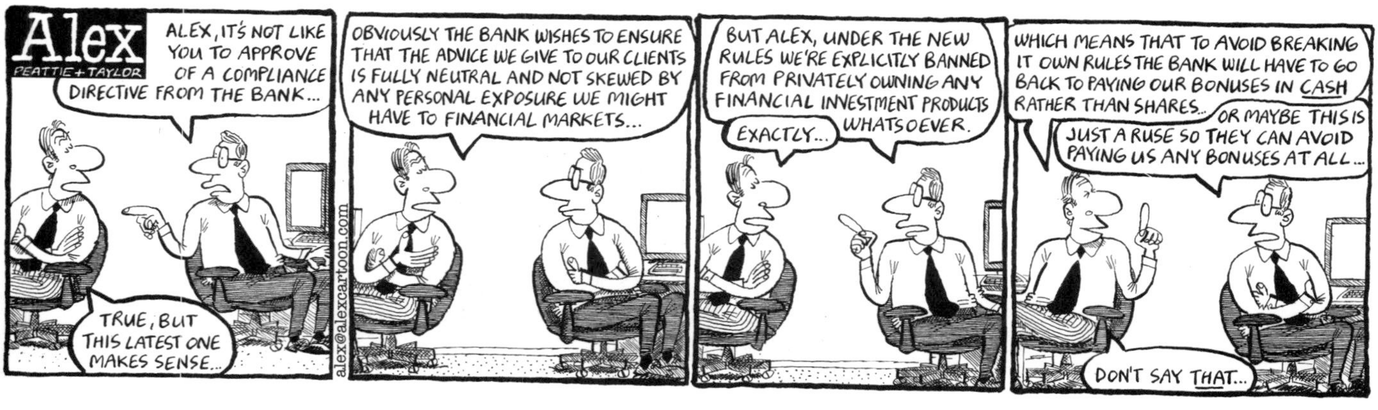
Alex
PEATTIE+TAYLOR
ALEX, IT'S NOT LIKE YOU TO APPROVE OF A COMPLIANCE DIRECTIVE FROM THE BANK...
TRUE, BUT THIS LATEST ONE MAKES SENSE...
alex@alexcartoon.com
OBVIOUSLY THE BANK WISHES TO ENSURE THAT THE ADVICE WE GIVE TO OUR CLIENTS IS FULLY NEUTRAL AND NOT SKEWED BY ANY PERSONAL EXPOSURE WE MIGHT HAVE TO FINANCIAL MARKETS...
BUT ALEX, UNDER THE NEW RULES WE'RE EXPLICITLY BANNED FROM PRIVATELY OWNING ANY FINANCIAL INVESTMENT PRODUCTS WHATSOEVER.
EXACTLY...
WHICH MEANS THAT TO AVOID BREAKING IT OWN RULES THE BANK WILL HAVE TO GO BACK TO PAYING OUR BONUSES IN CASH RATHER THAN SHARES...
OR MAYBE THIS IS JUST A RUSE SO THEY CAN AVOID PAYING US ANY BONUSES AT ALL...
DON'T SAY THAT...

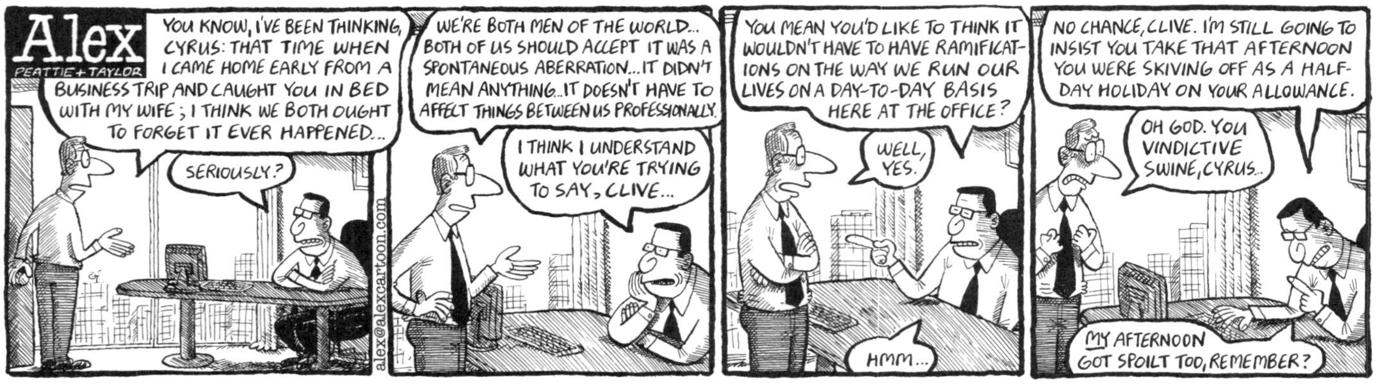
Alex
PEATTIE + TAYLOR
YOU KNOW, I'VE BEEN THINKING, CYRUS: THAT TIME WHEN I CAME HOME EARLY FROM A BUSINESS TRIP AND CAUGHT YOU IN BED WITH MY WIFE; I THINK WE BOTH OUGHT TO FORGET IT EVER HAPPENED...
SERIOUSLY?
alex@alexcartoon.com
WE'RE BOTH MEN OF THE WORLD... BOTH OF US SHOULD ACCEPT IT WAS A SPONTANEOUS ABERRATION... IT DIDN'T MEAN ANYTHING.. IT DOESN'T HAVE TO AFFECT THINGS BETWEEN US PROFESSIONALLY.
I THINK I UNDERSTAND WHAT YOU'RE TRYING TO SAY, CLIVE...
YOU MEAN YOU'D LIKE TO THINK IT WOULDN'T HAVE TO HAVE RAMIFICATIONS ON THE WAY WE RUN OUR LIVES ON A DAY-TO-DAY BASIS HERE AT THE OFFICE?
WELL, YES.
HMM...
NO CHANCE, CLIVE. I'M STILL GOING TO INSIST YOU TAKE THAT AFTERNOON YOU WERE SKIVING OFF AS A HALF-DAY HOLIDAY ON YOUR ALLOWANCE.
OH GOD. YOU VINDICTIVE SWINE, CYRUS..
MY AFTERNOON GOT SPOILT TOO, REMEMBER?

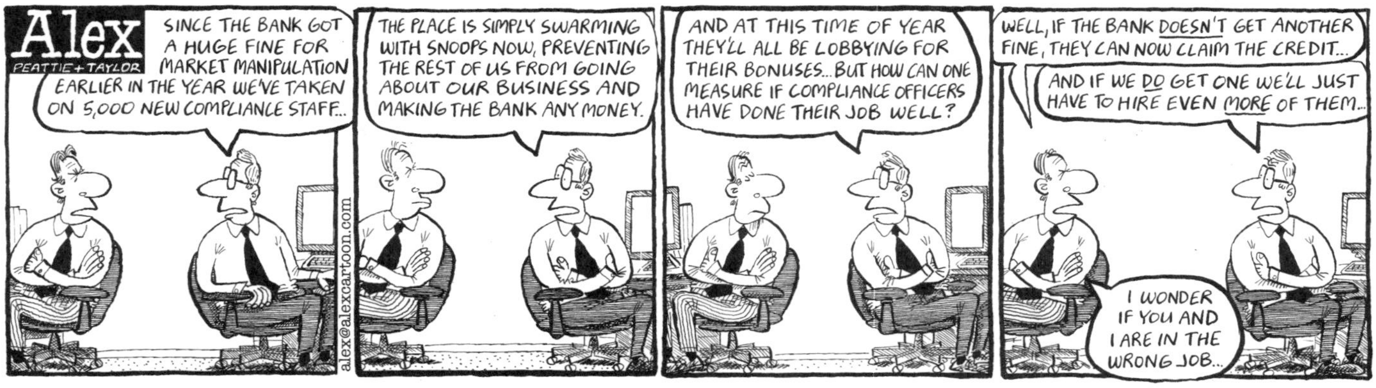
Alex
PEATTIE + TAYLOR
SINCE THE BANK GOT A HUGE FINE FOR MARKET MANIPULATION EARLIER IN THE YEAR WE'VE TAKEN ON 5,000 NEW COMPLIANCE STAFF...
alex@alexcartoon.com
THE PLACE IS SIMPLY SWARMING WITH SNOOPS NOW, PREVENTING THE REST OF US FROM GOING ABOUT OUR BUSINESS AND MAKING THE BANK ANY MONEY.
AND AT THIS TIME OF YEAR THEY'LL ALL BE LOBBYING FOR THEIR BONUSES... BUT HOW CAN ONE MEASURE IF COMPLIANCE OFFICERS HAVE DONE THEIR JOB WELL?
WELL, IF THE BANK DOESN'T GET ANOTHER FINE, THEY CAN NOW CLAIM THE CREDIT...
AND IF WE DO GET ONE WE'LL JUST HAVE TO HIRE EVEN MORE OF THEM...
I WONDER IF YOU AND I ARE IN THE WRONG JOB...

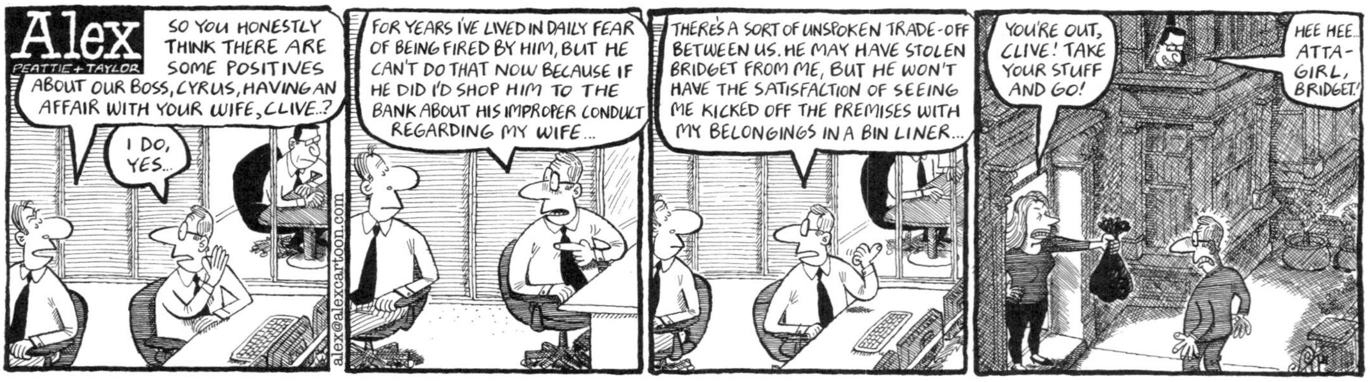
Alex
PEATTIE + TAYLOR
SO YOU HONESTLY THINK THERE ARE SOME POSITIVES ABOUT OUR BOSS, CYRUS, HAVING AN AFFAIR WITH YOUR WIFE, CLIVE..?
I DO, YES...
alex@alexcartoon.com
FOR YEARS I'VE LIVED IN DAILY FEAR OF BEING FIRED BY HIM, BUT HE CAN'T DO THAT NOW BECAUSE IF HE DID I'D SHOP HIM TO THE BANK ABOUT HIS IMPROPER CONDUCT REGARDING MY WIFE...
THERE'S A SORT OF UNSPOKEN TRADE-OFF BETWEEN US. HE MAY HAVE STOLEN BRIDGET FROM ME, BUT HE WON'T HAVE THE SATISFACTION OF SEEING ME KICKED OFF THE PREMISES WITH MY BELONGINGS IN A BIN LINER...
YOU'RE OUT, CLIVE! TAKE YOUR STUFF AND GO!
HEE HEE... ATTA-GIRL, BRIDGET!

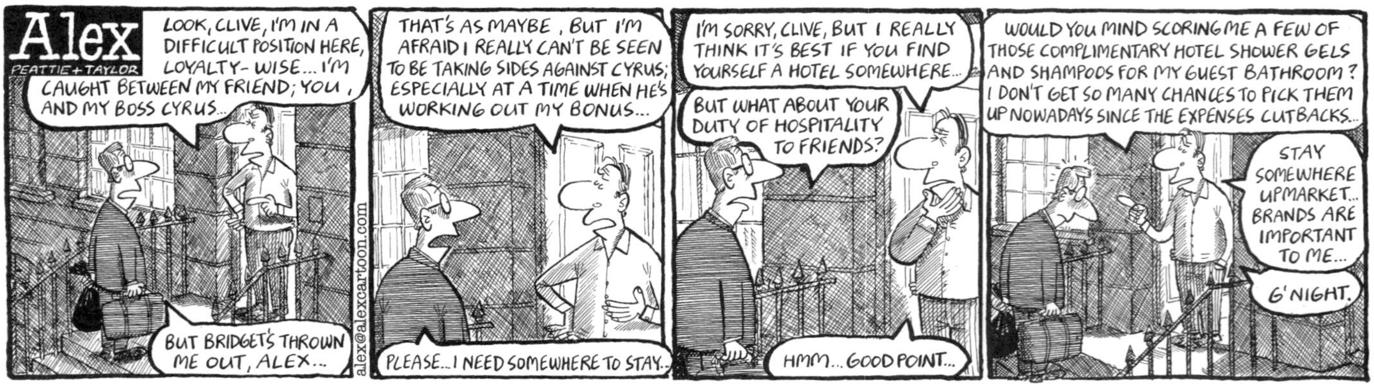
Alex
PEATTIE + TAYLOR
LOOK, CLIVE, I'M IN A DIFFICULT POSITION HERE, LOYALTY-WISE... I'M CAUGHT BETWEEN MY FRIEND; YOU, AND MY BOSS CYRUS...
BUT BRIDGET'S THROWN ME OUT, ALEX...
alex@alexcartoon.com
THAT'S AS MAYBE, BUT I'M AFRAID I REALLY CAN'T BE SEEN TO BE TAKING SIDES AGAINST CYRUS; ESPECIALLY AT A TIME WHEN HE'S WORKING OUT MY BONUS...
PLEASE... I NEED SOMEWHERE TO STAY...
I'M SORRY, CLIVE, BUT I REALLY THINK IT'S BEST IF YOU FIND YOURSELF A HOTEL SOMEWHERE...
BUT WHAT ABOUT YOUR DUTY OF HOSPITALITY TO FRIENDS?
HMM... GOOD POINT...
WOULD YOU MIND SCORING ME A FEW OF THOSE COMPLIMENTARY HOTEL SHOWER GELS AND SHAMPOOS FOR MY GUEST BATHROOM? I DON'T GET SO MANY CHANCES TO PICK THEM UP NOWADAYS SINCE THE EXPENSES CUTBACKS...
STAY SOMEWHERE UPMARKET... BRANDS ARE IMPORTANT TO ME...
G'NIGHT.

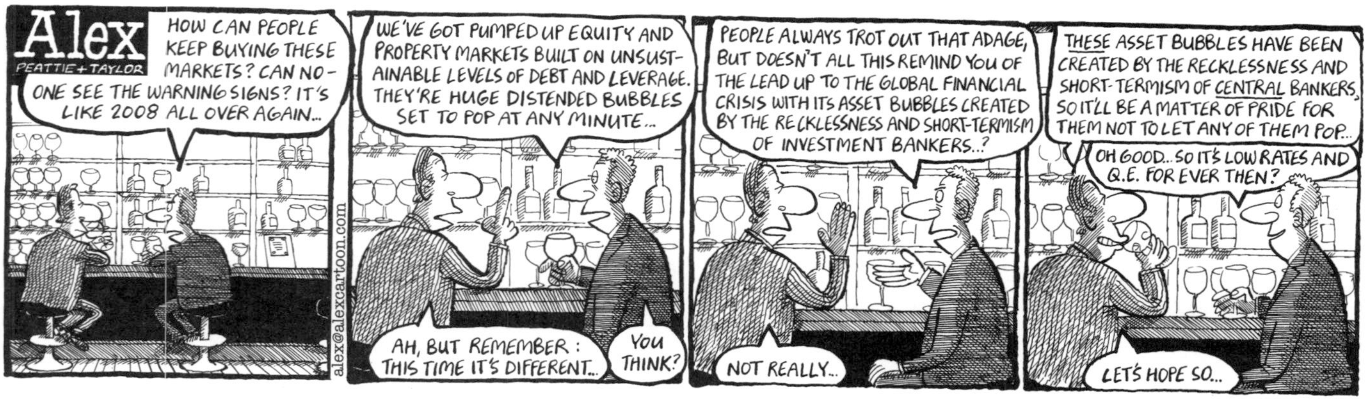
Alex
PEATTIE + TAYLOR
HOW CAN PEOPLE KEEP BUYING THESE MARKETS? CAN NO-ONE SEE THE WARNING SIGNS? IT'S LIKE 2008 ALL OVER AGAIN...
WE'VE GOT PUMPED UP EQUITY AND PROPERTY MARKETS BUILT ON UNSUSTAINABLE LEVELS OF DEBT AND LEVERAGE. THEY'RE HUGE DISTENDED BUBBLES SET TO POP AT ANY MINUTE...
AH, BUT REMEMBER: THIS TIME IT'S DIFFERENT...
YOU THINK?
alex@alexcartoon.com
PEOPLE ALWAYS TROT OUT THAT ADAGE, BUT DOESN'T ALL THIS REMIND YOU OF THE LEAD UP TO THE GLOBAL FINANCIAL CRISIS WITH ITS ASSET BUBBLES CREATED BY THE RECKLESSNESS AND SHORT-TERMISM OF INVESTMENT BANKERS...?
NOT REALLY...
THESE ASSET BUBBLES HAVE BEEN CREATED BY THE RECKLESSNESS AND SHORT-TERMISM OF CENTRAL BANKERS, SO IT'LL BE A MATTER OF PRIDE FOR THEM NOT TO LET ANY OF THEM POP...
OH GOOD... SO IT'S LOW RATES AND Q.E. FOR EVER THEN?
LET'S HOPE SO...

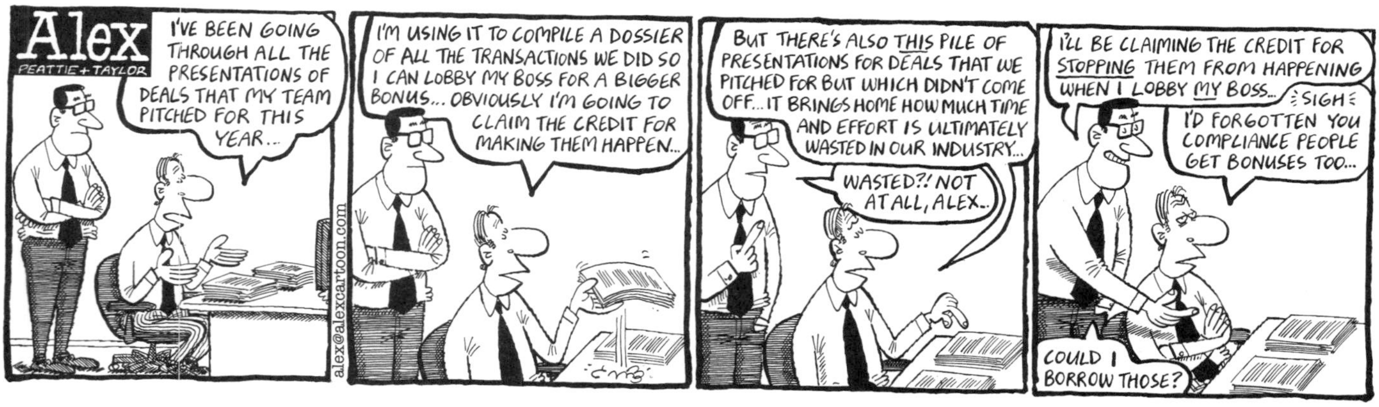
Alex
PEATTIE + TAYLOR
I'VE BEEN GOING THROUGH ALL THE PRESENTATIONS OF DEALS THAT MY TEAM PITCHED FOR THIS YEAR...
I'M USING IT TO COMPILE A DOSSIER OF ALL THE TRANSACTIONS WE DID SO I CAN LOBBY MY BOSS FOR A BIGGER BONUS... OBVIOUSLY I'M GOING TO CLAIM THE CREDIT FOR MAKING THEM HAPPEN...
alex@alexcartoon.com
BUT THERE'S ALSO THIS PILE OF PRESENTATIONS FOR DEALS THAT WE PITCHED FOR BUT WHICH DIDN'T COME OFF... IT BRINGS HOME HOW MUCH TIME AND EFFORT IS ULTIMATELY WASTED IN OUR INDUSTRY...
WASTED?! NOT AT ALL, ALEX...
I'LL BE CLAIMING THE CREDIT FOR STOPPING THEM FROM HAPPENING WHEN I LOBBY MY BOSS...
SIGH
I'D FORGOTTEN YOU COMPLIANCE PEOPLE GET BONUSES TOO...
COULD I BORROW THOSE?

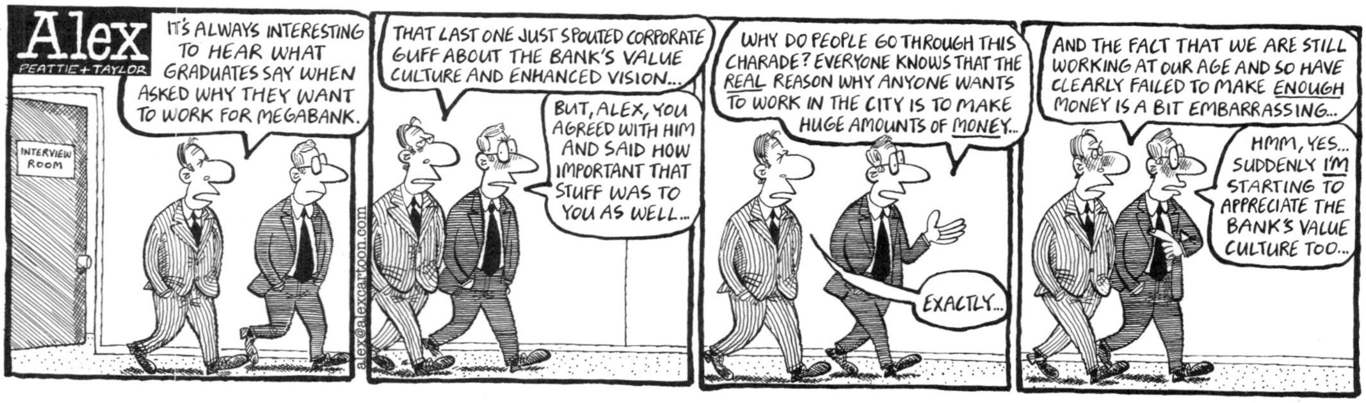
Alex
PEATTIE + TAYLOR
IT'S ALWAYS INTERESTING TO HEAR WHAT GRADUATES SAY WHEN ASKED WHY THEY WANT TO WORK FOR MEGABANK.
INTERVIEW ROOM
THAT LAST ONE JUST SPOUTED CORPORATE GUFF ABOUT THE BANK'S VALUE CULTURE AND ENHANCED VISION...
BUT, ALEX, YOU AGREED WITH HIM AND SAID HOW IMPORTANT THAT STUFF WAS TO YOU AS WELL...
alex@alexcartoon.com
WHY DO PEOPLE GO THROUGH THIS CHARADE? EVERYONE KNOWS THAT THE REAL REASON WHY ANYONE WANTS TO WORK IN THE CITY IS TO MAKE HUGE AMOUNTS OF MONEY...
EXACTLY...
AND THE FACT THAT WE ARE STILL WORKING AT OUR AGE AND SO HAVE CLEARLY FAILED TO MAKE ENOUGH MONEY IS A BIT EMBARRASSING...
HMM, YES... SUDDENLY I'M STARTING TO APPRECIATE THE BANK'S VALUE CULTURE TOO...

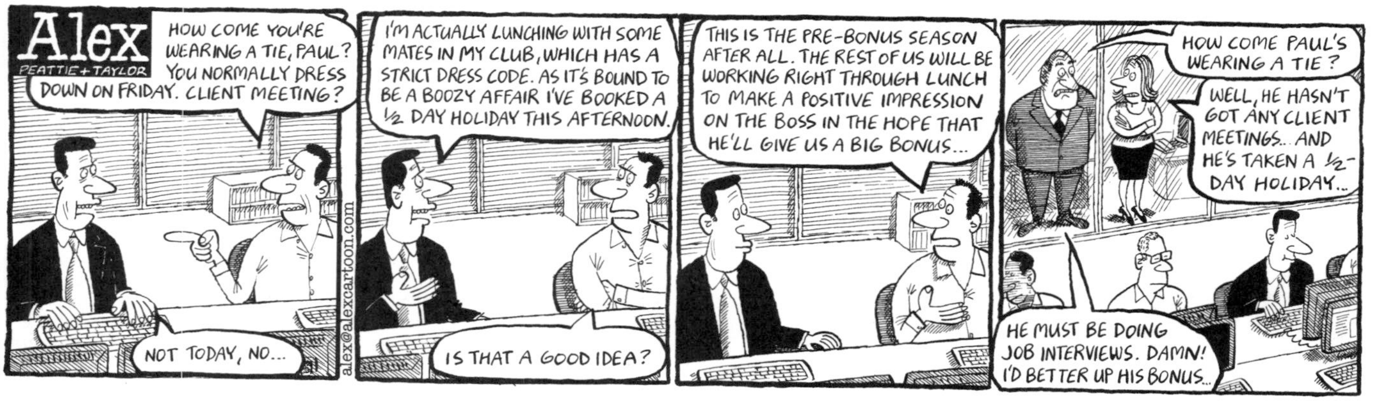
Alex
PEATTIE + TAYLOR
HOW COME YOU'RE WEARING A TIE, PAUL? YOU NORMALLY DRESS DOWN ON FRIDAY. CLIENT MEETING?
NOT TODAY, NO...
I'M ACTUALLY LUNCHING WITH SOME MATES IN MY CLUB, WHICH HAS A STRICT DRESS CODE. AS IT'S BOUND TO BE A BOOZY AFFAIR I'VE BOOKED A ½ DAY HOLIDAY THIS AFTERNOON.
IS THAT A GOOD IDEA?
alex@alexcartoon.com
THIS IS THE PRE-BONUS SEASON AFTER ALL. THE REST OF US WILL BE WORKING RIGHT THROUGH LUNCH TO MAKE A POSITIVE IMPRESSION ON THE BOSS IN THE HOPE THAT HE'LL GIVE US A BIG BONUS...
HOW COME PAUL'S WEARING A TIE?
WELL, HE HASN'T GOT ANY CLIENT MEETINGS... AND HE'S TAKEN A ½-DAY HOLIDAY...
HE MUST BE DOING JOB INTERVIEWS. DAMN! I'D BETTER UP HIS BONUS...

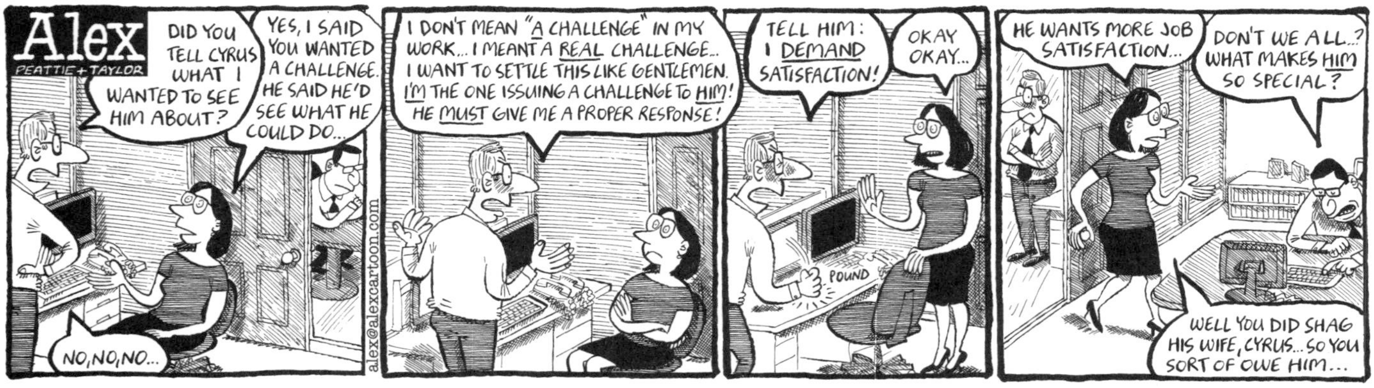
Alex
PEATTIE + TAYLOR
DID YOU TELL CYRUS WHAT I WANTED TO SEE HIM ABOUT?
YES, I SAID YOU WANTED A CHALLENGE. HE SAID HE'D SEE WHAT HE COULD DO...
NO, NO, NO...
alex@alexcartoon.com
I DON'T MEAN "A CHALLENGE" IN MY WORK... I MEANT A REAL CHALLENGE... I WANT TO SETTLE THIS LIKE GENTLEMEN. I'M THE ONE ISSUING A CHALLENGE TO HIM! HE MUST GIVE ME A PROPER RESPONSE!
TELL HIM: I DEMAND SATISFACTION!
OKAY OKAY...
POUND
HE WANTS MORE JOB SATISFACTION...
DON'T WE ALL..? WHAT MAKES HIM SO SPECIAL?
WELL YOU DID SHAG HIS WIFE, CYRUS... SO YOU SORT OF OWE HIM...

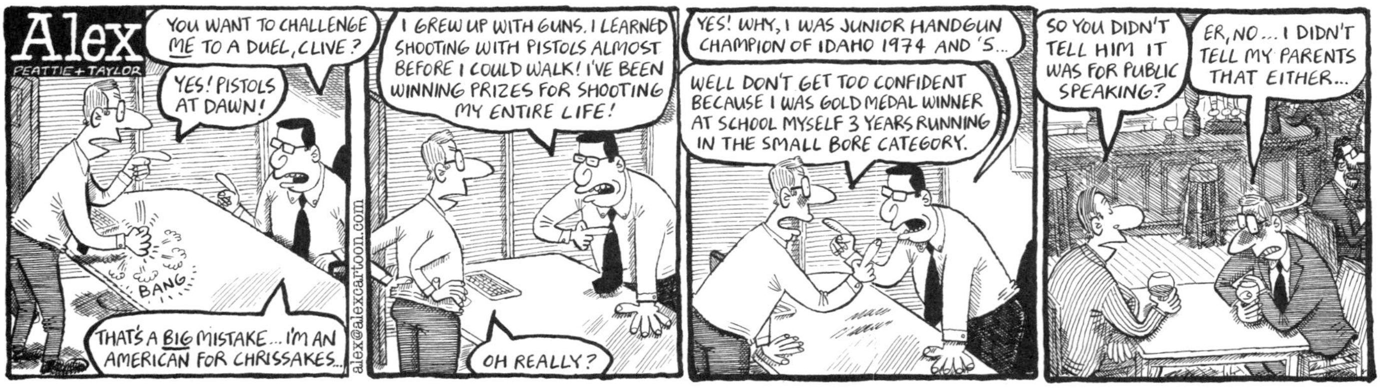
Alex
PEATTIE + TAYLOR
YOU WANT TO CHALLENGE ME TO A DUEL, CLIVE?
YES! PISTOLS AT DAWN!
BANG
THAT'S A BIG MISTAKE... I'M AN AMERICAN FOR CHRISSAKES...
alex@alexcartoon.com
I GREW UP WITH GUNS. I LEARNED SHOOTING WITH PISTOLS ALMOST BEFORE I COULD WALK! I'VE BEEN WINNING PRIZES FOR SHOOTING MY ENTIRE LIFE!
OH REALLY?
YES! WHY, I WAS JUNIOR HANDGUN CHAMPION OF IDAHO 1974 AND '5...
WELL DON'T GET TOO CONFIDENT BECAUSE I WAS GOLD MEDAL WINNER AT SCHOOL MYSELF 3 YEARS RUNNING IN THE SMALL BORE CATEGORY.
SO YOU DIDN'T TELL HIM IT WAS FOR PUBLIC SPEAKING?
ER, NO... I DIDN'T TELL MY PARENTS THAT EITHER...

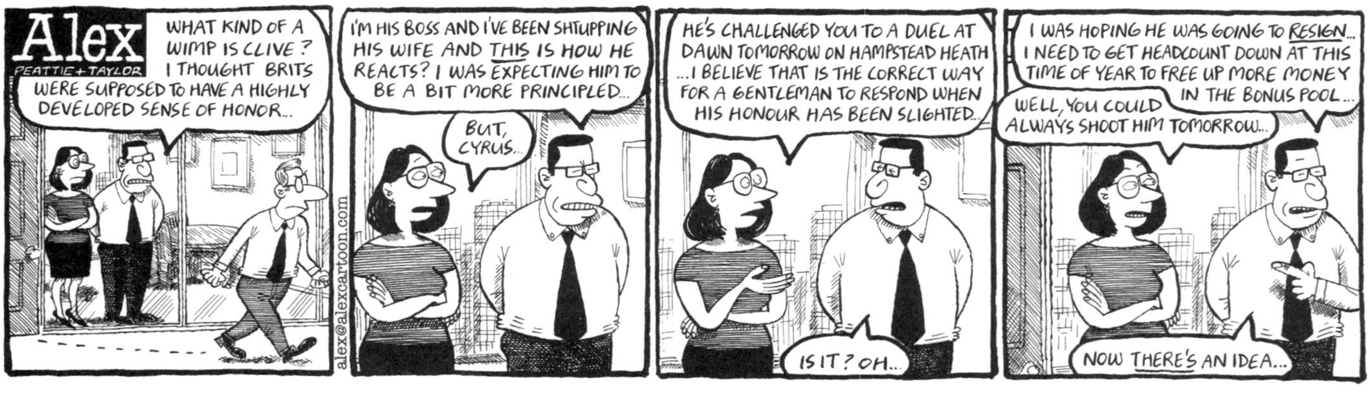
Alex
PEATTIE + TAYLOR
WHAT KIND OF A WIMP IS CLIVE? I THOUGHT BRITS WERE SUPPOSED TO HAVE A HIGHLY DEVELOPED SENSE OF HONOR...
alex@alexcartoon.com
I'M HIS BOSS AND I'VE BEEN SHTUPPING HIS WIFE AND THIS IS HOW HE REACTS? I WAS EXPECTING HIM TO BE A BIT MORE PRINCIPLED...
BUT, CYRUS...
HE'S CHALLENGED YOU TO A DUEL AT DAWN TOMORROW ON HAMPSTEAD HEATH ...I BELIEVE THAT IS THE CORRECT WAY FOR A GENTLEMAN TO RESPOND WHEN HIS HONOUR HAS BEEN SLIGHTED...
IS IT? OH..
I WAS HOPING HE WAS GOING TO RESIGN... I NEED TO GET HEADCOUNT DOWN AT THIS TIME OF YEAR TO FREE UP MORE MONEY IN THE BONUS POOL...
WELL, YOU COULD ALWAYS SHOOT HIM TOMORROW...
NOW THERE'S AN IDEA...

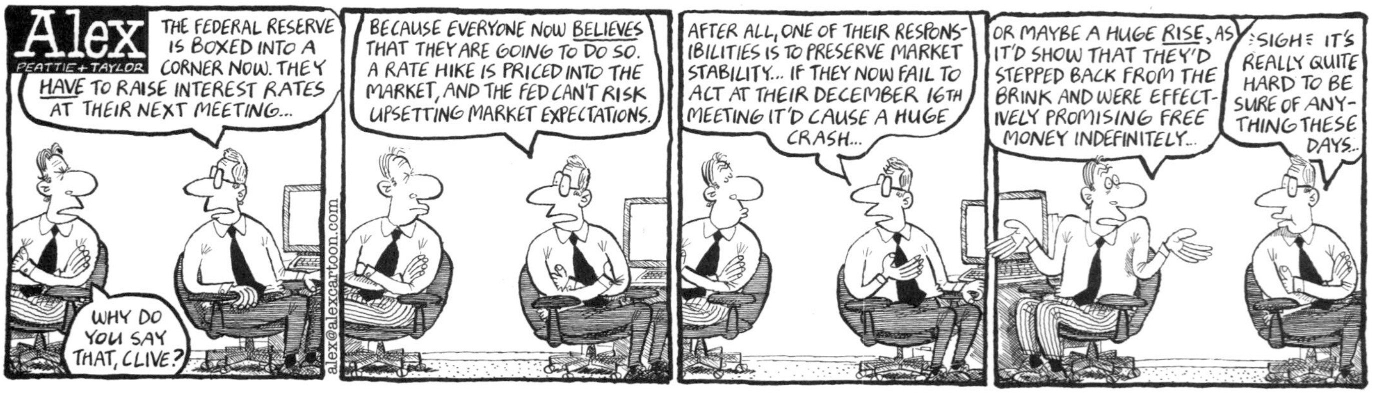
Alex
PEATTIE + TAYLOR
THE FEDERAL RESERVE IS BOXED INTO A CORNER NOW. THEY HAVE TO RAISE INTEREST RATES AT THEIR NEXT MEETING...
WHY DO YOU SAY THAT, CLIVE?
alex@alexcartoon.com
BECAUSE EVERYONE NOW BELIEVES THAT THEY ARE GOING TO DO SO. A RATE HIKE IS PRICED INTO THE MARKET, AND THE FED CAN'T RISK UPSETTING MARKET EXPECTATIONS.
AFTER ALL, ONE OF THEIR RESPONSIBILITIES IS TO PRESERVE MARKET STABILITY... IF THEY NOW FAIL TO ACT AT THEIR DECEMBER 16TH MEETING IT'D CAUSE A HUGE CRASH...
OR MAYBE A HUGE RISE, AS IT'D SHOW THAT THEY'D STEPPED BACK FROM THE BRINK AND WERE EFFECTIVELY PROMISING FREE MONEY INDEFINITELY...
SIGH IT'S REALLY QUITE HARD TO BE SURE OF ANYTHING THESE DAYS..

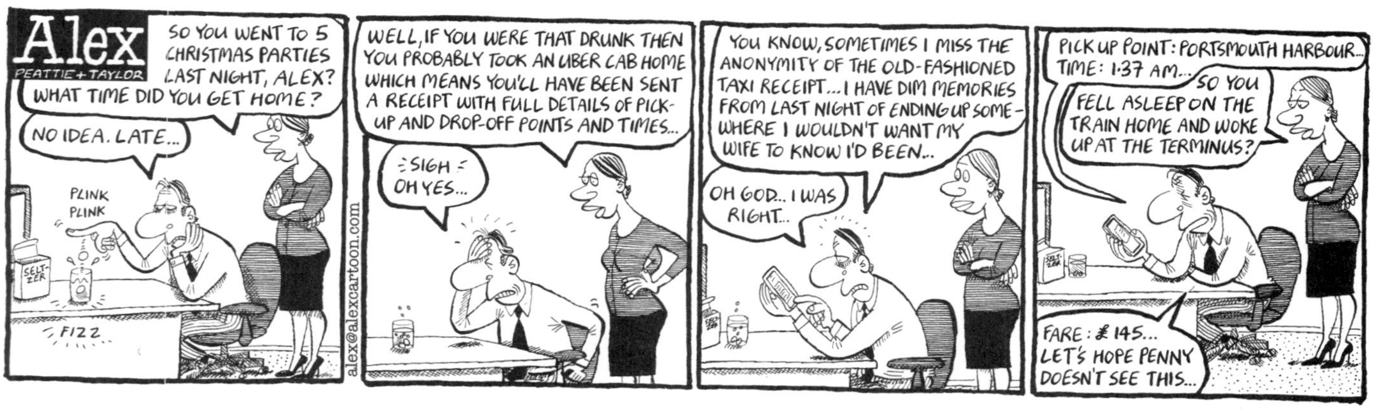
Alex
PEATTIE + TAYLOR
SO YOU WENT TO 5 CHRISTMAS PARTIES LAST NIGHT, ALEX? WHAT TIME DID YOU GET HOME?
NO IDEA. LATE...
PLINK PLINK
SELTZER
FIZZ
WELL, IF YOU WERE THAT DRUNK THEN YOU PROBABLY TOOK AN UBER CAB HOME WHICH MEANS YOU'LL HAVE BEEN SENT A RECEIPT WITH FULL DETAILS OF PICK-UP AND DROP-OFF POINTS AND TIMES...
SIGH OH YES...
alex@alexcartoon.com
YOU KNOW, SOMETIMES I MISS THE ANONYMITY OF THE OLD-FASHIONED TAXI RECEIPT... I HAVE DIM MEMORIES FROM LAST NIGHT OF ENDING UP SOMEWHERE I WOULDN'T WANT MY WIFE TO KNOW I'D BEEN...
OH GOD... I WAS RIGHT...
PICK UP POINT: PORTSMOUTH HARBOUR... TIME: 1.37 AM...
SO YOU FELL ASLEEP ON THE TRAIN HOME AND WOKE UP AT THE TERMINUS?
FARE: £145... LET'S HOPE PENNY DOESN'T SEE THIS...

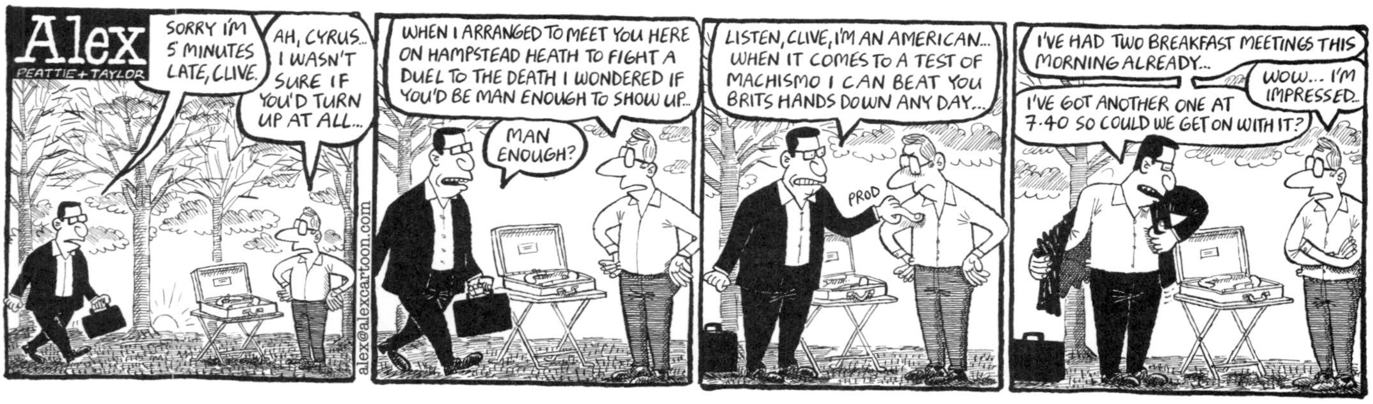
Alex
PEATTIE + TAYLOR
SORRY I'M 5 MINUTES LATE, CLIVE.
AH, CYRUS... I WASN'T SURE IF YOU'D TURN UP AT ALL...
alex@alexcartoon.com
WHEN I ARRANGED TO MEET YOU HERE ON HAMPSTEAD HEATH TO FIGHT A DUEL TO THE DEATH I WONDERED IF YOU'D BE MAN ENOUGH TO SHOW UP...
MAN ENOUGH?
LISTEN, CLIVE, I'M AN AMERICAN... WHEN IT COMES TO A TEST OF MACHISMO I CAN BEAT YOU BRITS HANDS DOWN ANY DAY...
PROD
I'VE HAD TWO BREAKFAST MEETINGS THIS MORNING ALREADY...
WOW... I'M IMPRESSED...
I'VE GOT ANOTHER ONE AT 7.40 SO COULD WE GET ON WITH IT?

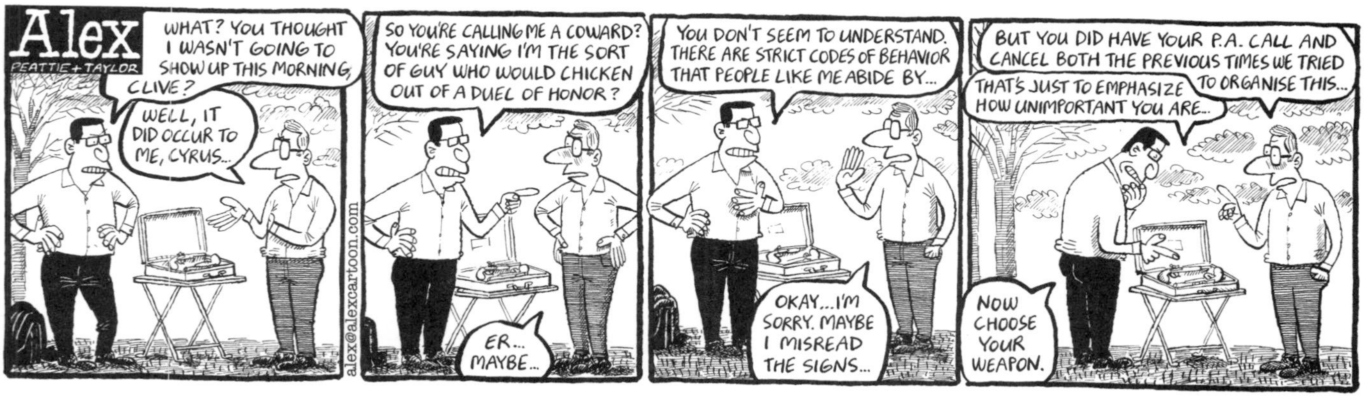
Alex
PEATTIE + TAYLOR
WHAT? YOU THOUGHT I WASN'T GOING TO SHOW UP THIS MORNING, CLIVE?
WELL, IT DID OCCUR TO ME, CYRUS...
alex@alexcartoon.com
SO YOU'RE CALLING ME A COWARD? YOU'RE SAYING I'M THE SORT OF GUY WHO WOULD CHICKEN OUT OF A DUEL OF HONOR?
ER... MAYBE...
YOU DON'T SEEM TO UNDERSTAND. THERE ARE STRICT CODES OF BEHAVIOR THAT PEOPLE LIKE ME ABIDE BY...
OKAY... I'M SORRY. MAYBE I MISREAD THE SIGNS...
BUT YOU DID HAVE YOUR P.A. CALL AND CANCEL BOTH THE PREVIOUS TIMES WE TRIED TO ORGANISE THIS...
THAT'S JUST TO EMPHASIZE HOW UNIMPORTANT YOU ARE...
NOW CHOOSE YOUR WEAPON.

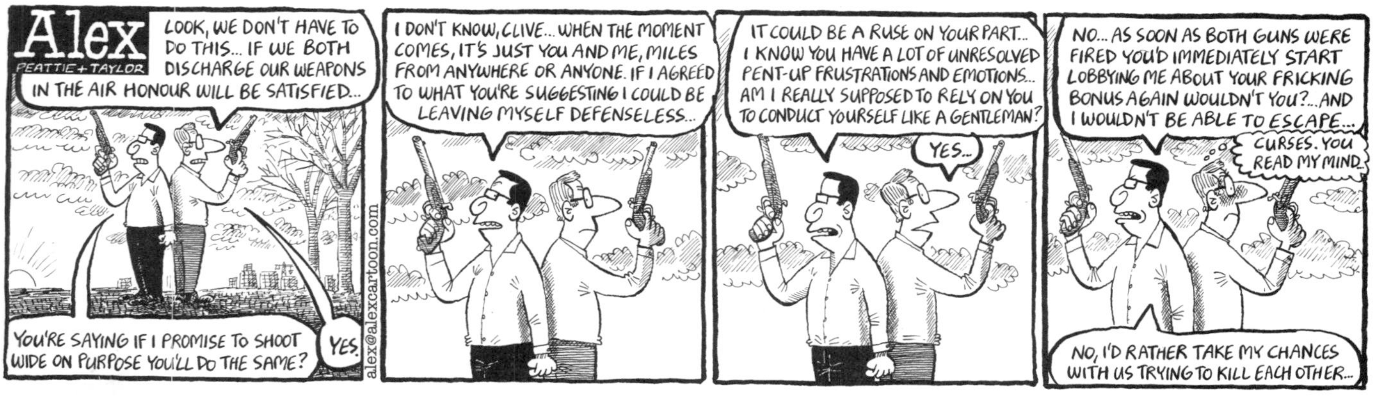
Alex
PEATTIE + TAYLOR
LOOK, WE DON'T HAVE TO DO THIS... IF WE BOTH DISCHARGE OUR WEAPONS IN THE AIR HONOUR WILL BE SATISFIED...
YOU'RE SAYING IF I PROMISE TO SHOOT WIDE ON PURPOSE YOU'LL DO THE SAME?
YES.
alex@alexcartoon.com
I DON'T KNOW, CLIVE... WHEN THE MOMENT COMES, IT'S JUST YOU AND ME, MILES FROM ANYWHERE OR ANYONE. IF I AGREED TO WHAT YOU'RE SUGGESTING I COULD BE LEAVING MYSELF DEFENSELESS...
IT COULD BE A RUSE ON YOUR PART... I KNOW YOU HAVE A LOT OF UNRESOLVED PENT-UP FRUSTRATIONS AND EMOTIONS... AM I REALLY SUPPOSED TO RELY ON YOU TO CONDUCT YOURSELF LIKE A GENTLEMAN?
YES...
NO... AS SOON AS BOTH GUNS WERE FIRED YOU'D IMMEDIATELY START LOBBYING ME ABOUT YOUR FRICKING BONUS AGAIN WOULDN'T YOU?... AND I WOULDN'T BE ABLE TO ESCAPE...
CURSES. YOU READ MY MIND.
NO, I'D RATHER TAKE MY CHANCES WITH US TRYING TO KILL EACH OTHER...

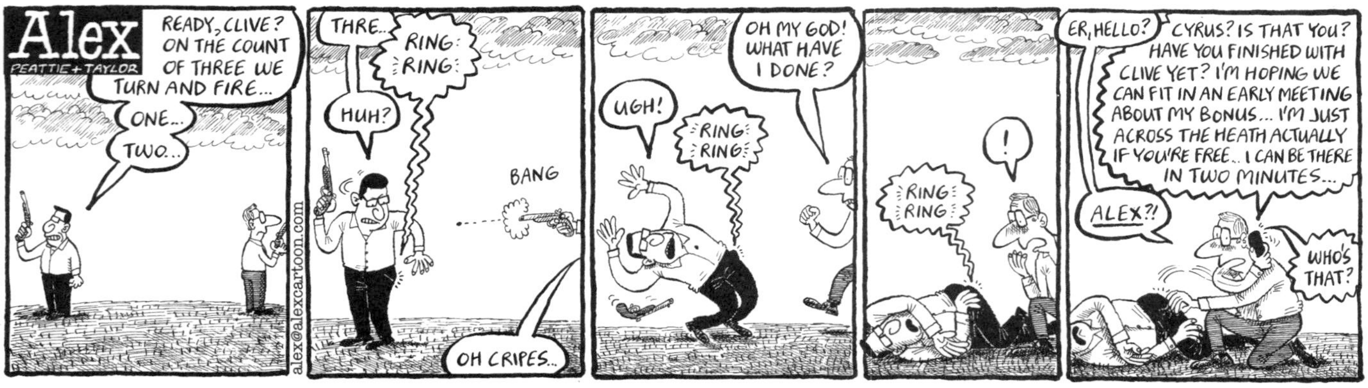
Alex
PEATTIE+TAYLOR
READY, CLIVE? ON THE COUNT OF THREE WE TURN AND FIRE...
ONE...
TWO...
alex@alexcartoon.com
THRE..
RING RING
HUH?
BANG
OH CRIPES..
UGH!
RING RING
OH MY GOD! WHAT HAVE I DONE?
RING RING
!
ER, HELLO?
CYRUS? IS THAT YOU? HAVE YOU FINISHED WITH CLIVE YET? I'M HOPING WE CAN FIT IN AN EARLY MEETING ABOUT MY BONUS... I'M JUST ACROSS THE HEATH ACTUALLY IF YOU'RE FREE.. I CAN BE THERE IN TWO MINUTES...
ALEX?!
WHO'S THAT?

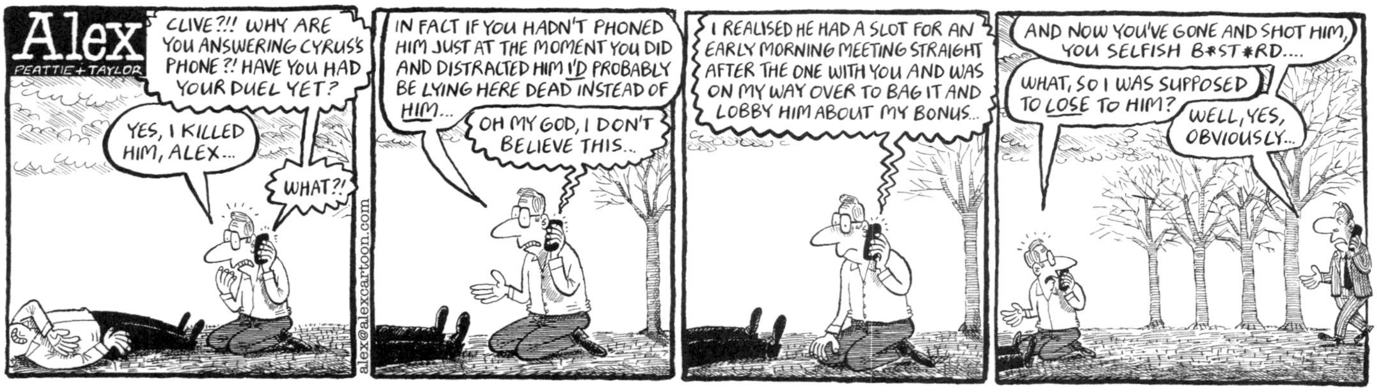
Alex
PEATTIE+TAYLOR
CLIVE?!! WHY ARE YOU ANSWERING CYRUS'S PHONE?! HAVE YOU HAD YOUR DUEL YET?
YES, I KILLED HIM, ALEX...
WHAT?!
alex@alexcartoon.com
IN FACT IF YOU HADN'T PHONED HIM JUST AT THE MOMENT YOU DID AND DISTRACTED HIM I'D PROBABLY BE LYING HERE DEAD INSTEAD OF HIM...
OH MY GOD, I DON'T BELIEVE THIS...
I REALISED HE HAD A SLOT FOR AN EARLY MORNING MEETING STRAIGHT AFTER THE ONE WITH YOU AND WAS ON MY WAY OVER TO BAG IT AND LOBBY HIM ABOUT MY BONUS...
AND NOW YOU'VE GONE AND SHOT HIM, YOU SELFISH B*ST*RD....
WHAT, SO I WAS SUPPOSED TO LOSE TO HIM?
WELL, YES, OBVIOUSLY...

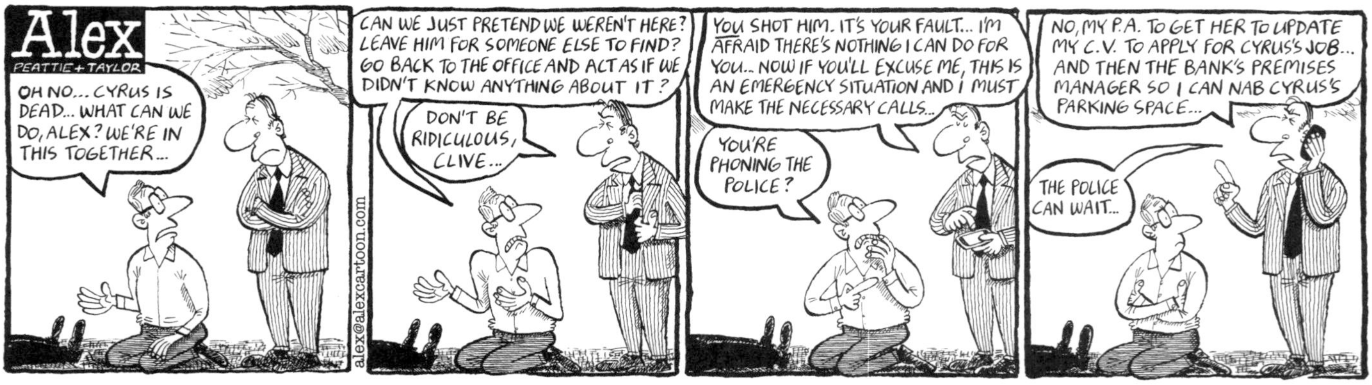
Alex
PEATTIE+TAYLOR
OH NO... CYRUS IS DEAD... WHAT CAN WE DO, ALEX? WE'RE IN THIS TOGETHER...
alex@alexcartoon.com
CAN WE JUST PRETEND WE WEREN'T HERE? LEAVE HIM FOR SOMEONE ELSE TO FIND? GO BACK TO THE OFFICE AND ACT AS IF WE DIDN'T KNOW ANYTHING ABOUT IT?
DON'T BE RIDICULOUS, CLIVE...
YOU SHOT HIM. IT'S YOUR FAULT... I'M AFRAID THERE'S NOTHING I CAN DO FOR YOU... NOW IF YOU'LL EXCUSE ME, THIS IS AN EMERGENCY SITUATION AND I MUST MAKE THE NECESSARY CALLS...
YOU'RE PHONING THE POLICE?
NO, MY P.A. TO GET HER TO UPDATE MY C.V. TO APPLY FOR CYRUS'S JOB... AND THEN THE BANK'S PREMISES MANAGER SO I CAN NAB CYRUS'S PARKING SPACE...
THE POLICE CAN WAIT...

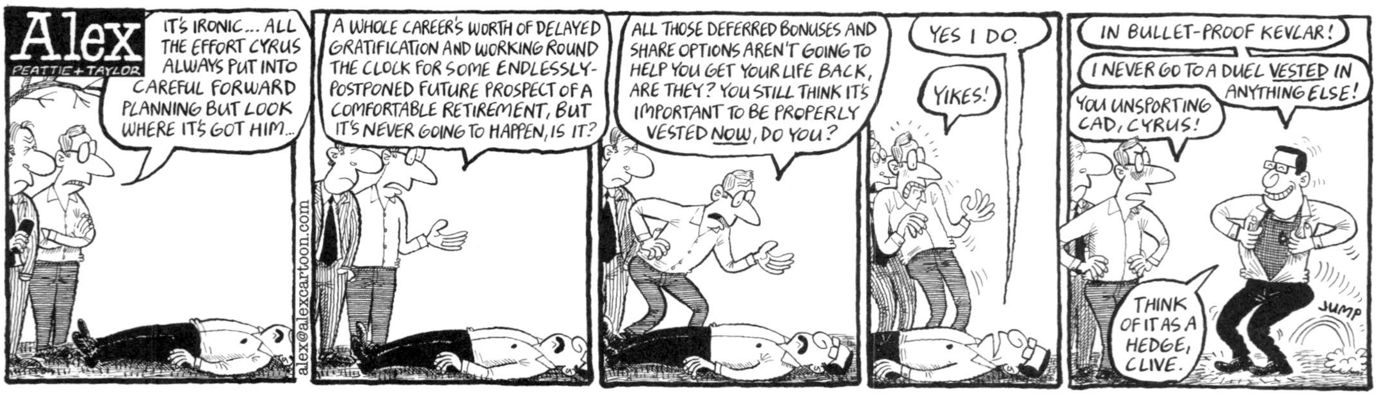
Alex
PEATTIE+TAYLOR
IT'S IRONIC... ALL THE EFFORT CYRUS ALWAYS PUT INTO CAREFUL FORWARD PLANNING BUT LOOK WHERE IT'S GOT HIM...
alex@alexcartoon.com
A WHOLE CAREER'S WORTH OF DELAYED GRATIFICATION AND WORKING ROUND THE CLOCK FOR SOME ENDLESSLY-POSTPONED FUTURE PROSPECT OF A COMFORTABLE RETIREMENT, BUT IT'S NEVER GOING TO HAPPEN, IS IT?
ALL THOSE DEFERRED BONUSES AND SHARE OPTIONS AREN'T GOING TO HELP YOU GET YOUR LIFE BACK, ARE THEY? YOU STILL THINK IT'S IMPORTANT TO BE PROPERLY VESTED NOW, DO YOU?
YES I DO.
YIKES!
IN BULLET-PROOF KEVLAR!
I NEVER GO TO A DUEL VESTED IN ANYTHING ELSE!
YOU UNSPORTING CAD, CYRUS!
THINK OF IT AS A HEDGE, CLIVE.
JUMP

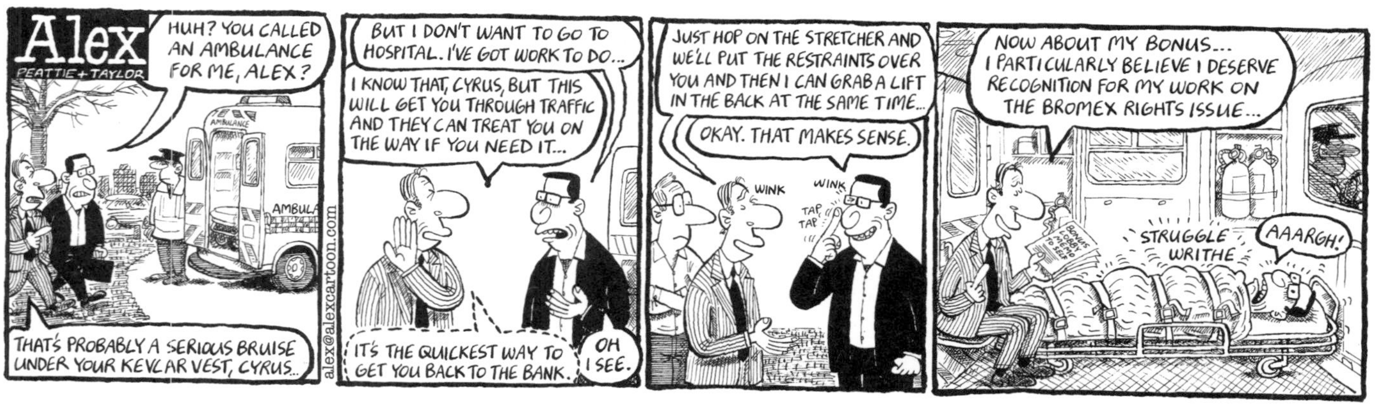
Alex
PEATTIE + TAYLOR
HUH? YOU CALLED AN AMBULANCE FOR ME, ALEX?
THAT'S PROBABLY A SERIOUS BRUISE UNDER YOUR KEVLAR VEST, CYRUS...
alex@alexcartoon.com
BUT I DON'T WANT TO GO TO HOSPITAL. I'VE GOT WORK TO DO...
I KNOW THAT, CYRUS, BUT THIS WILL GET YOU THROUGH TRAFFIC AND THEY CAN TREAT YOU ON THE WAY IF YOU NEED IT...
IT'S THE QUICKEST WAY TO GET YOU BACK TO THE BANK.
OH I SEE.
JUST HOP ON THE STRETCHER AND WE'LL PUT THE RESTRAINTS OVER YOU AND THEN I CAN GRAB A LIFT IN THE BACK AT THE SAME TIME...
OKAY. THAT MAKES SENSE.
WINK
WINK
TAP TAP
NOW ABOUT MY BONUS... I PARTICULARLY BELIEVE I DESERVE RECOGNITION FOR MY WORK ON THE BROMEX RIGHTS ISSUE...
STRUGGLE
WRITHE
AAARGH!

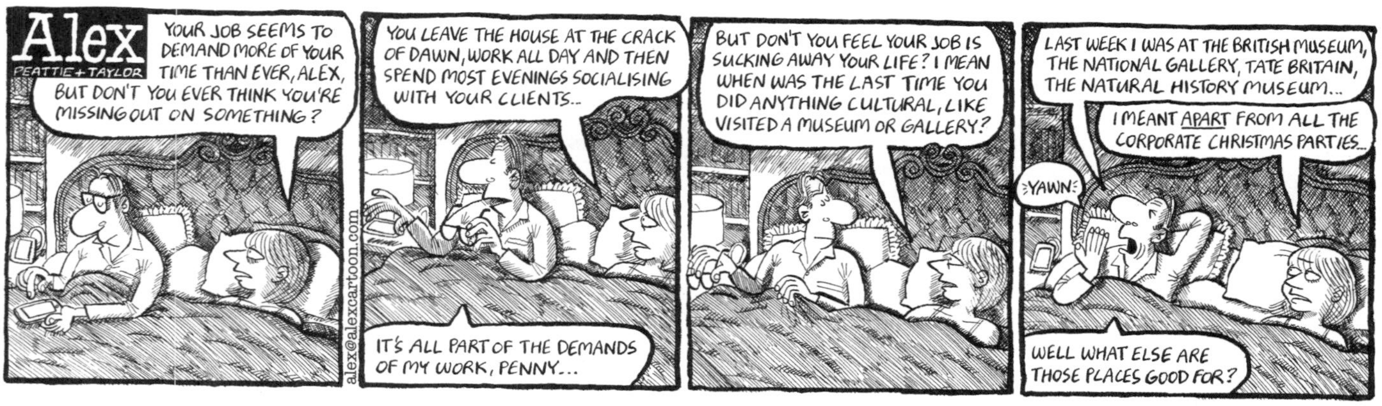
Alex
PEATTIE + TAYLOR
YOUR JOB SEEMS TO DEMAND MORE OF YOUR TIME THAN EVER, ALEX, BUT DON'T YOU EVER THINK YOU'RE MISSING OUT ON SOMETHING?
alex@alexcartoon.com
YOU LEAVE THE HOUSE AT THE CRACK OF DAWN, WORK ALL DAY AND THEN SPEND MOST EVENINGS SOCIALISING WITH YOUR CLIENTS...
IT'S ALL PART OF THE DEMANDS OF MY WORK, PENNY...
BUT DON'T YOU FEEL YOUR JOB IS SUCKING AWAY YOUR LIFE? I MEAN WHEN WAS THE LAST TIME YOU DID ANYTHING CULTURAL, LIKE VISITED A MUSEUM OR GALLERY?
LAST WEEK I WAS AT THE BRITISH MUSEUM, THE NATIONAL GALLERY, TATE BRITAIN, THE NATURAL HISTORY MUSEUM...
I MEANT APART FROM ALL THE CORPORATE CHRISTMAS PARTIES...
YAWN
WELL WHAT ELSE ARE THOSE PLACES GOOD FOR?

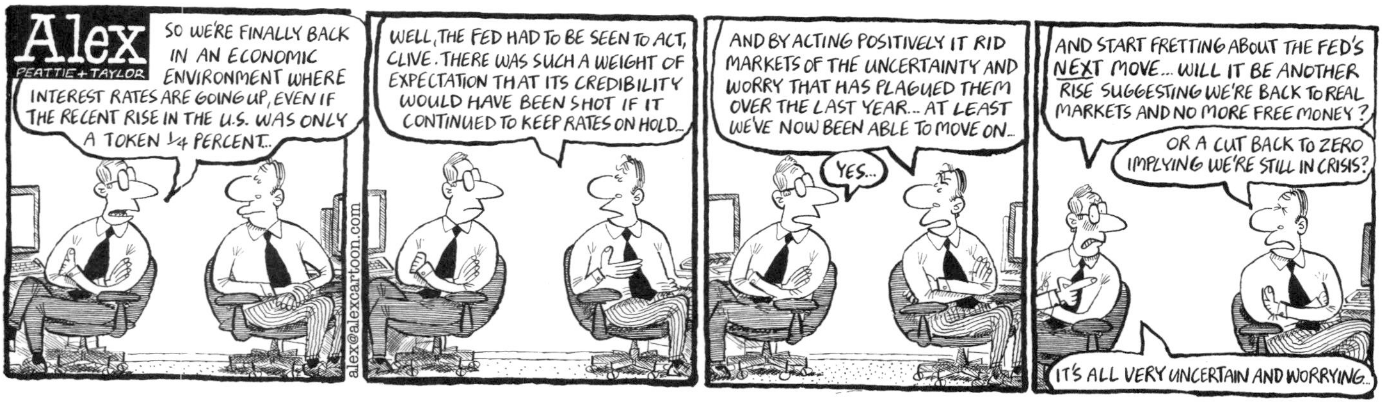
Alex
PEATTIE + TAYLOR
SO WE'RE FINALLY BACK IN AN ECONOMIC ENVIRONMENT WHERE INTEREST RATES ARE GOING UP, EVEN IF THE RECENT RISE IN THE U.S. WAS ONLY A TOKEN 1/4 PERCENT...
alex@alexcartoon.com
WELL, THE FED HAD TO BE SEEN TO ACT, CLIVE. THERE WAS SUCH A WEIGHT OF EXPECTATION THAT ITS CREDIBILITY WOULD HAVE BEEN SHOT IF IT CONTINUED TO KEEP RATES ON HOLD...
AND BY ACTING POSITIVELY IT RID MARKETS OF THE UNCERTAINTY AND WORRY THAT HAS PLAGUED THEM OVER THE LAST YEAR... AT LEAST WE'VE NOW BEEN ABLE TO MOVE ON...
YES...
AND START FRETTING ABOUT THE FED'S NEXT MOVE... WILL IT BE ANOTHER RISE SUGGESTING WE'RE BACK TO REAL MARKETS AND NO MORE FREE MONEY?
OR A CUT BACK TO ZERO IMPLYING WE'RE STILL IN CRISIS?
IT'S ALL VERY UNCERTAIN AND WORRYING...

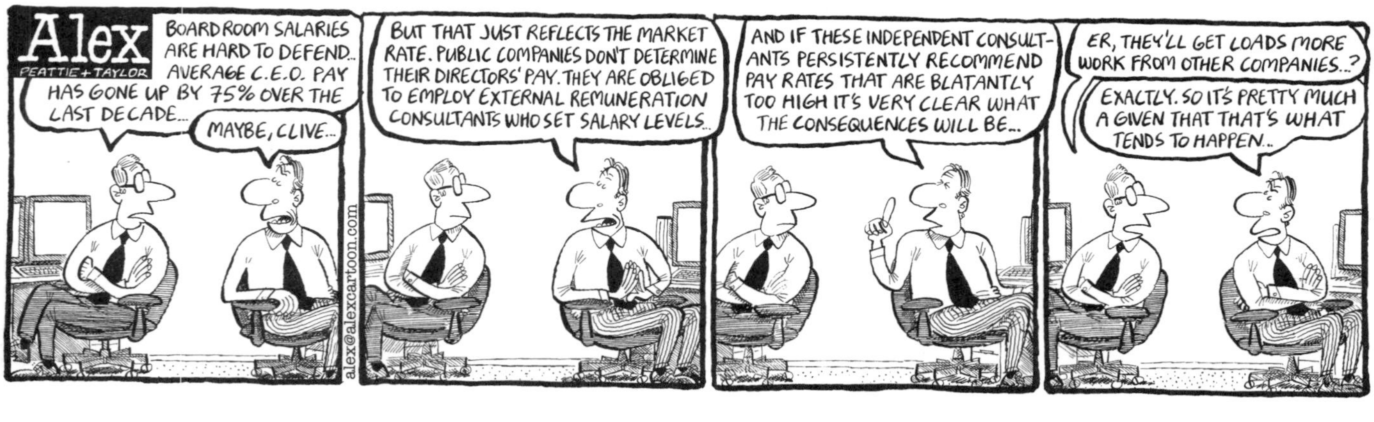
Alex
PEATTIE + TAYLOR
BOARDROOM SALARIES ARE HARD TO DEFEND... AVERAGE C.E.O. PAY HAS GONE UP BY 75% OVER THE LAST DECADE...
MAYBE, CLIVE...
alex@alexcartoon.com
BUT THAT JUST REFLECTS THE MARKET RATE. PUBLIC COMPANIES DON'T DETERMINE THEIR DIRECTORS' PAY. THEY ARE OBLIGED TO EMPLOY EXTERNAL REMUNERATION CONSULTANTS WHO SET SALARY LEVELS...
AND IF THESE INDEPENDENT CONSULT-ANTS PERSISTENTLY RECOMMEND PAY RATES THAT ARE BLATANTLY TOO HIGH IT'S VERY CLEAR WHAT THE CONSEQUENCES WILL BE...
ER, THEY'LL GET LOADS MORE WORK FROM OTHER COMPANIES..?
EXACTLY. SO IT'S PRETTY MUCH A GIVEN THAT THAT'S WHAT TENDS TO HAPPEN...

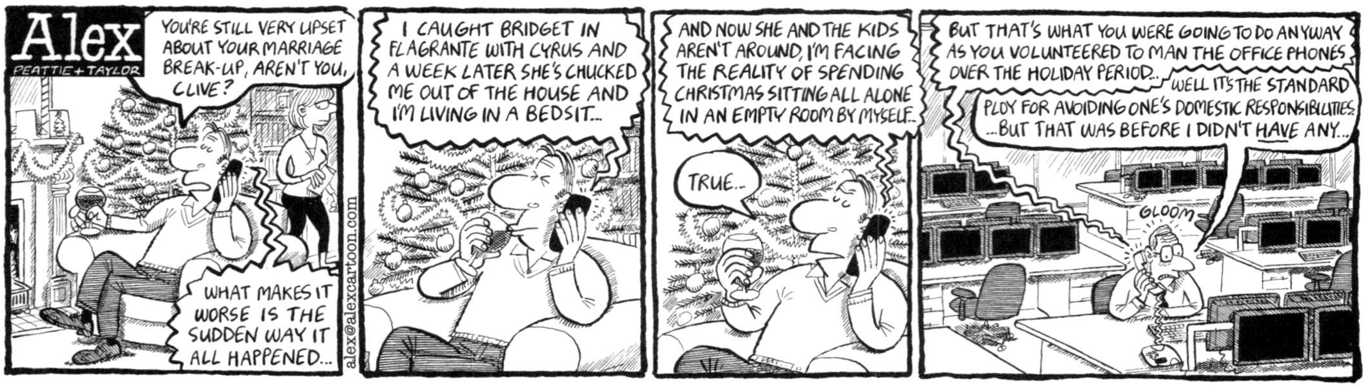
Alex
PEATTIE + TAYLOR
YOU'RE STILL VERY UPSET ABOUT YOUR MARRIAGE BREAK-UP, AREN'T YOU, CLIVE?
WHAT MAKES IT WORSE IS THE SUDDEN WAY IT ALL HAPPENED...
I CAUGHT BRIDGET IN FLAGRANTE WITH CYRUS AND A WEEK LATER SHE'S CHUCKED ME OUT OF THE HOUSE AND I'M LIVING IN A BEDSIT...
alex@alexcartoon.com
AND NOW SHE AND THE KIDS AREN'T AROUND, I'M FACING THE REALITY OF SPENDING CHRISTMAS SITTING ALL ALONE IN AN EMPTY ROOM BY MYSELF...
TRUE...
BUT THAT'S WHAT YOU WERE GOING TO DO ANYWAY AS YOU VOLUNTEERED TO MAN THE OFFICE PHONES OVER THE HOLIDAY PERIOD...
WELL IT'S THE STANDARD PLOY FOR AVOIDING ONE'S DOMESTIC RESPONSIBILITIES. ...BUT THAT WAS BEFORE I DIDN'T HAVE ANY...
GLOOM

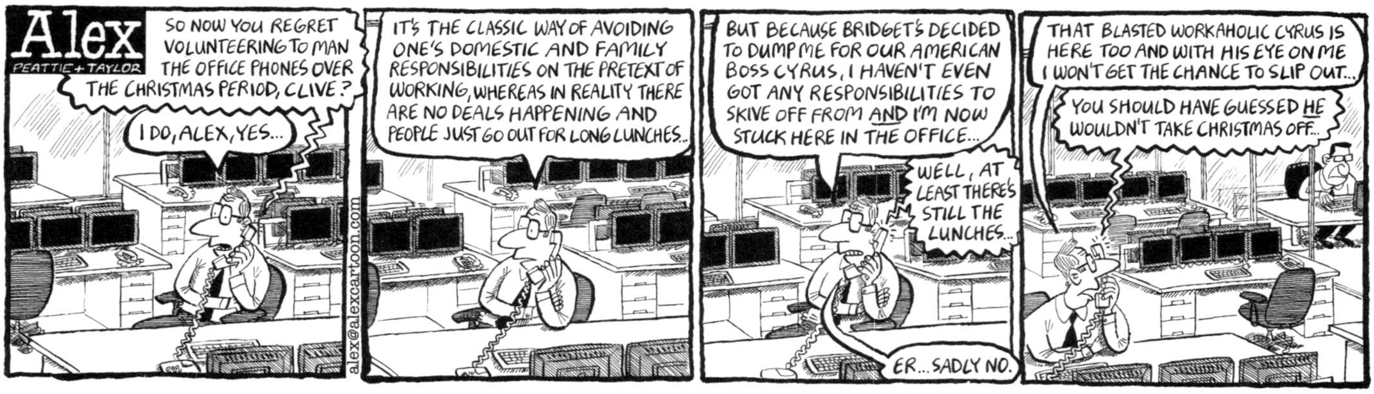
Alex
PEATTIE + TAYLOR
SO NOW YOU REGRET VOLUNTEERING TO MAN THE OFFICE PHONES OVER THE CHRISTMAS PERIOD, CLIVE?
I DO, ALEX, YES...
alex@alexcartoon.com
IT'S THE CLASSIC WAY OF AVOIDING ONE'S DOMESTIC AND FAMILY RESPONSIBILITIES ON THE PRETEXT OF WORKING, WHEREAS IN REALITY THERE ARE NO DEALS HAPPENING AND PEOPLE JUST GO OUT FOR LONG LUNCHES...
BUT BECAUSE BRIDGET'S DECIDED TO DUMP ME FOR OUR AMERICAN BOSS CYRUS, I HAVEN'T EVEN GOT ANY RESPONSIBILITIES TO SKIVE OFF FROM AND I'M NOW STUCK HERE IN THE OFFICE...
WELL, AT LEAST THERE'S STILL THE LUNCHES...
ER...SADLY NO.
THAT BLASTED WORKAHOLIC CYRUS IS HERE TOO AND WITH HIS EYE ON ME I WON'T GET THE CHANCE TO SLIP OUT...
YOU SHOULD HAVE GUESSED HE WOULDN'T TAKE CHRISTMAS OFF...

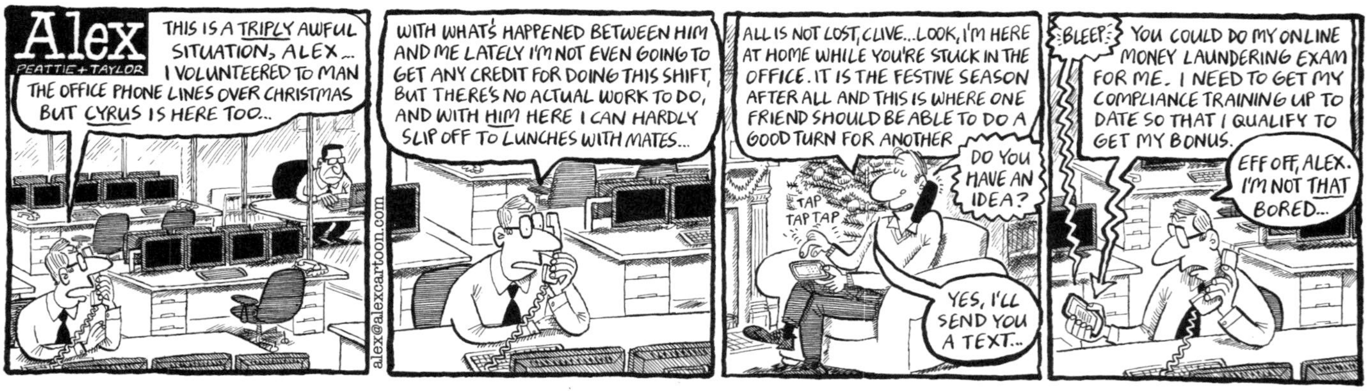
Alex
PEATTIE + TAYLOR
THIS IS A TRIPLY AWFUL SITUATION, ALEX... I VOLUNTEERED TO MAN THE OFFICE PHONE LINES OVER CHRISTMAS BUT CYRUS IS HERE TOO...
alex@alexcartoon.com
WITH WHAT'S HAPPENED BETWEEN HIM AND ME LATELY I'M NOT EVEN GOING TO GET ANY CREDIT FOR DOING THIS SHIFT, BUT THERE'S NO ACTUAL WORK TO DO, AND WITH HIM HERE I CAN HARDLY SLIP OFF TO LUNCHES WITH MATES...
ALL IS NOT LOST, CLIVE...LOOK, I'M HERE AT HOME WHILE YOU'RE STUCK IN THE OFFICE. IT IS THE FESTIVE SEASON AFTER ALL AND THIS IS WHERE ONE FRIEND SHOULD BE ABLE TO DO A GOOD TURN FOR ANOTHER
DO YOU HAVE AN IDEA?
TAP TAP TAP
YES, I'LL SEND YOU A TEXT...
BLEEP
YOU COULD DO MY ONLINE MONEY LAUNDERING EXAM FOR ME. I NEED TO GET MY COMPLIANCE TRAINING UP TO DATE SO THAT I QUALIFY TO GET MY BONUS.
EFF OFF, ALEX. I'M NOT THAT BORED...

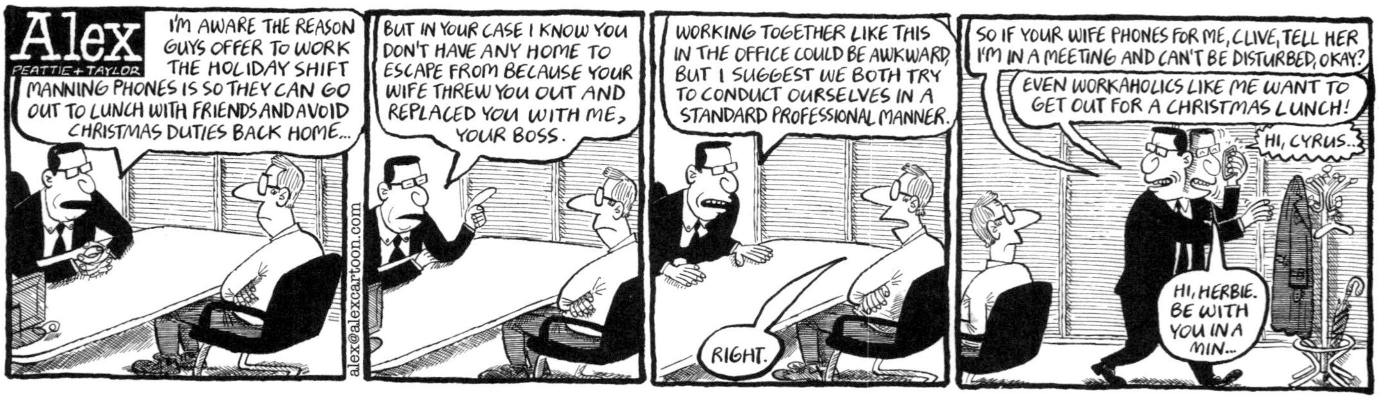
Alex
PEATTIE + TAYLOR
I'M AWARE THE REASON GUYS OFFER TO WORK THE HOLIDAY SHIFT MANNING PHONES IS SO THEY CAN GO OUT TO LUNCH WITH FRIENDS AND AVOID CHRISTMAS DUTIES BACK HOME...
alex@alexcartoon.com
BUT IN YOUR CASE I KNOW YOU DON'T HAVE ANY HOME TO ESCAPE FROM BECAUSE YOUR WIFE THREW YOU OUT AND REPLACED YOU WITH ME, YOUR BOSS.
WORKING TOGETHER LIKE THIS IN THE OFFICE COULD BE AWKWARD, BUT I SUGGEST WE BOTH TRY TO CONDUCT OURSELVES IN A STANDARD PROFESSIONAL MANNER.
RIGHT.
SO IF YOUR WIFE PHONES FOR ME, CLIVE, TELL HER I'M IN A MEETING AND CAN'T BE DISTURBED, OKAY?
EVEN WORKAHOLICS LIKE ME WANT TO GET OUT FOR A CHRISTMAS LUNCH!
HI, CYRUS...
HI, HERBIE. BE WITH YOU IN A MIN...

CLIVE IS ON HIS OWN THIS CHRISTMAS...

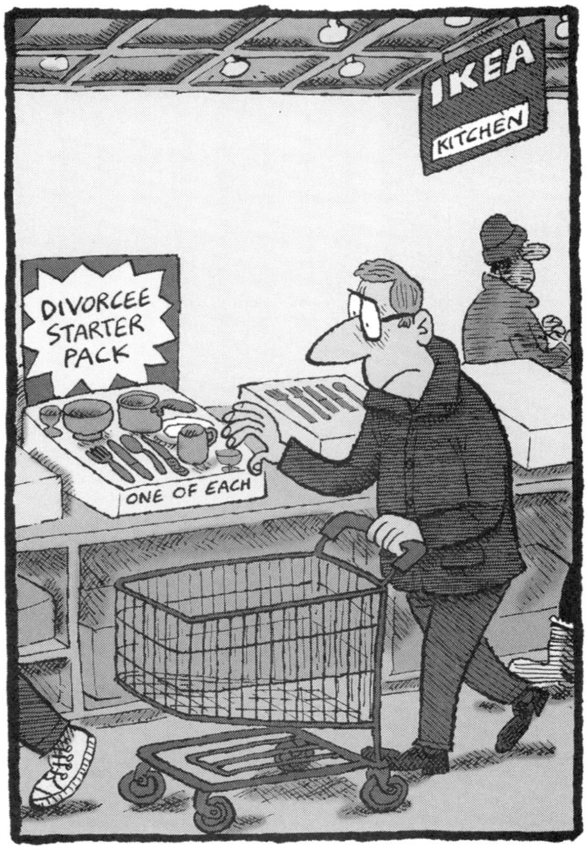
IKEA
KITCHEN
DIVORCEE STARTER PACK
ONE OF EACH

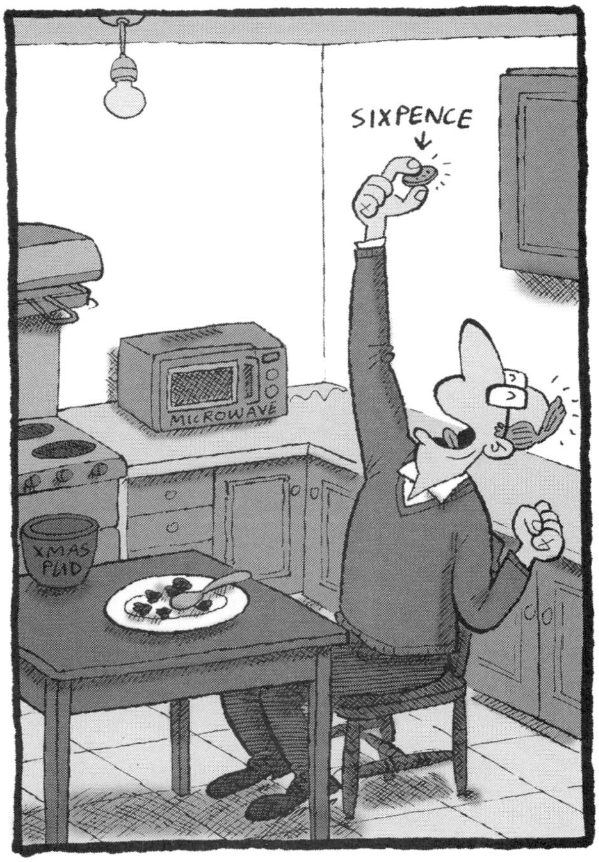
SIXPENCE
MICROWAVE
XMAS PUD

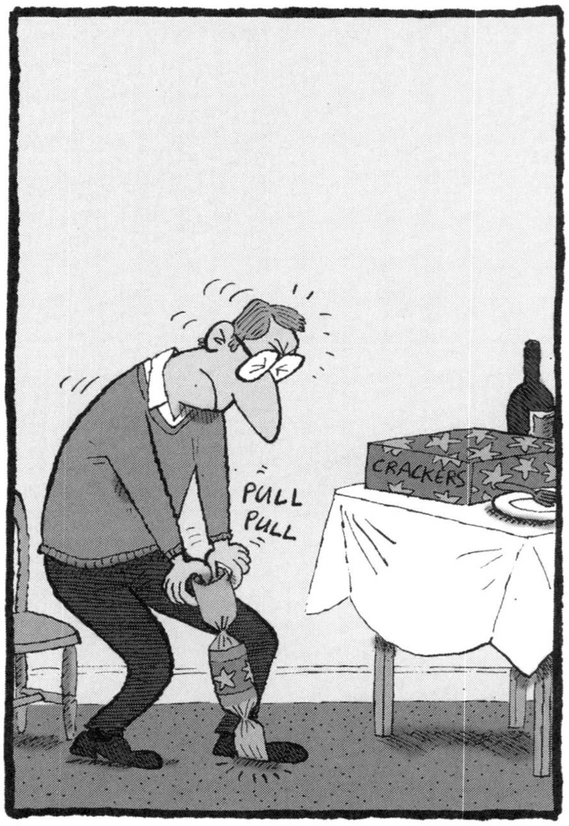
PULL
PULL
CRACKERS

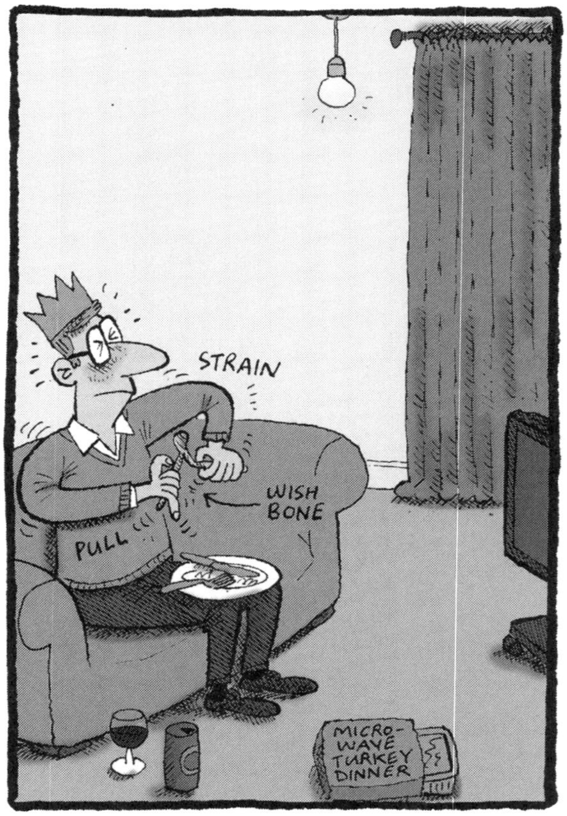
STRAIN
WISH BONE
PULL
MICRO-WAVE TURKEY DINNER

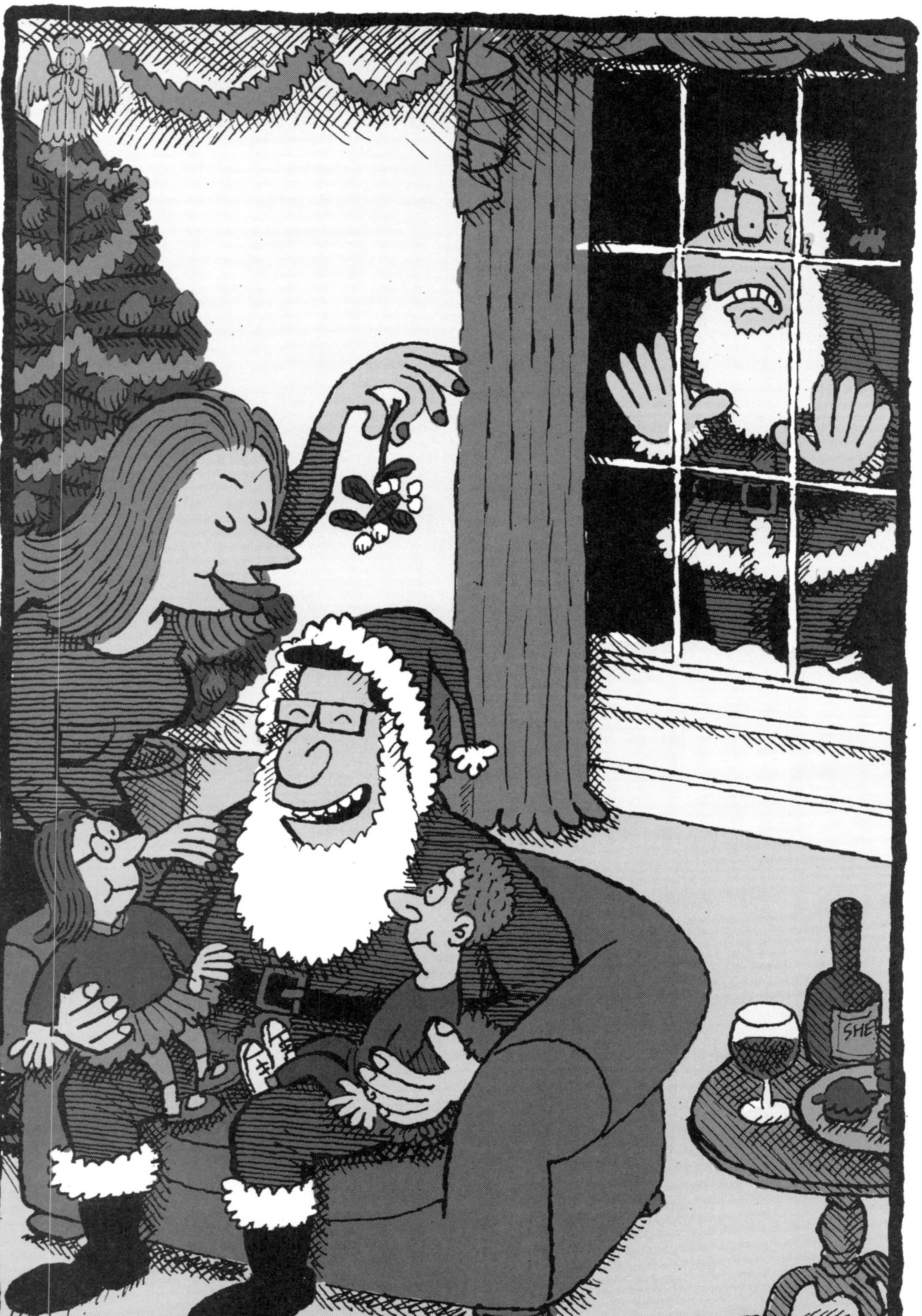

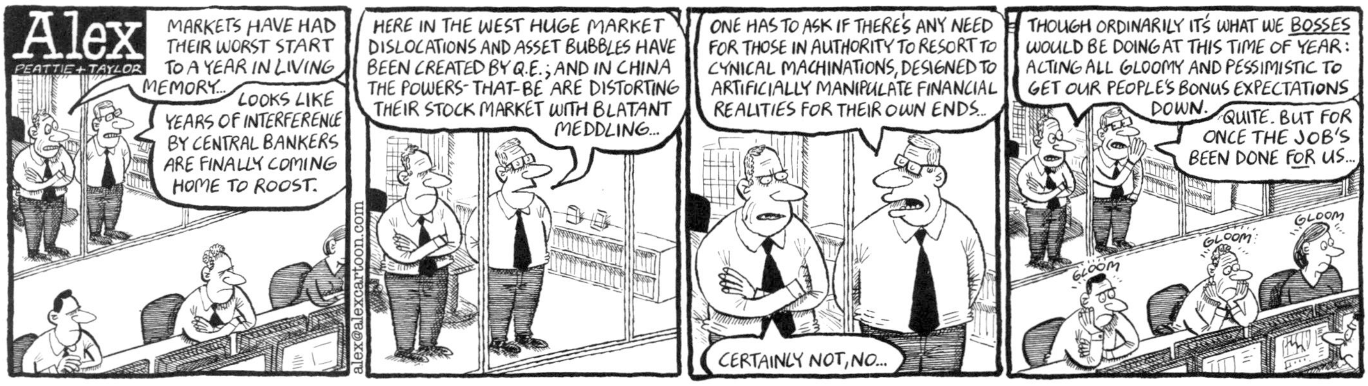
Alex
PEATTIE+TAYLOR
MARKETS HAVE HAD THEIR WORST START TO A YEAR IN LIVING MEMORY...
LOOKS LIKE YEARS OF INTERFERENCE BY CENTRAL BANKERS ARE FINALLY COMING HOME TO ROOST.
alex@alexcartoon.com
HERE IN THE WEST HUGE MARKET DISLOCATIONS AND ASSET BUBBLES HAVE BEEN CREATED BY Q.E.; AND IN CHINA THE POWERS-THAT-BE ARE DISTORTING THEIR STOCK MARKET WITH BLATANT MEDDLING...
ONE HAS TO ASK IF THERE'S ANY NEED FOR THOSE IN AUTHORITY TO RESORT TO CYNICAL MACHINATIONS, DESIGNED TO ARTIFICIALLY MANIPULATE FINANCIAL REALITIES FOR THEIR OWN ENDS...
CERTAINLY NOT, NO...
THOUGH ORDINARILY IT'S WHAT WE BOSSES WOULD BE DOING AT THIS TIME OF YEAR: ACTING ALL GLOOMY AND PESSIMISTIC TO GET OUR PEOPLE'S BONUS EXPECTATIONS DOWN.
QUITE. BUT FOR ONCE THE JOB'S BEEN DONE FOR US...
GLOOM
GLOOM
GLOOM

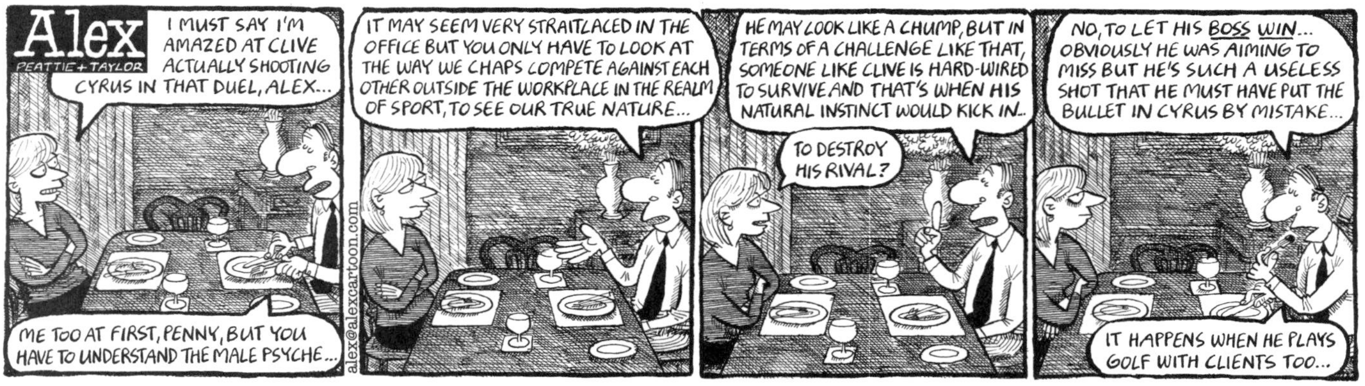
Alex
PEATTIE+TAYLOR
I MUST SAY I'M AMAZED AT CLIVE ACTUALLY SHOOTING CYRUS IN THAT DUEL, ALEX...
ME TOO AT FIRST, PENNY, BUT YOU HAVE TO UNDERSTAND THE MALE PSYCHE...
alex@alexcartoon.com
IT MAY SEEM VERY STRAITLACED IN THE OFFICE BUT YOU ONLY HAVE TO LOOK AT THE WAY WE CHAPS COMPETE AGAINST EACH OTHER OUTSIDE THE WORKPLACE IN THE REALM OF SPORT, TO SEE OUR TRUE NATURE...
HE MAY LOOK LIKE A CHUMP, BUT IN TERMS OF A CHALLENGE LIKE THAT, SOMEONE LIKE CLIVE IS HARD-WIRED TO SURVIVE AND THAT'S WHEN HIS NATURAL INSTINCT WOULD KICK IN...
TO DESTROY HIS RIVAL?
NO, TO LET HIS BOSS WIN... OBVIOUSLY HE WAS AIMING TO MISS BUT HE'S SUCH A USELESS SHOT THAT HE MUST HAVE PUT THE BULLET IN CYRUS BY MISTAKE...
IT HAPPENS WHEN HE PLAYS GOLF WITH CLIENTS TOO...

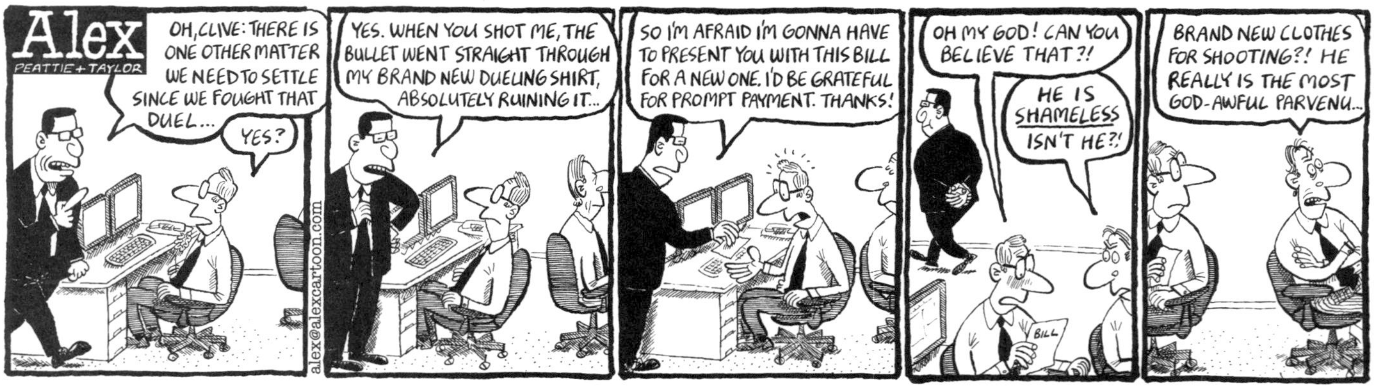
Alex
PEATTIE+TAYLOR
OH, CLIVE: THERE IS ONE OTHER MATTER WE NEED TO SETTLE SINCE WE FOUGHT THAT DUEL...
YES?
alex@alexcartoon.com
YES. WHEN YOU SHOT ME, THE BULLET WENT STRAIGHT THROUGH MY BRAND NEW DUELING SHIRT, ABSOLUTELY RUINING IT...
SO I'M AFRAID I'M GONNA HAVE TO PRESENT YOU WITH THIS BILL FOR A NEW ONE. I'D BE GRATEFUL FOR PROMPT PAYMENT. THANKS!
OH MY GOD! CAN YOU BELIEVE THAT?!
HE IS SHAMELESS ISN'T HE?!
BILL
BRAND NEW CLOTHES FOR SHOOTING?! HE REALLY IS THE MOST GOD-AWFUL PARVENU...

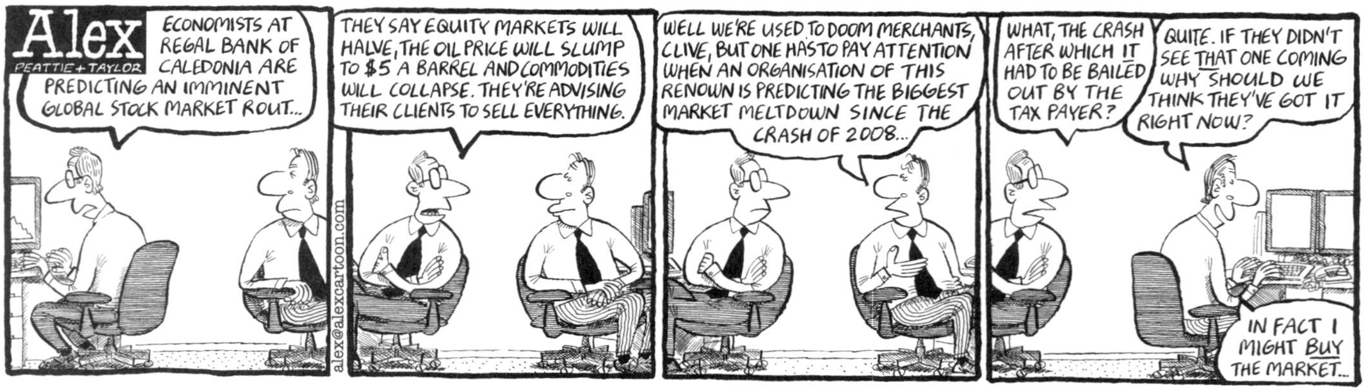
Alex
PEATTIE+TAYLOR
ECONOMISTS AT REGAL BANK OF CALEDONIA ARE PREDICTING AN IMMINENT GLOBAL STOCK MARKET ROUT...
alex@alexcartoon.com
THEY SAY EQUITY MARKETS WILL HALVE, THE OIL PRICE WILL SLUMP TO $5 A BARREL AND COMMODITIES WILL COLLAPSE. THEY'RE ADVISING THEIR CLIENTS TO SELL EVERYTHING.
WELL WE'RE USED TO DOOM MERCHANTS, CLIVE, BUT ONE HAS TO PAY ATTENTION WHEN AN ORGANISATION OF THIS RENOWN IS PREDICTING THE BIGGEST MARKET MELTDOWN SINCE THE CRASH OF 2008...
WHAT, THE CRASH AFTER WHICH IT HAD TO BE BAILED OUT BY THE TAX PAYER?
QUITE. IF THEY DIDN'T SEE THAT ONE COMING WHY SHOULD WE THINK THEY'VE GOT IT RIGHT NOW?
IN FACT I MIGHT BUY THE MARKET...

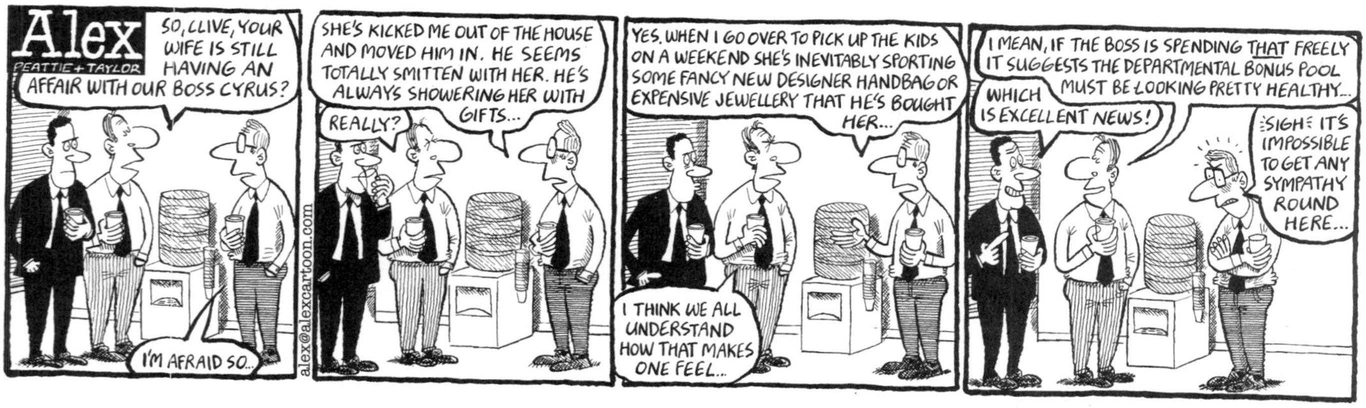
Alex
PEATTIE + TAYLOR
SO, CLIVE, YOUR WIFE IS STILL HAVING AN AFFAIR WITH OUR BOSS CYRUS?
I'M AFRAID SO...
alex@alexcartoon.com
SHE'S KICKED ME OUT OF THE HOUSE AND MOVED HIM IN. HE SEEMS TOTALLY SMITTEN WITH HER. HE'S ALWAYS SHOWERING HER WITH GIFTS...
REALLY?
YES. WHEN I GO OVER TO PICK UP THE KIDS ON A WEEKEND SHE'S INEVITABLY SPORTING SOME FANCY NEW DESIGNER HANDBAG OR EXPENSIVE JEWELLERY THAT HE'S BOUGHT HER...
I THINK WE ALL UNDERSTAND HOW THAT MAKES ONE FEEL...
I MEAN, IF THE BOSS IS SPENDING THAT FREELY IT SUGGESTS THE DEPARTMENTAL BONUS POOL MUST BE LOOKING PRETTY HEALTHY...
WHICH IS EXCELLENT NEWS!
SIGH IT'S IMPOSSIBLE TO GET ANY SYMPATHY ROUND HERE...

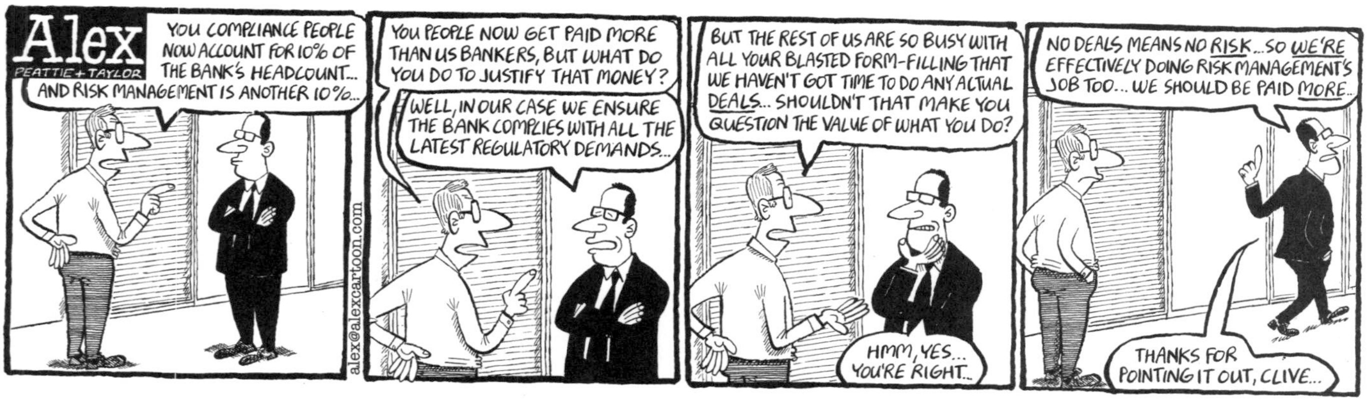
Alex
PEATTIE + TAYLOR
YOU COMPLIANCE PEOPLE NOW ACCOUNT FOR 10% OF THE BANK'S HEADCOUNT... AND RISK MANAGEMENT IS ANOTHER 10%...
alex@alexcartoon.com
YOU PEOPLE NOW GET PAID MORE THAN US BANKERS, BUT WHAT DO YOU DO TO JUSTIFY THAT MONEY?
WELL, IN OUR CASE WE ENSURE THE BANK COMPLIES WITH ALL THE LATEST REGULATORY DEMANDS...
BUT THE REST OF US ARE SO BUSY WITH ALL YOUR BLASTED FORM-FILLING THAT WE HAVEN'T GOT TIME TO DO ANY ACTUAL DEALS... SHOULDN'T THAT MAKE YOU QUESTION THE VALUE OF WHAT YOU DO?
HMM, YES... YOU'RE RIGHT...
NO DEALS MEANS NO RISK... SO WE'RE EFFECTIVELY DOING RISK MANAGEMENT'S JOB TOO... WE SHOULD BE PAID MORE...
THANKS FOR POINTING IT OUT, CLIVE...

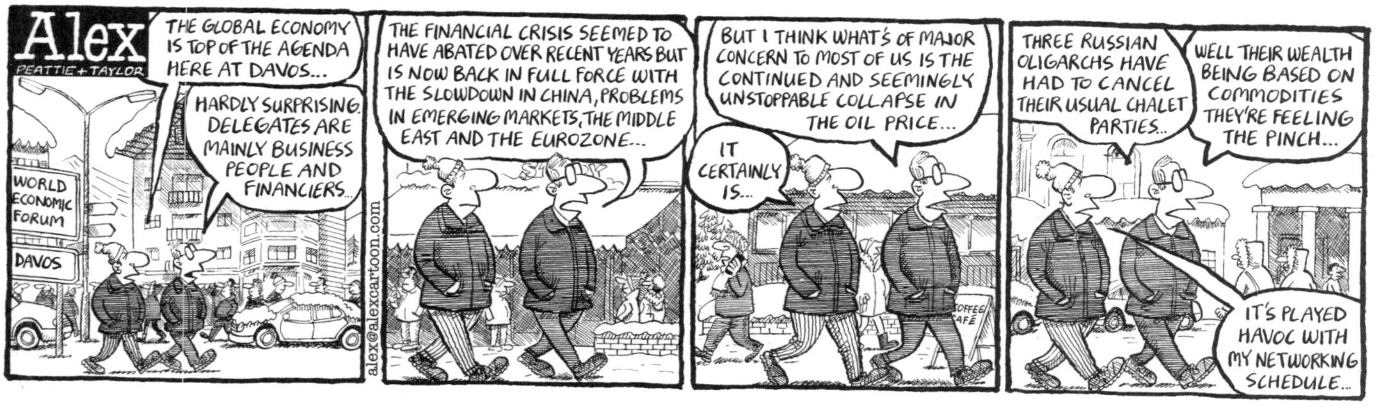
Alex
PEATTIE + TAYLOR
THE GLOBAL ECONOMY IS TOP OF THE AGENDA HERE AT DAVOS...
HARDLY SURPRISING. DELEGATES ARE MAINLY BUSINESS PEOPLE AND FINANCIERS...
WORLD ECONOMIC FORUM
DAVOS
alex@alexcartoon.com
THE FINANCIAL CRISIS SEEMED TO HAVE ABATED OVER RECENT YEARS BUT IS NOW BACK IN FULL FORCE WITH THE SLOWDOWN IN CHINA, PROBLEMS IN EMERGING MARKETS, THE MIDDLE EAST AND THE EUROZONE...
BUT I THINK WHAT'S OF MAJOR CONCERN TO MOST OF US IS THE CONTINUED AND SEEMINGLY UNSTOPPABLE COLLAPSE IN THE OIL PRICE...
IT CERTAINLY IS...
COFFEE CAFÉ
THREE RUSSIAN OLIGARCHS HAVE HAD TO CANCEL THEIR USUAL CHALET PARTIES...
WELL THEIR WEALTH BEING BASED ON COMMODITIES THEY'RE FEELING THE PINCH...
IT'S PLAYED HAVOC WITH MY NETWORKING SCHEDULE...

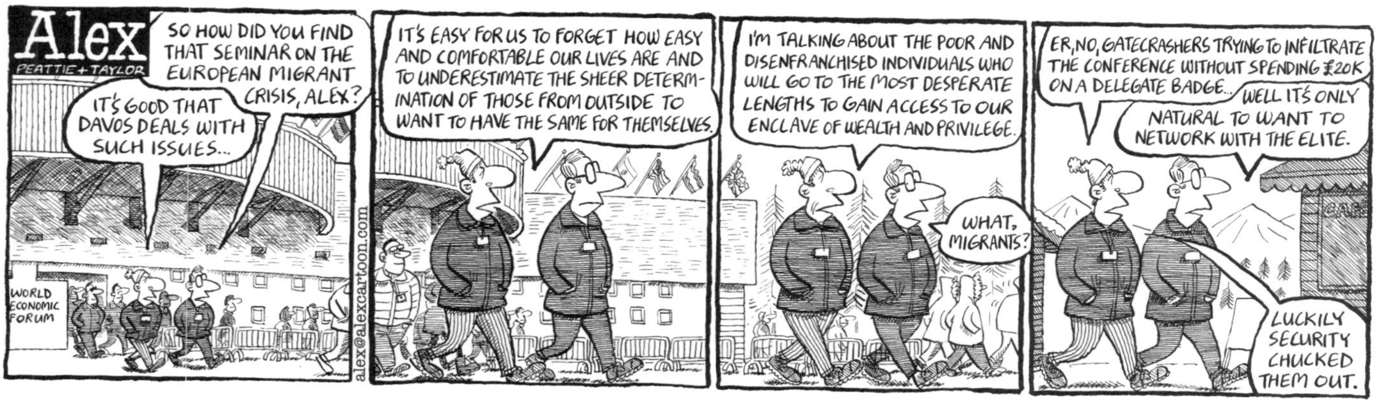
Alex
PEATTIE + TAYLOR
SO HOW DID YOU FIND THAT SEMINAR ON THE EUROPEAN MIGRANT CRISIS, ALEX?
IT'S GOOD THAT DAVOS DEALS WITH SUCH ISSUES...
WORLD ECONOMIC FORUM
alex@alexcartoon.com
IT'S EASY FOR US TO FORGET HOW EASY AND COMFORTABLE OUR LIVES ARE AND TO UNDERESTIMATE THE SHEER DETERMINATION OF THOSE FROM OUTSIDE TO WANT TO HAVE THE SAME FOR THEMSELVES.
I'M TALKING ABOUT THE POOR AND DISENFRANCHISED INDIVIDUALS WHO WILL GO TO THE MOST DESPERATE LENGTHS TO GAIN ACCESS TO OUR ENCLAVE OF WEALTH AND PRIVILEGE.
WHAT, MIGRANTS?
ER, NO, GATECRASHERS TRYING TO INFILTRATE THE CONFERENCE WITHOUT SPENDING £20K ON A DELEGATE BADGE...
WELL IT'S ONLY NATURAL TO WANT TO NETWORK WITH THE ELITE.
LUCKILY SECURITY CHUCKED THEM OUT.

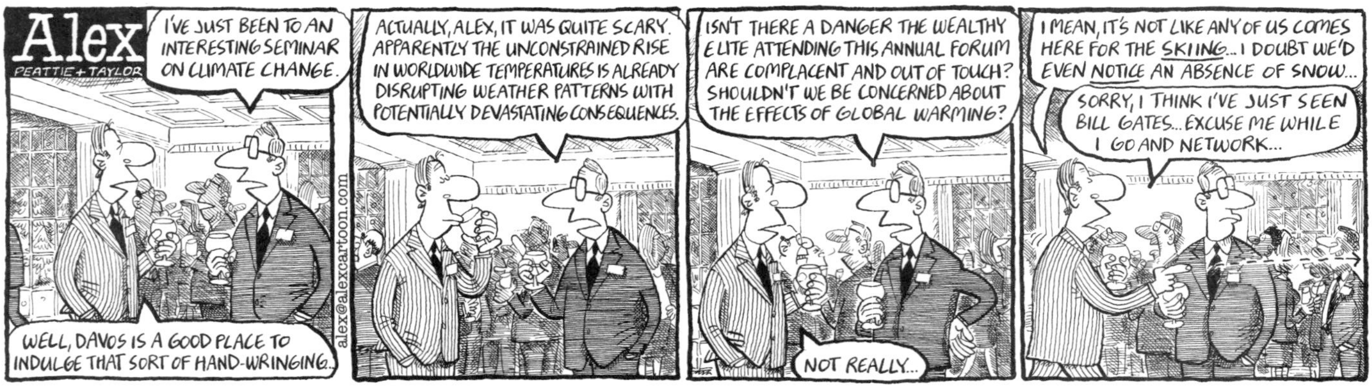
Alex
PEATTIE + TAYLOR
I'VE JUST BEEN TO AN INTERESTING SEMINAR ON CLIMATE CHANGE.
WELL, DAVOS IS A GOOD PLACE TO INDULGE THAT SORT OF HAND-WRINGING...
alex@alexcartoon.com
ACTUALLY, ALEX, IT WAS QUITE SCARY. APPARENTLY THE UNCONSTRAINED RISE IN WORLDWIDE TEMPERATURES IS ALREADY DISRUPTING WEATHER PATTERNS WITH POTENTIALLY DEVASTATING CONSEQUENCES.
ISN'T THERE A DANGER THE WEALTHY ELITE ATTENDING THIS ANNUAL FORUM ARE COMPLACENT AND OUT OF TOUCH? SHOULDN'T WE BE CONCERNED ABOUT THE EFFECTS OF GLOBAL WARMING?
NOT REALLY...
I MEAN, IT'S NOT LIKE ANY OF US COMES HERE FOR THE SKIING... I DOUBT WE'D EVEN NOTICE AN ABSENCE OF SNOW...
SORRY, I THINK I'VE JUST SEEN BILL GATES... EXCUSE ME WHILE I GO AND NETWORK...

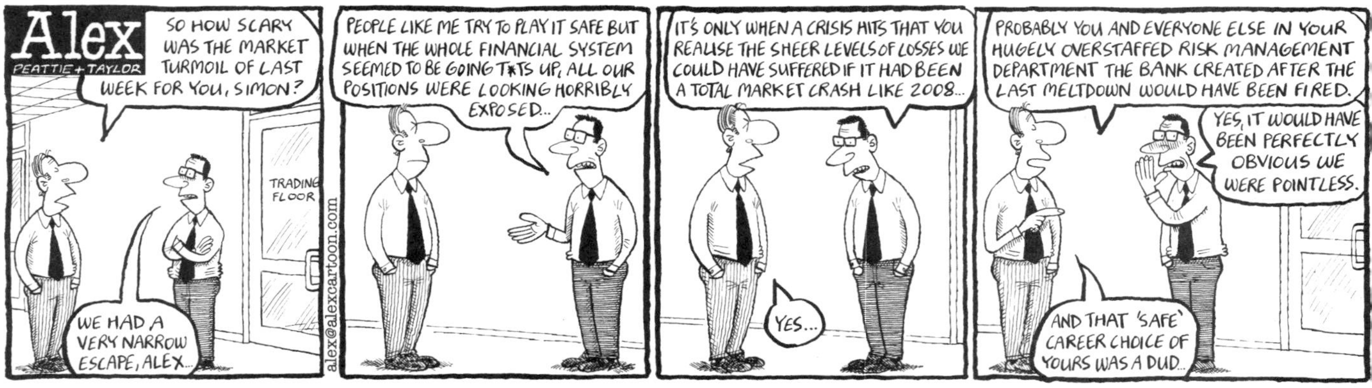
Alex
PEATTIE + TAYLOR
SO HOW SCARY WAS THE MARKET TURMOIL OF LAST WEEK FOR YOU, SIMON?
WE HAD A VERY NARROW ESCAPE, ALEX...
TRADING FLOOR
alex@alexcartoon.com
PEOPLE LIKE ME TRY TO PLAY IT SAFE BUT WHEN THE WHOLE FINANCIAL SYSTEM SEEMED TO BE GOING T*TS UP, ALL OUR POSITIONS WERE LOOKING HORRIBLY EXPOSED...
IT'S ONLY WHEN A CRISIS HITS THAT YOU REALISE THE SHEER LEVELS OF LOSSES WE COULD HAVE SUFFERED IF IT HAD BEEN A TOTAL MARKET CRASH LIKE 2008...
YES...
PROBABLY YOU AND EVERYONE ELSE IN YOUR HUGELY OVERSTAFFED RISK MANAGEMENT DEPARTMENT THE BANK CREATED AFTER THE LAST MELTDOWN WOULD HAVE BEEN FIRED.
YES, IT WOULD HAVE BEEN PERFECTLY OBVIOUS WE WERE POINTLESS.
AND THAT 'SAFE' CAREER CHOICE OF YOURS WAS A DUD...

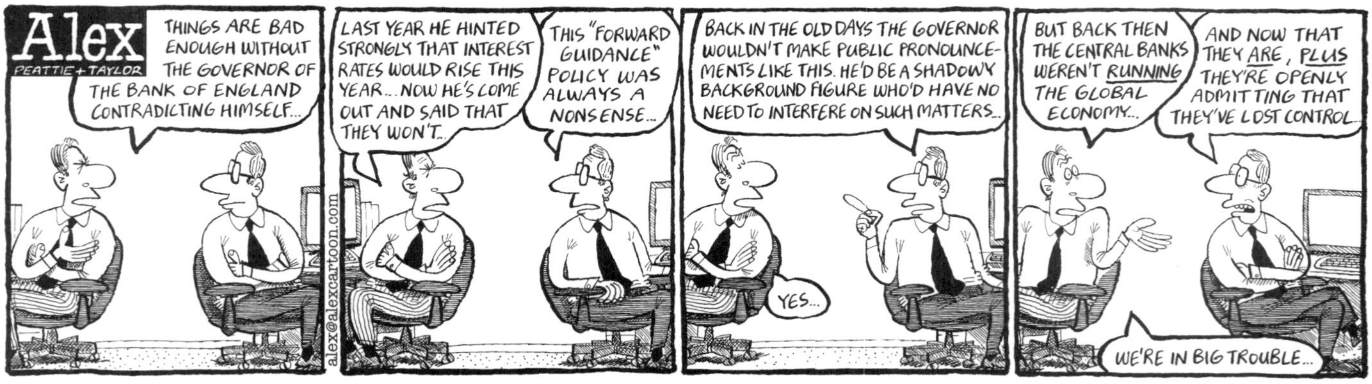
Alex
PEATTIE + TAYLOR
THINGS ARE BAD ENOUGH WITHOUT THE GOVERNOR OF THE BANK OF ENGLAND CONTRADICTING HIMSELF...
alex@alexcartoon.com
LAST YEAR HE HINTED STRONGLY THAT INTEREST RATES WOULD RISE THIS YEAR... NOW HE'S COME OUT AND SAID THAT THEY WON'T...
THIS "FORWARD GUIDANCE" POLICY WAS ALWAYS A NONSENSE...
BACK IN THE OLD DAYS THE GOVERNOR WOULDN'T MAKE PUBLIC PRONOUNCEMENTS LIKE THIS. HE'D BE A SHADOWY BACKGROUND FIGURE WHO'D HAVE NO NEED TO INTERFERE ON SUCH MATTERS...
YES...
BUT BACK THEN THE CENTRAL BANKS WEREN'T RUNNING THE GLOBAL ECONOMY...
AND NOW THAT THEY ARE, PLUS THEY'RE OPENLY ADMITTING THAT THEY'VE LOST CONTROL...
WE'RE IN BIG TROUBLE...

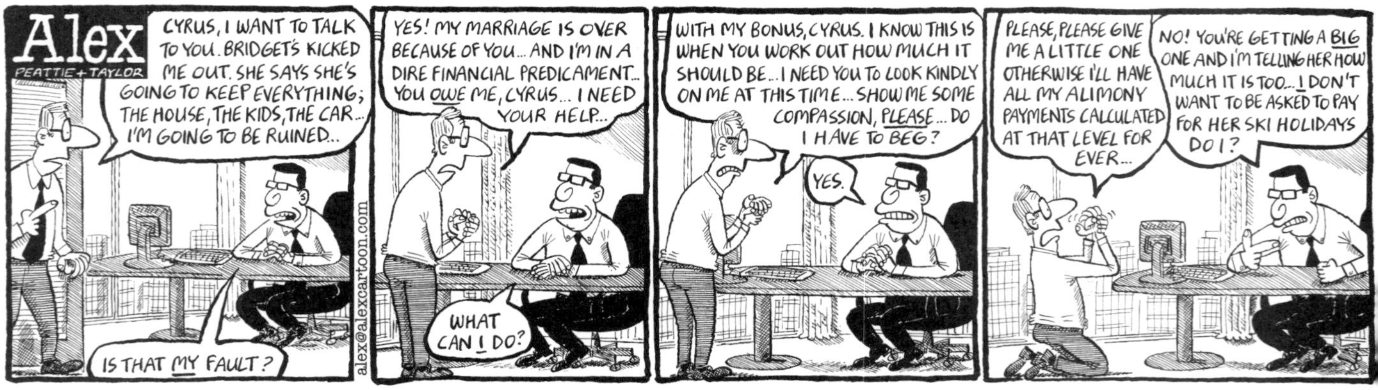
Alex
PEATTIE + TAYLOR
CYRUS, I WANT TO TALK TO YOU. BRIDGET'S KICKED ME OUT. SHE SAYS SHE'S GOING TO KEEP EVERYTHING; THE HOUSE, THE KIDS, THE CAR... I'M GOING TO BE RUINED...
IS THAT MY FAULT?
alex@alexcartoon.com
YES! MY MARRIAGE IS OVER BECAUSE OF YOU... AND I'M IN A DIRE FINANCIAL PREDICAMENT... YOU OWE ME, CYRUS... I NEED YOUR HELP...
WHAT CAN I DO?
WITH MY BONUS, CYRUS. I KNOW THIS IS WHEN YOU WORK OUT HOW MUCH IT SHOULD BE... I NEED YOU TO LOOK KINDLY ON ME AT THIS TIME... SHOW ME SOME COMPASSION, PLEASE... DO I HAVE TO BEG?
YES.
PLEASE, PLEASE GIVE ME A LITTLE ONE OTHERWISE I'LL HAVE ALL MY ALIMONY PAYMENTS CALCULATED AT THAT LEVEL FOR EVER...
NO! YOU'RE GETTING A BIG ONE AND I'M TELLING HER HOW MUCH IT IS TOO... I DON'T WANT TO BE ASKED TO PAY FOR HER SKI HOLIDAYS DO I?

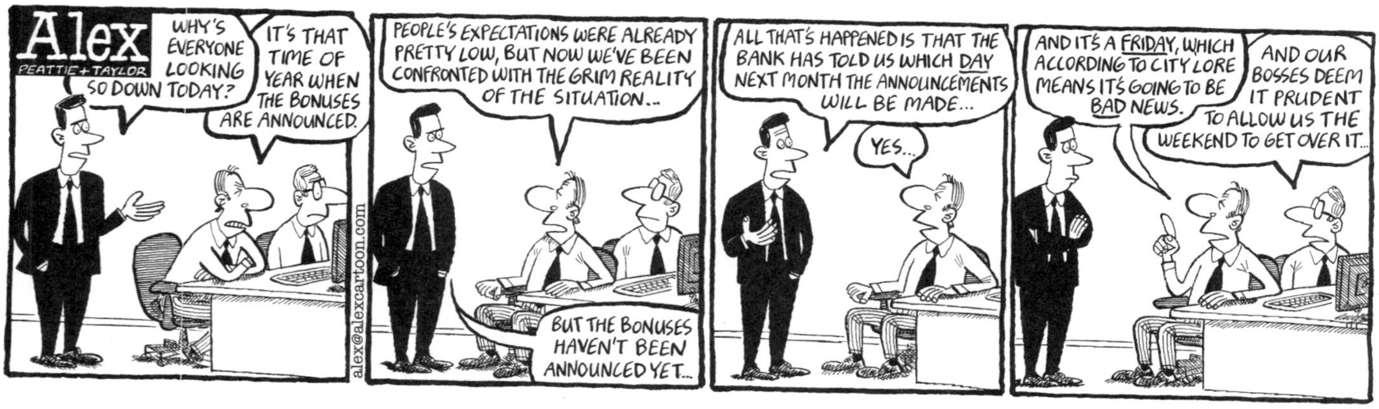
Alex
PEATTIE + TAYLOR
WHY'S EVERYONE LOOKING SO DOWN TODAY?
IT'S THAT TIME OF YEAR WHEN THE BONUSES ARE ANNOUNCED.
alex@alexcartoon.com
PEOPLE'S EXPECTATIONS WERE ALREADY PRETTY LOW, BUT NOW WE'VE BEEN CONFRONTED WITH THE GRIM REALITY OF THE SITUATION...
BUT THE BONUSES HAVEN'T BEEN ANNOUNCED YET...
ALL THAT'S HAPPENED IS THAT THE BANK HAS TOLD US WHICH DAY NEXT MONTH THE ANNOUNCEMENTS WILL BE MADE...
YES...
AND IT'S A FRIDAY, WHICH ACCORDING TO CITY LORE MEANS IT'S GOING TO BE BAD NEWS.
AND OUR BOSSES DEEM IT PRUDENT TO ALLOW US THE WEEKEND TO GET OVER IT...

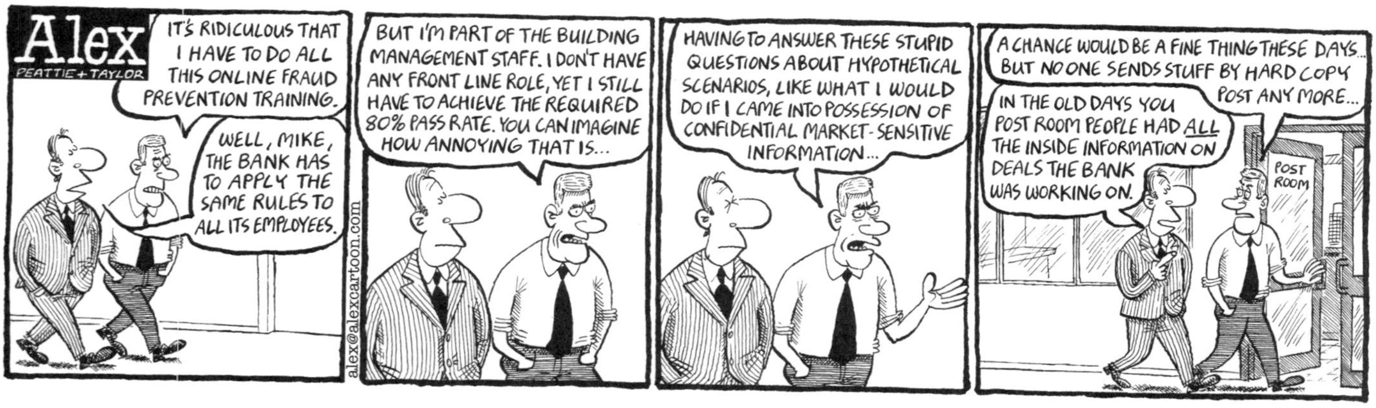
Alex
PEATTIE + TAYLOR
IT'S RIDICULOUS THAT I HAVE TO DO ALL THIS ONLINE FRAUD PREVENTION TRAINING.
WELL, MIKE, THE BANK HAS TO APPLY THE SAME RULES TO ALL ITS EMPLOYEES.
alex@alexcartoon.com
BUT I'M PART OF THE BUILDING MANAGEMENT STAFF. I DON'T HAVE ANY FRONT LINE ROLE, YET I STILL HAVE TO ACHIEVE THE REQUIRED 80% PASS RATE. YOU CAN IMAGINE HOW ANNOYING THAT IS...
HAVING TO ANSWER THESE STUPID QUESTIONS ABOUT HYPOTHETICAL SCENARIOS, LIKE WHAT I WOULD DO IF I CAME INTO POSSESSION OF CONFIDENTIAL MARKET-SENSITIVE INFORMATION...
A CHANCE WOULD BE A FINE THING THESE DAYS... BUT NO ONE SENDS STUFF BY HARD COPY POST ANY MORE...
IN THE OLD DAYS YOU POST ROOM PEOPLE HAD ALL THE INSIDE INFORMATION ON DEALS THE BANK WAS WORKING ON.
POST ROOM

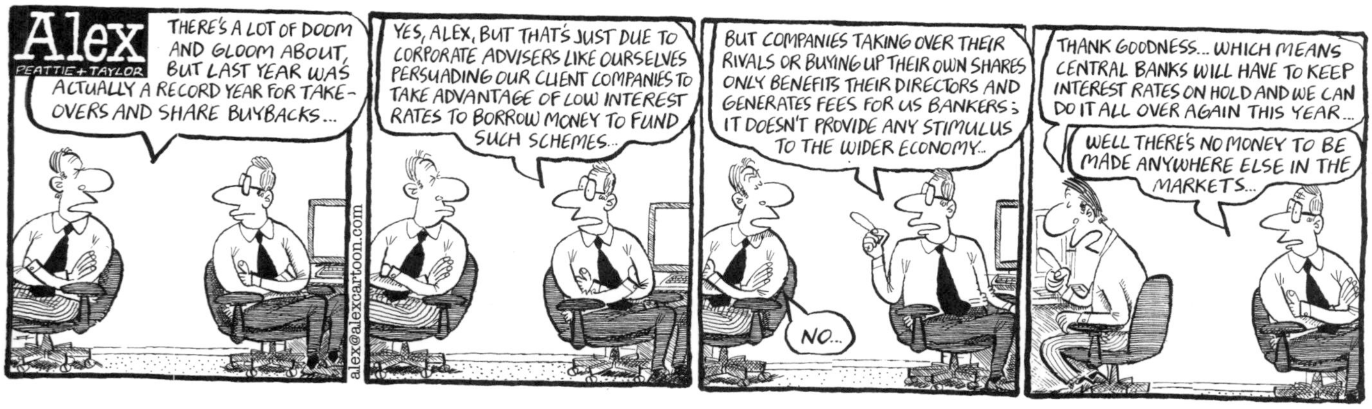
Alex
PEATTIE + TAYLOR
THERE'S A LOT OF DOOM AND GLOOM ABOUT, BUT LAST YEAR WAS ACTUALLY A RECORD YEAR FOR TAKE-OVERS AND SHARE BUYBACKS...
alex@alexcartoon.com
YES, ALEX, BUT THAT'S JUST DUE TO CORPORATE ADVISERS LIKE OURSELVES PERSUADING OUR CLIENT COMPANIES TO TAKE ADVANTAGE OF LOW INTEREST RATES TO BORROW MONEY TO FUND SUCH SCHEMES...
BUT COMPANIES TAKING OVER THEIR RIVALS OR BUYING UP THEIR OWN SHARES ONLY BENEFITS THEIR DIRECTORS AND GENERATES FEES FOR US BANKERS; IT DOESN'T PROVIDE ANY STIMULUS TO THE WIDER ECONOMY...
NO...
THANK GOODNESS... WHICH MEANS CENTRAL BANKS WILL HAVE TO KEEP INTEREST RATES ON HOLD AND WE CAN DO IT ALL OVER AGAIN THIS YEAR...
WELL THERE'S NO MONEY TO BE MADE ANYWHERE ELSE IN THE MARKETS...

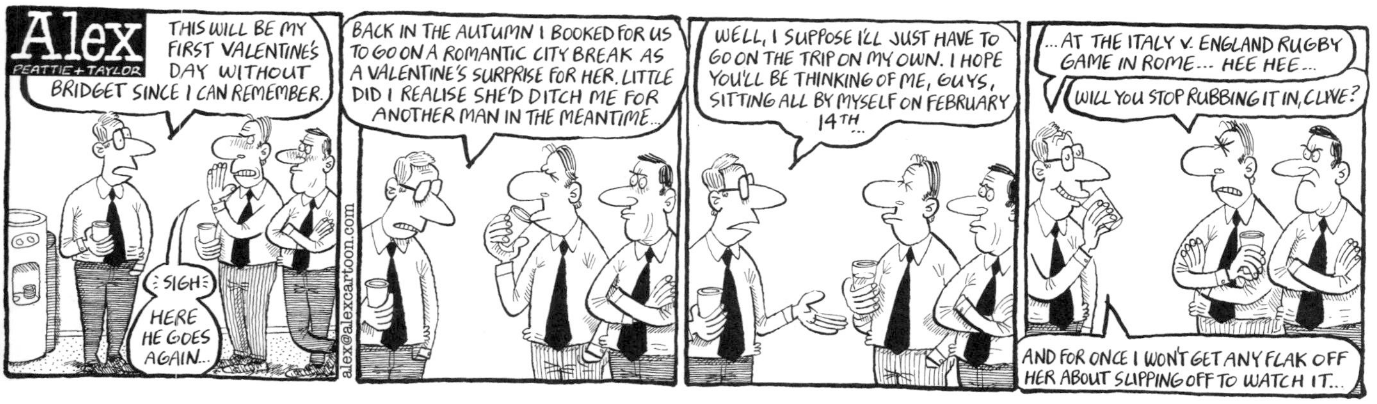
Alex
PEATTIE + TAYLOR
THIS WILL BE MY FIRST VALENTINE'S DAY WITHOUT BRIDGET SINCE I CAN REMEMBER.
SIGH
HERE HE GOES AGAIN...
alex@alexcartoon.com
BACK IN THE AUTUMN I BOOKED FOR US TO GO ON A ROMANTIC CITY BREAK AS A VALENTINE'S SURPRISE FOR HER. LITTLE DID I REALISE SHE'D DITCH ME FOR ANOTHER MAN IN THE MEANTIME...
WELL, I SUPPOSE I'LL JUST HAVE TO GO ON THE TRIP ON MY OWN. I HOPE YOU'LL BE THINKING OF ME, GUYS, SITTING ALL BY MYSELF ON FEBRUARY 14TH...
...AT THE ITALY V. ENGLAND RUGBY GAME IN ROME... HEE HEE...
WILL YOU STOP RUBBING IT IN, CLIVE?
AND FOR ONCE I WON'T GET ANY FLAK OFF HER ABOUT SLIPPING OFF TO WATCH IT...

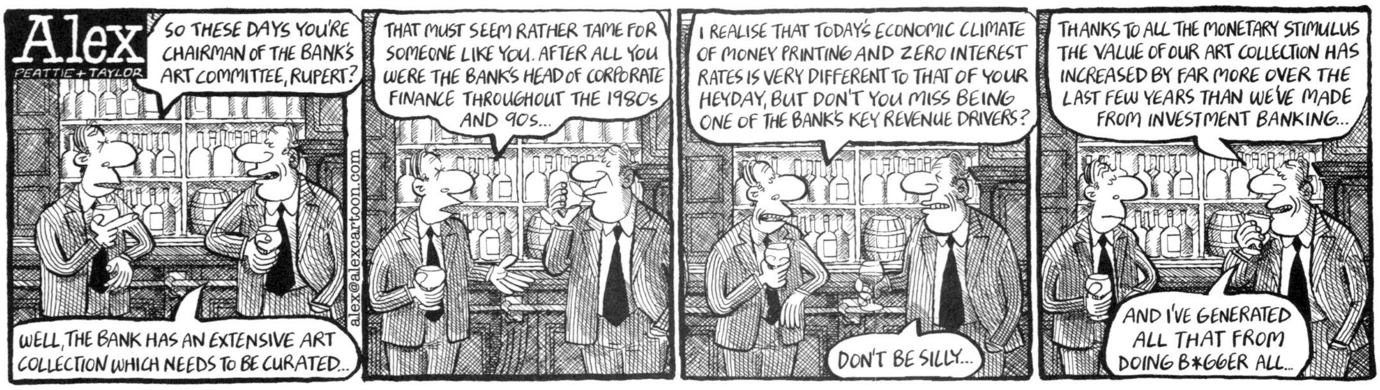
Alex
PEATTIE + TAYLOR
SO THESE DAYS YOU'RE CHAIRMAN OF THE BANK'S ART COMMITTEE, RUPERT?
WELL, THE BANK HAS AN EXTENSIVE ART COLLECTION WHICH NEEDS TO BE CURATED...
alex@alexcartoon.com
THAT MUST SEEM RATHER TAME FOR SOMEONE LIKE YOU. AFTER ALL YOU WERE THE BANK'S HEAD OF CORPORATE FINANCE THROUGHOUT THE 1980s AND 90s...
I REALISE THAT TODAY'S ECONOMIC CLIMATE OF MONEY PRINTING AND ZERO INTEREST RATES IS VERY DIFFERENT TO THAT OF YOUR HEYDAY, BUT DON'T YOU MISS BEING ONE OF THE BANK'S KEY REVENUE DRIVERS?
DON'T BE SILLY...
THANKS TO ALL THE MONETARY STIMULUS THE VALUE OF OUR ART COLLECTION HAS INCREASED BY FAR MORE OVER THE LAST FEW YEARS THAN WE'VE MADE FROM INVESTMENT BANKING...
AND I'VE GENERATED ALL THAT FROM DOING B*GGER ALL...

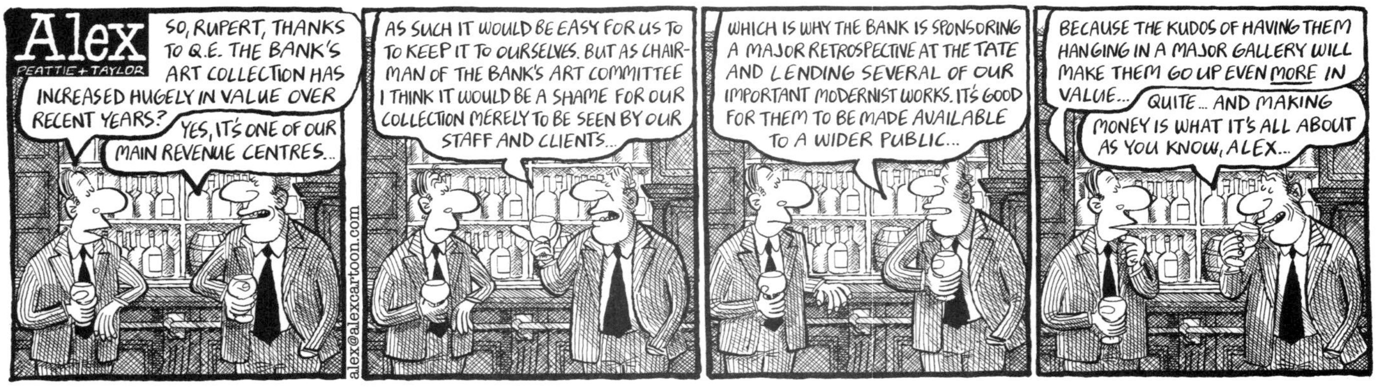
Alex
PEATTIE + TAYLOR
SO, RUPERT, THANKS TO Q.E. THE BANK'S ART COLLECTION HAS INCREASED HUGELY IN VALUE OVER RECENT YEARS?
YES, IT'S ONE OF OUR MAIN REVENUE CENTRES...
alex@alexcartoon.com
AS SUCH IT WOULD BE EASY FOR US TO TO KEEP IT TO OURSELVES. BUT AS CHAIRMAN OF THE BANK'S ART COMMITTEE I THINK IT WOULD BE A SHAME FOR OUR COLLECTION MERELY TO BE SEEN BY OUR STAFF AND CLIENTS...
WHICH IS WHY THE BANK IS SPONSORING A MAJOR RETROSPECTIVE AT THE TATE AND LENDING SEVERAL OF OUR IMPORTANT MODERNIST WORKS. IT'S GOOD FOR THEM TO BE MADE AVAILABLE TO A WIDER PUBLIC...
BECAUSE THE KUDOS OF HAVING THEM HANGING IN A MAJOR GALLERY WILL MAKE THEM GO UP EVEN MORE IN VALUE...
QUITE... AND MAKING MONEY IS WHAT IT'S ALL ABOUT AS YOU KNOW, ALEX...

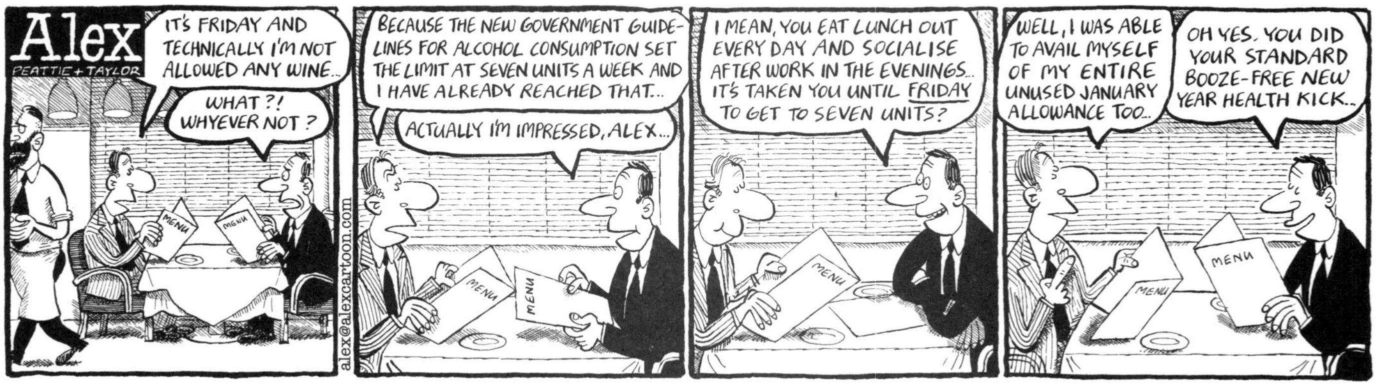
Alex
PEATTIE + TAYLOR
IT'S FRIDAY AND TECHNICALLY I'M NOT ALLOWED ANY WINE...
WHAT?! WHYEVER NOT?
MENU
alex@alexcartoon.com
BECAUSE THE NEW GOVERNMENT GUIDELINES FOR ALCOHOL CONSUMPTION SET THE LIMIT AT SEVEN UNITS A WEEK AND I HAVE ALREADY REACHED THAT...
ACTUALLY I'M IMPRESSED, ALEX...
I MEAN, YOU EAT LUNCH OUT EVERY DAY AND SOCIALISE AFTER WORK IN THE EVENINGS... IT'S TAKEN YOU UNTIL FRIDAY TO GET TO SEVEN UNITS?
WELL, I WAS ABLE TO AVAIL MYSELF OF MY ENTIRE UNUSED JANUARY ALLOWANCE TOO...
OH YES. YOU DID YOUR STANDARD BOOZE-FREE NEW YEAR HEALTH KICK...

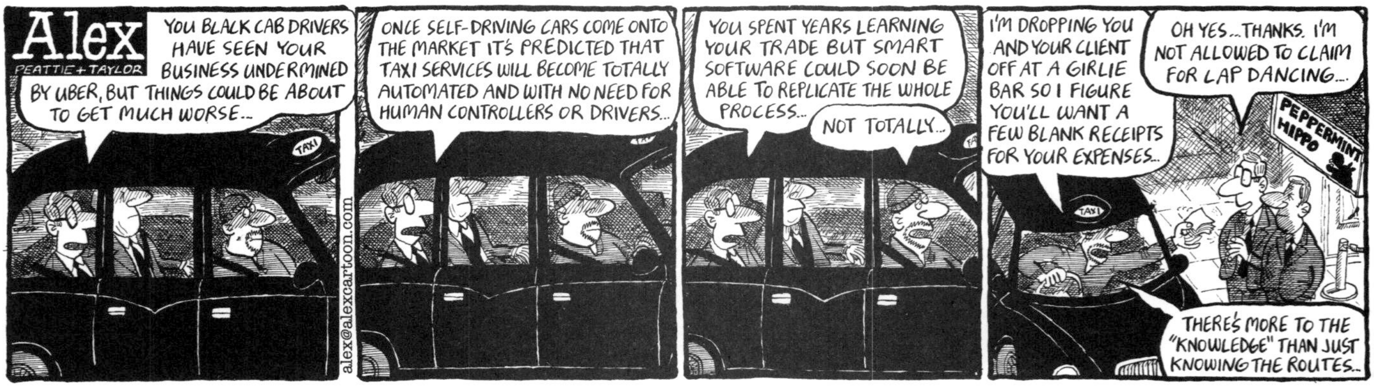
Alex
PEATTIE + TAYLOR
YOU BLACK CAB DRIVERS HAVE SEEN YOUR BUSINESS UNDERMINED BY UBER, BUT THINGS COULD BE ABOUT TO GET MUCH WORSE...
TAXI
alex@alexcartoon.com
ONCE SELF-DRIVING CARS COME ONTO THE MARKET IT'S PREDICTED THAT TAXI SERVICES WILL BECOME TOTALLY AUTOMATED AND WITH NO NEED FOR HUMAN CONTROLLERS OR DRIVERS...
YOU SPENT YEARS LEARNING YOUR TRADE BUT SMART SOFTWARE COULD SOON BE ABLE TO REPLICATE THE WHOLE PROCESS...
NOT TOTALLY...
I'M DROPPING YOU AND YOUR CLIENT OFF AT A GIRLIE BAR SO I FIGURE YOU'LL WANT A FEW BLANK RECEIPTS FOR YOUR EXPENSES...
OH YES... THANKS. I'M NOT ALLOWED TO CLAIM FOR LAP DANCING...
PEPPERMINT HIPPO
THERE'S MORE TO THE "KNOWLEDGE" THAN JUST KNOWING THE ROUTES...

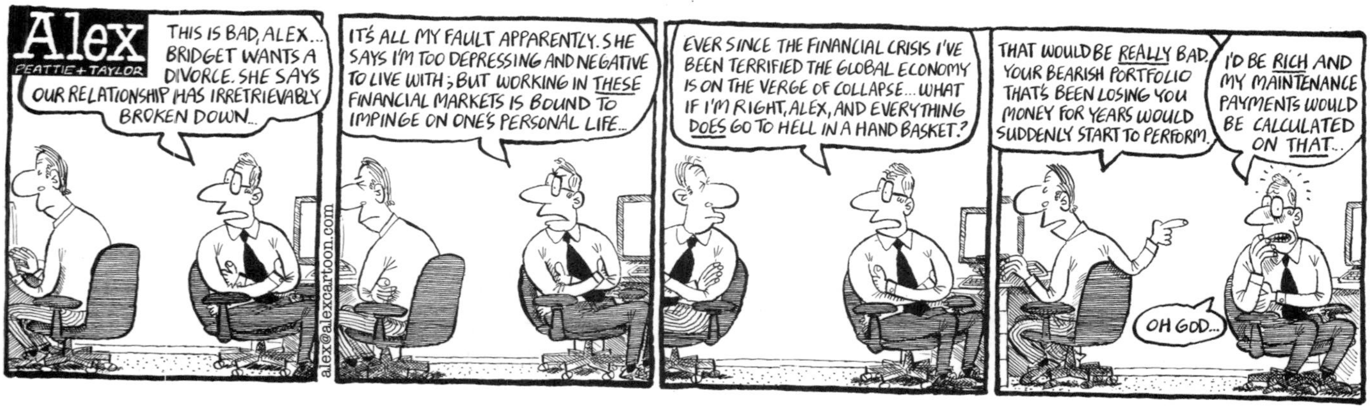
Alex
PEATTIE + TAYLOR
THIS IS BAD, ALEX... BRIDGET WANTS A DIVORCE. SHE SAYS OUR RELATIONSHIP HAS IRRETRIEVABLY BROKEN DOWN...
IT'S ALL MY FAULT APPARENTLY. SHE SAYS I'M TOO DEPRESSING AND NEGATIVE TO LIVE WITH; BUT WORKING IN THESE FINANCIAL MARKETS IS BOUND TO IMPINGE ON ONE'S PERSONAL LIFE...
EVER SINCE THE FINANCIAL CRISIS I'VE BEEN TERRIFIED THE GLOBAL ECONOMY IS ON THE VERGE OF COLLAPSE... WHAT IF I'M RIGHT, ALEX, AND EVERYTHING DOES GO TO HELL IN A HAND BASKET.?
THAT WOULD BE REALLY BAD. YOUR BEARISH PORTFOLIO THAT'S BEEN LOSING YOU MONEY FOR YEARS WOULD SUDDENLY START TO PERFORM.
I'D BE RICH AND MY MAINTENANCE PAYMENTS WOULD BE CALCULATED ON THAT...
OH GOD...
alex@alexcartoon.com

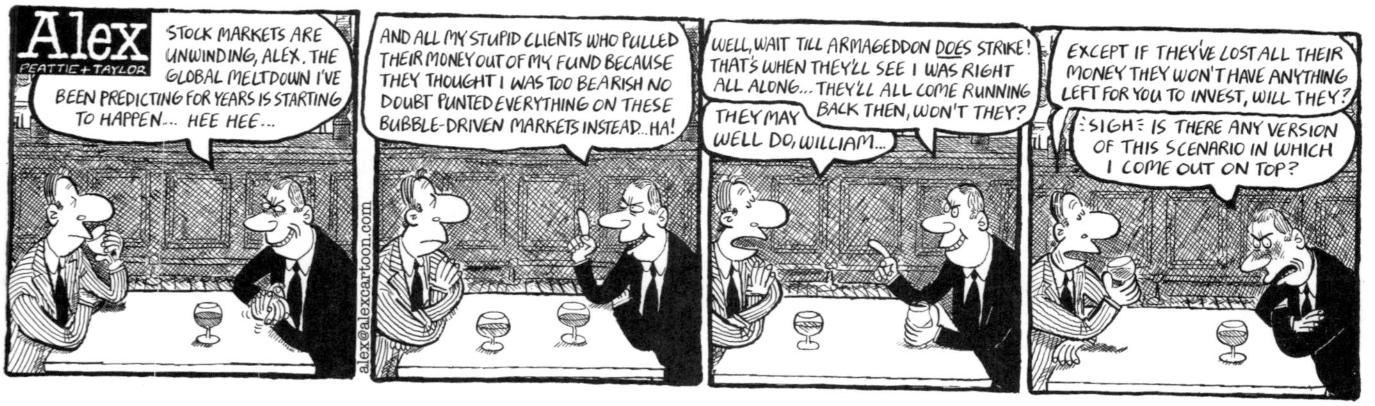
Alex
PEATTIE + TAYLOR
STOCK MARKETS ARE UNWINDING, ALEX. THE GLOBAL MELTDOWN I'VE BEEN PREDICTING FOR YEARS IS STARTING TO HAPPEN.... HEE HEE...
AND ALL MY STUPID CLIENTS WHO PULLED THEIR MONEY OUT OF MY FUND BECAUSE THEY THOUGHT I WAS TOO BEARISH NO DOUBT PUNTED EVERYTHING ON THESE BUBBLE-DRIVEN MARKETS INSTEAD...HA!
WELL, WAIT TILL ARMAGEDDON DOES STRIKE! THAT'S WHEN THEY'LL SEE I WAS RIGHT ALL ALONG... THEY'LL ALL COME RUNNING BACK THEN, WON'T THEY?
THEY MAY WELL DO, WILLIAM...
EXCEPT IF THEY'VE LOST ALL THEIR MONEY THEY WON'T HAVE ANYTHING LEFT FOR YOU TO INVEST, WILL THEY?
SIGH IS THERE ANY VERSION OF THIS SCENARIO IN WHICH I COME OUT ON TOP?
alex@alexcartoon.com

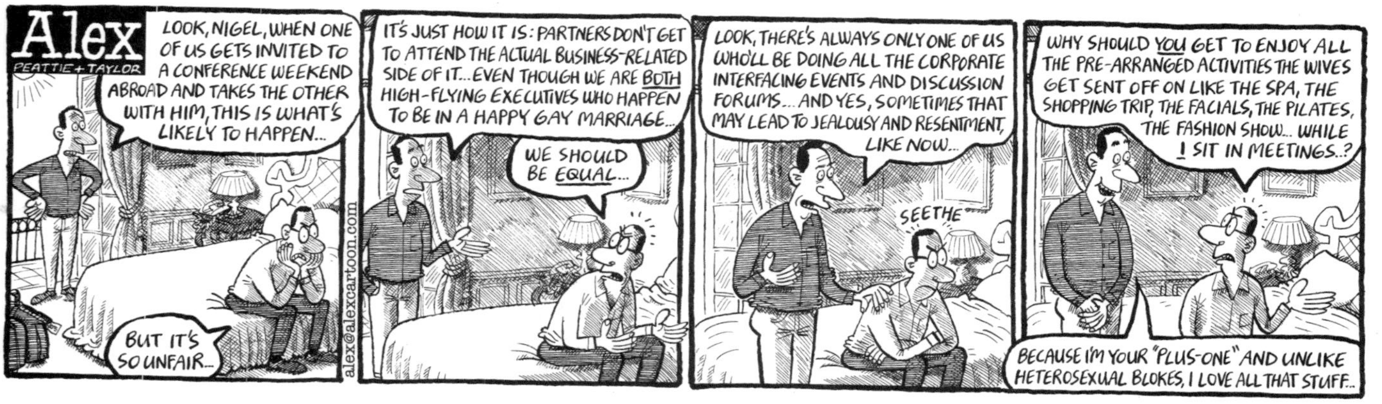
Alex
PEATTIE + TAYLOR
LOOK, NIGEL, WHEN ONE OF US GETS INVITED TO A CONFERENCE WEEKEND ABROAD AND TAKES THE OTHER WITH HIM, THIS IS WHAT'S LIKELY TO HAPPEN...
BUT IT'S SO UNFAIR...
IT'S JUST HOW IT IS: PARTNERS DON'T GET TO ATTEND THE ACTUAL BUSINESS-RELATED SIDE OF IT... EVEN THOUGH WE ARE BOTH HIGH-FLYING EXECUTIVES WHO HAPPEN TO BE IN A HAPPY GAY MARRIAGE...
WE SHOULD BE EQUAL...
LOOK, THERE'S ALWAYS ONLY ONE OF US WHO'LL BE DOING ALL THE CORPORATE INTERFACING EVENTS AND DISCUSSION FORUMS... AND YES, SOMETIMES THAT MAY LEAD TO JEALOUSY AND RESENTMENT, LIKE NOW...
SEETHE
WHY SHOULD YOU GET TO ENJOY ALL THE PRE-ARRANGED ACTIVITIES THE WIVES GET SENT OFF ON LIKE THE SPA, THE SHOPPING TRIP, THE FACIALS, THE PILATES, THE FASHION SHOW... WHILE I SIT IN MEETINGS..?
BECAUSE I'M YOUR "PLUS-ONE" AND UNLIKE HETEROSEXUAL BLOKES, I LOVE ALL THAT STUFF...
alex@alexcartoon.com

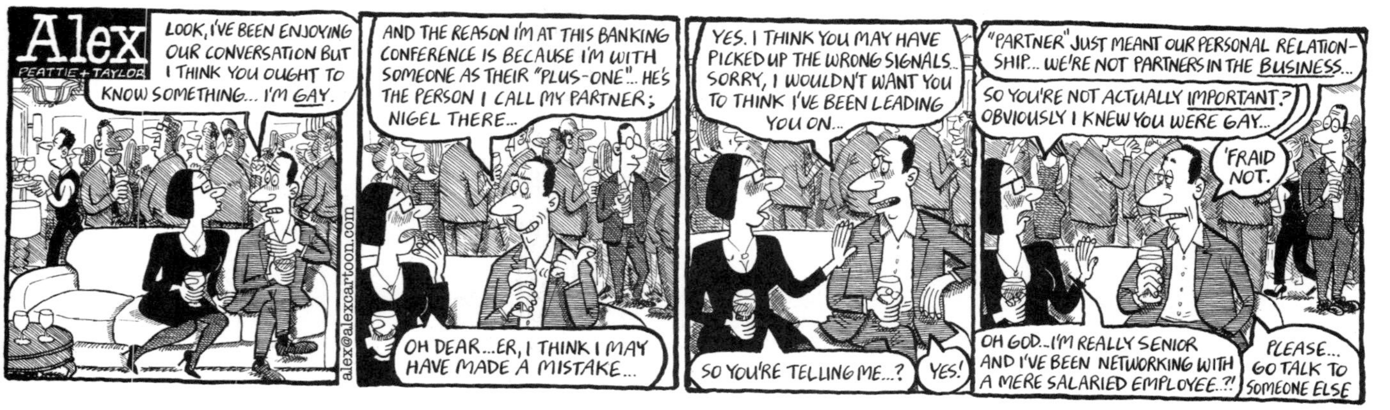
Alex
PEATTIE + TAYLOR
LOOK, I'VE BEEN ENJOYING OUR CONVERSATION BUT I THINK YOU OUGHT TO KNOW SOMETHING... I'M GAY.
AND THE REASON I'M AT THIS BANKING CONFERENCE IS BECAUSE I'M WITH SOMEONE AS THEIR "PLUS-ONE"... HE'S THE PERSON I CALL MY PARTNER; NIGEL THERE...
OH DEAR...ER, I THINK I MAY HAVE MADE A MISTAKE...
YES. I THINK YOU MAY HAVE PICKED UP THE WRONG SIGNALS... SORRY, I WOULDN'T WANT YOU TO THINK I'VE BEEN LEADING YOU ON...
SO YOU'RE TELLING ME...?
YES!
"PARTNER" JUST MEANT OUR PERSONAL RELATIONSHIP... WE'RE NOT PARTNERS IN THE BUSINESS...
SO YOU'RE NOT ACTUALLY IMPORTANT.?
OBVIOUSLY I KNEW YOU WERE GAY...
'FRAID NOT.
OH GOD...I'M REALLY SENIOR AND I'VE BEEN NETWORKING WITH A MERE SALARIED EMPLOYEE..?!
PLEASE... GO TALK TO SOMEONE ELSE
alex@alexcartoon.com

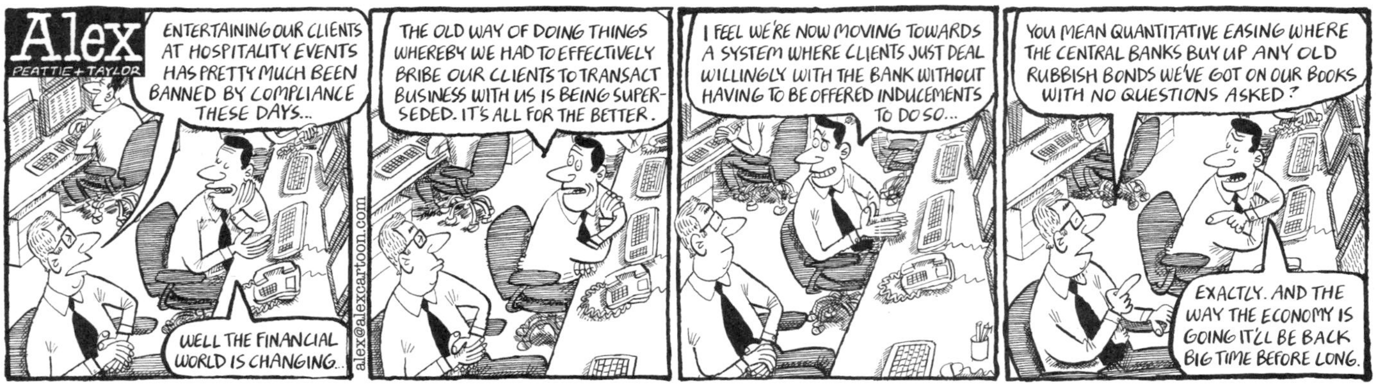
Alex
PEATTIE + TAYLOR
ENTERTAINING OUR CLIENTS AT HOSPITALITY EVENTS HAS PRETTY MUCH BEEN BANNED BY COMPLIANCE THESE DAYS...
WELL THE FINANCIAL WORLD IS CHANGING...
alex@alexcartoon.com
THE OLD WAY OF DOING THINGS WHEREBY WE HAD TO EFFECTIVELY BRIBE OUR CLIENTS TO TRANSACT BUSINESS WITH US IS BEING SUPER-SEDED. IT'S ALL FOR THE BETTER.
I FEEL WE'RE NOW MOVING TOWARDS A SYSTEM WHERE CLIENTS JUST DEAL WILLINGLY WITH THE BANK WITHOUT HAVING TO BE OFFERED INDUCEMENTS TO DO SO...
YOU MEAN QUANTITATIVE EASING WHERE THE CENTRAL BANKS BUY UP ANY OLD RUBBISH BONDS WE'VE GOT ON OUR BOOKS WITH NO QUESTIONS ASKED?
EXACTLY. AND THE WAY THE ECONOMY IS GOING IT'LL BE BACK BIG TIME BEFORE LONG.

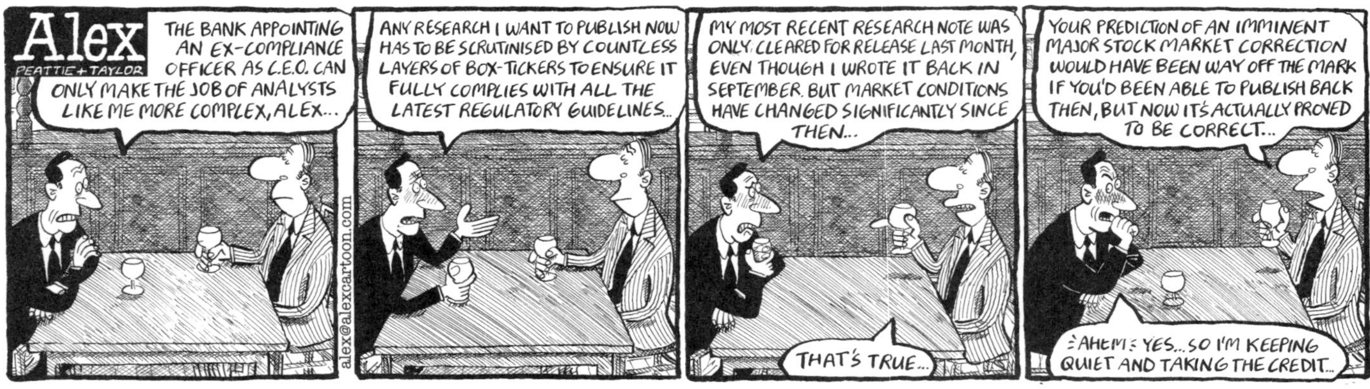
Alex
PEATTIE + TAYLOR
THE BANK APPOINTING AN EX-COMPLIANCE OFFICER AS C.E.O. CAN ONLY MAKE THE JOB OF ANALYSTS LIKE ME MORE COMPLEX, ALEX...
alex@alexcartoon.com
ANY RESEARCH I WANT TO PUBLISH NOW HAS TO BE SCRUTINISED BY COUNTLESS LAYERS OF BOX-TICKERS TO ENSURE IT FULLY COMPLIES WITH ALL THE LATEST REGULATORY GUIDELINES...
MY MOST RECENT RESEARCH NOTE WAS ONLY CLEARED FOR RELEASE LAST MONTH, EVEN THOUGH I WROTE IT BACK IN SEPTEMBER. BUT MARKET CONDITIONS HAVE CHANGED SIGNIFICANTLY SINCE THEN...
THAT'S TRUE...
YOUR PREDICTION OF AN IMMINENT MAJOR STOCK MARKET CORRECTION WOULD HAVE BEEN WAY OFF THE MARK IF YOU'D BEEN ABLE TO PUBLISH BACK THEN, BUT NOW IT'S ACTUALLY PROVED TO BE CORRECT...
AHEM: YES... SO I'M KEEPING QUIET AND TAKING THE CREDIT...

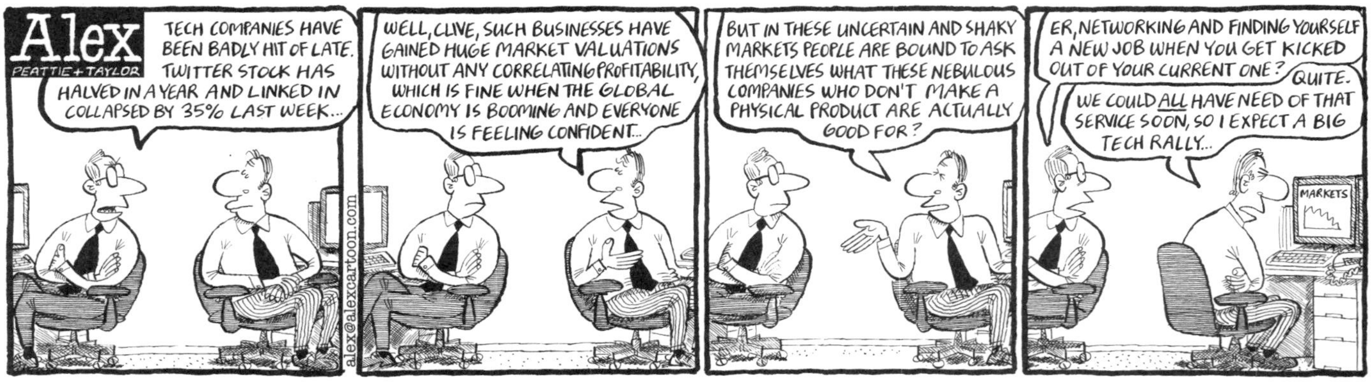
Alex
PEATTIE + TAYLOR
TECH COMPANIES HAVE BEEN BADLY HIT OF LATE. TWITTER STOCK HAS HALVED IN A YEAR AND LINKED IN COLLAPSED BY 35% LAST WEEK...
alex@alexcartoon.com
WELL, CLIVE, SUCH BUSINESSES HAVE GAINED HUGE MARKET VALUATIONS WITHOUT ANY CORRELATING PROFITABILITY, WHICH IS FINE WHEN THE GLOBAL ECONOMY IS BOOMING AND EVERYONE IS FEELING CONFIDENT...
BUT IN THESE UNCERTAIN AND SHAKY MARKETS PEOPLE ARE BOUND TO ASK THEMSELVES WHAT THESE NEBULOUS COMPANIES WHO DON'T MAKE A PHYSICAL PRODUCT ARE ACTUALLY GOOD FOR?
ER, NETWORKING AND FINDING YOURSELF A NEW JOB WHEN YOU GET KICKED OUT OF YOUR CURRENT ONE?
QUITE. WE COULD ALL HAVE NEED OF THAT SERVICE SOON, SO I EXPECT A BIG TECH RALLY...
MARKETS

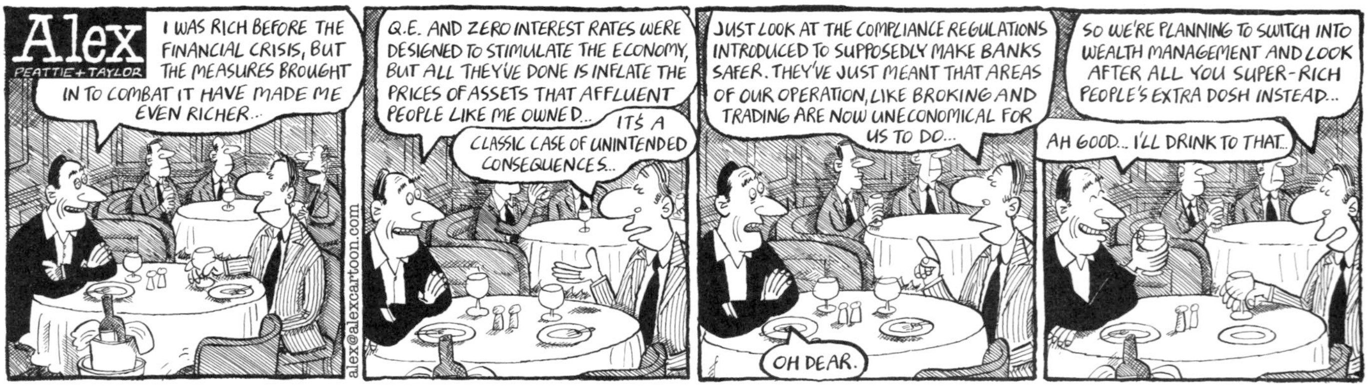
Alex
PEATTIE + TAYLOR
I WAS RICH BEFORE THE FINANCIAL CRISIS, BUT THE MEASURES BROUGHT IN TO COMBAT IT HAVE MADE ME EVEN RICHER...
alex@alexcartoon.com
Q.E. AND ZERO INTEREST RATES WERE DESIGNED TO STIMULATE THE ECONOMY, BUT ALL THEY'VE DONE IS INFLATE THE PRICES OF ASSETS THAT AFFLUENT PEOPLE LIKE ME OWNED...
IT'S A CLASSIC CASE OF UNINTENDED CONSEQUENCES...
JUST LOOK AT THE COMPLIANCE REGULATIONS INTRODUCED TO SUPPOSEDLY MAKE BANKS SAFER. THEY'VE JUST MEANT THAT AREAS OF OUR OPERATION, LIKE BROKING AND TRADING ARE NOW UNECONOMICAL FOR US TO DO...
OH DEAR.
SO WE'RE PLANNING TO SWITCH INTO WEALTH MANAGEMENT AND LOOK AFTER ALL YOU SUPER-RICH PEOPLE'S EXTRA DOSH INSTEAD...
AH GOOD... I'LL DRINK TO THAT...

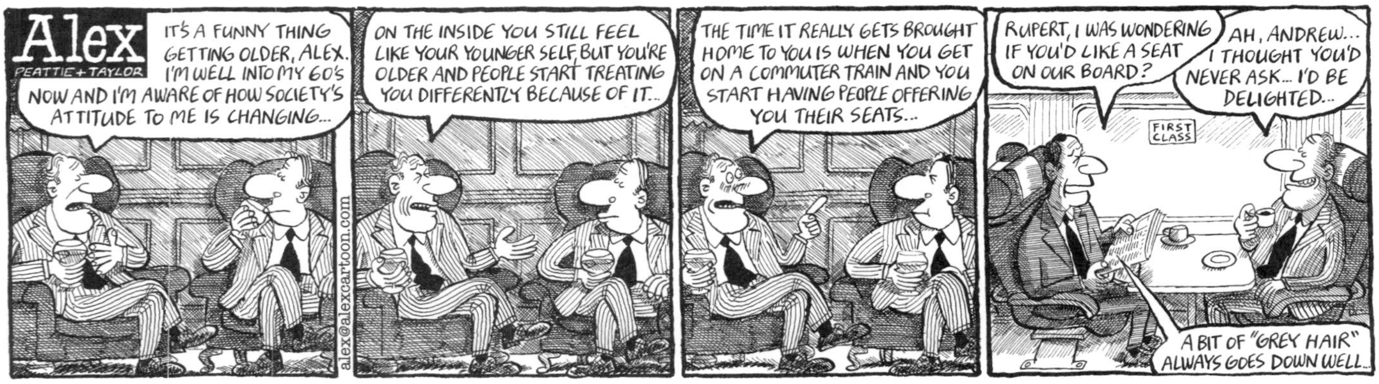
Alex
PEATTIE+TAYLOR
IT'S A FUNNY THING GETTING OLDER, ALEX. I'M WELL INTO MY 60'S NOW AND I'M AWARE OF HOW SOCIETY'S ATTITUDE TO ME IS CHANGING...
ON THE INSIDE YOU STILL FEEL LIKE YOUR YOUNGER SELF, BUT YOU'RE OLDER AND PEOPLE START TREATING YOU DIFFERENTLY BECAUSE OF IT...
alex@alexcartoon.com
THE TIME IT REALLY GETS BROUGHT HOME TO YOU IS WHEN YOU GET ON A COMMUTER TRAIN AND YOU START HAVING PEOPLE OFFERING YOU THEIR SEATS...
RUPERT, I WAS WONDERING IF YOU'D LIKE A SEAT ON OUR BOARD?
AH, ANDREW... I THOUGHT YOU'D NEVER ASK... I'D BE DELIGHTED...
FIRST CLASS
A BIT OF "GREY HAIR" ALWAYS GOES DOWN WELL...

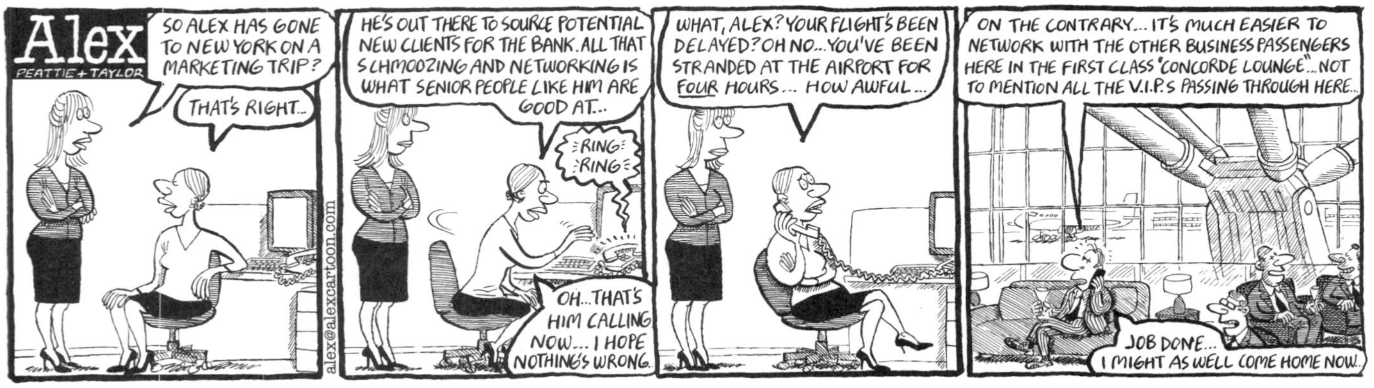
Alex
PEATTIE+TAYLOR
SO ALEX HAS GONE TO NEW YORK ON A MARKETING TRIP?
THAT'S RIGHT...
alex@alexcartoon.com
HE'S OUT THERE TO SOURCE POTENTIAL NEW CLIENTS FOR THE BANK. ALL THAT SCHMOOZING AND NETWORKING IS WHAT SENIOR PEOPLE LIKE HIM ARE GOOD AT...
RING RING
OH... THAT'S HIM CALLING NOW... I HOPE NOTHING'S WRONG.
WHAT, ALEX? YOUR FLIGHT'S BEEN DELAYED? OH NO... YOU'VE BEEN STRANDED AT THE AIRPORT FOR FOUR HOURS... HOW AWFUL...
ON THE CONTRARY... IT'S MUCH EASIER TO NETWORK WITH THE OTHER BUSINESS PASSENGERS HERE IN THE FIRST CLASS "CONCORDE LOUNGE"... NOT TO MENTION ALL THE V.I.P.S PASSING THROUGH HERE...
JOB DONE... I MIGHT AS WELL COME HOME NOW...

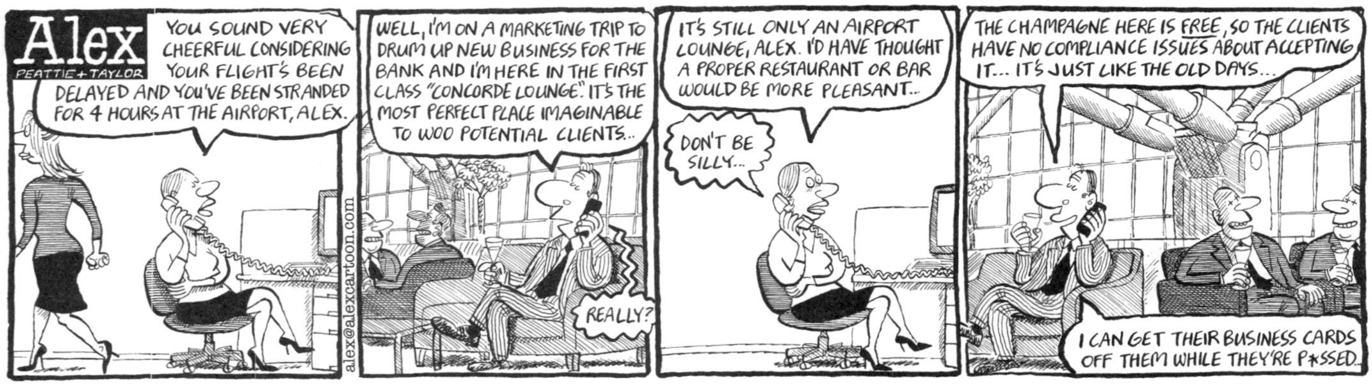
Alex
PEATTIE+TAYLOR
YOU SOUND VERY CHEERFUL CONSIDERING YOUR FLIGHT'S BEEN DELAYED AND YOU'VE BEEN STRANDED FOR 4 HOURS AT THE AIRPORT, ALEX.
alex@alexcartoon.com
WELL, I'M ON A MARKETING TRIP TO DRUM UP NEW BUSINESS FOR THE BANK AND I'M HERE IN THE FIRST CLASS "CONCORDE LOUNGE". IT'S THE MOST PERFECT PLACE IMAGINABLE TO WOO POTENTIAL CLIENTS...
REALLY?
IT'S STILL ONLY AN AIRPORT LOUNGE, ALEX. I'D HAVE THOUGHT A PROPER RESTAURANT OR BAR WOULD BE MORE PLEASANT...
DON'T BE SILLY...
THE CHAMPAGNE HERE IS FREE, SO THE CLIENTS HAVE NO COMPLIANCE ISSUES ABOUT ACCEPTING IT... IT'S JUST LIKE THE OLD DAYS...
I CAN GET THEIR BUSINESS CARDS OFF THEM WHILE THEY'RE P*SSED.

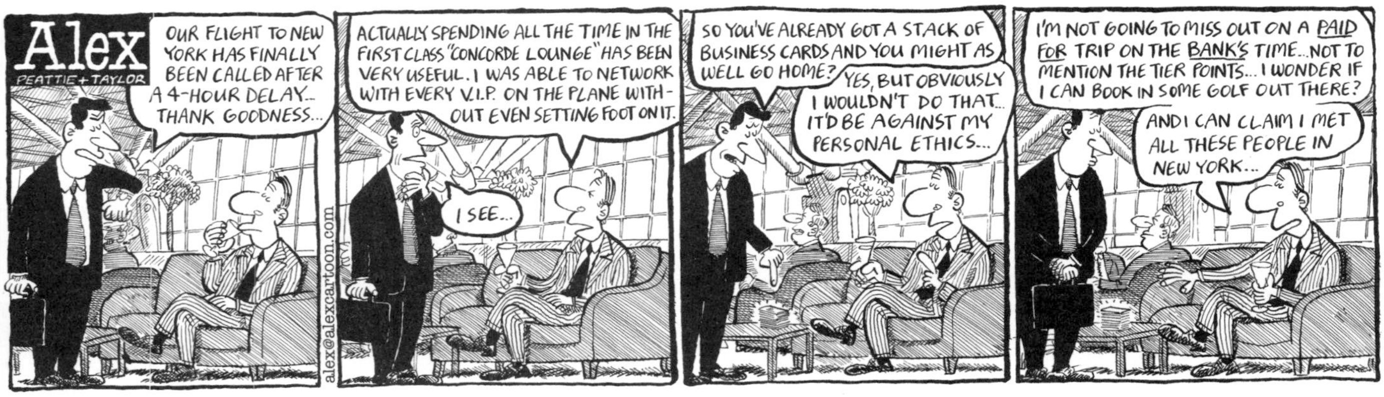
Alex
PEATTIE+TAYLOR
OUR FLIGHT TO NEW YORK HAS FINALLY BEEN CALLED AFTER A 4-HOUR DELAY... THANK GOODNESS...
alex@alexcartoon.com
ACTUALLY SPENDING ALL THE TIME IN THE FIRST CLASS "CONCORDE LOUNGE" HAS BEEN VERY USEFUL. I WAS ABLE TO NETWORK WITH EVERY V.I.P. ON THE PLANE WITHOUT EVEN SETTING FOOT ON IT.
I SEE...
SO YOU'VE ALREADY GOT A STACK OF BUSINESS CARDS AND YOU MIGHT AS WELL GO HOME?
YES, BUT OBVIOUSLY I WOULDN'T DO THAT... IT'D BE AGAINST MY PERSONAL ETHICS...
I'M NOT GOING TO MISS OUT ON A PAID FOR TRIP ON THE BANK'S TIME... NOT TO MENTION THE TIER POINTS... I WONDER IF I CAN BOOK IN SOME GOLF OUT THERE?
AND I CAN CLAIM I MET ALL THESE PEOPLE IN NEW YORK...

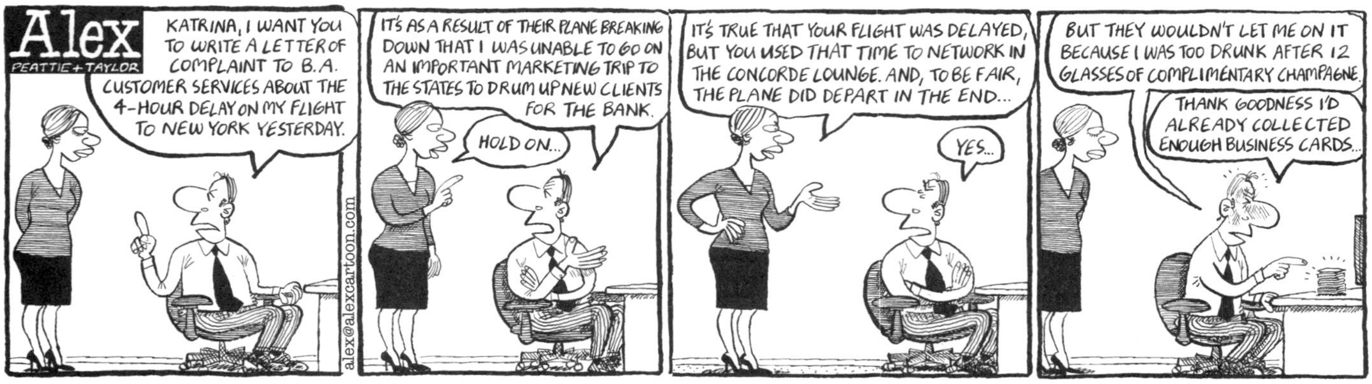
Alex
PEATTIE+TAYLOR
KATRINA, I WANT YOU TO WRITE A LETTER OF COMPLAINT TO B.A. CUSTOMER SERVICES ABOUT THE 4-HOUR DELAY ON MY FLIGHT TO NEW YORK YESTERDAY.
alex@alexcartoon.com
IT'S AS A RESULT OF THEIR PLANE BREAKING DOWN THAT I WAS UNABLE TO GO ON AN IMPORTANT MARKETING TRIP TO THE STATES TO DRUM UP NEW CLIENTS FOR THE BANK.
HOLD ON...
IT'S TRUE THAT YOUR FLIGHT WAS DELAYED, BUT YOU USED THAT TIME TO NETWORK IN THE CONCORDE LOUNGE. AND, TO BE FAIR, THE PLANE DID DEPART IN THE END...
YES...
BUT THEY WOULDN'T LET ME ON IT BECAUSE I WAS TOO DRUNK AFTER 12 GLASSES OF COMPLIMENTARY CHAMPAGNE.
THANK GOODNESS I'D ALREADY COLLECTED ENOUGH BUSINESS CARDS...

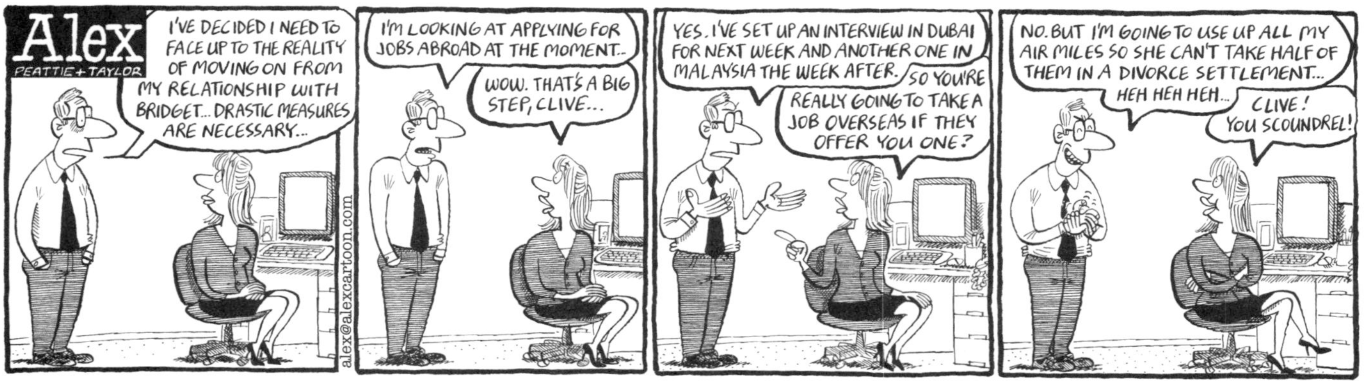
Alex
PEATTIE+TAYLOR
I'VE DECIDED I NEED TO FACE UP TO THE REALITY OF MOVING ON FROM MY RELATIONSHIP WITH BRIDGET... DRASTIC MEASURES ARE NECESSARY...
alex@alexcartoon.com
I'M LOOKING AT APPLYING FOR JOBS ABROAD AT THE MOMENT...
WOW. THAT'S A BIG STEP, CLIVE...
YES. I'VE SET UP AN INTERVIEW IN DUBAI FOR NEXT WEEK AND ANOTHER ONE IN MALAYSIA THE WEEK AFTER.
SO YOU'RE REALLY GOING TO TAKE A JOB OVERSEAS IF THEY OFFER YOU ONE?
NO. BUT I'M GOING TO USE UP ALL MY AIR MILES SO SHE CAN'T TAKE HALF OF THEM IN A DIVORCE SETTLEMENT...
HEH HEH HEH...
CLIVE! YOU SCOUNDREL!

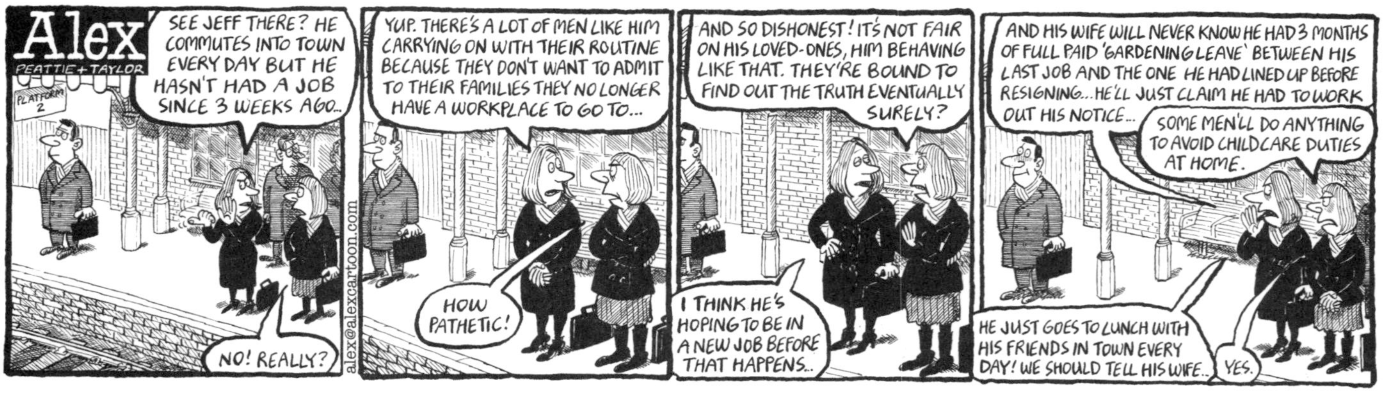
Alex
PEATTIE+TAYLOR
PLATFORM 2
SEE JEFF THERE? HE COMMUTES INTO TOWN EVERY DAY BUT HE HASN'T HAD A JOB SINCE 3 WEEKS AGO...
NO! REALLY?
alex@alexcartoon.com
YUP. THERE'S A LOT OF MEN LIKE HIM CARRYING ON WITH THEIR ROUTINE BECAUSE THEY DON'T WANT TO ADMIT TO THEIR FAMILIES THEY NO LONGER HAVE A WORKPLACE TO GO TO...
HOW PATHETIC!
AND SO DISHONEST! IT'S NOT FAIR ON HIS LOVED-ONES, HIM BEHAVING LIKE THAT. THEY'RE BOUND TO FIND OUT THE TRUTH EVENTUALLY SURELY?
I THINK HE'S HOPING TO BE IN A NEW JOB BEFORE THAT HAPPENS...
AND HIS WIFE WILL NEVER KNOW HE HAD 3 MONTHS OF FULL PAID 'GARDENING LEAVE' BETWEEN HIS LAST JOB AND THE ONE HE HAD LINED UP BEFORE RESIGNING... HE'LL JUST CLAIM HE HAD TO WORK OUT HIS NOTICE...
SOME MEN'LL DO ANYTHING TO AVOID CHILDCARE DUTIES AT HOME.
HE JUST GOES TO LUNCH WITH HIS FRIENDS IN TOWN EVERY DAY! WE SHOULD TELL HIS WIFE...
YES.

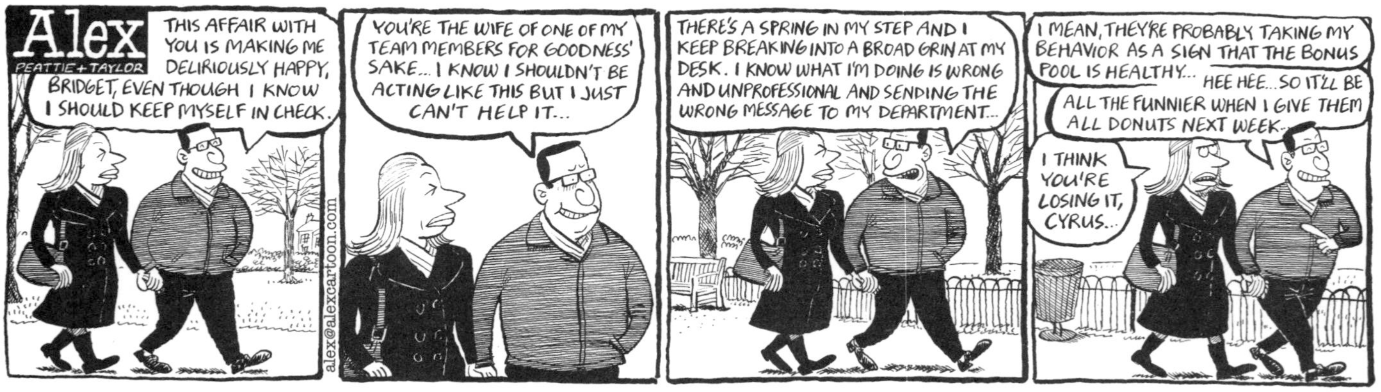
Alex
PEATTIE+TAYLOR
THIS AFFAIR WITH YOU IS MAKING ME DELIRIOUSLY HAPPY, BRIDGET, EVEN THOUGH I KNOW I SHOULD KEEP MYSELF IN CHECK.
alex@alexcartoon.com
YOU'RE THE WIFE OF ONE OF MY TEAM MEMBERS FOR GOODNESS' SAKE... I KNOW I SHOULDN'T BE ACTING LIKE THIS BUT I JUST CAN'T HELP IT...
THERE'S A SPRING IN MY STEP AND I KEEP BREAKING INTO A BROAD GRIN AT MY DESK. I KNOW WHAT I'M DOING IS WRONG AND UNPROFESSIONAL AND SENDING THE WRONG MESSAGE TO MY DEPARTMENT...
I MEAN, THEY'RE PROBABLY TAKING MY BEHAVIOR AS A SIGN THAT THE BONUS POOL IS HEALTHY...
HEE HEE... SO IT'LL BE ALL THE FUNNIER WHEN I GIVE THEM ALL DONUTS NEXT WEEK...
I THINK YOU'RE LOSING IT, CYRUS...

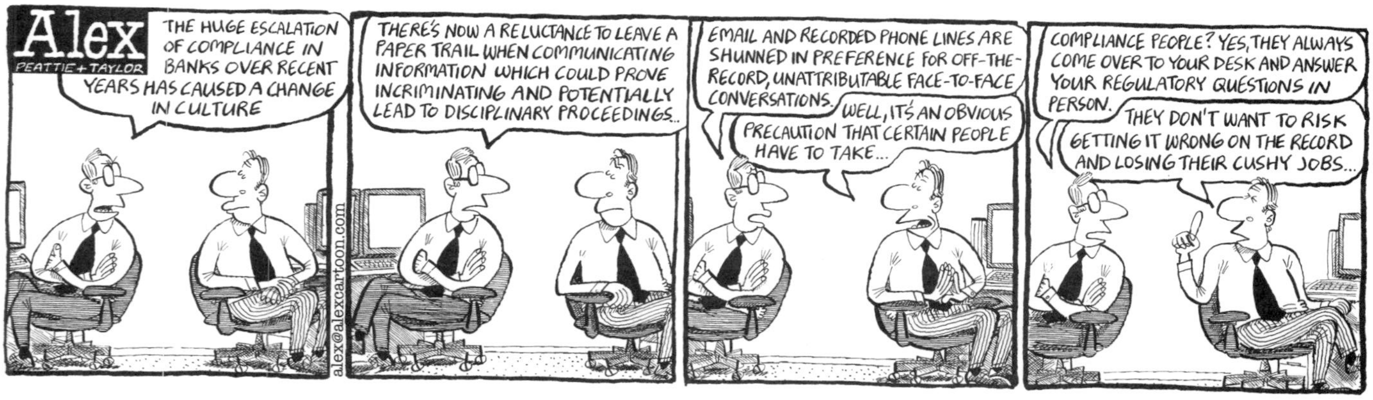
Alex
PEATTIE + TAYLOR
THE HUGE ESCALATION OF COMPLIANCE IN BANKS OVER RECENT YEARS HAS CAUSED A CHANGE IN CULTURE
alex@alexcartoon.com
THERE'S NOW A RELUCTANCE TO LEAVE A PAPER TRAIL WHEN COMMUNICATING INFORMATION WHICH COULD PROVE INCRIMINATING AND POTENTIALLY LEAD TO DISCIPLINARY PROCEEDINGS...
EMAIL AND RECORDED PHONE LINES ARE SHUNNED IN PREFERENCE FOR OFF-THE-RECORD, UNATTRIBUTABLE FACE-TO-FACE CONVERSATIONS.
WELL, IT'S AN OBVIOUS PRECAUTION THAT CERTAIN PEOPLE HAVE TO TAKE...
COMPLIANCE PEOPLE? YES, THEY ALWAYS COME OVER TO YOUR DESK AND ANSWER YOUR REGULATORY QUESTIONS IN PERSON.
THEY DON'T WANT TO RISK GETTING IT WRONG ON THE RECORD AND LOSING THEIR CUSHY JOBS...

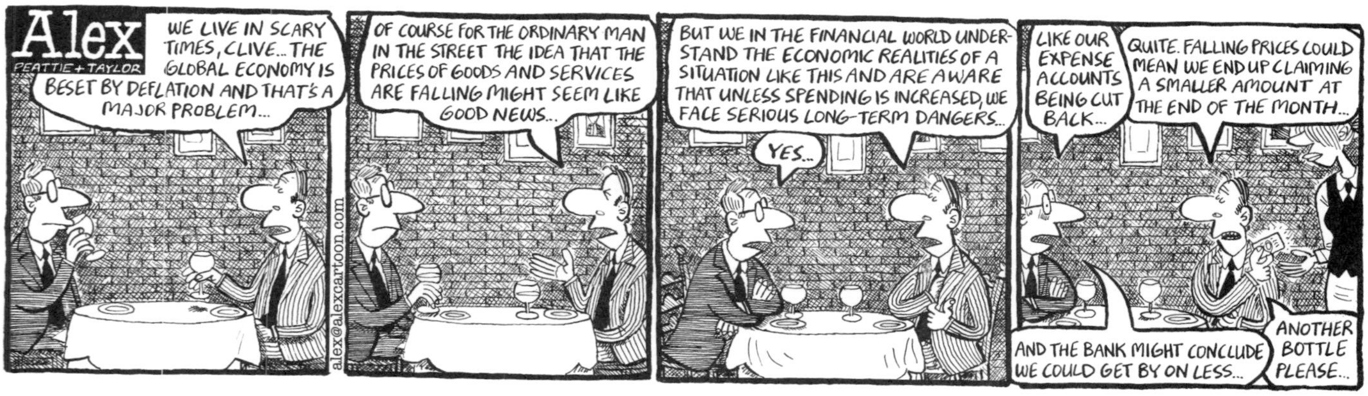
Alex
PEATTIE + TAYLOR
WE LIVE IN SCARY TIMES, CLIVE... THE GLOBAL ECONOMY IS BESET BY DEFLATION AND THAT'S A MAJOR PROBLEM...
alex@alexcartoon.com
OF COURSE FOR THE ORDINARY MAN IN THE STREET THE IDEA THAT THE PRICES OF GOODS AND SERVICES ARE FALLING MIGHT SEEM LIKE GOOD NEWS...
BUT WE IN THE FINANCIAL WORLD UNDERSTAND THE ECONOMIC REALITIES OF A SITUATION LIKE THIS AND ARE AWARE THAT UNLESS SPENDING IS INCREASED, WE FACE SERIOUS LONG-TERM DANGERS...
YES...
LIKE OUR EXPENSE ACCOUNTS BEING CUT BACK...
QUITE. FALLING PRICES COULD MEAN WE END UP CLAIMING A SMALLER AMOUNT AT THE END OF THE MONTH...
AND THE BANK MIGHT CONCLUDE WE COULD GET BY ON LESS...
ANOTHER BOTTLE PLEASE...

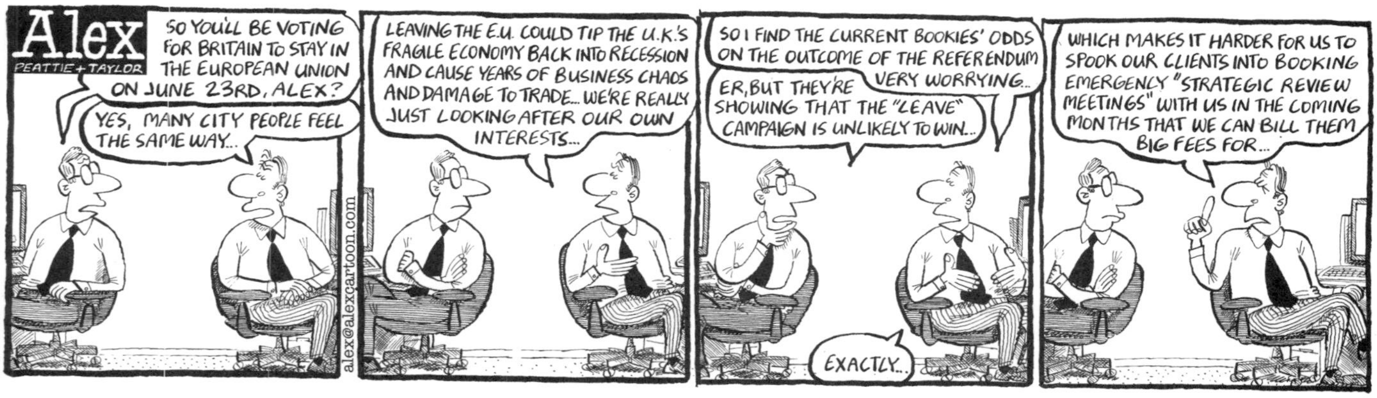
Alex
PEATTIE + TAYLOR
SO YOU'LL BE VOTING FOR BRITAIN TO STAY IN THE EUROPEAN UNION ON JUNE 23RD, ALEX?
YES, MANY CITY PEOPLE FEEL THE SAME WAY...
alex@alexcartoon.com
LEAVING THE E.U. COULD TIP THE U.K.'S FRAGILE ECONOMY BACK INTO RECESSION AND CAUSE YEARS OF BUSINESS CHAOS AND DAMAGE TO TRADE... WE'RE REALLY JUST LOOKING AFTER OUR OWN INTERESTS...
SO I FIND THE CURRENT BOOKIES' ODDS ON THE OUTCOME OF THE REFERENDUM VERY WORRYING...
ER, BUT THEY'RE SHOWING THAT THE "LEAVE" CAMPAIGN IS UNLIKELY TO WIN...
EXACTLY...
WHICH MAKES IT HARDER FOR US TO SPOOK OUR CLIENTS INTO BOOKING EMERGENCY "STRATEGIC REVIEW MEETINGS" WITH US IN THE COMING MONTHS THAT WE CAN BILL THEM BIG FEES FOR...

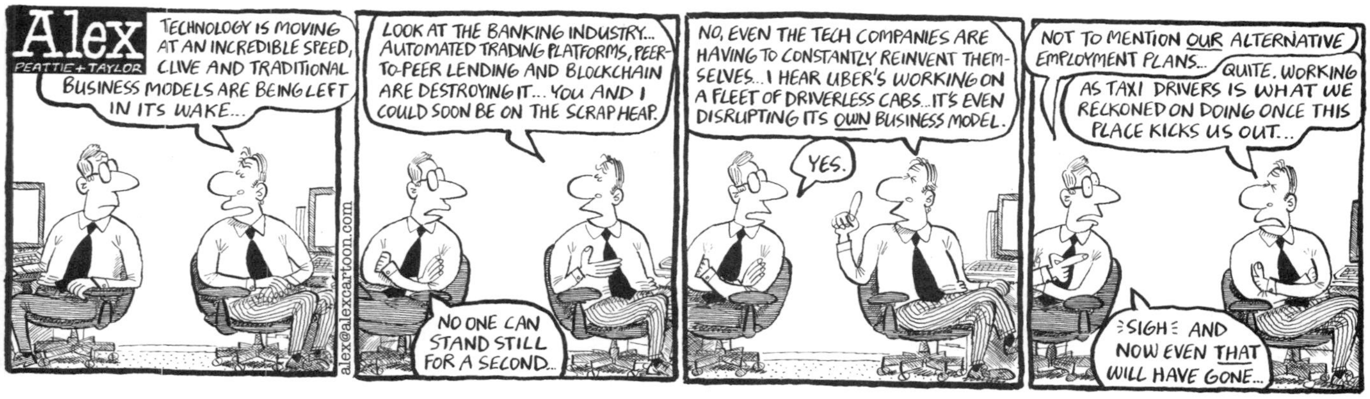
Alex
PEATTIE + TAYLOR
TECHNOLOGY IS MOVING AT AN INCREDIBLE SPEED, CLIVE AND TRADITIONAL BUSINESS MODELS ARE BEING LEFT IN ITS WAKE...
alex@alexcartoon.com
LOOK AT THE BANKING INDUSTRY... AUTOMATED TRADING PLATFORMS, PEER-TO-PEER LENDING AND BLOCKCHAIN ARE DESTROYING IT... YOU AND I COULD SOON BE ON THE SCRAP HEAP.
NO ONE CAN STAND STILL FOR A SECOND...
NO, EVEN THE TECH COMPANIES ARE HAVING TO CONSTANTLY REINVENT THEMSELVES... I HEAR UBER'S WORKING ON A FLEET OF DRIVERLESS CABS... IT'S EVEN DISRUPTING ITS OWN BUSINESS MODEL.
YES.
NOT TO MENTION OUR ALTERNATIVE EMPLOYMENT PLANS...
QUITE. WORKING AS TAXI DRIVERS IS WHAT WE RECKONED ON DOING ONCE THIS PLACE KICKS US OUT...
SIGH AND NOW EVEN THAT WILL HAVE GONE...

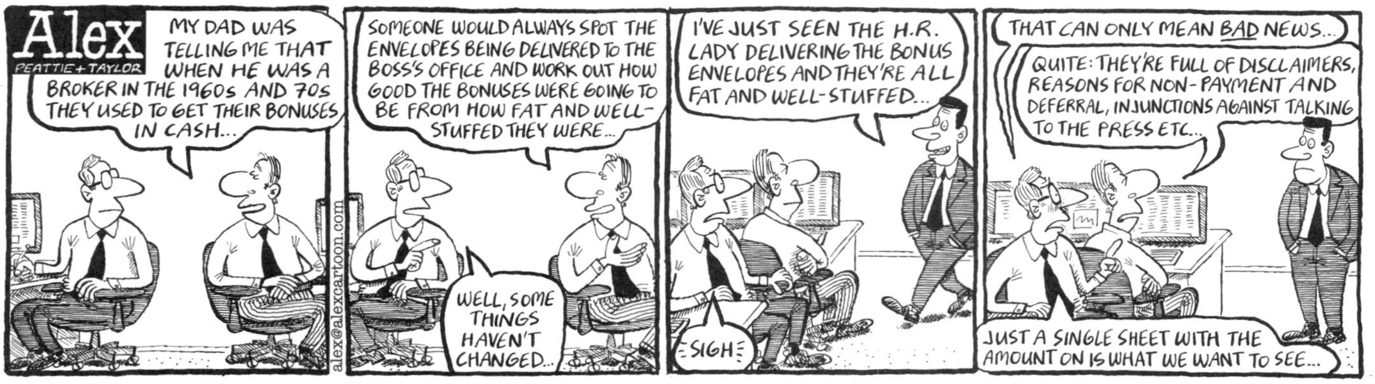
Alex
PEATTIE + TAYLOR
MY DAD WAS TELLING ME THAT WHEN HE WAS A BROKER IN THE 1960s AND 70s THEY USED TO GET THEIR BONUSES IN CASH...
SOMEONE WOULD ALWAYS SPOT THE ENVELOPES BEING DELIVERED TO THE BOSS'S OFFICE AND WORK OUT HOW GOOD THE BONUSES WERE GOING TO BE FROM HOW FAT AND WELL-STUFFED THEY WERE...
WELL, SOME THINGS HAVEN'T CHANGED...
alex@alexcartoon.com
I'VE JUST SEEN THE H.R. LADY DELIVERING THE BONUS ENVELOPES AND THEY'RE ALL FAT AND WELL-STUFFED...
SIGH
THAT CAN ONLY MEAN BAD NEWS...
QUITE: THEY'RE FULL OF DISCLAIMERS, REASONS FOR NON-PAYMENT AND DEFERRAL, INJUNCTIONS AGAINST TALKING TO THE PRESS ETC...
JUST A SINGLE SHEET WITH THE AMOUNT ON IS WHAT WE WANT TO SEE...

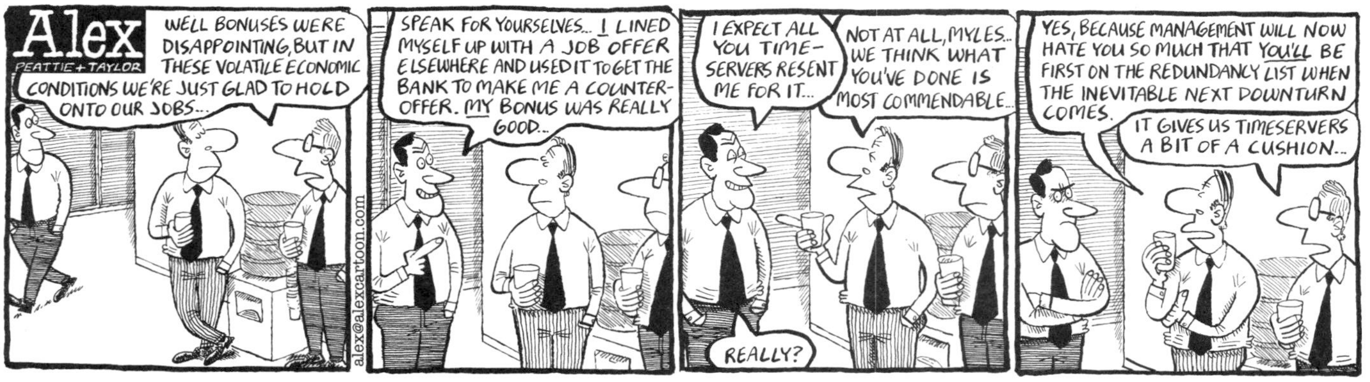
Alex
PEATTIE + TAYLOR
WELL BONUSES WERE DISAPPOINTING, BUT IN THESE VOLATILE ECONOMIC CONDITIONS WE'RE JUST GLAD TO HOLD ONTO OUR JOBS...
alex@alexcartoon.com
SPEAK FOR YOURSELVES... I LINED MYSELF UP WITH A JOB OFFER ELSEWHERE AND USED IT TO GET THE BANK TO MAKE ME A COUNTER-OFFER. MY BONUS WAS REALLY GOOD...
I EXPECT ALL YOU TIME-SERVERS RESENT ME FOR IT...
NOT AT ALL, MYLES... WE THINK WHAT YOU'VE DONE IS MOST COMMENDABLE...
REALLY?
YES, BECAUSE MANAGEMENT WILL NOW HATE YOU SO MUCH THAT YOU'LL BE FIRST ON THE REDUNDANCY LIST WHEN THE INEVITABLE NEXT DOWNTURN COMES.
IT GIVES US TIMESERVERS A BIT OF A CUSHION...

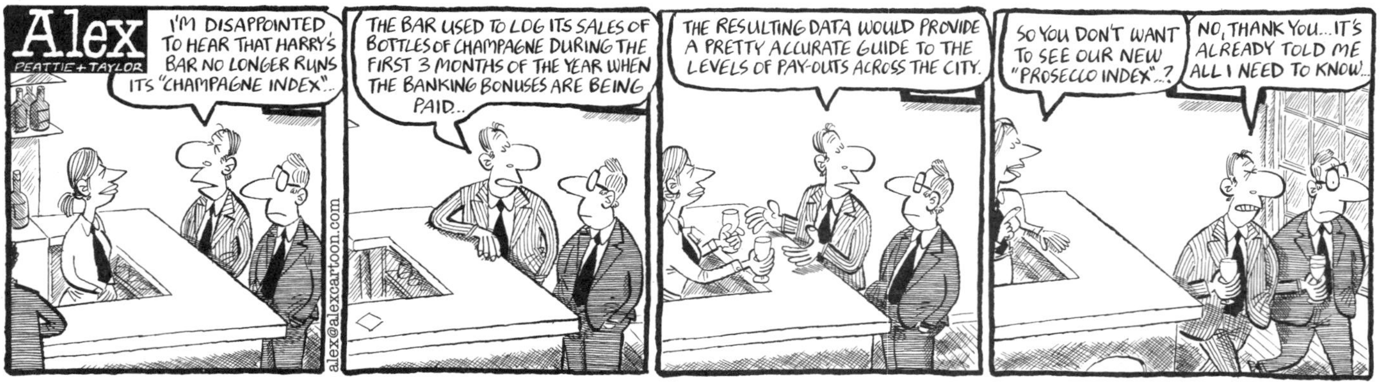
Alex
PEATTIE + TAYLOR
I'M DISAPPOINTED TO HEAR THAT HARRY'S BAR NO LONGER RUNS ITS "CHAMPAGNE INDEX"...
alex@alexcartoon.com
THE BAR USED TO LOG ITS SALES OF BOTTLES OF CHAMPAGNE DURING THE FIRST 3 MONTHS OF THE YEAR WHEN THE BANKING BONUSES ARE BEING PAID...
THE RESULTING DATA WOULD PROVIDE A PRETTY ACCURATE GUIDE TO THE LEVELS OF PAY-OUTS ACROSS THE CITY.
SO YOU DON'T WANT TO SEE OUR NEW "PROSECCO INDEX"..?
NO, THANK YOU... IT'S ALREADY TOLD ME ALL I NEED TO KNOW...

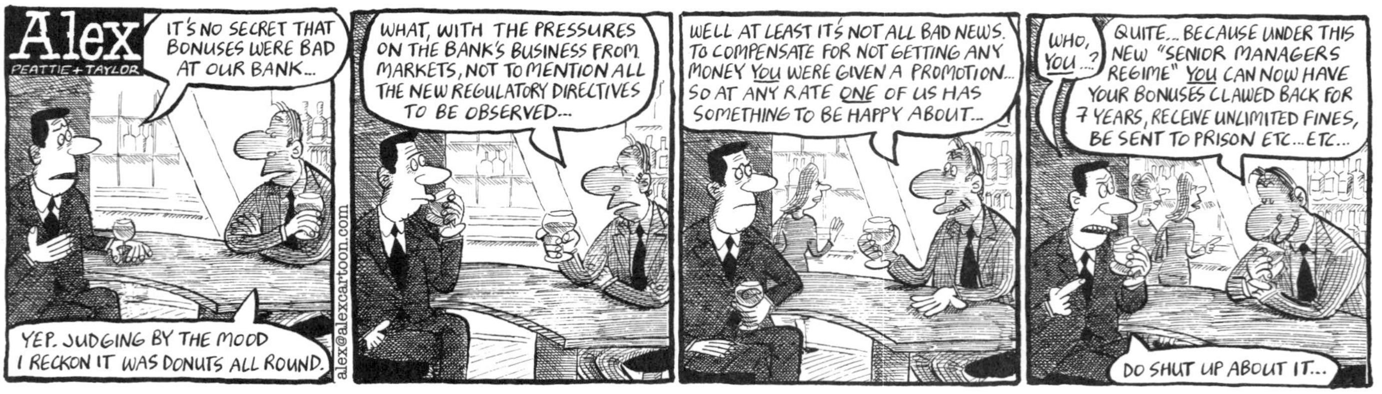
Alex
PEATTIE + TAYLOR
IT'S NO SECRET THAT BONUSES WERE BAD AT OUR BANK...
YEP. JUDGING BY THE MOOD I RECKON IT WAS DONUTS ALL ROUND.
alex@alexcartoon.com
WHAT, WITH THE PRESSURES ON THE BANK'S BUSINESS FROM MARKETS, NOT TO MENTION ALL THE NEW REGULATORY DIRECTIVES TO BE OBSERVED...
WELL AT LEAST IT'S NOT ALL BAD NEWS. TO COMPENSATE FOR NOT GETTING ANY MONEY YOU WERE GIVEN A PROMOTION... SO AT ANY RATE ONE OF US HAS SOMETHING TO BE HAPPY ABOUT...
WHO, YOU...?
QUITE... BECAUSE UNDER THIS NEW "SENIOR MANAGERS REGIME" YOU CAN NOW HAVE YOUR BONUSES CLAWED BACK FOR 7 YEARS, RECEIVE UNLIMITED FINES, BE SENT TO PRISON ETC...ETC...
DO SHUT UP ABOUT IT...

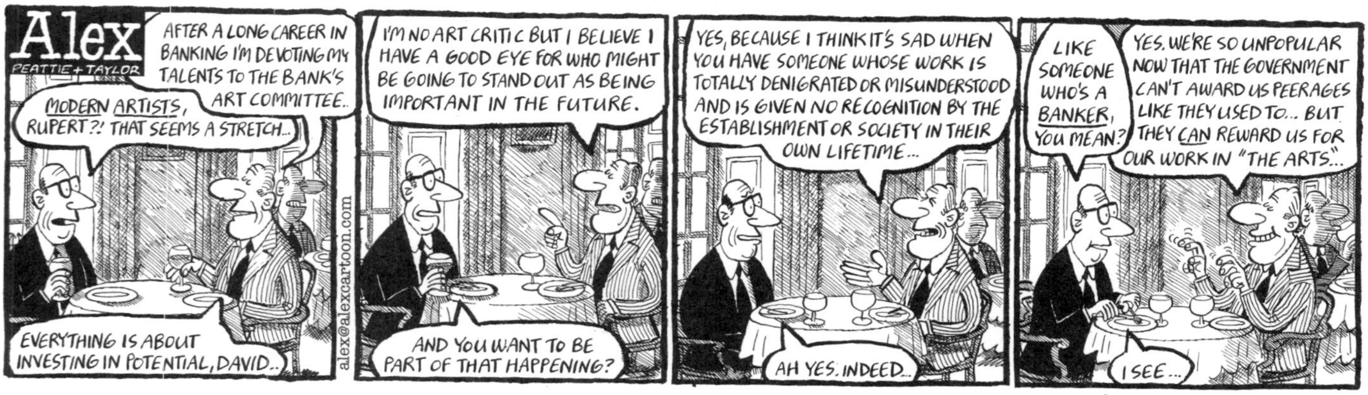
Alex
PEATTIE + TAYLOR
AFTER A LONG CAREER IN BANKING I'M DEVOTING MY TALENTS TO THE BANK'S ART COMMITTEE..
MODERN ARTISTS, RUPERT?! THAT SEEMS A STRETCH...
EVERYTHING IS ABOUT INVESTING IN POTENTIAL, DAVID...
alex@alexcartoon.com
I'M NO ART CRITIC BUT I BELIEVE I HAVE A GOOD EYE FOR WHO MIGHT BE GOING TO STAND OUT AS BEING IMPORTANT IN THE FUTURE.
AND YOU WANT TO BE PART OF THAT HAPPENING?
YES, BECAUSE I THINK IT'S SAD WHEN YOU HAVE SOMEONE WHOSE WORK IS TOTALLY DENIGRATED OR MISUNDERSTOOD AND IS GIVEN NO RECOGNITION BY THE ESTABLISHMENT OR SOCIETY IN THEIR OWN LIFETIME...
AH YES. INDEED...
LIKE SOMEONE WHO'S A BANKER, YOU MEAN?
YES. WE'RE SO UNPOPULAR NOW THAT THE GOVERNMENT CAN'T AWARD US PEERAGES LIKE THEY USED TO... BUT THEY CAN REWARD US FOR OUR WORK IN "THE ARTS"...
I SEE...

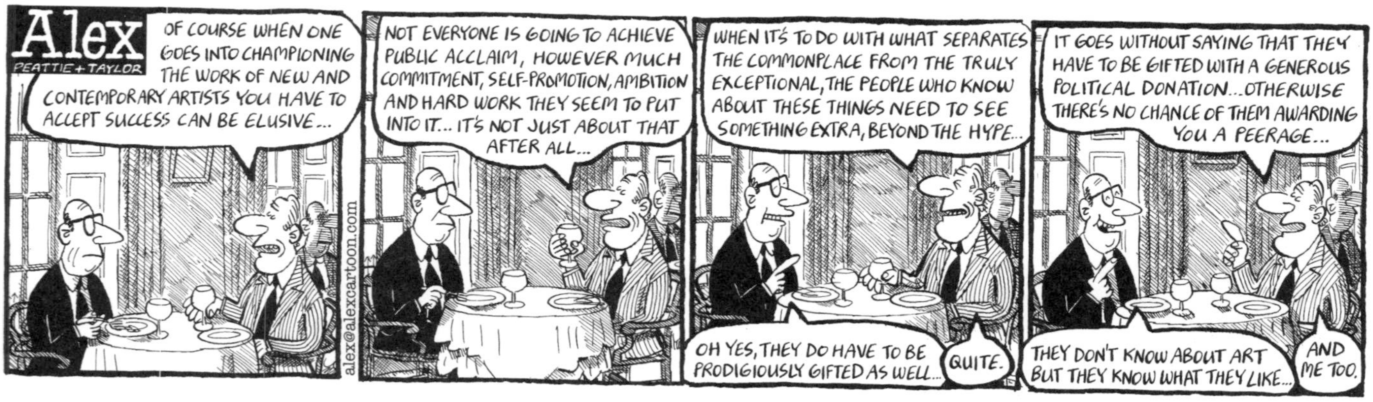
Alex
PEATTIE + TAYLOR
OF COURSE WHEN ONE GOES INTO CHAMPIONING THE WORK OF NEW AND CONTEMPORARY ARTISTS YOU HAVE TO ACCEPT SUCCESS CAN BE ELUSIVE...
alex@alexcartoon.com
NOT EVERYONE IS GOING TO ACHIEVE PUBLIC ACCLAIM, HOWEVER MUCH COMMITMENT, SELF-PROMOTION, AMBITION AND HARD WORK THEY SEEM TO PUT INTO IT... IT'S NOT JUST ABOUT THAT AFTER ALL...
WHEN IT'S TO DO WITH WHAT SEPARATES THE COMMONPLACE FROM THE TRULY EXCEPTIONAL, THE PEOPLE WHO KNOW ABOUT THESE THINGS NEED TO SEE SOMETHING EXTRA, BEYOND THE HYPE...
OH YES, THEY DO HAVE TO BE PRODIGIOUSLY GIFTED AS WELL...
QUITE.
IT GOES WITHOUT SAYING THAT THEY HAVE TO BE GIFTED WITH A GENEROUS POLITICAL DONATION... OTHERWISE THERE'S NO CHANCE OF THEM AWARDING YOU A PEERAGE...
THEY DON'T KNOW ABOUT ART BUT THEY KNOW WHAT THEY LIKE...
AND ME TOO.

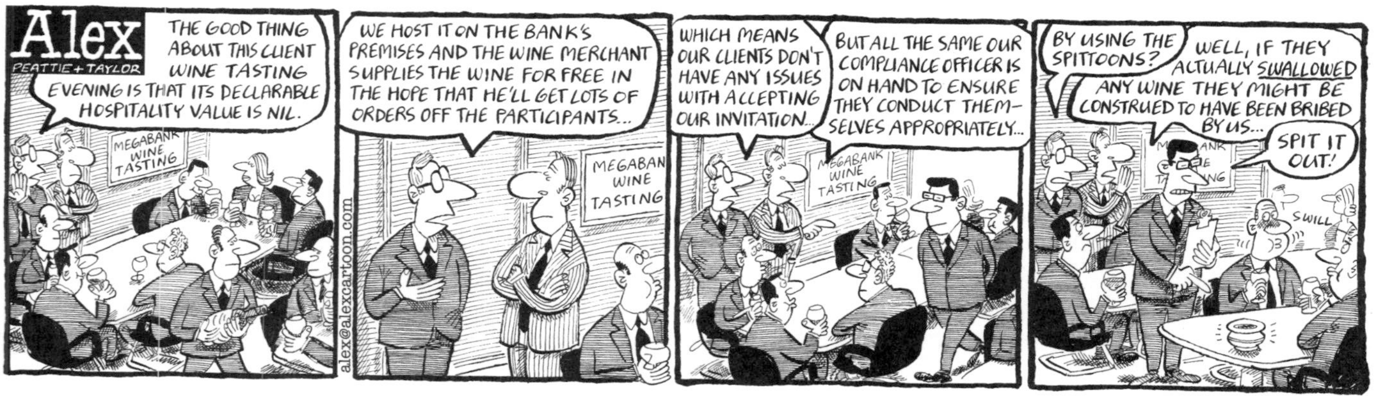
Alex
PEATTIE + TAYLOR
THE GOOD THING ABOUT THIS CLIENT WINE TASTING EVENING IS THAT ITS DECLARABLE HOSPITALITY VALUE IS NIL.
MEGABANK WINE TASTING
alex@alexcartoon.com
WE HOST IT ON THE BANK'S PREMISES AND THE WINE MERCHANT SUPPLIES THE WINE FOR FREE IN THE HOPE THAT HE'LL GET LOTS OF ORDERS OFF THE PARTICIPANTS...
MEGABAN WINE TASTING
WHICH MEANS OUR CLIENTS DON'T HAVE ANY ISSUES WITH ACCEPTING OUR INVITATION.
BUT ALL THE SAME OUR COMPLIANCE OFFICER IS ON HAND TO ENSURE THEY CONDUCT THEMSELVES APPROPRIATELY...
MEGABANK WINE TASTING
BY USING THE SPITTOONS?
WELL, IF THEY ACTUALLY SWALLOWED ANY WINE THEY MIGHT BE CONSTRUED TO HAVE BEEN BRIBED BY US...
SPIT IT OUT!
SWILL

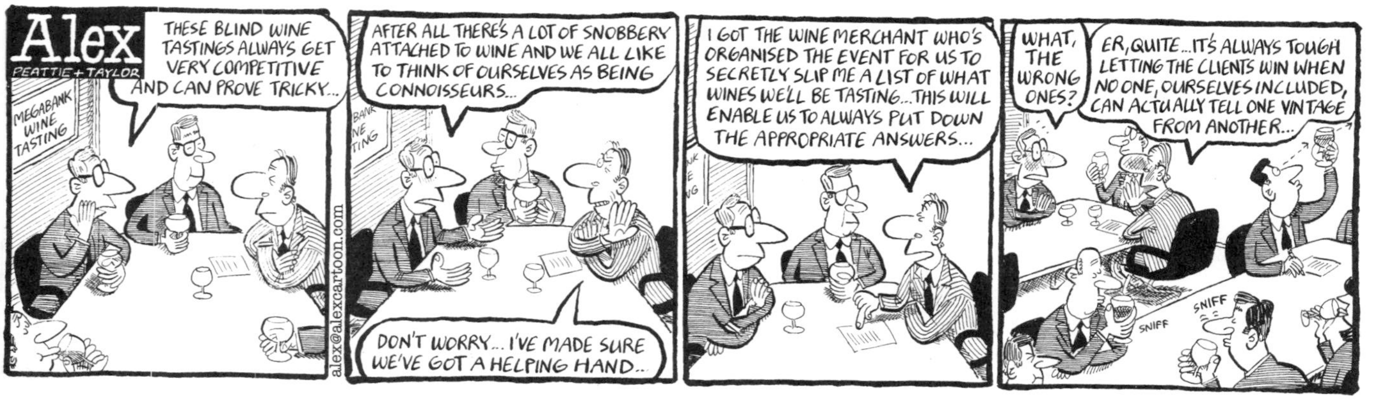
Alex
PEATTIE + TAYLOR
THESE BLIND WINE TASTINGS ALWAYS GET VERY COMPETITIVE AND CAN PROVE TRICKY...
MEGABANK WINE TASTING
alex@alexcartoon.com
AFTER ALL THERE'S A LOT OF SNOBBERY ATTACHED TO WINE AND WE ALL LIKE TO THINK OF OURSELVES AS BEING CONNOISSEURS...
DON'T WORRY... I'VE MADE SURE WE'VE GOT A HELPING HAND..
I GOT THE WINE MERCHANT WHO'S ORGANISED THE EVENT FOR US TO SECRETLY SLIP ME A LIST OF WHAT WINES WE'LL BE TASTING... THIS WILL ENABLE US TO ALWAYS PUT DOWN THE APPROPRIATE ANSWERS...
WHAT, THE WRONG ONES?
ER, QUITE... IT'S ALWAYS TOUGH LETTING THE CLIENTS WIN WHEN NO ONE, OURSELVES INCLUDED, CAN ACTUALLY TELL ONE VINTAGE FROM ANOTHER...
SNIFF
SNIFF

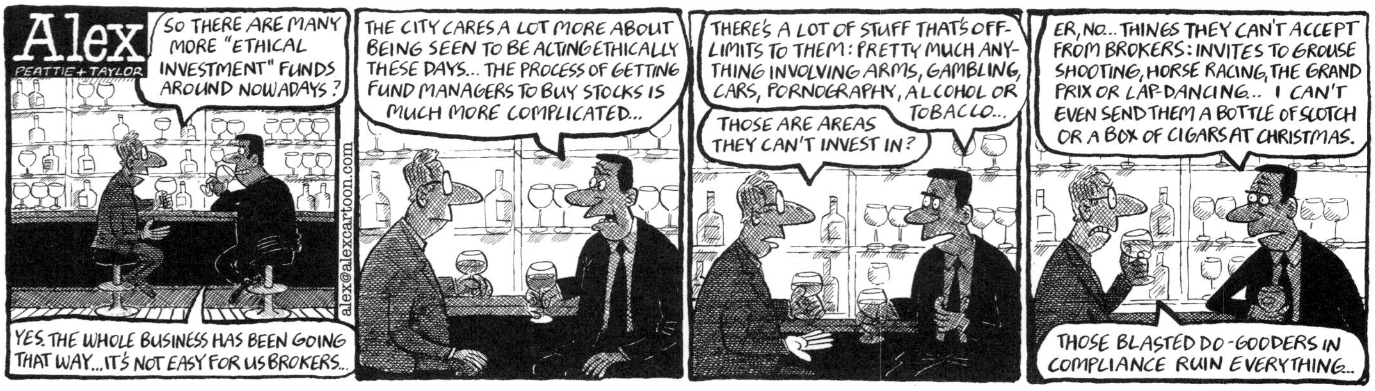
Alex
PEATTIE + TAYLOR
SO THERE ARE MANY MORE "ETHICAL INVESTMENT" FUNDS AROUND NOWADAYS?
YES. THE WHOLE BUSINESS HAS BEEN GOING THAT WAY... IT'S NOT EASY FOR US BROKERS...
alex@alexcartoon.com
THE CITY CARES A LOT MORE ABOUT BEING SEEN TO BE ACTING ETHICALLY THESE DAYS... THE PROCESS OF GETTING FUND MANAGERS TO BUY STOCKS IS MUCH MORE COMPLICATED...
THERE'S A LOT OF STUFF THAT'S OFF-LIMITS TO THEM: PRETTY MUCH ANYTHING INVOLVING ARMS, GAMBLING, CARS, PORNOGRAPHY, ALCOHOL OR TOBACCO...
THOSE ARE AREAS THEY CAN'T INVEST IN?
ER, NO... THINGS THEY CAN'T ACCEPT FROM BROKERS: INVITES TO GROUSE SHOOTING, HORSE RACING, THE GRAND PRIX OR LAP-DANCING... I CAN'T EVEN SEND THEM A BOTTLE OF SCOTCH OR A BOX OF CIGARS AT CHRISTMAS.
THOSE BLASTED DO-GOODERS IN COMPLIANCE RUIN EVERYTHING...

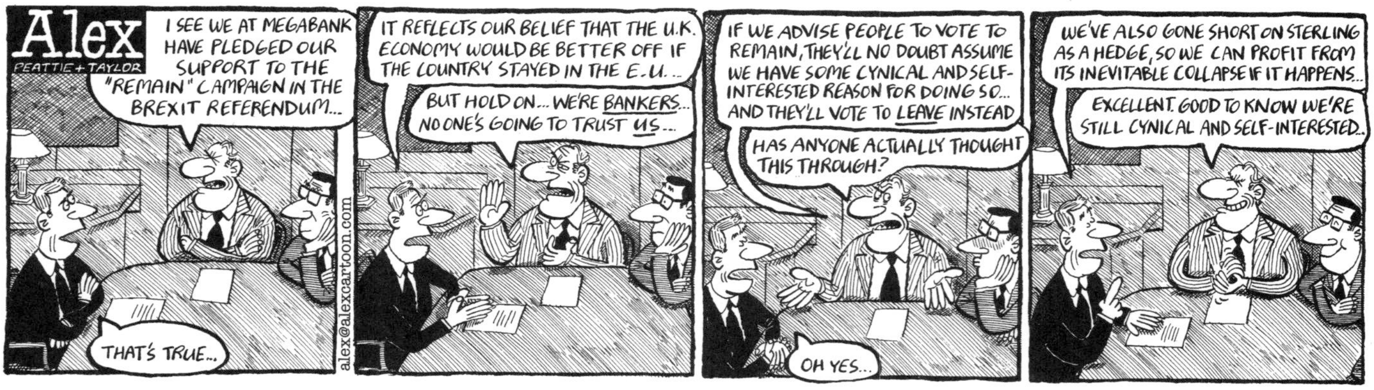
Alex
PEATTIE + TAYLOR
I SEE WE AT MEGABANK HAVE PLEDGED OUR SUPPORT TO THE "REMAIN" CAMPAIGN IN THE BREXIT REFERENDUM...
THAT'S TRUE...
alex@alexcartoon.com
IT REFLECTS OUR BELIEF THAT THE U.K. ECONOMY WOULD BE BETTER OFF IF THE COUNTRY STAYED IN THE E.U. ..
BUT HOLD ON... WE'RE BANKERS... NO ONE'S GOING TO TRUST US...
IF WE ADVISE PEOPLE TO VOTE TO REMAIN, THEY'LL NO DOUBT ASSUME WE HAVE SOME CYNICAL AND SELF-INTERESTED REASON FOR DOING SO... AND THEY'LL VOTE TO LEAVE INSTEAD
HAS ANYONE ACTUALLY THOUGHT THIS THROUGH?
OH YES...
WE'VE ALSO GONE SHORT ON STERLING AS A HEDGE, SO WE CAN PROFIT FROM ITS INEVITABLE COLLAPSE IF IT HAPPENS...
EXCELLENT. GOOD TO KNOW WE'RE STILL CYNICAL AND SELF-INTERESTED...

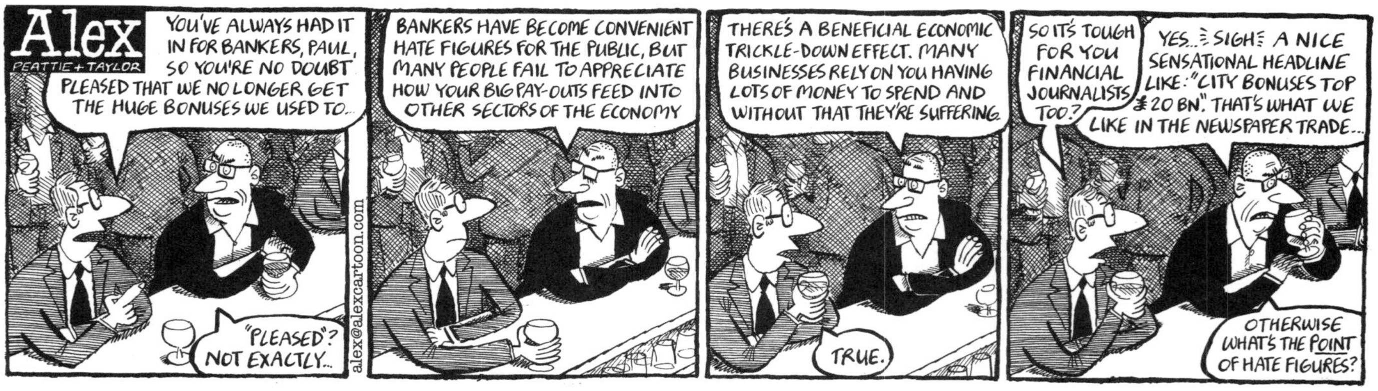
Alex
PEATTIE + TAYLOR
YOU'VE ALWAYS HAD IT IN FOR BANKERS, PAUL, SO YOU'RE NO DOUBT PLEASED THAT WE NO LONGER GET THE HUGE BONUSES WE USED TO...
"PLEASED"? NOT EXACTLY...
alex@alexcartoon.com
BANKERS HAVE BECOME CONVENIENT HATE FIGURES FOR THE PUBLIC, BUT MANY PEOPLE FAIL TO APPRECIATE HOW YOUR BIG PAY-OUTS FEED INTO OTHER SECTORS OF THE ECONOMY
THERE'S A BENEFICIAL ECONOMIC TRICKLE-DOWN EFFECT. MANY BUSINESSES RELY ON YOU HAVING LOTS OF MONEY TO SPEND AND WITHOUT THAT THEY'RE SUFFERING.
TRUE.
SO IT'S TOUGH FOR YOU FINANCIAL JOURNALISTS TOO?
YES... SIGH A NICE SENSATIONAL HEADLINE LIKE: "CITY BONUSES TOP £20 BN". THAT'S WHAT WE LIKE IN THE NEWSPAPER TRADE...
OTHERWISE WHAT'S THE POINT OF HATE FIGURES?

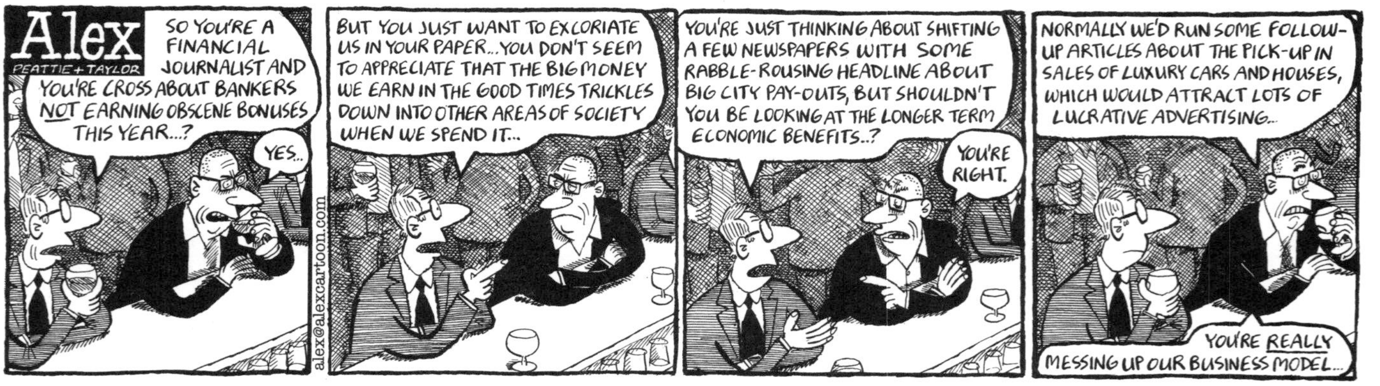
Alex
PEATTIE + TAYLOR
SO YOU'RE A FINANCIAL JOURNALIST AND YOU'RE CROSS ABOUT BANKERS NOT EARNING OBSCENE BONUSES THIS YEAR...?
YES...
alex@alexcartoon.com
BUT YOU JUST WANT TO EXCORIATE US IN YOUR PAPER... YOU DON'T SEEM TO APPRECIATE THAT THE BIG MONEY WE EARN IN THE GOOD TIMES TRICKLES DOWN INTO OTHER AREAS OF SOCIETY WHEN WE SPEND IT...
YOU'RE JUST THINKING ABOUT SHIFTING A FEW NEWSPAPERS WITH SOME RABBLE-ROUSING HEADLINE ABOUT BIG CITY PAY-OUTS, BUT SHOULDN'T YOU BE LOOKING AT THE LONGER TERM ECONOMIC BENEFITS..?
YOU'RE RIGHT.
NORMALLY WE'D RUN SOME FOLLOW-UP ARTICLES ABOUT THE PICK-UP IN SALES OF LUXURY CARS AND HOUSES, WHICH WOULD ATTRACT LOTS OF LUCRATIVE ADVERTISING...
YOU'RE REALLY MESSING UP OUR BUSINESS MODEL...

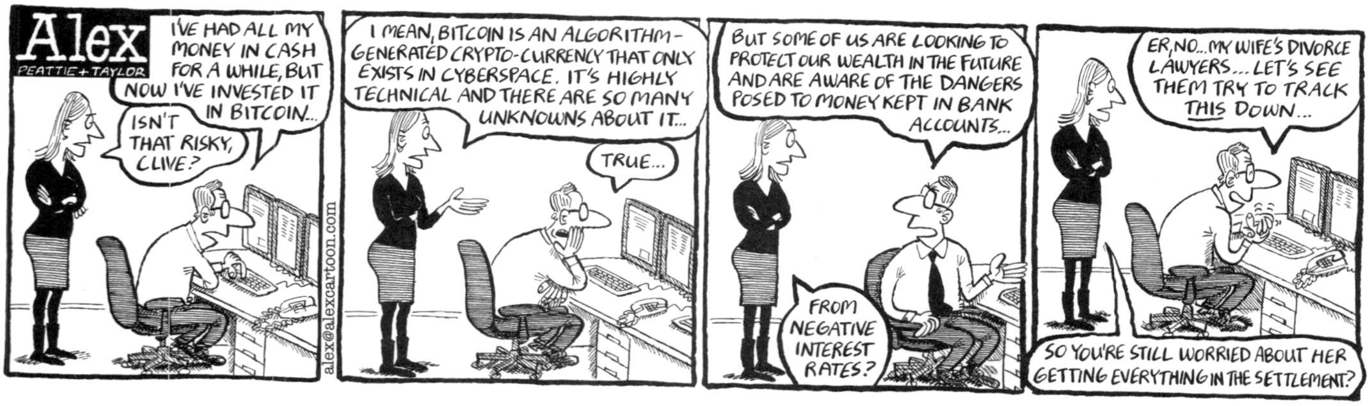
Alex
PEATTIE + TAYLOR
I'VE HAD ALL MY MONEY IN CASH FOR A WHILE, BUT NOW I'VE INVESTED IT IN BITCOIN...
ISN'T THAT RISKY, CLIVE?
alex@alexcartoon.com
I MEAN, BITCOIN IS AN ALGORITHM-GENERATED CRYPTO-CURRENCY THAT ONLY EXISTS IN CYBERSPACE. IT'S HIGHLY TECHNICAL AND THERE ARE SO MANY UNKNOWNS ABOUT IT...
TRUE...
BUT SOME OF US ARE LOOKING TO PROTECT OUR WEALTH IN THE FUTURE AND ARE AWARE OF THE DANGERS POSED TO MONEY KEPT IN BANK ACCOUNTS...
FROM NEGATIVE INTEREST RATES?
ER, NO... MY WIFE'S DIVORCE LAWYERS... LET'S SEE THEM TRY TO TRACK THIS DOWN...
SO YOU'RE STILL WORRIED ABOUT HER GETTING EVERYTHING IN THE SETTLEMENT?

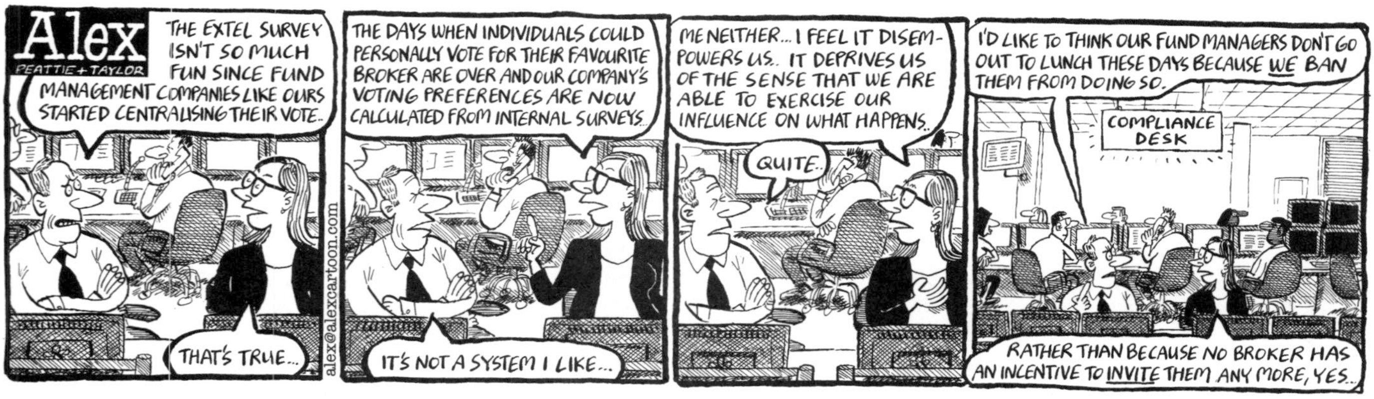
Alex
PEATTIE + TAYLOR
THE EXTEL SURVEY ISN'T SO MUCH FUN SINCE FUND MANAGEMENT COMPANIES LIKE OURS STARTED CENTRALISING THEIR VOTE...
THAT'S TRUE...
alex@alexcartoon.com
THE DAYS WHEN INDIVIDUALS COULD PERSONALLY VOTE FOR THEIR FAVOURITE BROKER ARE OVER AND OUR COMPANY'S VOTING PREFERENCES ARE NOW CALCULATED FROM INTERNAL SURVEYS...
IT'S NOT A SYSTEM I LIKE...
ME NEITHER... I FEEL IT DISEMPOWERS US.. IT DEPRIVES US OF THE SENSE THAT WE ARE ABLE TO EXERCISE OUR INFLUENCE ON WHAT HAPPENS..
QUITE..
I'D LIKE TO THINK OUR FUND MANAGERS DON'T GO OUT TO LUNCH THESE DAYS BECAUSE WE BAN THEM FROM DOING SO.
COMPLIANCE DESK
RATHER THAN BECAUSE NO BROKER HAS AN INCENTIVE TO INVITE THEM ANY MORE, YES..

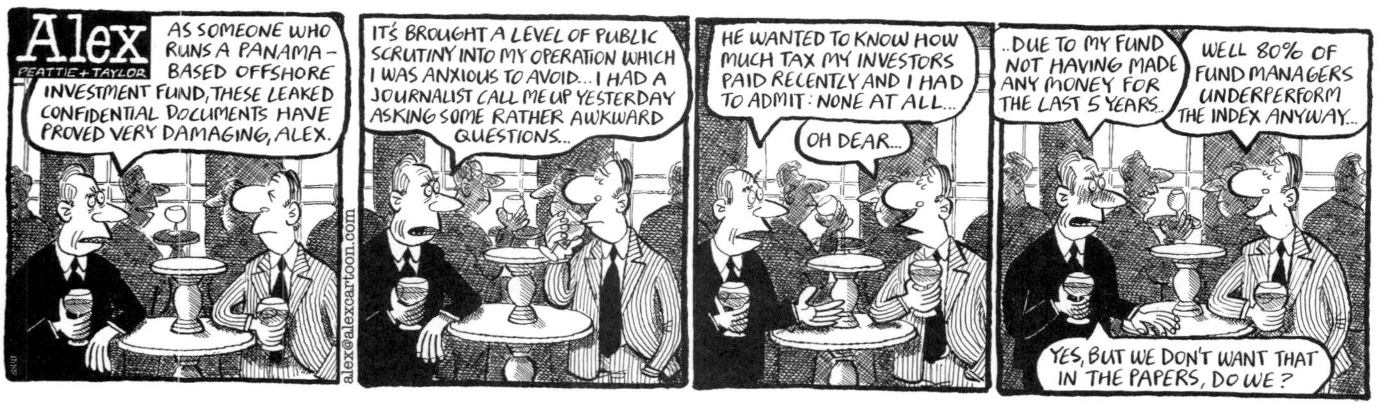
Alex
PEATTIE + TAYLOR
AS SOMEONE WHO RUNS A PANAMA-BASED OFFSHORE INVESTMENT FUND, THESE LEAKED CONFIDENTIAL DOCUMENTS HAVE PROVED VERY DAMAGING, ALEX.
alex@alexcartoon.com
IT'S BROUGHT A LEVEL OF PUBLIC SCRUTINY INTO MY OPERATION WHICH I WAS ANXIOUS TO AVOID... I HAD A JOURNALIST CALL ME UP YESTERDAY ASKING SOME RATHER AWKWARD QUESTIONS...
HE WANTED TO KNOW HOW MUCH TAX MY INVESTORS PAID RECENTLY AND I HAD TO ADMIT: NONE AT ALL...
OH DEAR...
..DUE TO MY FUND NOT HAVING MADE ANY MONEY FOR THE LAST 5 YEARS..
WELL 80% OF FUND MANAGERS UNDERPERFORM THE INDEX ANYWAY...
YES, BUT WE DON'T WANT THAT IN THE PAPERS, DO WE?

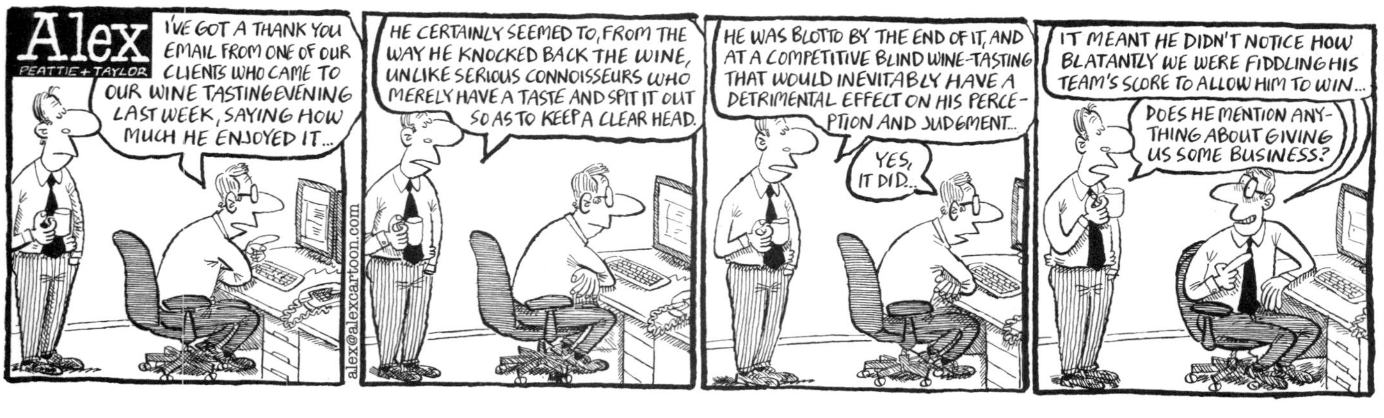
Alex
PEATTIE + TAYLOR
I'VE GOT A THANK YOU EMAIL FROM ONE OF OUR CLIENTS WHO CAME TO OUR WINE TASTING EVENING LAST WEEK, SAYING HOW MUCH HE ENJOYED IT...
alex@alexcartoon.com
HE CERTAINLY SEEMED TO, FROM THE WAY HE KNOCKED BACK THE WINE, UNLIKE SERIOUS CONNOISSEURS WHO MERELY HAVE A TASTE AND SPIT IT OUT SO AS TO KEEP A CLEAR HEAD.
HE WAS BLOTTO BY THE END OF IT, AND AT A COMPETITIVE BLIND WINE-TASTING THAT WOULD INEVITABLY HAVE A DETRIMENTAL EFFECT ON HIS PERCEPTION AND JUDGEMENT...
YES, IT DID..
IT MEANT HE DIDN'T NOTICE HOW BLATANTLY WE WERE FIDDLING HIS TEAM'S SCORE TO ALLOW HIM TO WIN...
DOES HE MENTION ANYTHING ABOUT GIVING US SOME BUSINESS?

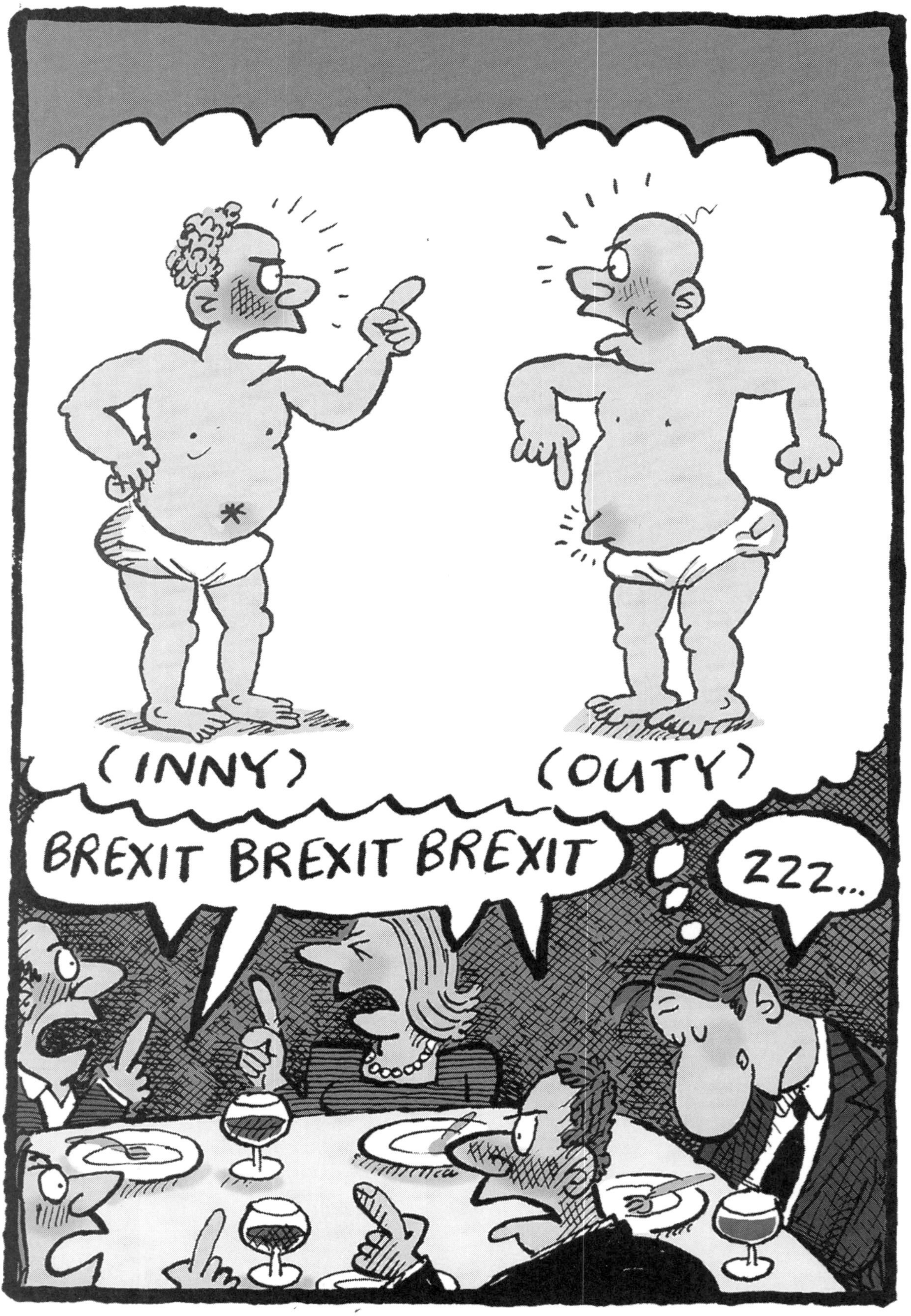
(INNY)
(OUTY)
BREXIT BREXIT BREXIT
ZZZ...

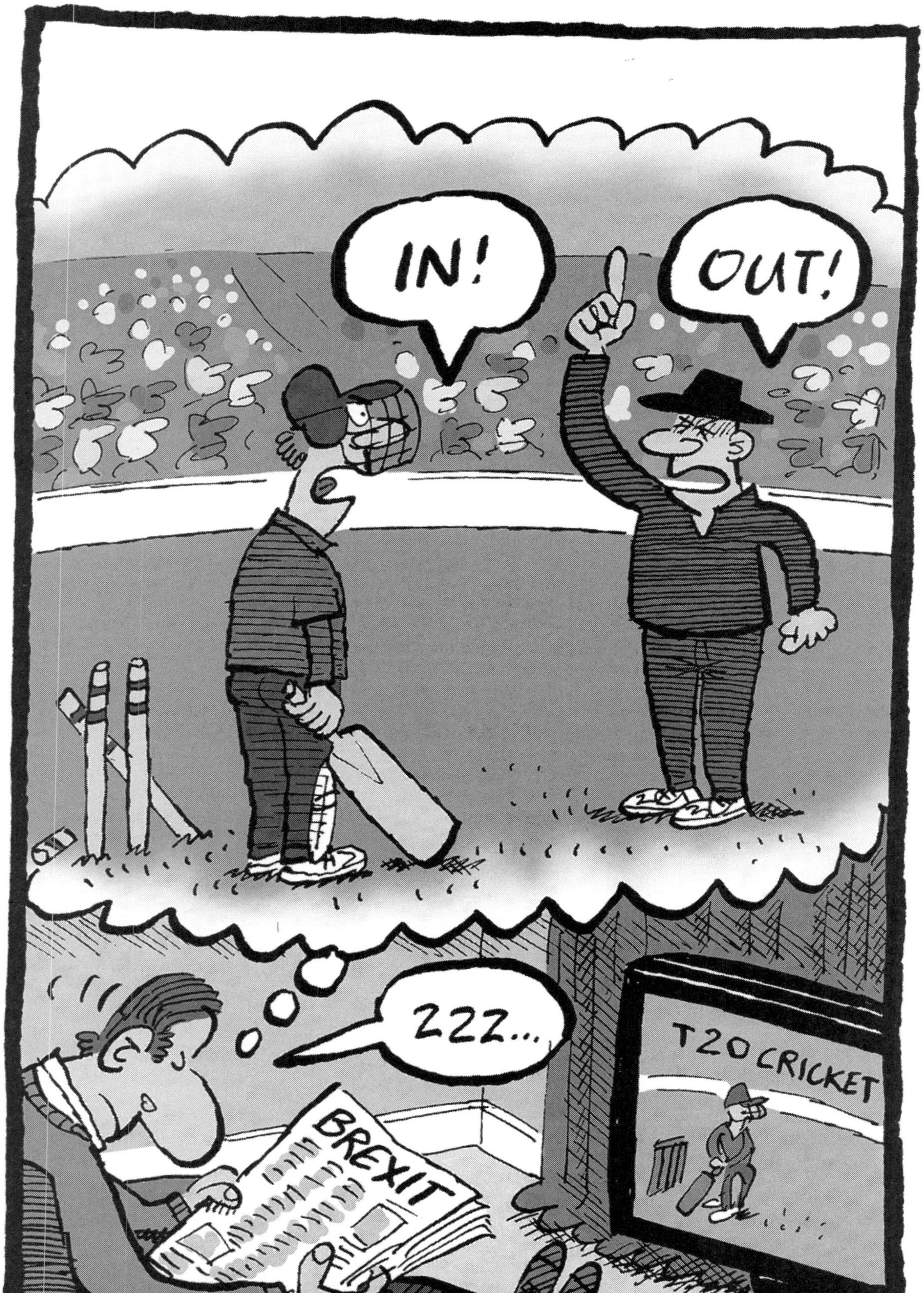
IN!
OUT!
ZZZ...
BREXIT
T20 CRICKET

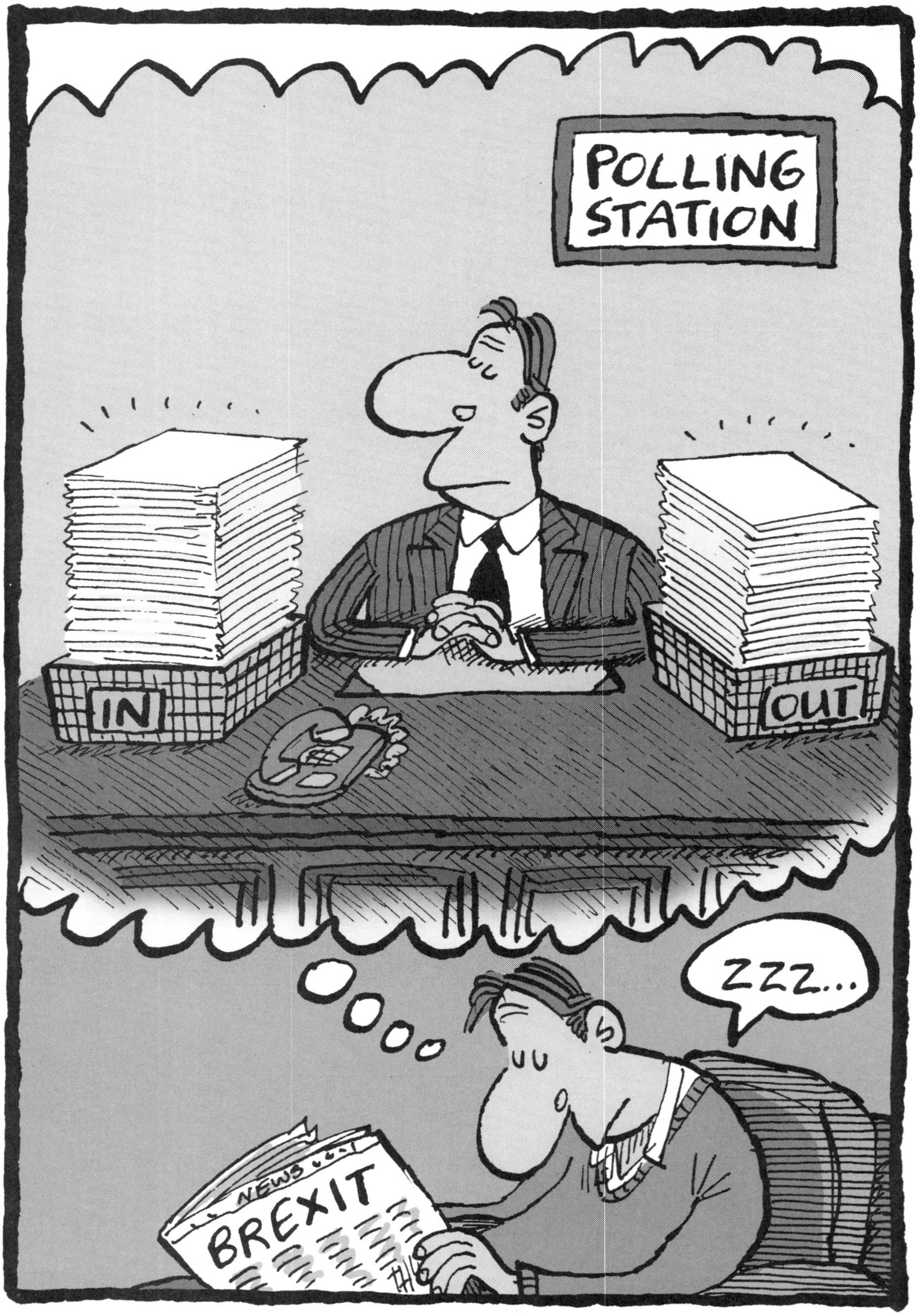
POLLING STATION
IN
OUT
ZZZ...
BREXIT

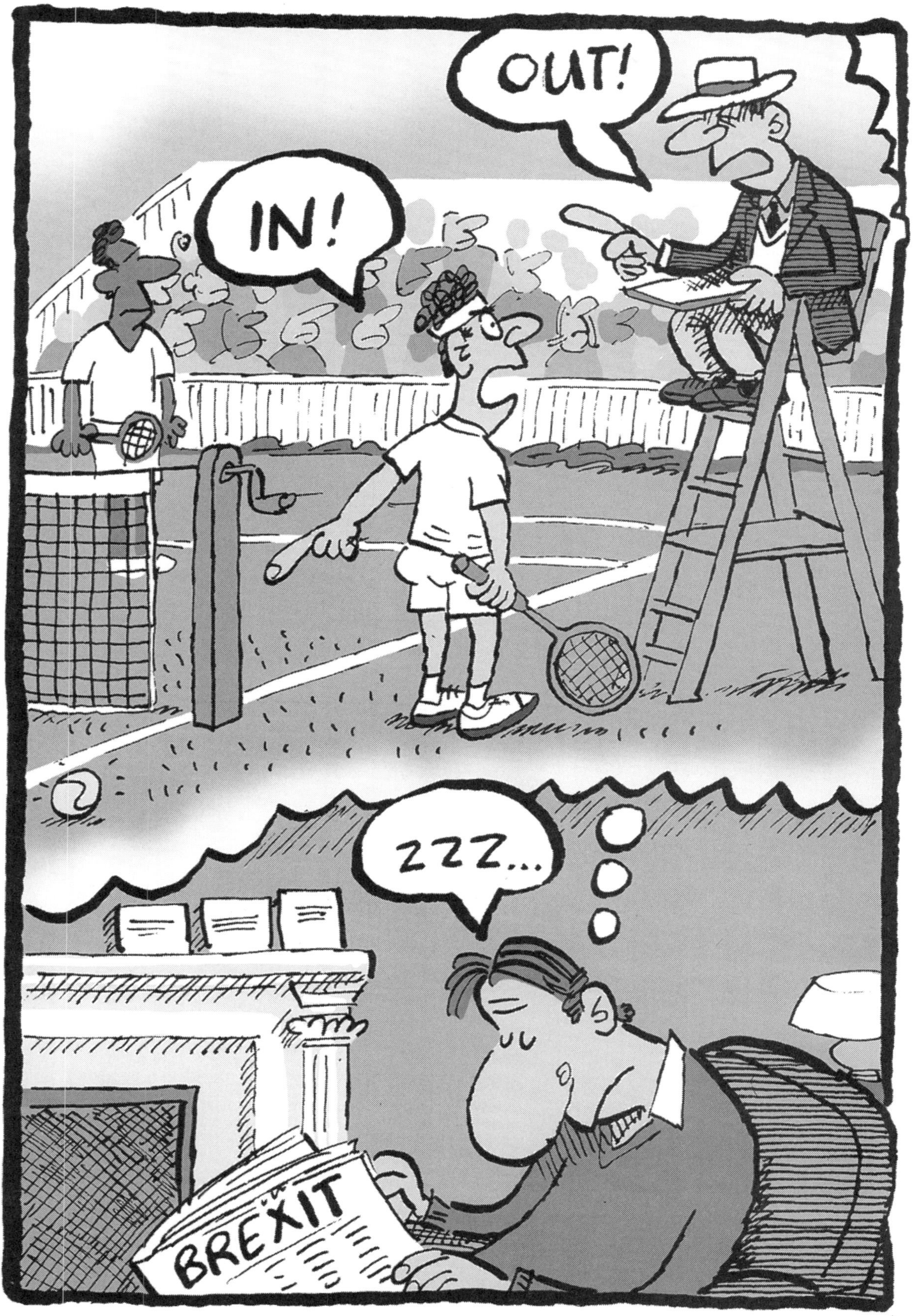
OUT!
IN!
ZZZ...
BREXIT

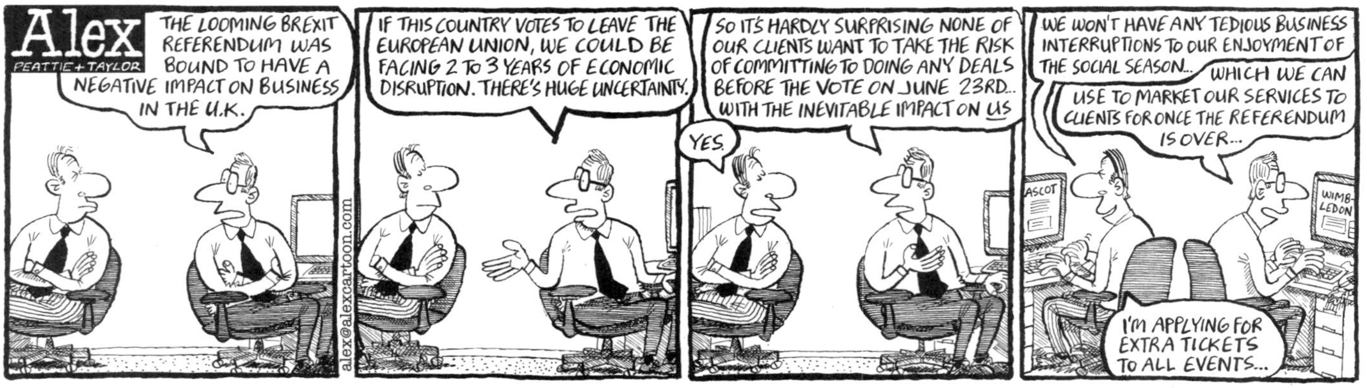
Alex
PEATTIE + TAYLOR
THE LOOMING BREXIT REFERENDUM WAS BOUND TO HAVE A NEGATIVE IMPACT ON BUSINESS IN THE U.K.
alex@alexcartoon.com
IF THIS COUNTRY VOTES TO LEAVE THE EUROPEAN UNION, WE COULD BE FACING 2 TO 3 YEARS OF ECONOMIC DISRUPTION. THERE'S HUGE UNCERTAINTY.
SO IT'S HARDLY SURPRISING NONE OF OUR CLIENTS WANT TO TAKE THE RISK OF COMMITTING TO DOING ANY DEALS BEFORE THE VOTE ON JUNE 23RD... WITH THE INEVITABLE IMPACT ON US
YES.
WE WON'T HAVE ANY TEDIOUS BUSINESS INTERRUPTIONS TO OUR ENJOYMENT OF THE SOCIAL SEASON...
WHICH WE CAN USE TO MARKET OUR SERVICES TO CLIENTS FOR ONCE THE REFERENDUM IS OVER...
ASCOT
WIMB-LEDON
I'M APPLYING FOR EXTRA TICKETS TO ALL EVENTS...

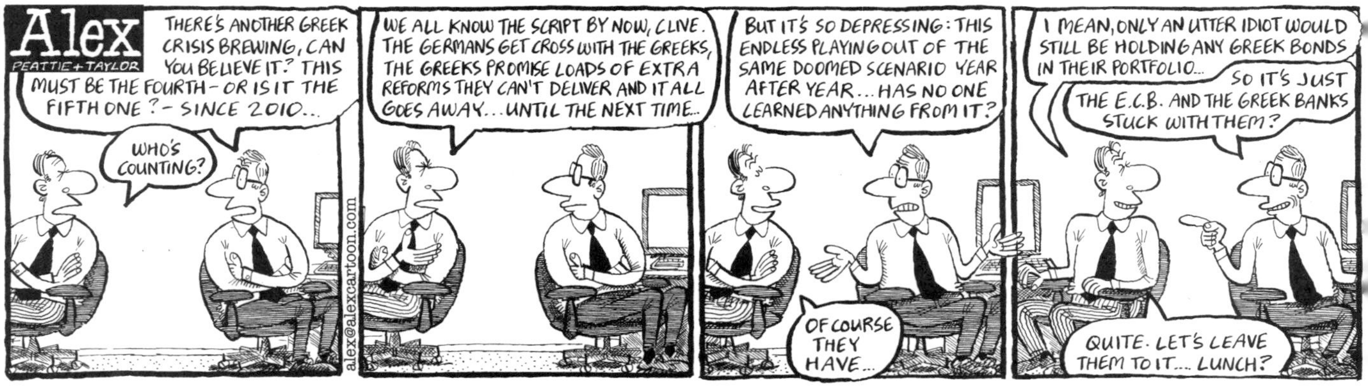
Alex
PEATTIE + TAYLOR
THERE'S ANOTHER GREEK CRISIS BREWING, CAN YOU BELIEVE IT? THIS MUST BE THE FOURTH - OR IS IT THE FIFTH ONE? - SINCE 2010...
WHO'S COUNTING?
alex@alexcartoon.com
WE ALL KNOW THE SCRIPT BY NOW, CLIVE. THE GERMANS GET CROSS WITH THE GREEKS, THE GREEKS PROMISE LOADS OF EXTRA REFORMS THEY CAN'T DELIVER AND IT ALL GOES AWAY... UNTIL THE NEXT TIME...
BUT IT'S SO DEPRESSING: THIS ENDLESS PLAYING OUT OF THE SAME DOOMED SCENARIO YEAR AFTER YEAR... HAS NO ONE LEARNED ANYTHING FROM IT?
OF COURSE THEY HAVE...
I MEAN, ONLY AN UTTER IDIOT WOULD STILL BE HOLDING ANY GREEK BONDS IN THEIR PORTFOLIO...
SO IT'S JUST THE E.C.B. AND THE GREEK BANKS STUCK WITH THEM?
QUITE. LET'S LEAVE THEM TO IT... LUNCH?

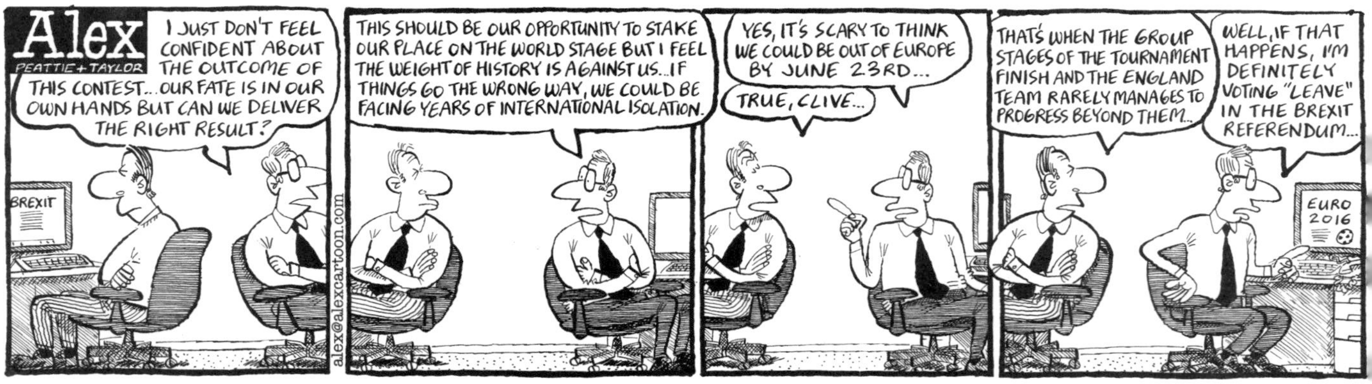
Alex
PEATTIE + TAYLOR
I JUST DON'T FEEL CONFIDENT ABOUT THE OUTCOME OF THIS CONTEST... OUR FATE IS IN OUR OWN HANDS BUT CAN WE DELIVER THE RIGHT RESULT?
BREXIT
alex@alexcartoon.com
THIS SHOULD BE OUR OPPORTUNITY TO STAKE OUR PLACE ON THE WORLD STAGE BUT I FEEL THE WEIGHT OF HISTORY IS AGAINST US... IF THINGS GO THE WRONG WAY, WE COULD BE FACING YEARS OF INTERNATIONAL ISOLATION.
YES, IT'S SCARY TO THINK WE COULD BE OUT OF EUROPE BY JUNE 23RD...
TRUE, CLIVE...
THAT'S WHEN THE GROUP STAGES OF THE TOURNAMENT FINISH AND THE ENGLAND TEAM RARELY MANAGES TO PROGRESS BEYOND THEM...
WELL, IF THAT HAPPENS, I'M DEFINITELY VOTING "LEAVE" IN THE BREXIT REFERENDUM...
EURO 2016

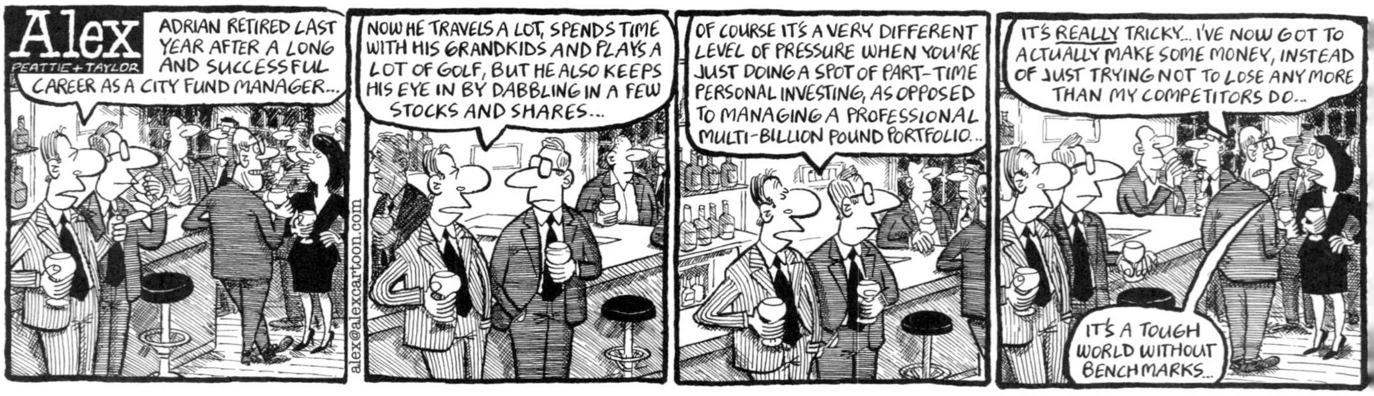
Alex
PEATTIE + TAYLOR
ADRIAN RETIRED LAST YEAR AFTER A LONG AND SUCCESSFUL CAREER AS A CITY FUND MANAGER...
alex@alexcartoon.com
NOW HE TRAVELS A LOT, SPENDS TIME WITH HIS GRANDKIDS AND PLAYS A LOT OF GOLF, BUT HE ALSO KEEPS HIS EYE IN BY DABBLING IN A FEW STOCKS AND SHARES...
OF COURSE IT'S A VERY DIFFERENT LEVEL OF PRESSURE WHEN YOU'RE JUST DOING A SPOT OF PART-TIME PERSONAL INVESTING, AS OPPOSED TO MANAGING A PROFESSIONAL MULTI-BILLION POUND PORTFOLIO...
IT'S REALLY TRICKY... I'VE NOW GOT TO ACTUALLY MAKE SOME MONEY, INSTEAD OF JUST TRYING NOT TO LOSE ANY MORE THAN MY COMPETITORS DO...
IT'S A TOUGH WORLD WITHOUT BENCHMARKS...

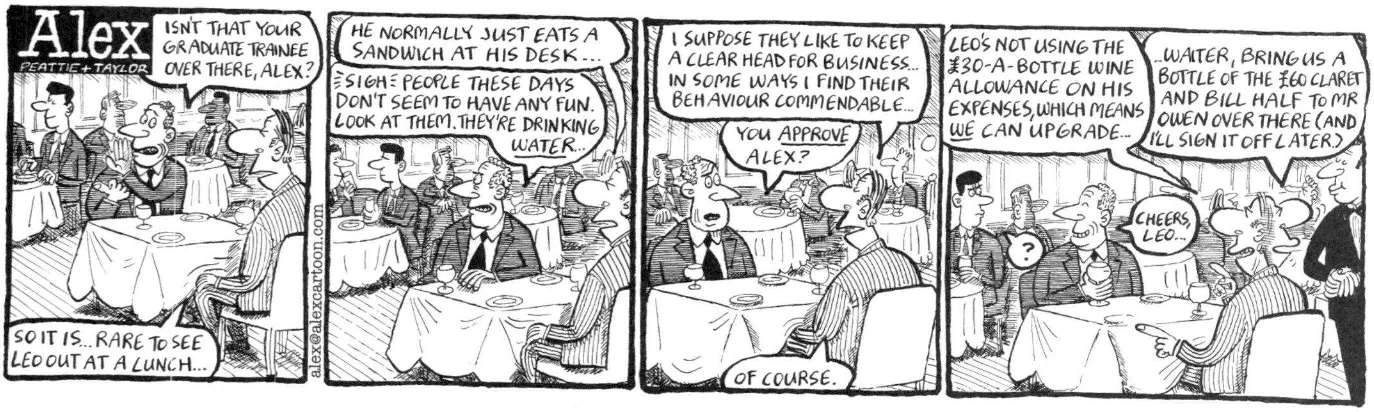
Alex
PEATTIE + TAYLOR
ISN'T THAT YOUR GRADUATE TRAINEE OVER THERE, ALEX?
SO IT IS... RARE TO SEE LEO OUT AT A LUNCH...
HE NORMALLY JUST EATS A SANDWICH AT HIS DESK...
≋SIGH≋ PEOPLE THESE DAYS DON'T SEEM TO HAVE ANY FUN. LOOK AT THEM. THEY'RE DRINKING WATER...
I SUPPOSE THEY LIKE TO KEEP A CLEAR HEAD FOR BUSINESS... IN SOME WAYS I FIND THEIR BEHAVIOUR COMMENDABLE...
YOU APPROVE ALEX?
OF COURSE.
LEO'S NOT USING THE £30-A-BOTTLE WINE ALLOWANCE ON HIS EXPENSES, WHICH MEANS WE CAN UPGRADE...
..WAITER, BRING US A BOTTLE OF THE £60 CLARET AND BILL HALF TO MR OWEN OVER THERE (AND I'LL SIGN IT OFF LATER).
?
CHEERS, LEO...
alex@alexcartoon.com

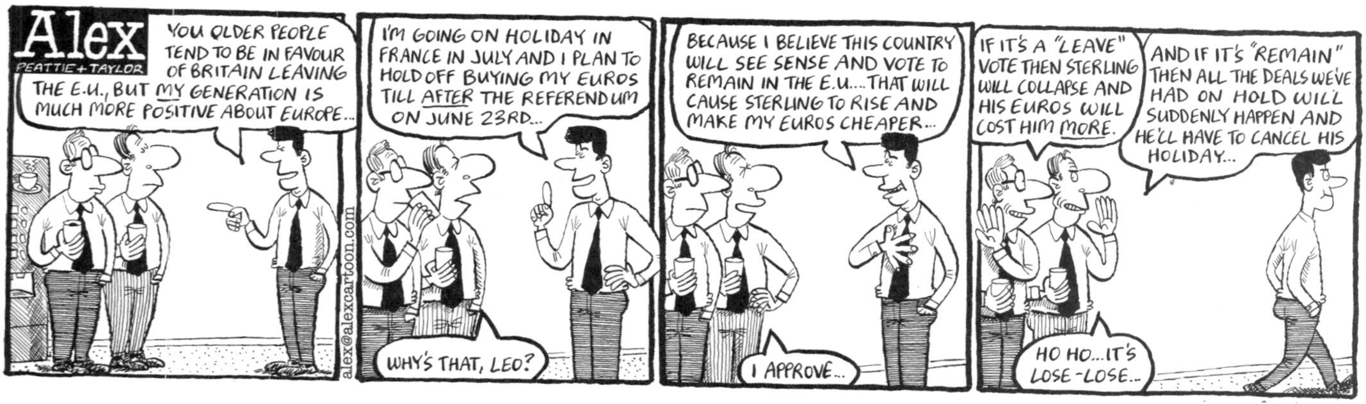
Alex
PEATTIE + TAYLOR
YOU OLDER PEOPLE TEND TO BE IN FAVOUR OF BRITAIN LEAVING THE E.U., BUT MY GENERATION IS MUCH MORE POSITIVE ABOUT EUROPE...
I'M GOING ON HOLIDAY IN FRANCE IN JULY AND I PLAN TO HOLD OFF BUYING MY EUROS TILL AFTER THE REFERENDUM ON JUNE 23RD...
WHY'S THAT, LEO?
BECAUSE I BELIEVE THIS COUNTRY WILL SEE SENSE AND VOTE TO REMAIN IN THE E.U.... THAT WILL CAUSE STERLING TO RISE AND MAKE MY EUROS CHEAPER...
I APPROVE...
IF IT'S A "LEAVE" VOTE THEN STERLING WILL COLLAPSE AND HIS EUROS WILL COST HIM MORE.
AND IF IT'S "REMAIN" THEN ALL THE DEALS WE'VE HAD ON HOLD WILL SUDDENLY HAPPEN AND HE'LL HAVE TO CANCEL HIS HOLIDAY...
HO HO... IT'S LOSE-LOSE...
alex@alexcartoon.com

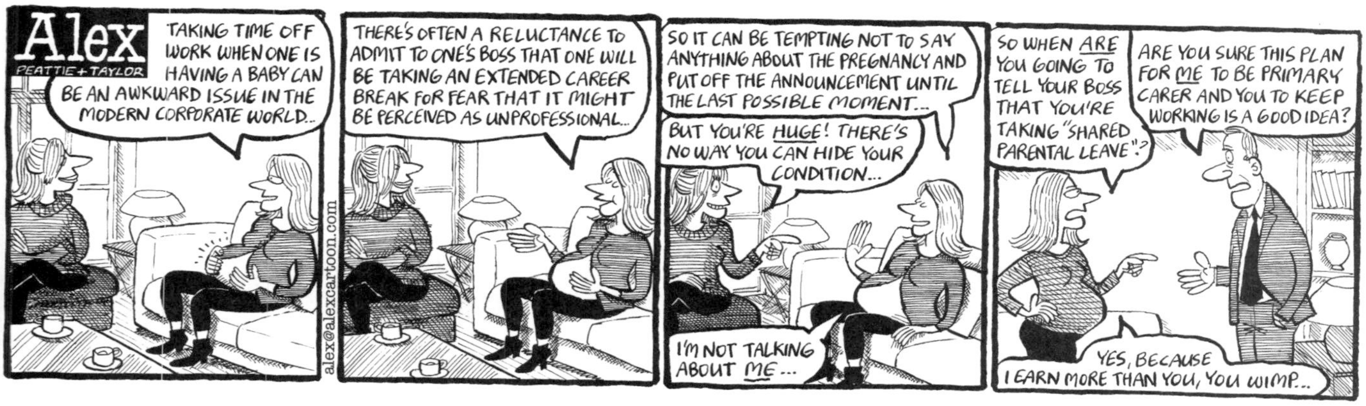
Alex
PEATTIE + TAYLOR
TAKING TIME OFF WORK WHEN ONE IS HAVING A BABY CAN BE AN AWKWARD ISSUE IN THE MODERN CORPORATE WORLD...
THERE'S OFTEN A RELUCTANCE TO ADMIT TO ONE'S BOSS THAT ONE WILL BE TAKING AN EXTENDED CAREER BREAK FOR FEAR THAT IT MIGHT BE PERCEIVED AS UNPROFESSIONAL...
SO IT CAN BE TEMPTING NOT TO SAY ANYTHING ABOUT THE PREGNANCY AND PUT OFF THE ANNOUNCEMENT UNTIL THE LAST POSSIBLE MOMENT...
BUT YOU'RE HUGE! THERE'S NO WAY YOU CAN HIDE YOUR CONDITION...
I'M NOT TALKING ABOUT ME...
SO WHEN ARE YOU GOING TO TELL YOUR BOSS THAT YOU'RE TAKING "SHARED PARENTAL LEAVE"?
ARE YOU SURE THIS PLAN FOR ME TO BE PRIMARY CARER AND YOU TO KEEP WORKING IS A GOOD IDEA?
YES, BECAUSE I EARN MORE THAN YOU, YOU WIMP...
alex@alexcartoon.com

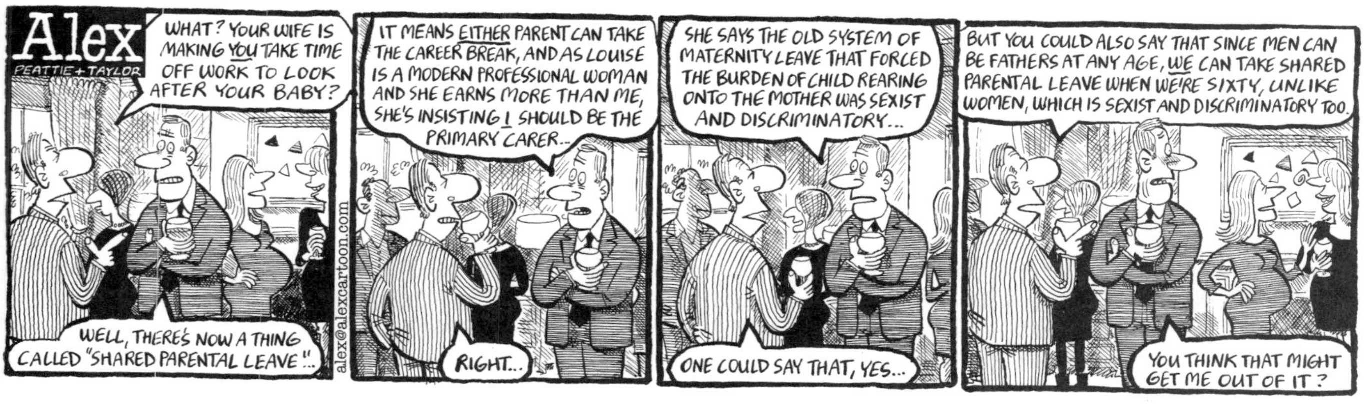
Alex
PEATTIE + TAYLOR
WHAT? YOUR WIFE IS MAKING YOU TAKE TIME OFF WORK TO LOOK AFTER YOUR BABY?
WELL, THERE'S NOW A THING CALLED "SHARED PARENTAL LEAVE"...
IT MEANS EITHER PARENT CAN TAKE THE CAREER BREAK, AND AS LOUISE IS A MODERN PROFESSIONAL WOMAN AND SHE EARNS MORE THAN ME, SHE'S INSISTING I SHOULD BE THE PRIMARY CARER...
RIGHT...
SHE SAYS THE OLD SYSTEM OF MATERNITY LEAVE THAT FORCED THE BURDEN OF CHILD REARING ONTO THE MOTHER WAS SEXIST AND DISCRIMINATORY...
ONE COULD SAY THAT, YES...
BUT YOU COULD ALSO SAY THAT SINCE MEN CAN BE FATHERS AT ANY AGE, WE CAN TAKE SHARED PARENTAL LEAVE WHEN WE'RE SIXTY, UNLIKE WOMEN, WHICH IS SEXIST AND DISCRIMINATORY TOO.
YOU THINK THAT MIGHT GET ME OUT OF IT?
alex@alexcartoon.com

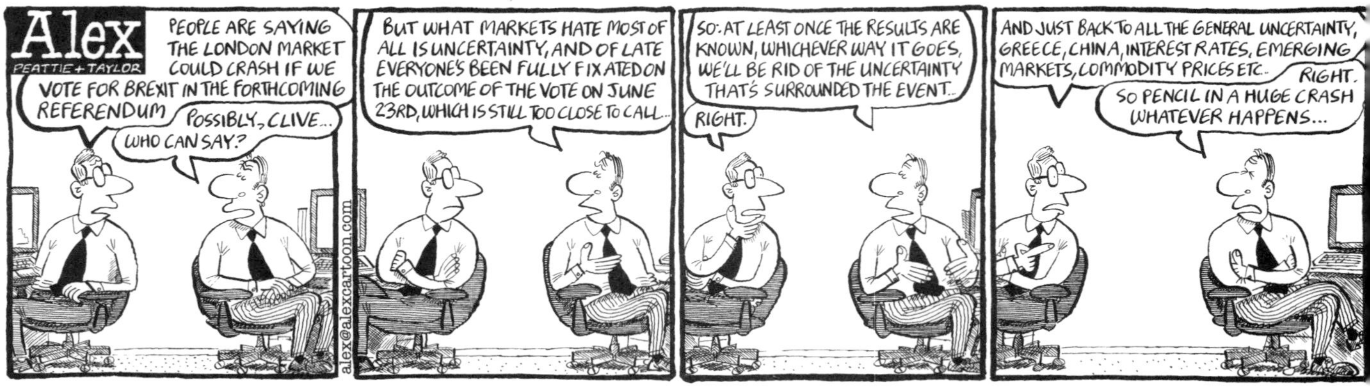
Alex
PEATTIE + TAYLOR
PEOPLE ARE SAYING THE LONDON MARKET COULD CRASH IF WE VOTE FOR BREXIT IN THE FORTHCOMING REFERENDUM
POSSIBLY, CLIVE... WHO CAN SAY?
BUT WHAT MARKETS HATE MOST OF ALL IS UNCERTAINTY, AND OF LATE EVERYONE'S BEEN FULLY FIXATED ON THE OUTCOME OF THE VOTE ON JUNE 23RD, WHICH IS STILL TOO CLOSE TO CALL...
alex@alexcartoon.com
SO: AT LEAST ONCE THE RESULTS ARE KNOWN, WHICHEVER WAY IT GOES, WE'LL BE RID OF THE UNCERTAINTY THAT'S SURROUNDED THE EVENT...
RIGHT.
AND JUST BACK TO ALL THE GENERAL UNCERTAINTY, GREECE, CHINA, INTEREST RATES, EMERGING MARKETS, COMMODITY PRICES ETC...
RIGHT.
SO PENCIL IN A HUGE CRASH WHATEVER HAPPENS...

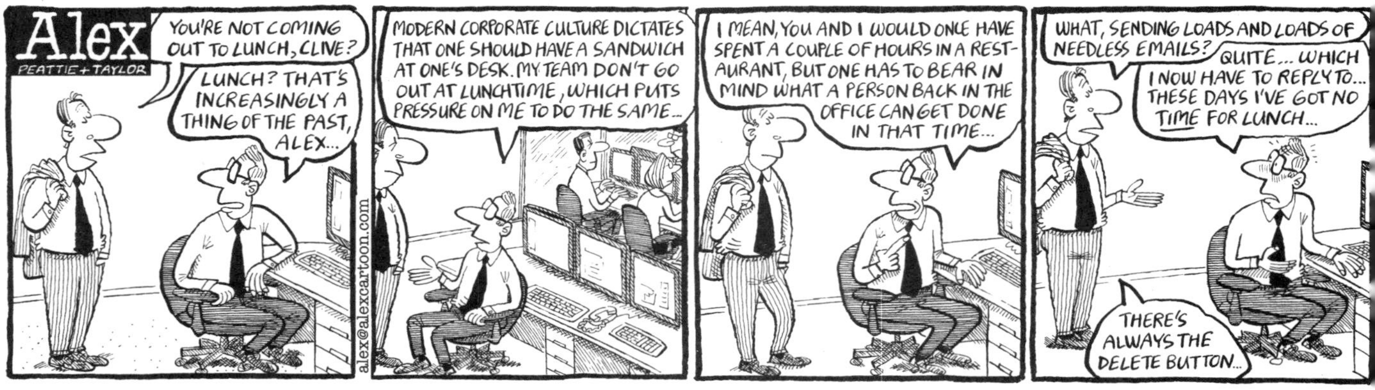
Alex
PEATTIE + TAYLOR
YOU'RE NOT COMING OUT TO LUNCH, CLIVE?
LUNCH? THAT'S INCREASINGLY A THING OF THE PAST, ALEX...
MODERN CORPORATE CULTURE DICTATES THAT ONE SHOULD HAVE A SANDWICH AT ONE'S DESK. MY TEAM DON'T GO OUT AT LUNCHTIME, WHICH PUTS PRESSURE ON ME TO DO THE SAME...
alex@alexcartoon.com
I MEAN, YOU AND I WOULD ONCE HAVE SPENT A COUPLE OF HOURS IN A RESTAURANT, BUT ONE HAS TO BEAR IN MIND WHAT A PERSON BACK IN THE OFFICE CAN GET DONE IN THAT TIME...
WHAT, SENDING LOADS AND LOADS OF NEEDLESS EMAILS?
QUITE... WHICH I NOW HAVE TO REPLY TO... THESE DAYS I'VE GOT NO TIME FOR LUNCH...
THERE'S ALWAYS THE DELETE BUTTON...

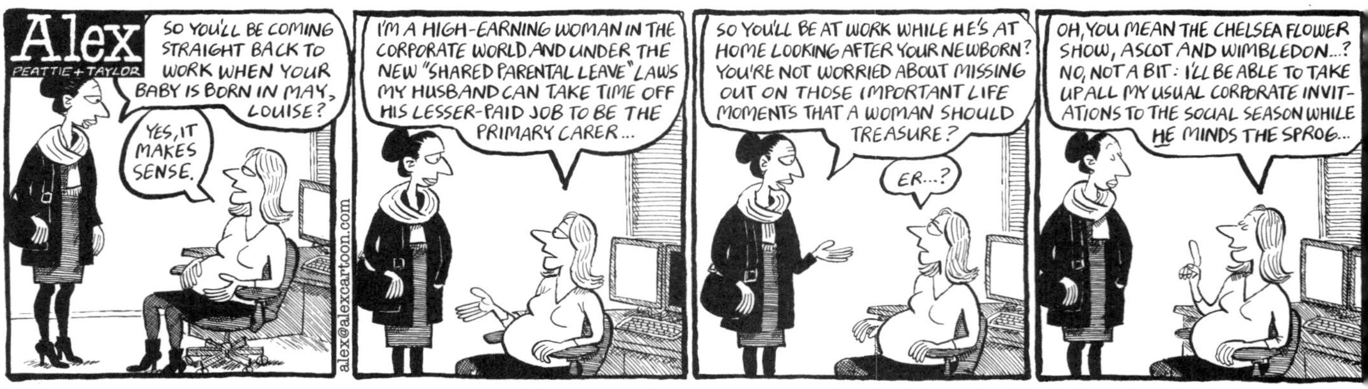
Alex
PEATTIE + TAYLOR
SO YOU'LL BE COMING STRAIGHT BACK TO WORK WHEN YOUR BABY IS BORN IN MAY, LOUISE?
YES, IT MAKES SENSE.
I'M A HIGH-EARNING WOMAN IN THE CORPORATE WORLD AND UNDER THE NEW "SHARED PARENTAL LEAVE" LAWS MY HUSBAND CAN TAKE TIME OFF HIS LESSER-PAID JOB TO BE THE PRIMARY CARER...
alex@alexcartoon.com
SO YOU'LL BE AT WORK WHILE HE'S AT HOME LOOKING AFTER YOUR NEWBORN? YOU'RE NOT WORRIED ABOUT MISSING OUT ON THOSE IMPORTANT LIFE MOMENTS THAT A WOMAN SHOULD TREASURE?
ER...?
OH, YOU MEAN THE CHELSEA FLOWER SHOW, ASCOT AND WIMBLEDON...? NO, NOT A BIT: I'LL BE ABLE TO TAKE UP ALL MY USUAL CORPORATE INVITATIONS TO THE SOCIAL SEASON WHILE HE MINDS THE SPROG...

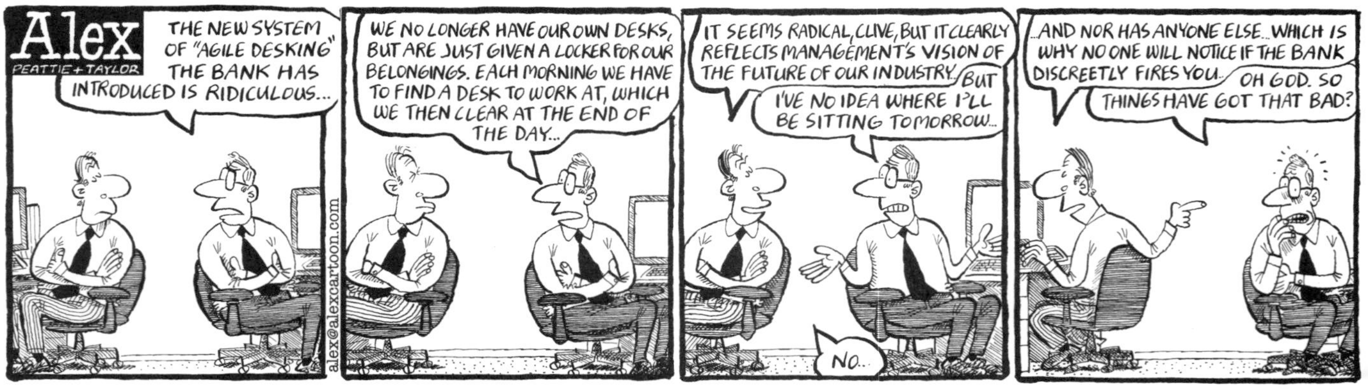
Alex
PEATTIE + TAYLOR
THE NEW SYSTEM OF "AGILE DESKING" THE BANK HAS INTRODUCED IS RIDICULOUS...
WE NO LONGER HAVE OUR OWN DESKS, BUT ARE JUST GIVEN A LOCKER FOR OUR BELONGINGS. EACH MORNING WE HAVE TO FIND A DESK TO WORK AT, WHICH WE THEN CLEAR AT THE END OF THE DAY...
alex@alexcartoon.com
IT SEEMS RADICAL, CLIVE, BUT IT CLEARLY REFLECTS MANAGEMENT'S VISION OF THE FUTURE OF OUR INDUSTRY.
BUT I'VE NO IDEA WHERE I'LL BE SITTING TOMORROW...
NO...
...AND NOR HAS ANYONE ELSE... WHICH IS WHY NO ONE WILL NOTICE IF THE BANK DISCREETLY FIRES YOU...
OH GOD. SO THINGS HAVE GOT THAT BAD?

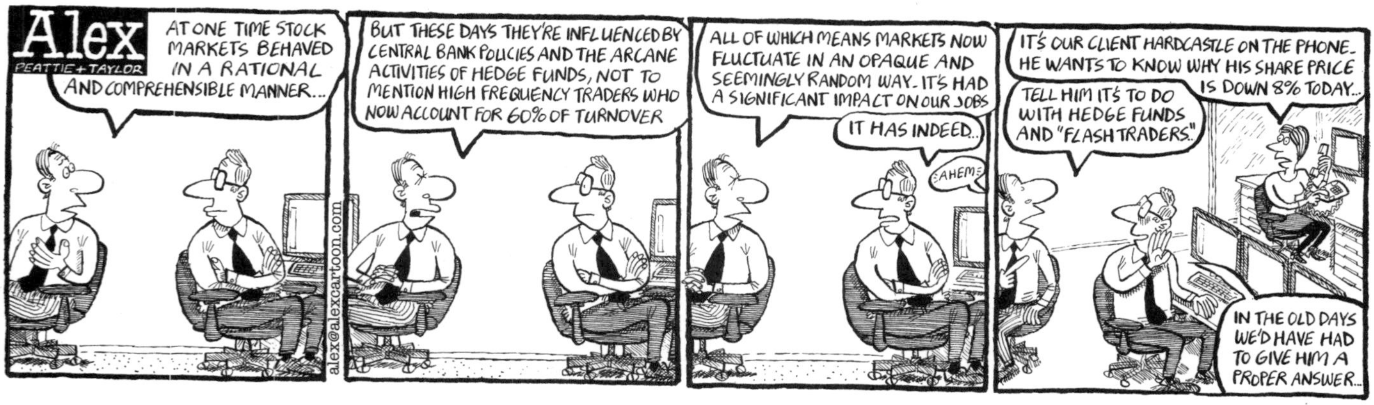
Alex
PEATTIE + TAYLOR
AT ONE TIME STOCK MARKETS BEHAVED IN A RATIONAL AND COMPREHENSIBLE MANNER...
BUT THESE DAYS THEY'RE INFLUENCED BY CENTRAL BANK POLICIES AND THE ARCANE ACTIVITIES OF HEDGE FUNDS, NOT TO MENTION HIGH FREQUENCY TRADERS WHO NOW ACCOUNT FOR 60% OF TURNOVER
alex@alexcartoon.com
ALL OF WHICH MEANS MARKETS NOW FLUCTUATE IN AN OPAQUE AND SEEMINGLY RANDOM WAY. IT'S HAD A SIGNIFICANT IMPACT ON OUR JOBS
IT HAS INDEED..
AHEM
IT'S OUR CLIENT HARDCASTLE ON THE PHONE. HE WANTS TO KNOW WHY HIS SHARE PRICE IS DOWN 8% TODAY...
TELL HIM IT'S TO DO WITH HEDGE FUNDS AND "FLASH TRADERS."
IN THE OLD DAYS WE'D HAVE HAD TO GIVE HIM A PROPER ANSWER...

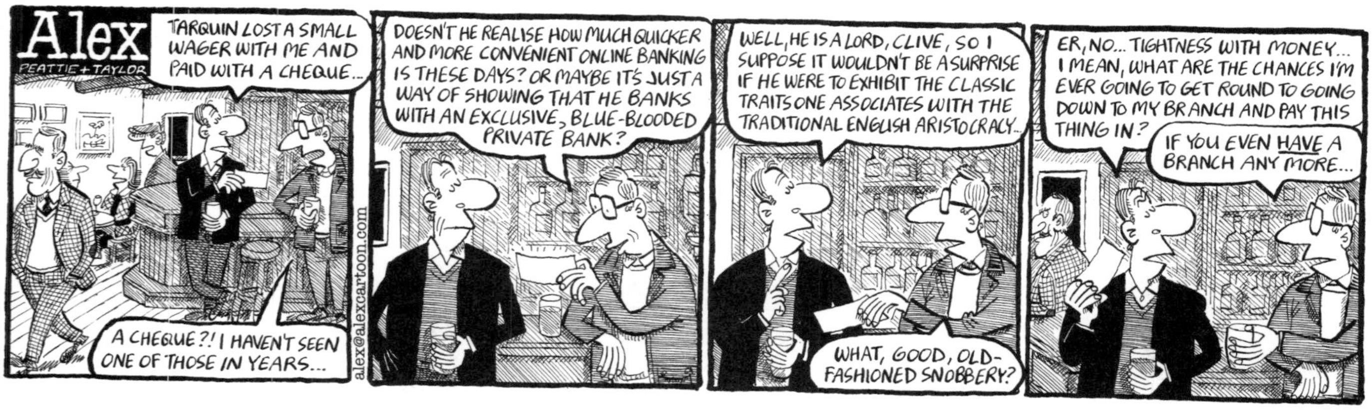
Alex
PEATTIE + TAYLOR
TARQUIN LOST A SMALL WAGER WITH ME AND PAID WITH A CHEQUE...
A CHEQUE?! I HAVEN'T SEEN ONE OF THOSE IN YEARS...
alex@alexcartoon.com
DOESN'T HE REALISE HOW MUCH QUICKER AND MORE CONVENIENT ONLINE BANKING IS THESE DAYS? OR MAYBE IT'S JUST A WAY OF SHOWING THAT HE BANKS WITH AN EXCLUSIVE, BLUE-BLOODED PRIVATE BANK?
WELL, HE IS A LORD, CLIVE, SO I SUPPOSE IT WOULDN'T BE A SURPRISE IF HE WERE TO EXHIBIT THE CLASSIC TRAITS ONE ASSOCIATES WITH THE TRADITIONAL ENGLISH ARISTOCRACY..
WHAT, GOOD, OLD-FASHIONED SNOBBERY?
ER, NO... TIGHTNESS WITH MONEY... I MEAN, WHAT ARE THE CHANCES I'M EVER GOING TO GET ROUND TO GOING DOWN TO MY BRANCH AND PAY THIS THING IN?
IF YOU EVEN HAVE A BRANCH ANY MORE...

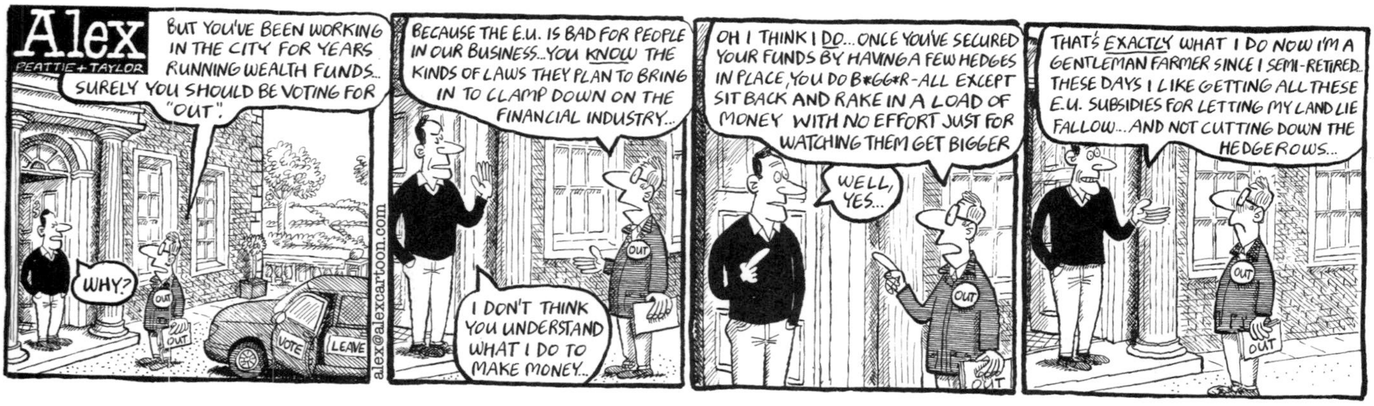
Alex
PEATTIE + TAYLOR
BUT YOU'VE BEEN WORKING IN THE CITY FOR YEARS RUNNING WEALTH FUNDS.. SURELY YOU SHOULD BE VOTING FOR "OUT".
WHY?
OUT
VOTE
LEAVE
alex@alexcartoon.com
BECAUSE THE E.U. IS BAD FOR PEOPLE IN OUR BUSINESS...YOU KNOW THE KINDS OF LAWS THEY PLAN TO BRING IN TO CLAMP DOWN ON THE FINANCIAL INDUSTRY...
I DON'T THINK YOU UNDERSTAND WHAT I DO TO MAKE MONEY...
OH I THINK I DO... ONCE YOU'VE SECURED YOUR FUNDS BY HAVING A FEW HEDGES IN PLACE, YOU DO B*GG*R-ALL EXCEPT SIT BACK AND RAKE IN A LOAD OF MONEY WITH NO EFFORT JUST FOR WATCHING THEM GET BIGGER
WELL, YES...
THAT'S EXACTLY WHAT I DO NOW I'M A GENTLEMAN FARMER SINCE I SEMI-RETIRED.. THESE DAYS I LIKE GETTING ALL THESE E.U. SUBSIDIES FOR LETTING MY LAND LIE FALLOW... AND NOT CUTTING DOWN THE HEDGEROWS...

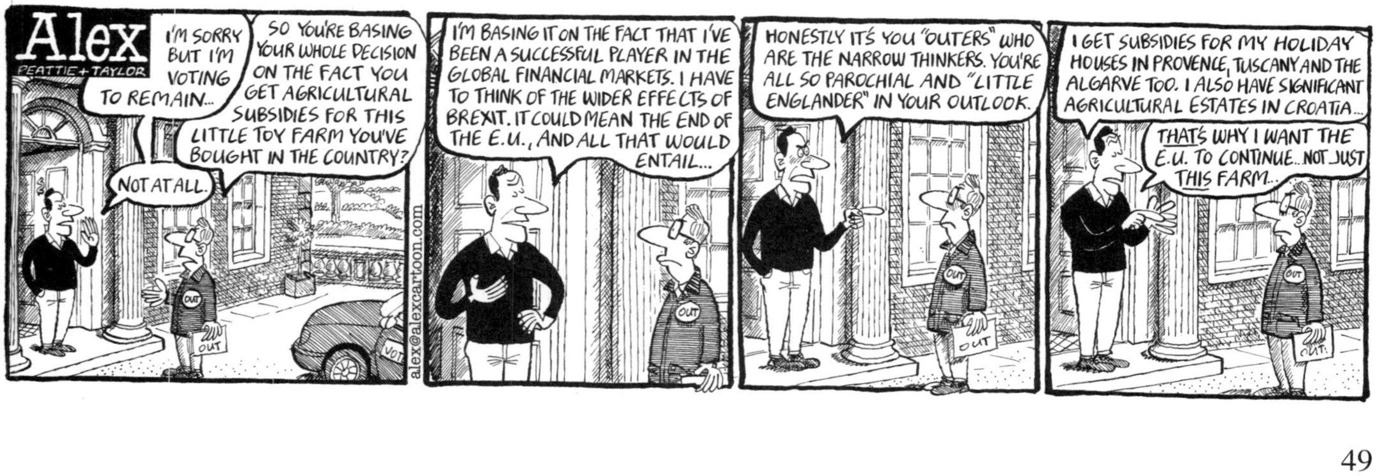
Alex
PEATTIE + TAYLOR
I'M SORRY BUT I'M VOTING TO REMAIN...
SO YOU'RE BASING YOUR WHOLE DECISION ON THE FACT YOU GET AGRICULTURAL SUBSIDIES FOR THIS LITTLE TOY FARM YOU'VE BOUGHT IN THE COUNTRY?
NOT AT ALL.
alex@alexcartoon.com
I'M BASING IT ON THE FACT THAT I'VE BEEN A SUCCESSFUL PLAYER IN THE GLOBAL FINANCIAL MARKETS. I HAVE TO THINK OF THE WIDER EFFECTS OF BREXIT. IT COULD MEAN THE END OF THE E.U., AND ALL THAT WOULD ENTAIL...
HONESTLY IT'S YOU "OUTERS" WHO ARE THE NARROW THINKERS. YOU'RE ALL SO PAROCHIAL AND "LITTLE ENGLANDER" IN YOUR OUTLOOK.
I GET SUBSIDIES FOR MY HOLIDAY HOUSES IN PROVENCE, TUSCANY AND THE ALGARVE TOO. I ALSO HAVE SIGNIFICANT AGRICULTURAL ESTATES IN CROATIA...
THAT'S WHY I WANT THE E.U. TO CONTINUE...NOT JUST THIS FARM...

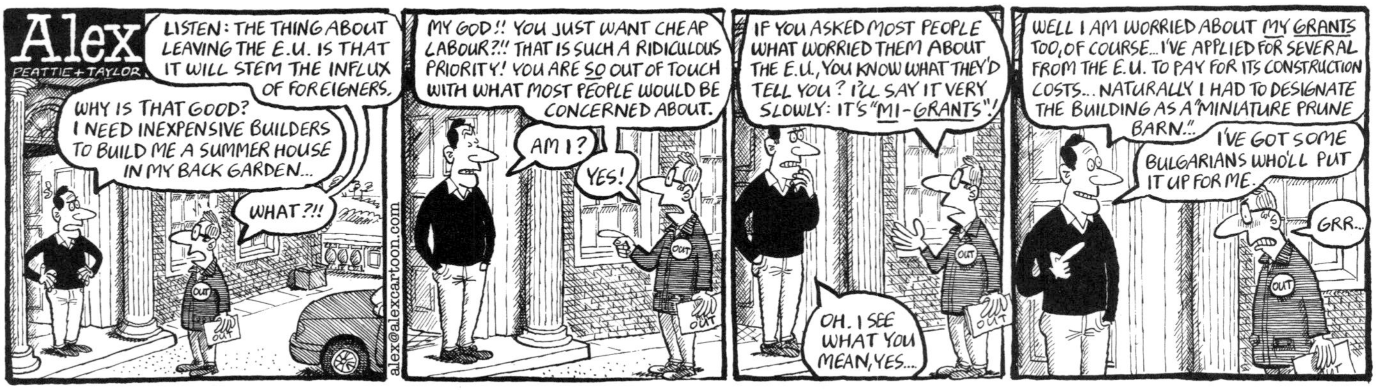
Alex
PEATTIE + TAYLOR
LISTEN: THE THING ABOUT LEAVING THE E.U. IS THAT IT WILL STEM THE INFLUX OF FOREIGNERS.
WHY IS THAT GOOD? I NEED INEXPENSIVE BUILDERS TO BUILD ME A SUMMER HOUSE IN MY BACK GARDEN...
WHAT?!!
MY GOD!! YOU JUST WANT CHEAP LABOUR?!! THAT IS SUCH A RIDICULOUS PRIORITY! YOU ARE SO OUT OF TOUCH WITH WHAT MOST PEOPLE WOULD BE CONCERNED ABOUT.
AM I?
YES!
alex@alexcartoon.com
IF YOU ASKED MOST PEOPLE WHAT WORRIED THEM ABOUT THE E.U., YOU KNOW WHAT THEY'D TELL YOU? I'LL SAY IT VERY SLOWLY: IT'S "MI-GRANTS"!
OH. I SEE WHAT YOU MEAN, YES...
WELL I AM WORRIED ABOUT MY GRANTS TOO, OF COURSE... I'VE APPLIED FOR SEVERAL FROM THE E.U. TO PAY FOR ITS CONSTRUCTION COSTS... NATURALLY I HAD TO DESIGNATE THE BUILDING AS A "MINIATURE PRUNE BARN."
I'VE GOT SOME BULGARIANS WHO'LL PUT IT UP FOR ME.
GRR...

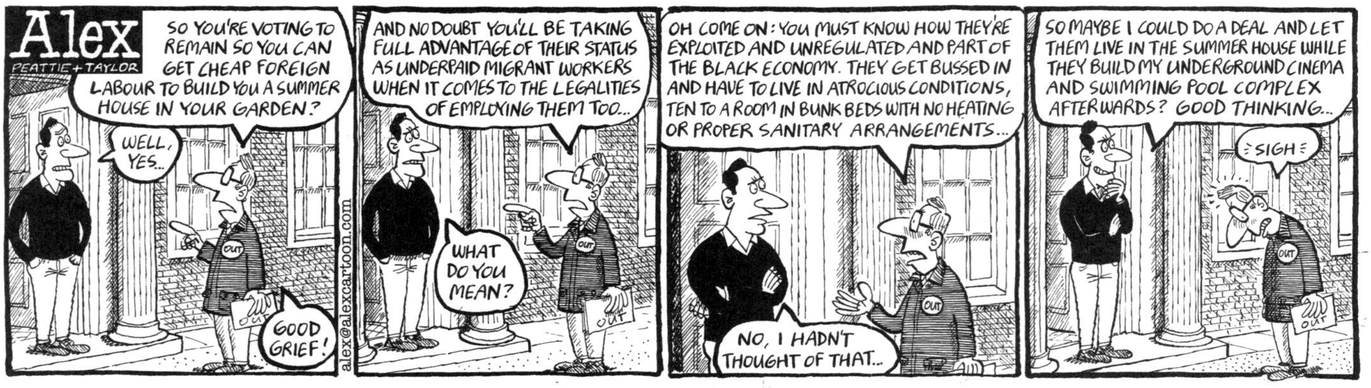
Alex
PEATTIE + TAYLOR
SO YOU'RE VOTING TO REMAIN SO YOU CAN GET CHEAP FOREIGN LABOUR TO BUILD YOU A SUMMER HOUSE IN YOUR GARDEN?
WELL, YES...
GOOD GRIEF!
alex@alexcartoon.com
AND NO DOUBT YOU'LL BE TAKING FULL ADVANTAGE OF THEIR STATUS AS UNDERPAID MIGRANT WORKERS WHEN IT COMES TO THE LEGALITIES OF EMPLOYING THEM TOO...
WHAT DO YOU MEAN?
OH COME ON: YOU MUST KNOW HOW THEY'RE EXPLOITED AND UNREGULATED AND PART OF THE BLACK ECONOMY. THEY GET BUSSED IN AND HAVE TO LIVE IN ATROCIOUS CONDITIONS, TEN TO A ROOM IN BUNK BEDS WITH NO HEATING OR PROPER SANITARY ARRANGEMENTS...
NO, I HADN'T THOUGHT OF THAT...
SO MAYBE I COULD DO A DEAL AND LET THEM LIVE IN THE SUMMER HOUSE WHILE THEY BUILD MY UNDERGROUND CINEMA AND SWIMMING POOL COMPLEX AFTERWARDS? GOOD THINKING...
SIGH

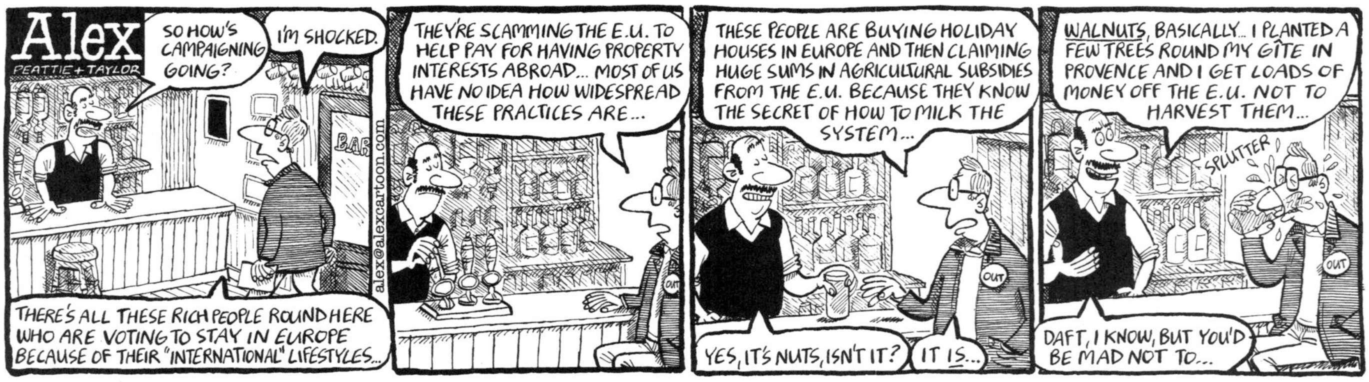
Alex
PEATTIE + TAYLOR
SO HOW'S CAMPAIGNING GOING?
I'M SHOCKED.
THERE'S ALL THESE RICH PEOPLE ROUND HERE WHO ARE VOTING TO STAY IN EUROPE BECAUSE OF THEIR "INTERNATIONAL" LIFESTYLES...
alex@alexcartoon.com
THEY'RE SCAMMING THE E.U. TO HELP PAY FOR HAVING PROPERTY INTERESTS ABROAD... MOST OF US HAVE NO IDEA HOW WIDESPREAD THESE PRACTICES ARE...
THESE PEOPLE ARE BUYING HOLIDAY HOUSES IN EUROPE AND THEN CLAIMING HUGE SUMS IN AGRICULTURAL SUBSIDIES FROM THE E.U. BECAUSE THEY KNOW THE SECRET OF HOW TO MILK THE SYSTEM...
YES, IT'S NUTS, ISN'T IT?
IT IS...
WALNUTS, BASICALLY... I PLANTED A FEW TREES ROUND MY GÎTE IN PROVENCE AND I GET LOADS OF MONEY OFF THE E.U. NOT TO HARVEST THEM...
SPLUTTER
DAFT, I KNOW, BUT YOU'D BE MAD NOT TO...

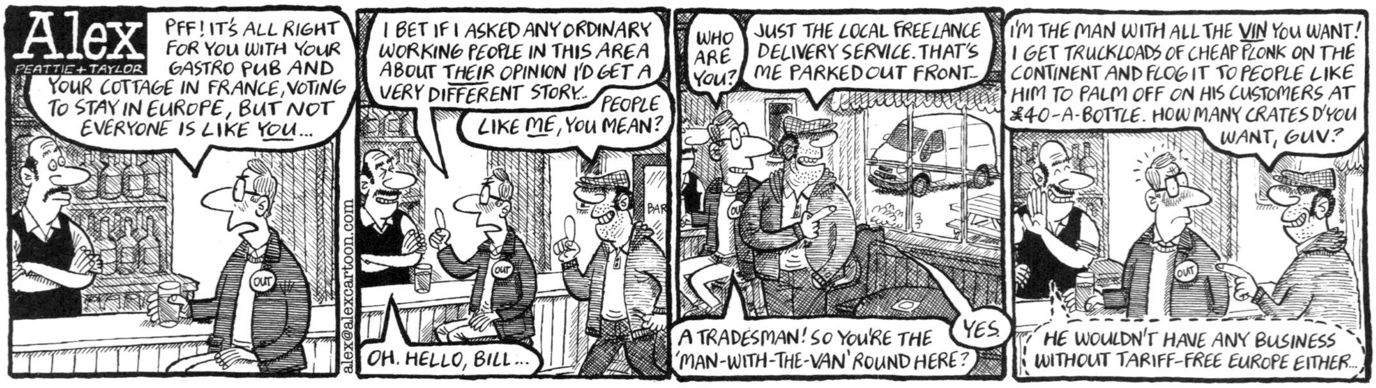
Alex
PEATTIE + TAYLOR
PFF! IT'S ALL RIGHT FOR YOU WITH YOUR GASTRO PUB AND YOUR COTTAGE IN FRANCE, VOTING TO STAY IN EUROPE, BUT NOT EVERYONE IS LIKE YOU...
alex@alexcartoon.com
I BET IF I ASKED ANY ORDINARY WORKING PEOPLE IN THIS AREA ABOUT THEIR OPINION I'D GET A VERY DIFFERENT STORY...
PEOPLE LIKE ME, YOU MEAN?
OH. HELLO, BILL...
WHO ARE YOU?
JUST THE LOCAL FREELANCE DELIVERY SERVICE. THAT'S ME PARKED OUT FRONT...
A TRADESMAN! SO YOU'RE THE 'MAN-WITH-THE-VAN' ROUND HERE?
YES.
I'M THE MAN WITH ALL THE VIN YOU WANT! I GET TRUCKLOADS OF CHEAP PLONK ON THE CONTINENT AND FLOG IT TO PEOPLE LIKE HIM TO PALM OFF ON HIS CUSTOMERS AT £40-A-BOTTLE. HOW MANY CRATES D'YOU WANT, GUV?
HE WOULDN'T HAVE ANY BUSINESS WITHOUT TARIFF-FREE EUROPE EITHER...

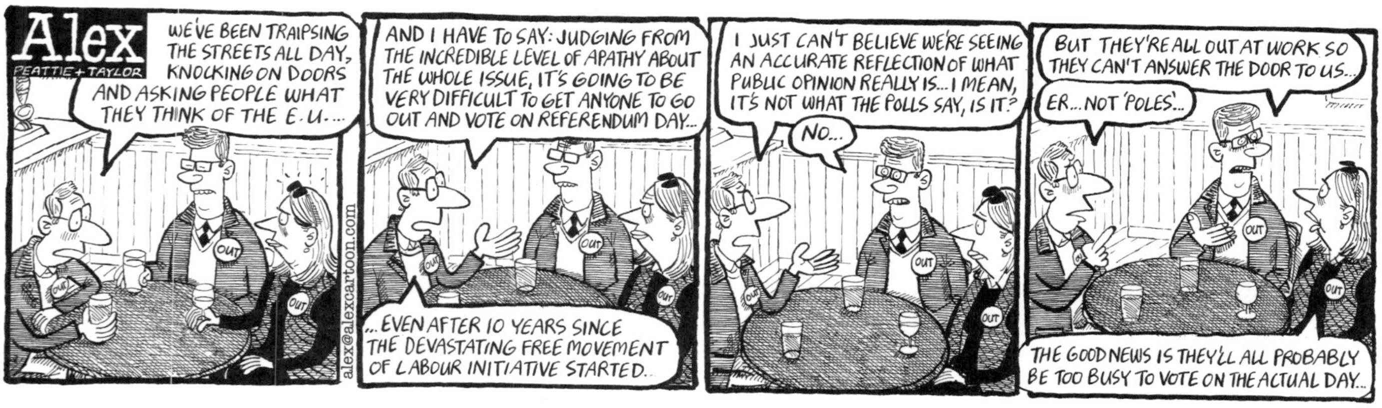
Alex
PEATTIE + TAYLOR
WE'VE BEEN TRAIPSING THE STREETS ALL DAY, KNOCKING ON DOORS AND ASKING PEOPLE WHAT THEY THINK OF THE E.U. ...
OUT
AND I HAVE TO SAY: JUDGING FROM THE INCREDIBLE LEVEL OF APATHY ABOUT THE WHOLE ISSUE, IT'S GOING TO BE VERY DIFFICULT TO GET ANYONE TO GO OUT AND VOTE ON REFERENDUM DAY...
...EVEN AFTER 10 YEARS SINCE THE DEVASTATING FREE MOVEMENT OF LABOUR INITIATIVE STARTED...
I JUST CAN'T BELIEVE WE'RE SEEING AN ACCURATE REFLECTION OF WHAT PUBLIC OPINION REALLY IS... I MEAN, IT'S NOT WHAT THE POLLS SAY, IS IT?
NO...
BUT THEY'RE ALL OUT AT WORK SO THEY CAN'T ANSWER THE DOOR TO US...
ER... NOT 'POLES'...
THE GOOD NEWS IS THEY'LL ALL PROBABLY BE TOO BUSY TO VOTE ON THE ACTUAL DAY...
alex@alexcartoon.com

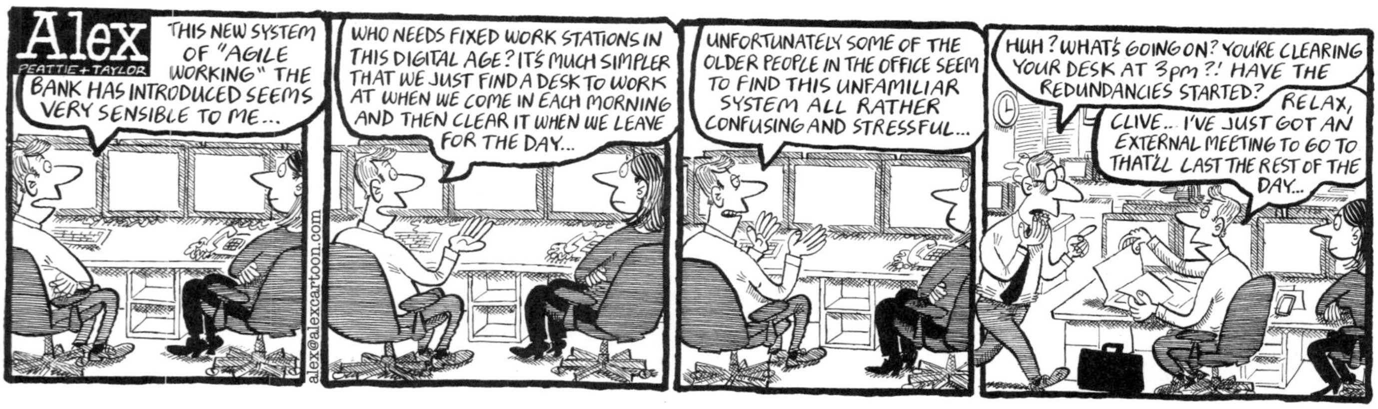
Alex
PEATTIE + TAYLOR
THIS NEW SYSTEM OF "AGILE WORKING" THE BANK HAS INTRODUCED SEEMS VERY SENSIBLE TO ME...
WHO NEEDS FIXED WORK STATIONS IN THIS DIGITAL AGE? IT'S MUCH SIMPLER THAT WE JUST FIND A DESK TO WORK AT WHEN WE COME IN EACH MORNING AND THEN CLEAR IT WHEN WE LEAVE FOR THE DAY...
UNFORTUNATELY SOME OF THE OLDER PEOPLE IN THE OFFICE SEEM TO FIND THIS UNFAMILIAR SYSTEM ALL RATHER CONFUSING AND STRESSFUL...
HUH? WHAT'S GOING ON? YOU'RE CLEARING YOUR DESK AT 3pm?! HAVE THE REDUNDANCIES STARTED?
RELAX, CLIVE... I'VE JUST GOT AN EXTERNAL MEETING TO GO TO THAT'LL LAST THE REST OF THE DAY...
alex@alexcartoon.com

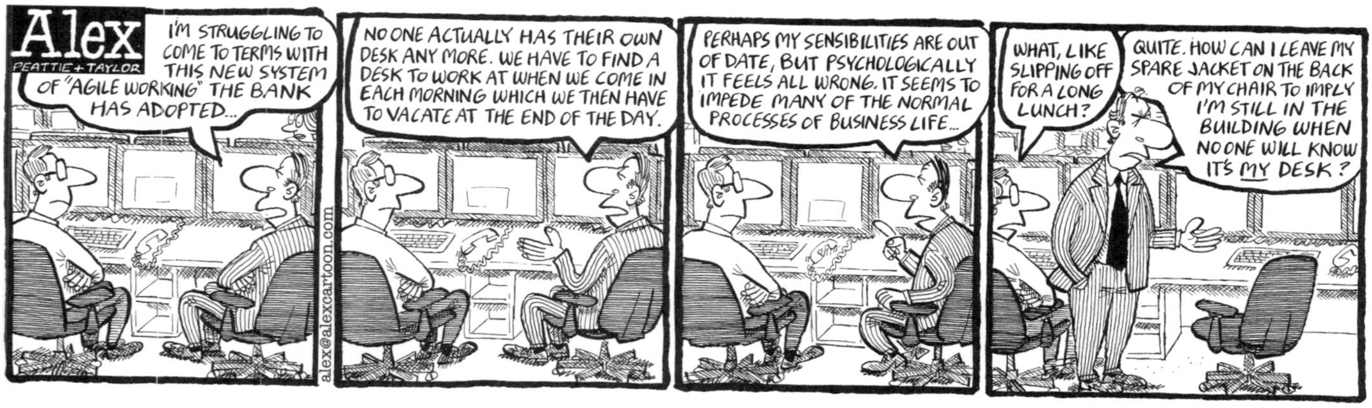
Alex
PEATTIE + TAYLOR
I'M STRUGGLING TO COME TO TERMS WITH THIS NEW SYSTEM OF "AGILE WORKING" THE BANK HAS ADOPTED...
NO ONE ACTUALLY HAS THEIR OWN DESK ANY MORE. WE HAVE TO FIND A DESK TO WORK AT WHEN WE COME IN EACH MORNING WHICH WE THEN HAVE TO VACATE AT THE END OF THE DAY.
PERHAPS MY SENSIBILITIES ARE OUT OF DATE, BUT PSYCHOLOGICALLY IT FEELS ALL WRONG. IT SEEMS TO IMPEDE MANY OF THE NORMAL PROCESSES OF BUSINESS LIFE...
WHAT, LIKE SLIPPING OFF FOR A LONG LUNCH?
QUITE. HOW CAN I LEAVE MY SPARE JACKET ON THE BACK OF MY CHAIR TO IMPLY I'M STILL IN THE BUILDING WHEN NO ONE WILL KNOW IT'S MY DESK?
alex@alexcartoon.com

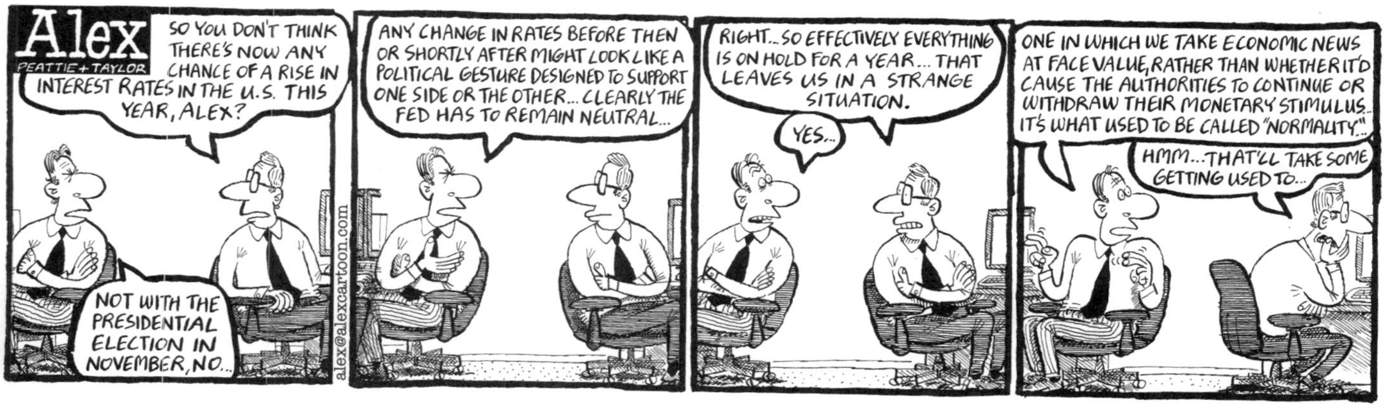
Alex
PEATTIE + TAYLOR
SO YOU DON'T THINK THERE'S NOW ANY CHANCE OF A RISE IN INTEREST RATES IN THE U.S. THIS YEAR, ALEX?
NOT WITH THE PRESIDENTIAL ELECTION IN NOVEMBER, NO...
ANY CHANGE IN RATES BEFORE THEN OR SHORTLY AFTER MIGHT LOOK LIKE A POLITICAL GESTURE DESIGNED TO SUPPORT ONE SIDE OR THE OTHER... CLEARLY THE FED HAS TO REMAIN NEUTRAL...
RIGHT... SO EFFECTIVELY EVERYTHING IS ON HOLD FOR A YEAR... THAT LEAVES US IN A STRANGE SITUATION.
YES...
ONE IN WHICH WE TAKE ECONOMIC NEWS AT FACE VALUE, RATHER THAN WHETHER IT'D CAUSE THE AUTHORITIES TO CONTINUE OR WITHDRAW THEIR MONETARY STIMULUS... IT'S WHAT USED TO BE CALLED "NORMALITY".
HMM... THAT'LL TAKE SOME GETTING USED TO...
alex@alexcartoon.com

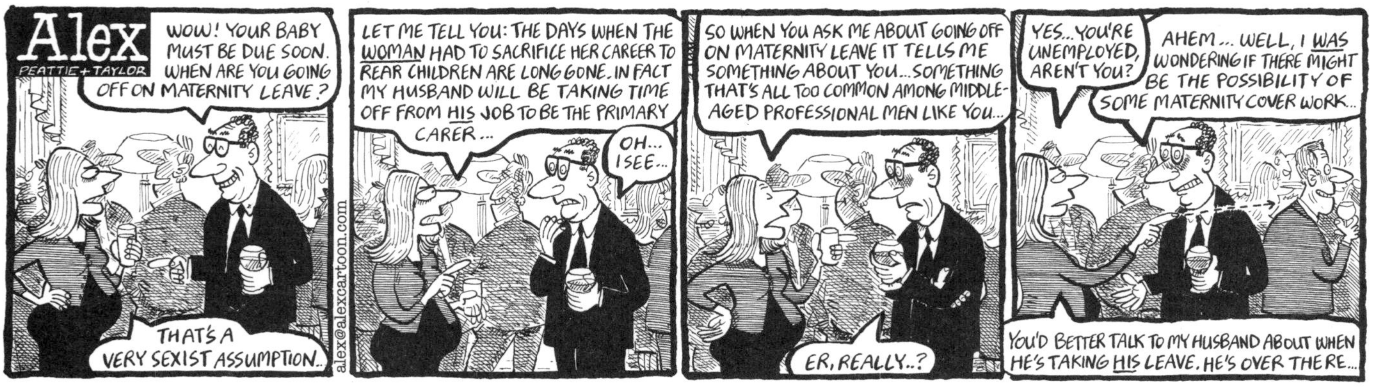
Alex
PEATTIE + TAYLOR
WOW! YOUR BABY MUST BE DUE SOON. WHEN ARE YOU GOING OFF ON MATERNITY LEAVE?
THAT'S A VERY SEXIST ASSUMPTION..
alex@alexcartoon.com
LET ME TELL YOU: THE DAYS WHEN THE WOMAN HAD TO SACRIFICE HER CAREER TO REAR CHILDREN ARE LONG GONE. IN FACT MY HUSBAND WILL BE TAKING TIME OFF FROM HIS JOB TO BE THE PRIMARY CARER...
OH... I SEE...
SO WHEN YOU ASK ME ABOUT GOING OFF ON MATERNITY LEAVE IT TELLS ME SOMETHING ABOUT YOU... SOMETHING THAT'S ALL TOO COMMON AMONG MIDDLE-AGED PROFESSIONAL MEN LIKE YOU...
ER, REALLY..?
YES... YOU'RE UNEMPLOYED, AREN'T YOU?
AHEM ... WELL, I WAS WONDERING IF THERE MIGHT BE THE POSSIBILITY OF SOME MATERNITY COVER WORK...
YOU'D BETTER TALK TO MY HUSBAND ABOUT WHEN HE'S TAKING HIS LEAVE. HE'S OVER THERE...

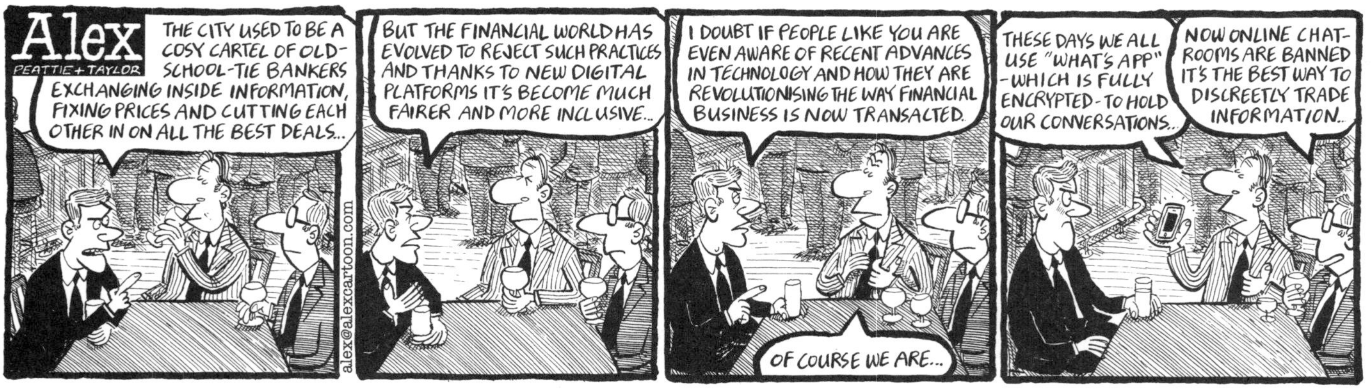
Alex
PEATTIE + TAYLOR
THE CITY USED TO BE A COSY CARTEL OF OLD-SCHOOL-TIE BANKERS EXCHANGING INSIDE INFORMATION, FIXING PRICES AND CUTTING EACH OTHER IN ON ALL THE BEST DEALS...
alex@alexcartoon.com
BUT THE FINANCIAL WORLD HAS EVOLVED TO REJECT SUCH PRACTICES AND THANKS TO NEW DIGITAL PLATFORMS IT'S BECOME MUCH FAIRER AND MORE INCLUSIVE...
I DOUBT IF PEOPLE LIKE YOU ARE EVEN AWARE OF RECENT ADVANCES IN TECHNOLOGY AND HOW THEY ARE REVOLUTIONISING THE WAY FINANCIAL BUSINESS IS NOW TRANSACTED.
OF COURSE WE ARE...
THESE DAYS WE ALL USE "WHAT'S APP" - WHICH IS FULLY ENCRYPTED - TO HOLD OUR CONVERSATIONS...
NOW ONLINE CHAT-ROOMS ARE BANNED IT'S THE BEST WAY TO DISCREETLY TRADE INFORMATION...

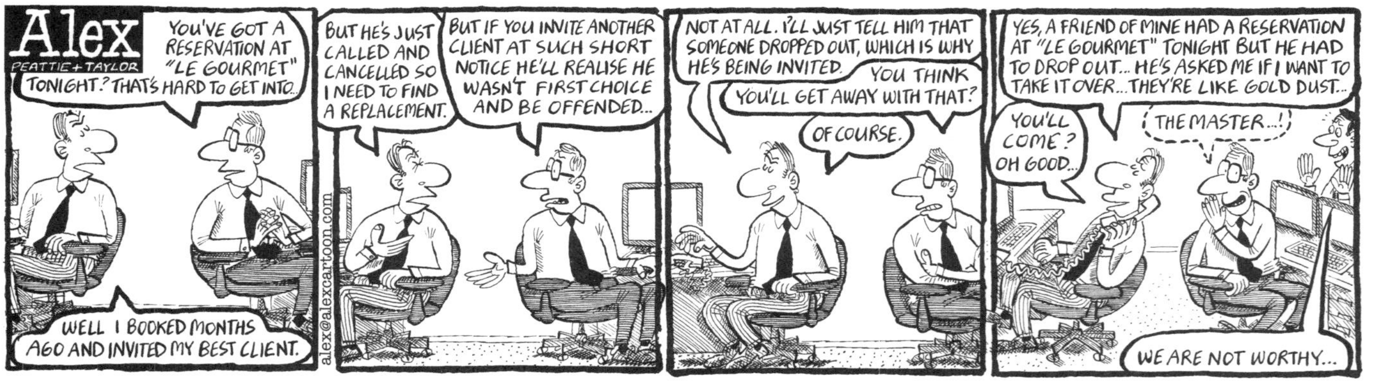
Alex
PEATTIE + TAYLOR
YOU'VE GOT A RESERVATION AT "LE GOURMET" TONIGHT? THAT'S HARD TO GET INTO.
WELL I BOOKED MONTHS AGO AND INVITED MY BEST CLIENT.
alex@alexcartoon.com
BUT HE'S JUST CALLED AND CANCELLED SO I NEED TO FIND A REPLACEMENT.
BUT IF YOU INVITE ANOTHER CLIENT AT SUCH SHORT NOTICE HE'LL REALISE HE WASN'T FIRST CHOICE AND BE OFFENDED...
NOT AT ALL. I'LL JUST TELL HIM THAT SOMEONE DROPPED OUT, WHICH IS WHY HE'S BEING INVITED.
YOU THINK YOU'LL GET AWAY WITH THAT?
OF COURSE.
YES, A FRIEND OF MINE HAD A RESERVATION AT "LE GOURMET" TONIGHT BUT HE HAD TO DROP OUT... HE'S ASKED ME IF I WANT TO TAKE IT OVER... THEY'RE LIKE GOLD DUST...
YOU'LL COME? OH GOOD...
THE MASTER...!
WE ARE NOT WORTHY...

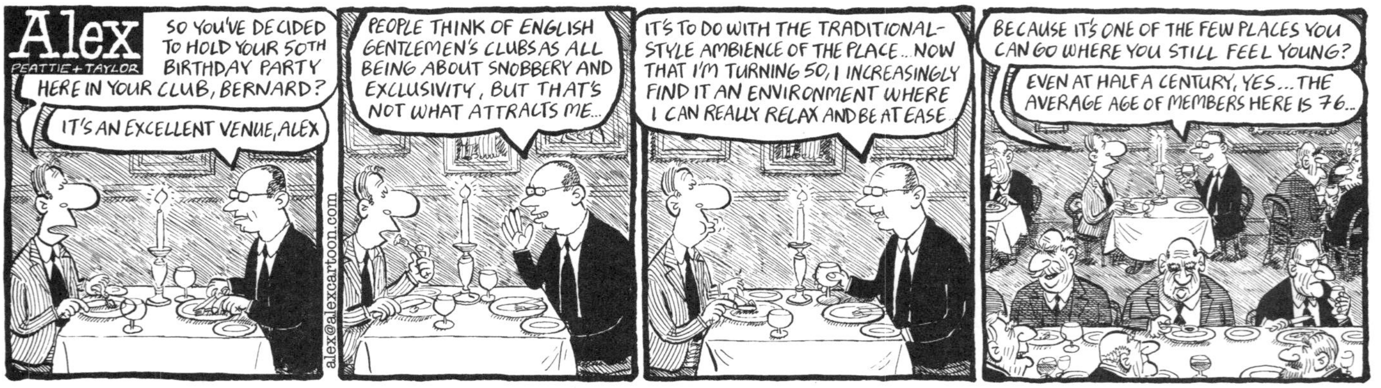
Alex
PEATTIE + TAYLOR
SO YOU'VE DECIDED TO HOLD YOUR 50TH BIRTHDAY PARTY HERE IN YOUR CLUB, BERNARD?
IT'S AN EXCELLENT VENUE, ALEX
alex@alexcartoon.com
PEOPLE THINK OF ENGLISH GENTLEMEN'S CLUBS AS ALL BEING ABOUT SNOBBERY AND EXCLUSIVITY, BUT THAT'S NOT WHAT ATTRACTS ME...
IT'S TO DO WITH THE TRADITIONAL-STYLE AMBIENCE OF THE PLACE... NOW THAT I'M TURNING 50, I INCREASINGLY FIND IT AN ENVIRONMENT WHERE I CAN REALLY RELAX AND BE AT EASE
BECAUSE IT'S ONE OF THE FEW PLACES YOU CAN GO WHERE YOU STILL FEEL YOUNG?
EVEN AT HALF A CENTURY, YES... THE AVERAGE AGE OF MEMBERS HERE IS 76...

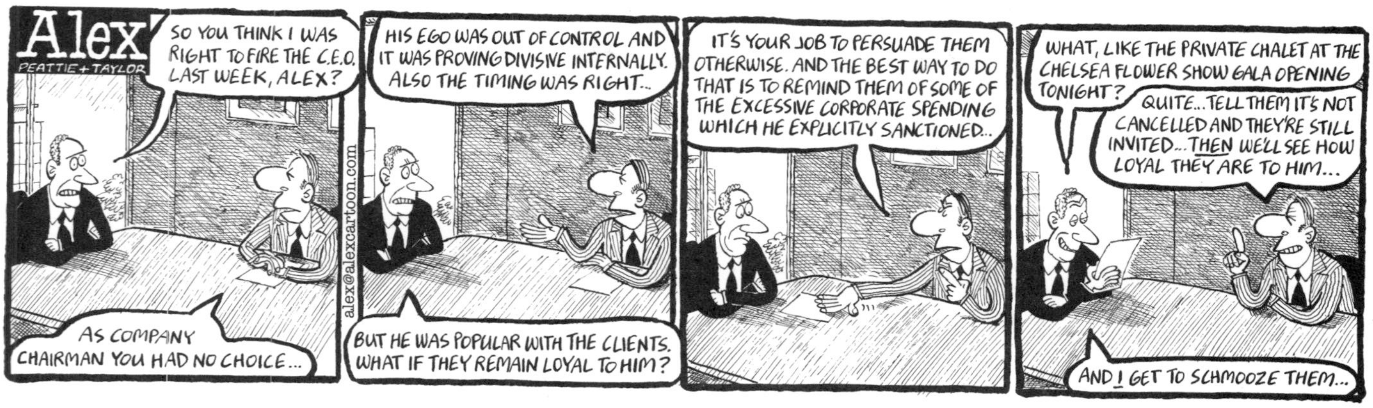
Alex
PEATTIE + TAYLOR
SO YOU THINK I WAS RIGHT TO FIRE THE C.E.O. LAST WEEK, ALEX?
AS COMPANY CHAIRMAN YOU HAD NO CHOICE...
HIS EGO WAS OUT OF CONTROL AND IT WAS PROVING DIVISIVE INTERNALLY. ALSO THE TIMING WAS RIGHT...
BUT HE WAS POPULAR WITH THE CLIENTS. WHAT IF THEY REMAIN LOYAL TO HIM?
alex@alexcartoon.com
IT'S YOUR JOB TO PERSUADE THEM OTHERWISE. AND THE BEST WAY TO DO THAT IS TO REMIND THEM OF SOME OF THE EXCESSIVE CORPORATE SPENDING WHICH HE EXPLICITLY SANCTIONED...
WHAT, LIKE THE PRIVATE CHALET AT THE CHELSEA FLOWER SHOW GALA OPENING TONIGHT?
QUITE... TELL THEM IT'S NOT CANCELLED AND THEY'RE STILL INVITED... THEN WE'LL SEE HOW LOYAL THEY ARE TO HIM...
AND I GET TO SCHMOOZE THEM...

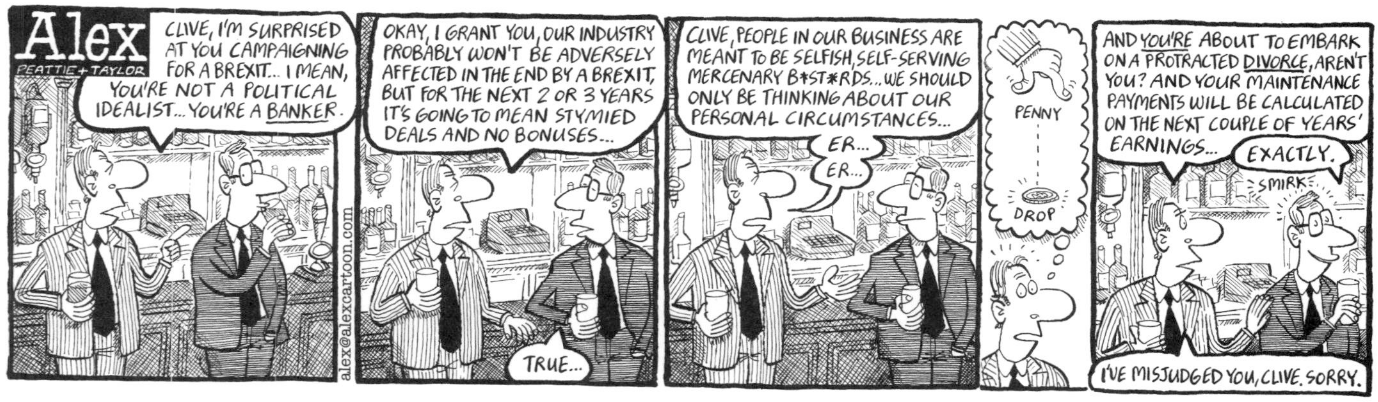
Alex
PEATTIE + TAYLOR
CLIVE, I'M SURPRISED AT YOU CAMPAIGNING FOR A BREXIT... I MEAN, YOU'RE NOT A POLITICAL IDEALIST... YOU'RE A BANKER.
OKAY, I GRANT YOU, OUR INDUSTRY PROBABLY WON'T BE ADVERSELY AFFECTED IN THE END BY A BREXIT, BUT FOR THE NEXT 2 OR 3 YEARS IT'S GOING TO MEAN STYMIED DEALS AND NO BONUSES...
TRUE...
alex@alexcartoon.com
CLIVE, PEOPLE IN OUR BUSINESS ARE MEANT TO BE SELFISH, SELF-SERVING MERCENARY B*ST*RDS... WE SHOULD ONLY BE THINKING ABOUT OUR PERSONAL CIRCUMSTANCES...
ER...
ER...
PENNY
DROP
AND YOU'RE ABOUT TO EMBARK ON A PROTRACTED DIVORCE, AREN'T YOU? AND YOUR MAINTENANCE PAYMENTS WILL BE CALCULATED ON THE NEXT COUPLE OF YEARS' EARNINGS...
EXACTLY.
SMIRK
I'VE MISJUDGED YOU, CLIVE. SORRY.

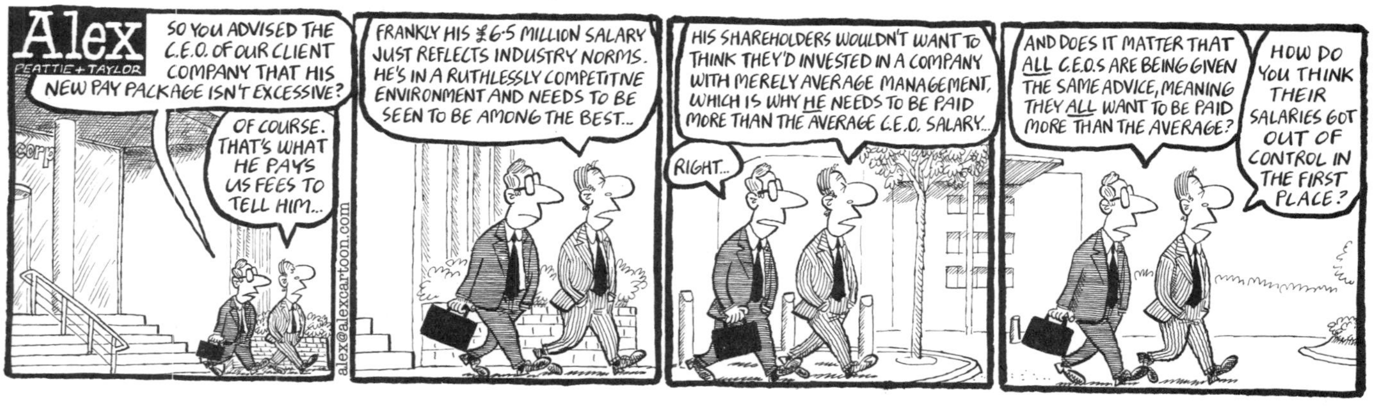
Alex
PEATTIE + TAYLOR
SO YOU ADVISED THE C.E.O. OF OUR CLIENT COMPANY THAT HIS NEW PAY PACKAGE ISN'T EXCESSIVE?
OF COURSE. THAT'S WHAT HE PAYS US FEES TO TELL HIM...
alex@alexcartoon.com
FRANKLY HIS £6·5 MILLION SALARY JUST REFLECTS INDUSTRY NORMS. HE'S IN A RUTHLESSLY COMPETITIVE ENVIRONMENT AND NEEDS TO BE SEEN TO BE AMONG THE BEST...
HIS SHAREHOLDERS WOULDN'T WANT TO THINK THEY'D INVESTED IN A COMPANY WITH MERELY AVERAGE MANAGEMENT, WHICH IS WHY HE NEEDS TO BE PAID MORE THAN THE AVERAGE C.E.O. SALARY...
RIGHT...
AND DOES IT MATTER THAT ALL C.E.O.S ARE BEING GIVEN THE SAME ADVICE, MEANING THEY ALL WANT TO BE PAID MORE THAN THE AVERAGE?
HOW DO YOU THINK THEIR SALARIES GOT OUT OF CONTROL IN THE FIRST PLACE?

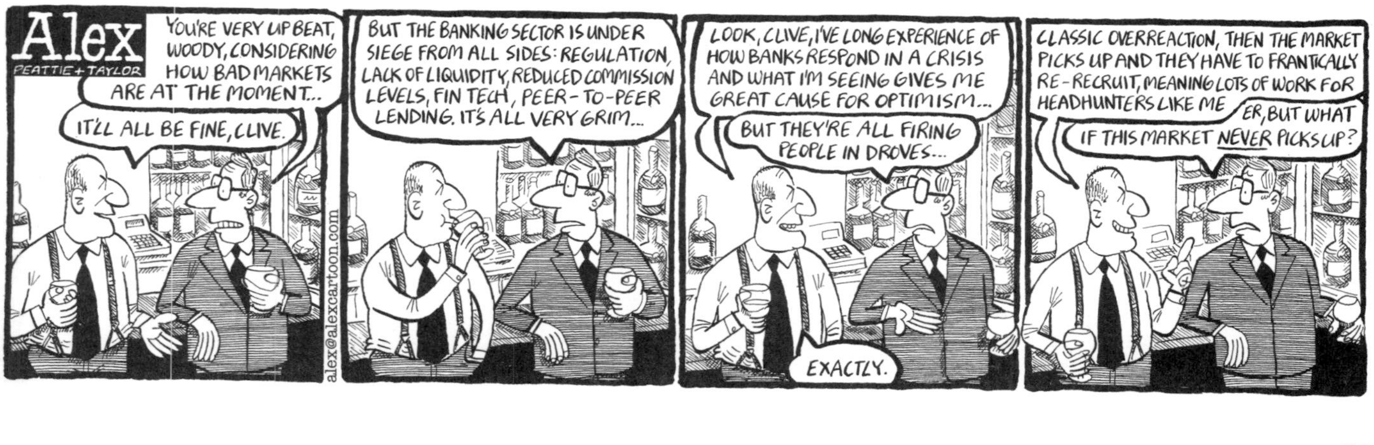
Alex
PEATTIE + TAYLOR
YOU'RE VERY UPBEAT, WOODY, CONSIDERING HOW BAD MARKETS ARE AT THE MOMENT...
IT'LL ALL BE FINE, CLIVE.
BUT THE BANKING SECTOR IS UNDER SIEGE FROM ALL SIDES: REGULATION, LACK OF LIQUIDITY, REDUCED COMMISSION LEVELS, FIN TECH, PEER-TO-PEER LENDING. IT'S ALL VERY GRIM...
alex@alexcartoon.com
LOOK, CLIVE, I'VE LONG EXPERIENCE OF HOW BANKS RESPOND IN A CRISIS AND WHAT I'M SEEING GIVES ME GREAT CAUSE FOR OPTIMISM...
BUT THEY'RE ALL FIRING PEOPLE IN DROVES...
EXACTLY.
CLASSIC OVERREACTION, THEN THE MARKET PICKS UP AND THEY HAVE TO FRANTICALLY RE-RECRUIT, MEANING LOTS OF WORK FOR HEADHUNTERS LIKE ME
ER, BUT WHAT IF THIS MARKET NEVER PICKS UP?

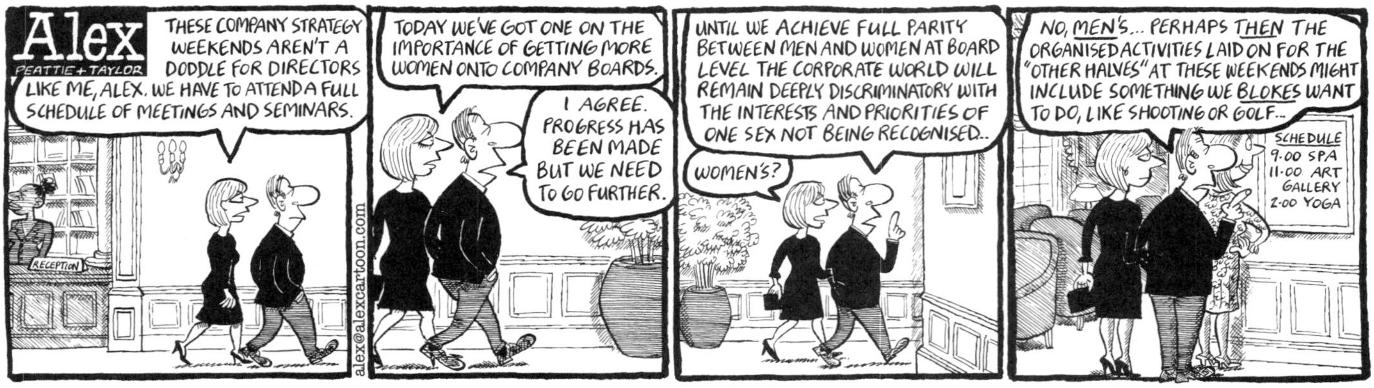
Alex
PEATTIE + TAYLOR
THESE COMPANY STRATEGY WEEKENDS AREN'T A DODDLE FOR DIRECTORS LIKE ME, ALEX. WE HAVE TO ATTEND A FULL SCHEDULE OF MEETINGS AND SEMINARS.
RECEPTION
TODAY WE'VE GOT ONE ON THE IMPORTANCE OF GETTING MORE WOMEN ONTO COMPANY BOARDS.
I AGREE. PROGRESS HAS BEEN MADE BUT WE NEED TO GO FURTHER.
alex@alexcartoon.com
UNTIL WE ACHIEVE FULL PARITY BETWEEN MEN AND WOMEN AT BOARD LEVEL THE CORPORATE WORLD WILL REMAIN DEEPLY DISCRIMINATORY WITH THE INTERESTS AND PRIORITIES OF ONE SEX NOT BEING RECOGNISED..
WOMEN'S?
NO, MEN'S... PERHAPS THEN THE ORGANISED ACTIVITIES LAID ON FOR THE "OTHER HALVES" AT THESE WEEKENDS MIGHT INCLUDE SOMETHING WE BLOKES WANT TO DO, LIKE SHOOTING OR GOLF...
SCHEDULE
9.00 SPA
11.00 ART GALLERY
2.00 YOGA

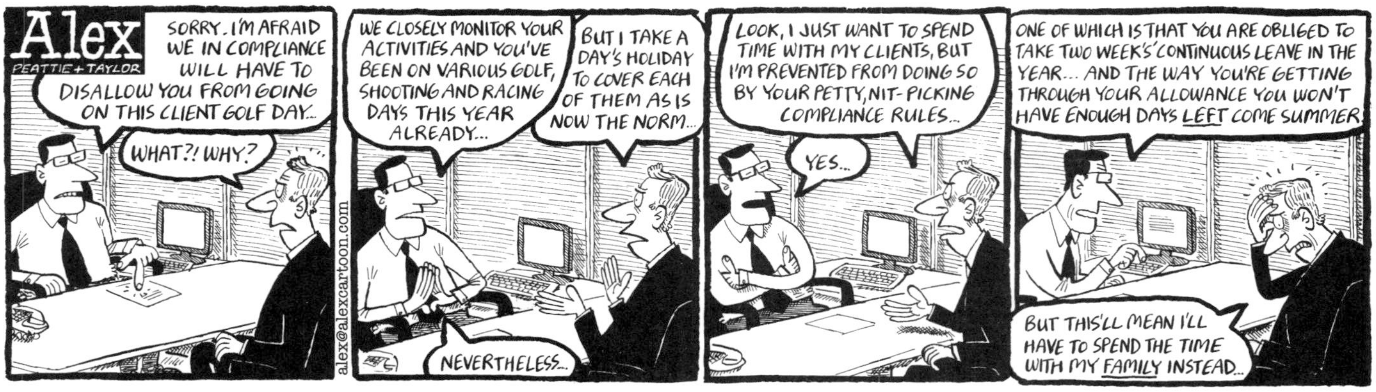
Alex
PEATTIE + TAYLOR
SORRY. I'M AFRAID WE IN COMPLIANCE WILL HAVE TO DISALLOW YOU FROM GOING ON THIS CLIENT GOLF DAY...
WHAT?! WHY?
WE CLOSELY MONITOR YOUR ACTIVITIES AND YOU'VE BEEN ON VARIOUS GOLF, SHOOTING AND RACING DAYS THIS YEAR ALREADY...
BUT I TAKE A DAY'S HOLIDAY TO COVER EACH OF THEM AS IS NOW THE NORM...
NEVERTHELESS...
alex@alexcartoon.com
LOOK, I JUST WANT TO SPEND TIME WITH MY CLIENTS, BUT I'M PREVENTED FROM DOING SO BY YOUR PETTY, NIT-PICKING COMPLIANCE RULES...
YES...
ONE OF WHICH IS THAT YOU ARE OBLIGED TO TAKE TWO WEEKS' CONTINUOUS LEAVE IN THE YEAR... AND THE WAY YOU'RE GETTING THROUGH YOUR ALLOWANCE YOU WON'T HAVE ENOUGH DAYS LEFT COME SUMMER
BUT THIS'LL MEAN I'LL HAVE TO SPEND THE TIME WITH MY FAMILY INSTEAD...

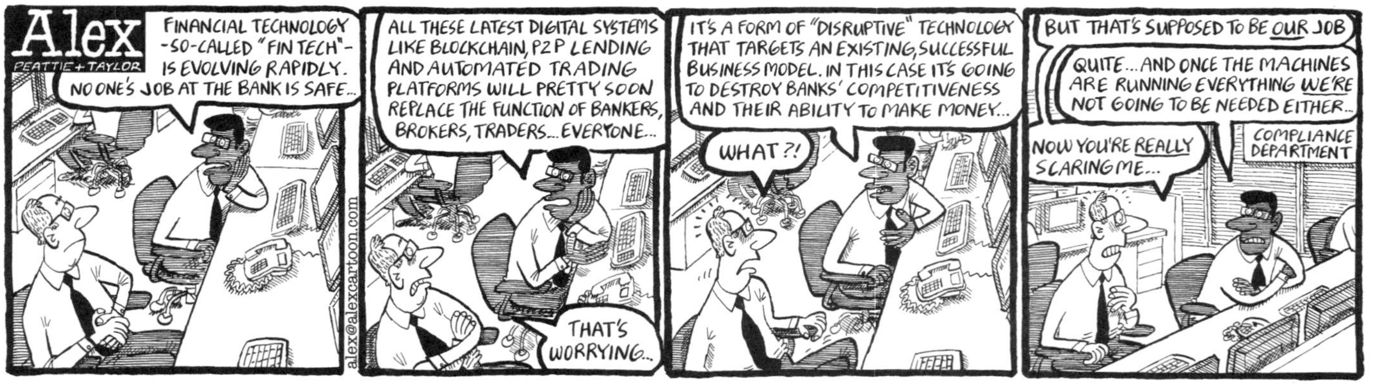
Alex
PEATTIE + TAYLOR
FINANCIAL TECHNOLOGY -SO-CALLED "FIN TECH"- IS EVOLVING RAPIDLY.
NO ONE'S JOB AT THE BANK IS SAFE...
ALL THESE LATEST DIGITAL SYSTEMS LIKE BLOCKCHAIN, P2P LENDING AND AUTOMATED TRADING PLATFORMS WILL PRETTY SOON REPLACE THE FUNCTION OF BANKERS, BROKERS, TRADERS... EVERYONE...
THAT'S WORRYING...
alex@alexcartoon.com
IT'S A FORM OF "DISRUPTIVE" TECHNOLOGY THAT TARGETS AN EXISTING, SUCCESSFUL BUSINESS MODEL. IN THIS CASE IT'S GOING TO DESTROY BANKS' COMPETITIVENESS AND THEIR ABILITY TO MAKE MONEY...
WHAT?!
BUT THAT'S SUPPOSED TO BE OUR JOB
QUITE... AND ONCE THE MACHINES ARE RUNNING EVERYTHING WE'RE NOT GOING TO BE NEEDED EITHER...
NOW YOU'RE REALLY SCARING ME...
COMPLIANCE DEPARTMENT

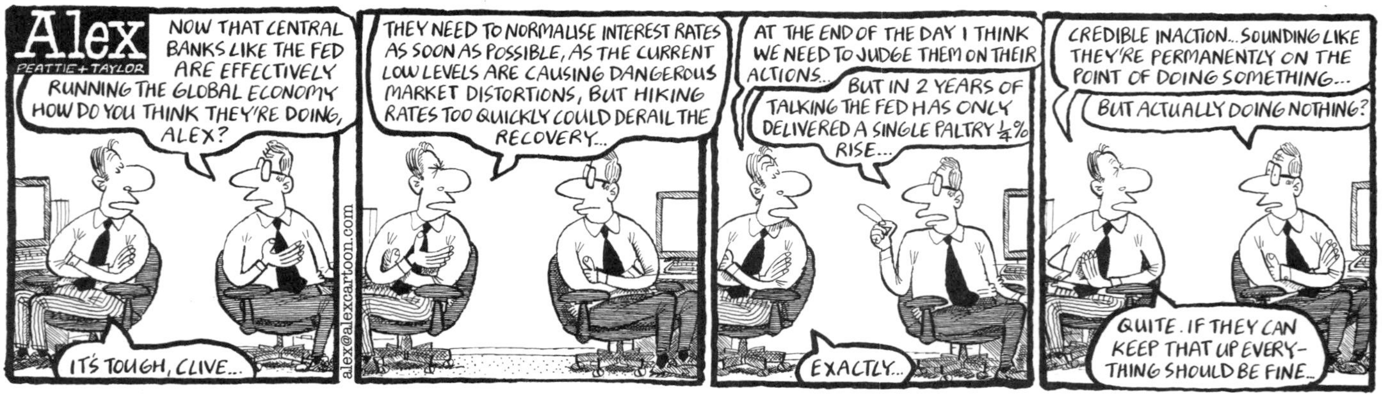
Alex
PEATTIE + TAYLOR
NOW THAT CENTRAL BANKS LIKE THE FED ARE EFFECTIVELY RUNNING THE GLOBAL ECONOMY HOW DO YOU THINK THEY'RE DOING, ALEX?
IT'S TOUGH, CLIVE...
alex@alexcartoon.com
THEY NEED TO NORMALISE INTEREST RATES AS SOON AS POSSIBLE, AS THE CURRENT LOW LEVELS ARE CAUSING DANGEROUS MARKET DISTORTIONS, BUT HIKING RATES TOO QUICKLY COULD DERAIL THE RECOVERY...
AT THE END OF THE DAY I THINK WE NEED TO JUDGE THEM ON THEIR ACTIONS...
BUT IN 2 YEARS OF TALKING THE FED HAS ONLY DELIVERED A SINGLE PALTRY ¼% RISE...
EXACTLY...
CREDIBLE INACTION... SOUNDING LIKE THEY'RE PERMANENTLY ON THE POINT OF DOING SOMETHING...
BUT ACTUALLY DOING NOTHING?
QUITE. IF THEY CAN KEEP THAT UP EVERYTHING SHOULD BE FINE...

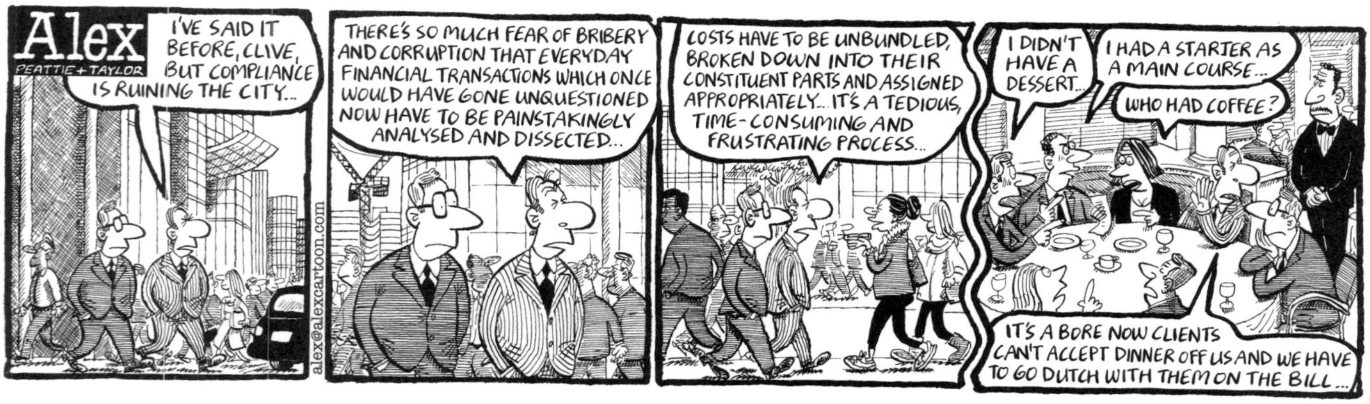
Alex
PEATTIE + TAYLOR
I'VE SAID IT BEFORE, CLIVE, BUT COMPLIANCE IS RUINING THE CITY...
alex@alexcartoon.com
THERE'S SO MUCH FEAR OF BRIBERY AND CORRUPTION THAT EVERYDAY FINANCIAL TRANSACTIONS WHICH ONCE WOULD HAVE GONE UNQUESTIONED NOW HAVE TO BE PAINSTAKINGLY ANALYSED AND DISSECTED...
COSTS HAVE TO BE UNBUNDLED, BROKEN DOWN INTO THEIR CONSTITUENT PARTS AND ASSIGNED APPROPRIATELY... IT'S A TEDIOUS, TIME-CONSUMING AND FRUSTRATING PROCESS...
I DIDN'T HAVE A DESSERT...
I HAD A STARTER AS A MAIN COURSE...
WHO HAD COFFEE?
IT'S A BORE NOW CLIENTS CAN'T ACCEPT DINNER OFF US AND WE HAVE TO GO DUTCH WITH THEM ON THE BILL...

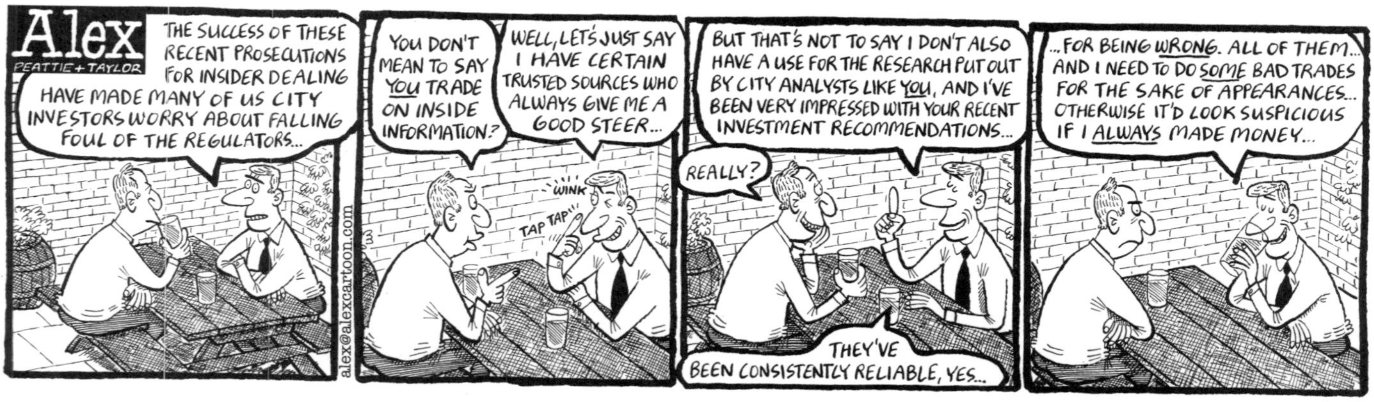
Alex
PEATTIE + TAYLOR
THE SUCCESS OF THESE RECENT PROSECUTIONS FOR INSIDER DEALING HAVE MADE MANY OF US CITY INVESTORS WORRY ABOUT FALLING FOUL OF THE REGULATORS...
alex@alexcartoon.com
YOU DON'T MEAN TO SAY YOU TRADE ON INSIDE INFORMATION?
WELL, LET'S JUST SAY I HAVE CERTAIN TRUSTED SOURCES WHO ALWAYS GIVE ME A GOOD STEER...
WINK
TAP TAP
BUT THAT'S NOT TO SAY I DON'T ALSO HAVE A USE FOR THE RESEARCH PUT OUT BY CITY ANALYSTS LIKE YOU, AND I'VE BEEN VERY IMPRESSED WITH YOUR RECENT INVESTMENT RECOMMENDATIONS...
REALLY?
THEY'VE BEEN CONSISTENTLY RELIABLE, YES...
...FOR BEING WRONG. ALL OF THEM... AND I NEED TO DO SOME BAD TRADES FOR THE SAKE OF APPEARANCES... OTHERWISE IT'D LOOK SUSPICIOUS IF I ALWAYS MADE MONEY...

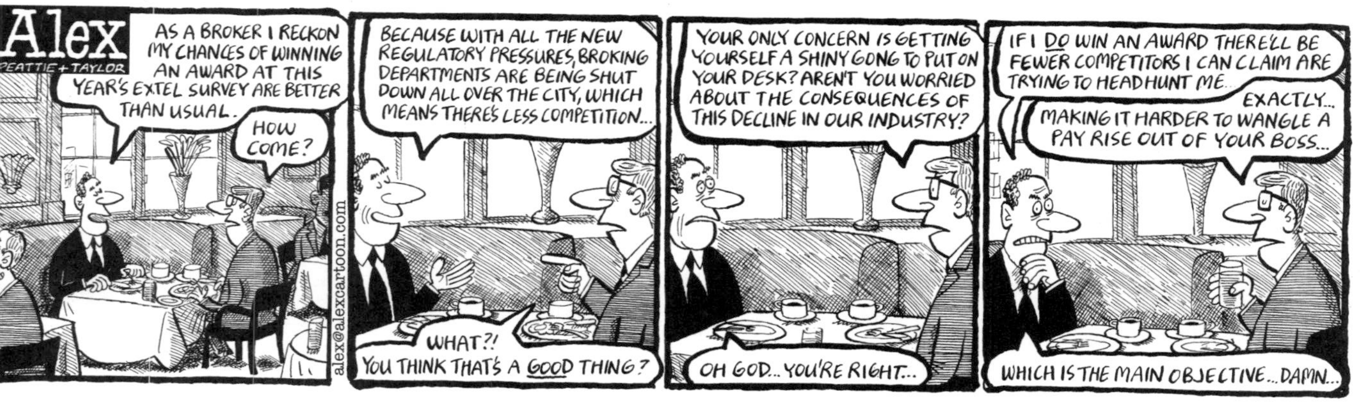
Alex
PEATTIE + TAYLOR
AS A BROKER I RECKON MY CHANCES OF WINNING AN AWARD AT THIS YEAR'S EXTEL SURVEY ARE BETTER THAN USUAL...
HOW COME?
alex@alexcartoon.com
BECAUSE WITH ALL THE NEW REGULATORY PRESSURES, BROKING DEPARTMENTS ARE BEING SHUT DOWN ALL OVER THE CITY, WHICH MEANS THERE'S LESS COMPETITION...
WHAT?! YOU THINK THAT'S A GOOD THING?
YOUR ONLY CONCERN IS GETTING YOURSELF A SHINY GONG TO PUT ON YOUR DESK? AREN'T YOU WORRIED ABOUT THE CONSEQUENCES OF THIS DECLINE IN OUR INDUSTRY?
OH GOD... YOU'RE RIGHT...
IF I DO WIN AN AWARD THERE'LL BE FEWER COMPETITORS I CAN CLAIM ARE TRYING TO HEADHUNT ME...
EXACTLY... MAKING IT HARDER TO WANGLE A PAY RISE OUT OF YOUR BOSS...
WHICH IS THE MAIN OBJECTIVE... DAMN...

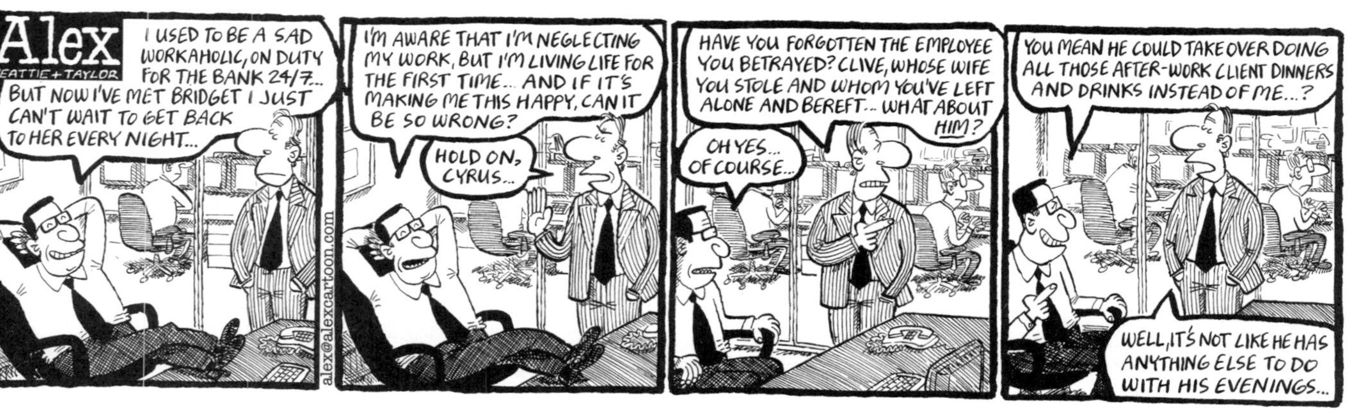
Alex
PEATTIE + TAYLOR
I USED TO BE A SAD WORKAHOLIC, ON DUTY FOR THE BANK 24/7... BUT NOW I'VE MET BRIDGET I JUST CAN'T WAIT TO GET BACK TO HER EVERY NIGHT...
alex@alexcartoon.com
I'M AWARE THAT I'M NEGLECTING MY WORK, BUT I'M LIVING LIFE FOR THE FIRST TIME... AND IF IT'S MAKING ME THIS HAPPY, CAN IT BE SO WRONG?
HOLD ON, CYRUS...
HAVE YOU FORGOTTEN THE EMPLOYEE YOU BETRAYED? CLIVE, WHOSE WIFE YOU STOLE AND WHOM YOU'VE LEFT ALONE AND BEREFT... WHAT ABOUT HIM?
OH YES... OF COURSE...
YOU MEAN HE COULD TAKE OVER DOING ALL THOSE AFTER-WORK CLIENT DINNERS AND DRINKS INSTEAD OF ME...?
WELL, IT'S NOT LIKE HE HAS ANYTHING ELSE TO DO WITH HIS EVENINGS...

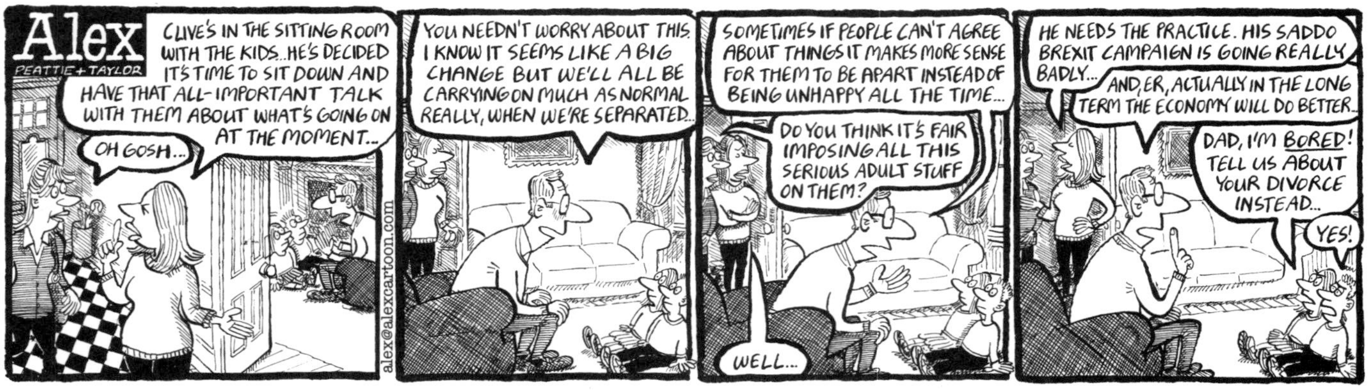
Alex
PEATTIE + TAYLOR
CLIVE'S IN THE SITTING ROOM WITH THE KIDS...HE'S DECIDED IT'S TIME TO SIT DOWN AND HAVE THAT ALL-IMPORTANT TALK WITH THEM ABOUT WHAT'S GOING ON AT THE MOMENT...
OH GOSH...
YOU NEEDN'T WORRY ABOUT THIS. I KNOW IT SEEMS LIKE A BIG CHANGE BUT WE'LL ALL BE CARRYING ON MUCH AS NORMAL REALLY, WHEN WE'RE SEPARATED...
alex@alexcartoon.com
SOMETIMES IF PEOPLE CAN'T AGREE ABOUT THINGS IT MAKES MORE SENSE FOR THEM TO BE APART INSTEAD OF BEING UNHAPPY ALL THE TIME...
DO YOU THINK IT'S FAIR IMPOSING ALL THIS SERIOUS ADULT STUFF ON THEM?
WELL...
HE NEEDS THE PRACTICE. HIS SADDO BREXIT CAMPAIGN IS GOING REALLY BADLY...
AND, ER, ACTUALLY IN THE LONG TERM THE ECONOMY WILL DO BETTER...
DAD, I'M BORED! TELL US ABOUT YOUR DIVORCE INSTEAD...
YES!

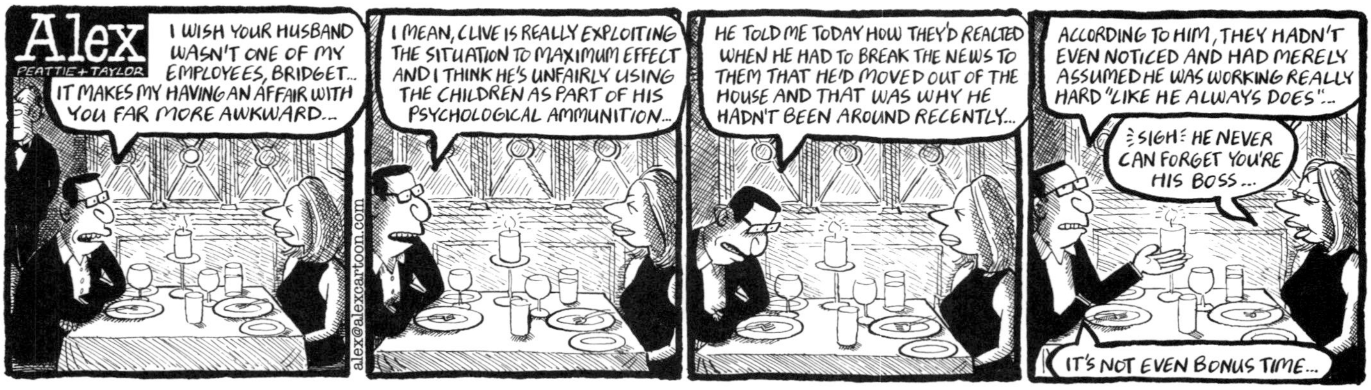
Alex
PEATTIE + TAYLOR
I WISH YOUR HUSBAND WASN'T ONE OF MY EMPLOYEES, BRIDGET... IT MAKES MY HAVING AN AFFAIR WITH YOU FAR MORE AWKWARD...
alex@alexcartoon.com
I MEAN, CLIVE IS REALLY EXPLOITING THE SITUATION TO MAXIMUM EFFECT AND I THINK HE'S UNFAIRLY USING THE CHILDREN AS PART OF HIS PSYCHOLOGICAL AMMUNITION...
HE TOLD ME TODAY HOW THEY'D REACTED WHEN HE HAD TO BREAK THE NEWS TO THEM THAT HE'D MOVED OUT OF THE HOUSE AND THAT WAS WHY HE HADN'T BEEN AROUND RECENTLY...
ACCORDING TO HIM, THEY HADN'T EVEN NOTICED AND HAD MERELY ASSUMED HE WAS WORKING REALLY HARD "LIKE HE ALWAYS DOES"...
SIGH HE NEVER CAN FORGET YOU'RE HIS BOSS...
IT'S NOT EVEN BONUS TIME...

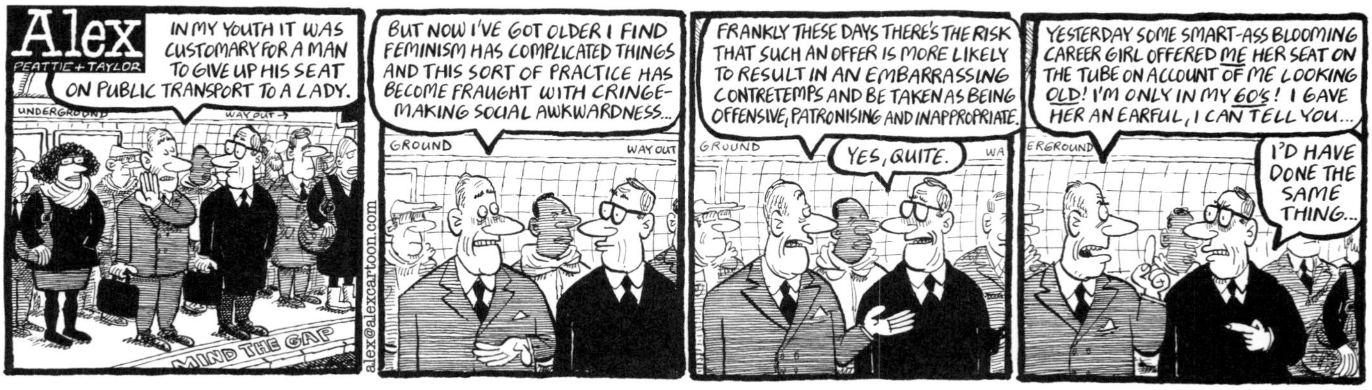
Alex
PEATTIE + TAYLOR
IN MY YOUTH IT WAS CUSTOMARY FOR A MAN TO GIVE UP HIS SEAT ON PUBLIC TRANSPORT TO A LADY.
UNDERGROUND
WAY OUT →
MIND THE GAP
alex@alexcartoon.com
BUT NOW I'VE GOT OLDER I FIND FEMINISM HAS COMPLICATED THINGS AND THIS SORT OF PRACTICE HAS BECOME FRAUGHT WITH CRINGE-MAKING SOCIAL AWKWARDNESS...
GROUND
WAY OUT
FRANKLY THESE DAYS THERE'S THE RISK THAT SUCH AN OFFER IS MORE LIKELY TO RESULT IN AN EMBARRASSING CONTRETEMPS AND BE TAKEN AS BEING OFFENSIVE, PATRONISING AND INAPPROPRIATE.
YES, QUITE.
YESTERDAY SOME SMART-ASS BLOOMING CAREER GIRL OFFERED ME HER SEAT ON THE TUBE ON ACCOUNT OF ME LOOKING OLD! I'M ONLY IN MY 60's! I GAVE HER AN EARFUL, I CAN TELL YOU...
I'D HAVE DONE THE SAME THING...

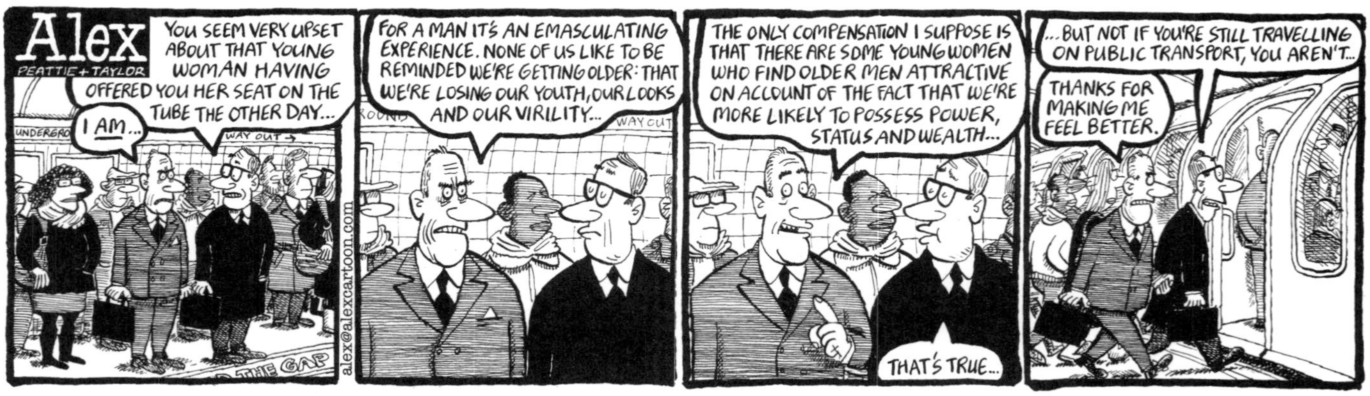
Alex
PEATTIE + TAYLOR
YOU SEEM VERY UPSET ABOUT THAT YOUNG WOMAN HAVING OFFERED YOU HER SEAT ON THE TUBE THE OTHER DAY...
I AM...
WAY OUT →
alex@alexcartoon.com
FOR A MAN IT'S AN EMASCULATING EXPERIENCE. NONE OF US LIKE TO BE REMINDED WE'RE GETTING OLDER: THAT WE'RE LOSING OUR YOUTH, OUR LOOKS AND OUR VIRILITY...
WAY OUT
THE ONLY COMPENSATION I SUPPOSE IS THAT THERE ARE SOME YOUNG WOMEN WHO FIND OLDER MEN ATTRACTIVE ON ACCOUNT OF THE FACT THAT WE'RE MORE LIKELY TO POSSESS POWER, STATUS AND WEALTH...
THAT'S TRUE...
...BUT NOT IF YOU'RE STILL TRAVELLING ON PUBLIC TRANSPORT, YOU AREN'T...
THANKS FOR MAKING ME FEEL BETTER.

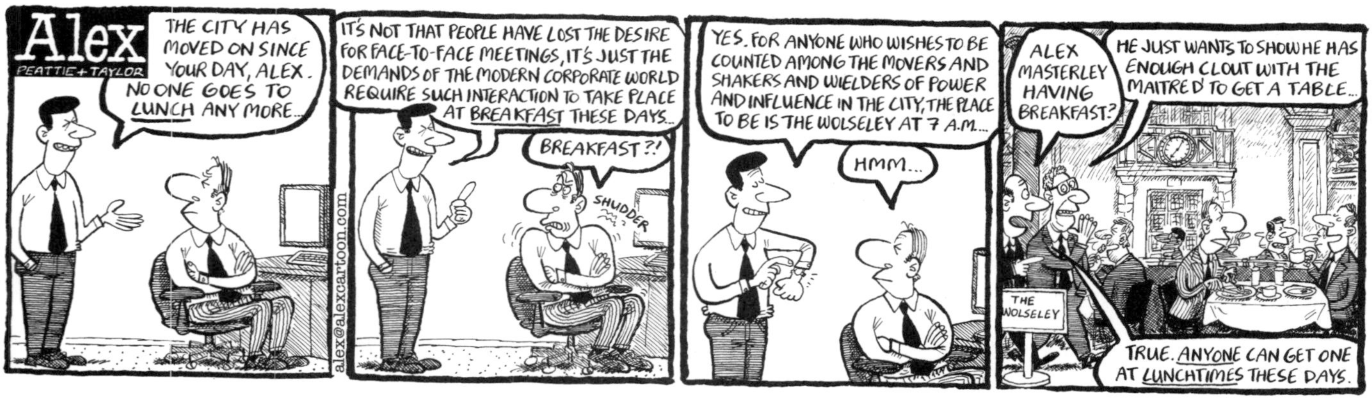
Alex
PEATTIE + TAYLOR
THE CITY HAS MOVED ON SINCE YOUR DAY, ALEX. NO ONE GOES TO LUNCH ANY MORE...
IT'S NOT THAT PEOPLE HAVE LOST THE DESIRE FOR FACE-TO-FACE MEETINGS, IT'S JUST THE DEMANDS OF THE MODERN CORPORATE WORLD REQUIRE SUCH INTERACTION TO TAKE PLACE AT BREAKFAST THESE DAYS...
BREAKFAST?!
SHUDDER
alex@alexcartoon.com
YES. FOR ANYONE WHO WISHES TO BE COUNTED AMONG THE MOVERS AND SHAKERS AND WIELDERS OF POWER AND INFLUENCE IN THE CITY, THE PLACE TO BE IS THE WOLSELEY AT 7 A.M....
HMM...
ALEX MASTERLEY HAVING BREAKFAST?
HE JUST WANTS TO SHOW HE HAS ENOUGH CLOUT WITH THE MAITRE D' TO GET A TABLE...
THE WOLSELEY
TRUE. ANYONE CAN GET ONE AT LUNCHTIMES THESE DAYS.

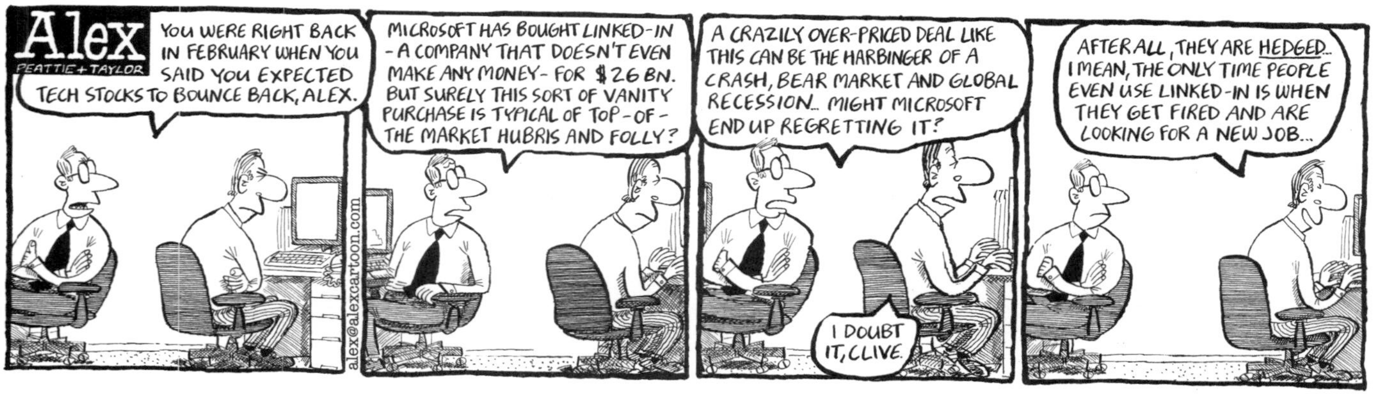
Alex
PEATTIE + TAYLOR
YOU WERE RIGHT BACK IN FEBRUARY WHEN YOU SAID YOU EXPECTED TECH STOCKS TO BOUNCE BACK, ALEX.
MICROSOFT HAS BOUGHT LINKED-IN - A COMPANY THAT DOESN'T EVEN MAKE ANY MONEY - FOR $26 BN. BUT SURELY THIS SORT OF VANITY PURCHASE IS TYPICAL OF TOP-OF-THE MARKET HUBRIS AND FOLLY?
alex@alexcartoon.com
A CRAZILY OVER-PRICED DEAL LIKE THIS CAN BE THE HARBINGER OF A CRASH, BEAR MARKET AND GLOBAL RECESSION... MIGHT MICROSOFT END UP REGRETTING IT?
I DOUBT IT, CLIVE.
AFTER ALL, THEY ARE HEDGED... I MEAN, THE ONLY TIME PEOPLE EVEN USE LINKED-IN IS WHEN THEY GET FIRED AND ARE LOOKING FOR A NEW JOB...

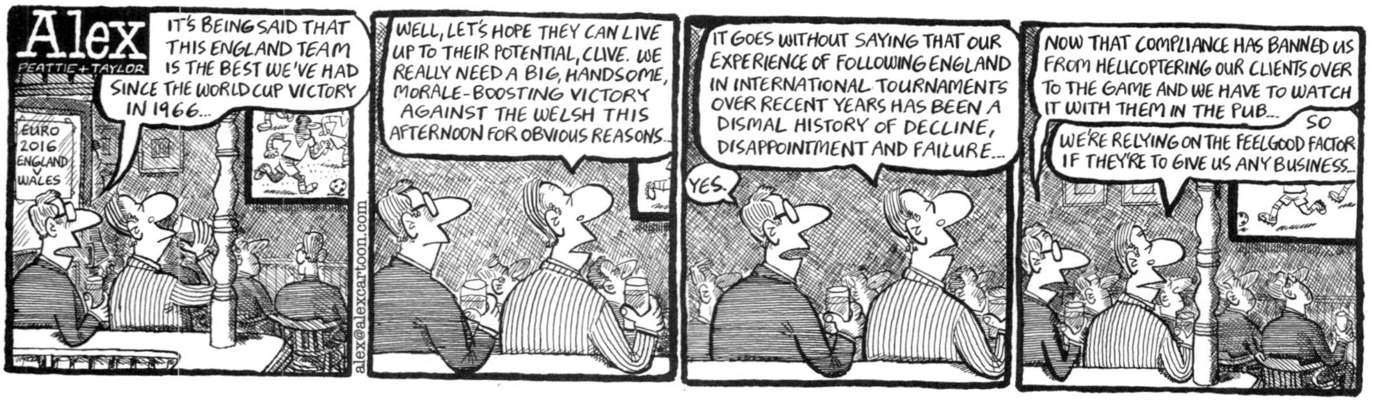
Alex
PEATTIE + TAYLOR
IT'S BEING SAID THAT THIS ENGLAND TEAM IS THE BEST WE'VE HAD SINCE THE WORLD CUP VICTORY IN 1966...
EURO 2016 ENGLAND v WALES
alex@alexcartoon.com
WELL, LET'S HOPE THEY CAN LIVE UP TO THEIR POTENTIAL, CLIVE. WE REALLY NEED A BIG, HANDSOME, MORALE-BOOSTING VICTORY AGAINST THE WELSH THIS AFTERNOON FOR OBVIOUS REASONS...
IT GOES WITHOUT SAYING THAT OUR EXPERIENCE OF FOLLOWING ENGLAND IN INTERNATIONAL TOURNAMENTS OVER RECENT YEARS HAS BEEN A DISMAL HISTORY OF DECLINE, DISAPPOINTMENT AND FAILURE...
YES.
NOW THAT COMPLIANCE HAS BANNED US FROM HELICOPTERING OUR CLIENTS OVER TO THE GAME AND WE HAVE TO WATCH IT WITH THEM IN THE PUB...
SO WE'RE RELYING ON THE FEELGOOD FACTOR IF THEY'RE TO GIVE US ANY BUSINESS...

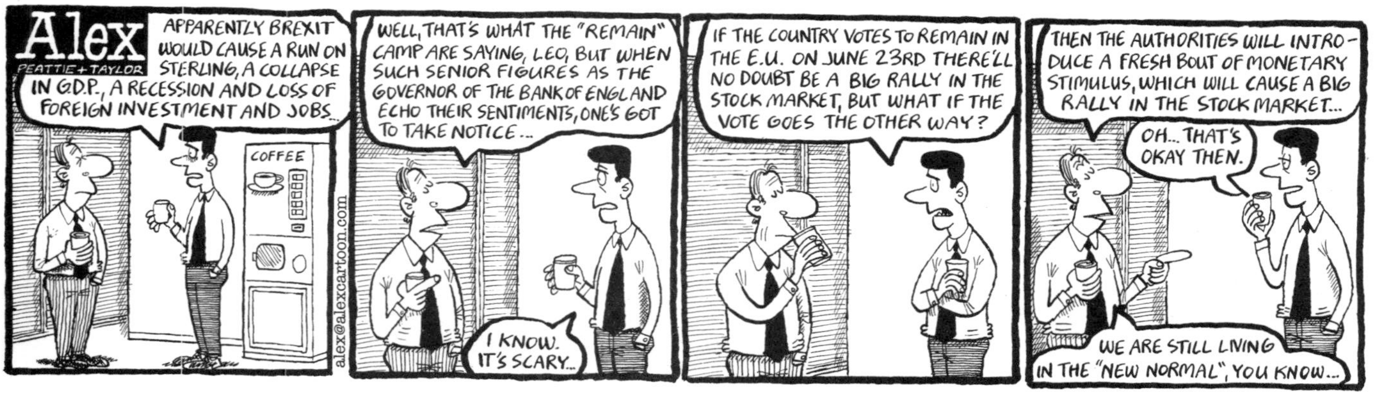
Alex
PEATTIE + TAYLOR
APPARENTLY BREXIT WOULD CAUSE A RUN ON STERLING, A COLLAPSE IN G.D.P., A RECESSION AND LOSS OF FOREIGN INVESTMENT AND JOBS...
COFFEE
alex@alexcartoon.com
WELL, THAT'S WHAT THE "REMAIN" CAMP ARE SAYING, LEO, BUT WHEN SUCH SENIOR FIGURES AS THE GOVERNOR OF THE BANK OF ENGLAND ECHO THEIR SENTIMENTS, ONE'S GOT TO TAKE NOTICE...
I KNOW. IT'S SCARY...
IF THE COUNTRY VOTES TO REMAIN IN THE E.U. ON JUNE 23RD THERE'LL NO DOUBT BE A BIG RALLY IN THE STOCK MARKET, BUT WHAT IF THE VOTE GOES THE OTHER WAY?
THEN THE AUTHORITIES WILL INTRODUCE A FRESH BOUT OF MONETARY STIMULUS, WHICH WILL CAUSE A BIG RALLY IN THE STOCK MARKET...
OH... THAT'S OKAY THEN.
WE ARE STILL LIVING IN THE "NEW NORMAL", YOU KNOW...

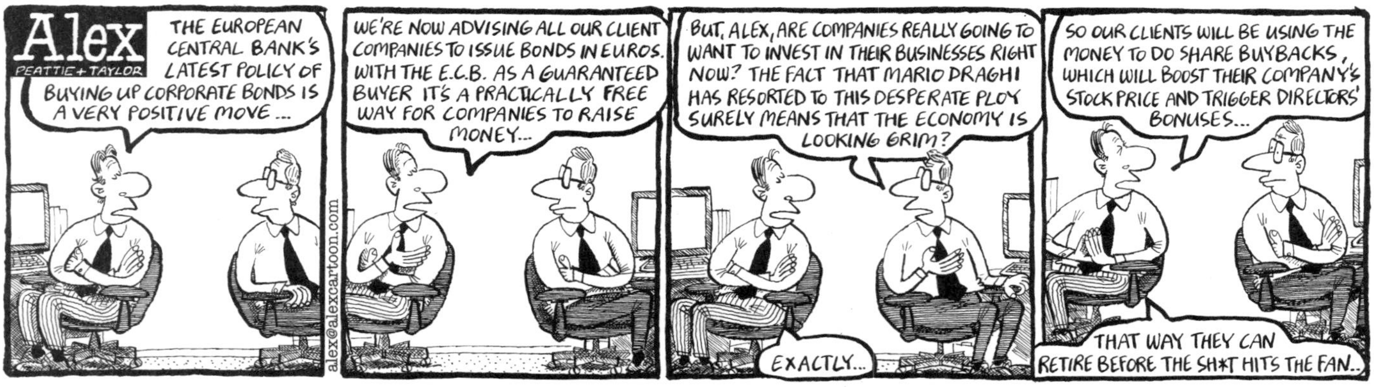
Alex
PEATTIE + TAYLOR
THE EUROPEAN CENTRAL BANK'S LATEST POLICY OF BUYING UP CORPORATE BONDS IS A VERY POSITIVE MOVE ...
WE'RE NOW ADVISING ALL OUR CLIENT COMPANIES TO ISSUE BONDS IN EUROS. WITH THE E.C.B. AS A GUARANTEED BUYER IT'S A PRACTICALLY FREE WAY FOR COMPANIES TO RAISE MONEY...
alex@alexcartoon.com
BUT, ALEX, ARE COMPANIES REALLY GOING TO WANT TO INVEST IN THEIR BUSINESSES RIGHT NOW? THE FACT THAT MARIO DRAGHI HAS RESORTED TO THIS DESPERATE PLOY SURELY MEANS THAT THE ECONOMY IS LOOKING GRIM?
EXACTLY...
SO OUR CLIENTS WILL BE USING THE MONEY TO DO SHARE BUYBACKS, WHICH WILL BOOST THEIR COMPANY'S STOCK PRICE AND TRIGGER DIRECTORS' BONUSES...
THAT WAY THEY CAN RETIRE BEFORE THE SH*T HITS THE FAN...

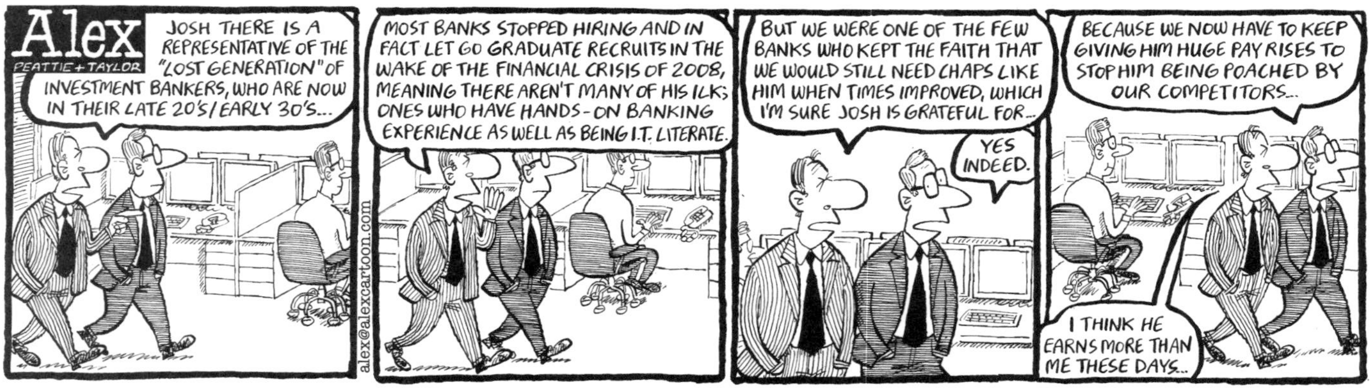
Alex
PEATTIE + TAYLOR
JOSH THERE IS A REPRESENTATIVE OF THE "LOST GENERATION" OF INVESTMENT BANKERS, WHO ARE NOW IN THEIR LATE 20'S / EARLY 30'S...
MOST BANKS STOPPED HIRING AND IN FACT LET GO GRADUATE RECRUITS IN THE WAKE OF THE FINANCIAL CRISIS OF 2008, MEANING THERE AREN'T MANY OF HIS ILK; ONES WHO HAVE HANDS-ON BANKING EXPERIENCE AS WELL AS BEING I.T. LITERATE.
alex@alexcartoon.com
BUT WE WERE ONE OF THE FEW BANKS WHO KEPT THE FAITH THAT WE WOULD STILL NEED CHAPS LIKE HIM WHEN TIMES IMPROVED, WHICH I'M SURE JOSH IS GRATEFUL FOR...
YES INDEED.
BECAUSE WE NOW HAVE TO KEEP GIVING HIM HUGE PAY RISES TO STOP HIM BEING POACHED BY OUR COMPETITORS...
I THINK HE EARNS MORE THAN ME THESE DAYS...

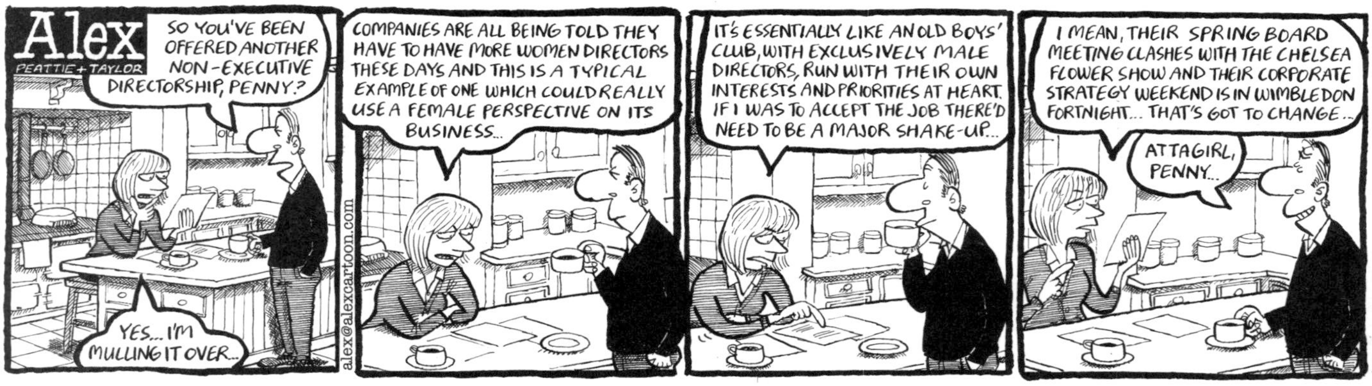
Alex
PEATTIE + TAYLOR
SO YOU'VE BEEN OFFERED ANOTHER NON-EXECUTIVE DIRECTORSHIP, PENNY?
YES... I'M MULLING IT OVER...
alex@alexcartoon.com
COMPANIES ARE ALL BEING TOLD THEY HAVE TO HAVE MORE WOMEN DIRECTORS THESE DAYS AND THIS IS A TYPICAL EXAMPLE OF ONE WHICH COULD REALLY USE A FEMALE PERSPECTIVE ON ITS BUSINESS...
IT'S ESSENTIALLY LIKE AN OLD BOYS' CLUB, WITH EXCLUSIVELY MALE DIRECTORS, RUN WITH THEIR OWN INTERESTS AND PRIORITIES AT HEART. IF I WAS TO ACCEPT THE JOB THERE'D NEED TO BE A MAJOR SHAKE-UP...
I MEAN, THEIR SPRING BOARD MEETING CLASHES WITH THE CHELSEA FLOWER SHOW AND THEIR CORPORATE STRATEGY WEEKEND IS IN WIMBLEDON FORTNIGHT... THAT'S GOT TO CHANGE...
ATTAGIRL, PENNY...

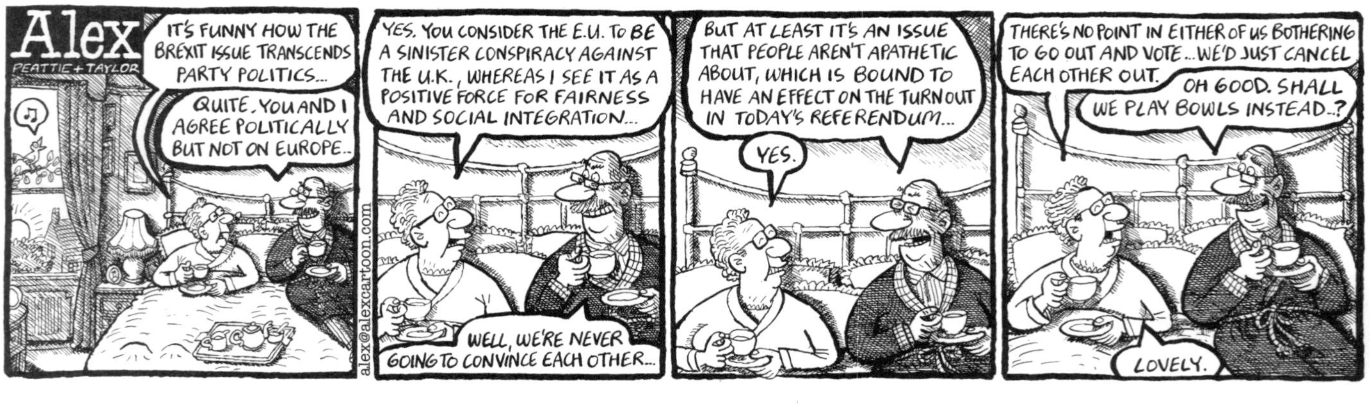
Alex
PEATTIE + TAYLOR
IT'S FUNNY HOW THE BREXIT ISSUE TRANSCENDS PARTY POLITICS...
QUITE. YOU AND I AGREE POLITICALLY BUT NOT ON EUROPE...
alex@alexcartoon.com
YES. YOU CONSIDER THE E.U. TO BE A SINISTER CONSPIRACY AGAINST THE U.K., WHEREAS I SEE IT AS A POSITIVE FORCE FOR FAIRNESS AND SOCIAL INTEGRATION...
WELL, WE'RE NEVER GOING TO CONVINCE EACH OTHER...
BUT AT LEAST IT'S AN ISSUE THAT PEOPLE AREN'T APATHETIC ABOUT, WHICH IS BOUND TO HAVE AN EFFECT ON THE TURNOUT IN TODAY'S REFERENDUM...
YES.
THERE'S NO POINT IN EITHER OF US BOTHERING TO GO OUT AND VOTE... WE'D JUST CANCEL EACH OTHER OUT.
OH GOOD. SHALL WE PLAY BOWLS INSTEAD..?
LOVELY.

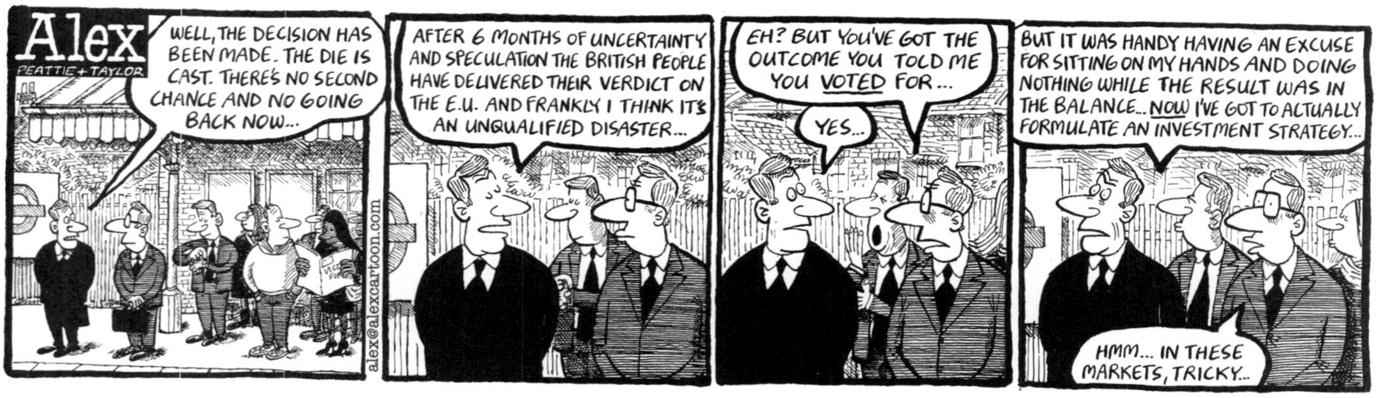
Alex
PEATTIE + TAYLOR
WELL, THE DECISION HAS BEEN MADE. THE DIE IS CAST. THERE'S NO SECOND CHANCE AND NO GOING BACK NOW...
AFTER 6 MONTHS OF UNCERTAINTY AND SPECULATION THE BRITISH PEOPLE HAVE DELIVERED THEIR VERDICT ON THE E.U. AND FRANKLY I THINK IT'S AN UNQUALIFIED DISASTER...
alex@alexcartoon.com
EH? BUT YOU'VE GOT THE OUTCOME YOU TOLD ME YOU VOTED FOR...
YES...
BUT IT WAS HANDY HAVING AN EXCUSE FOR SITTING ON MY HANDS AND DOING NOTHING WHILE THE RESULT WAS IN THE BALANCE... NOW I'VE GOT TO ACTUALLY FORMULATE AN INVESTMENT STRATEGY...
HMM... IN THESE MARKETS, TRICKY...

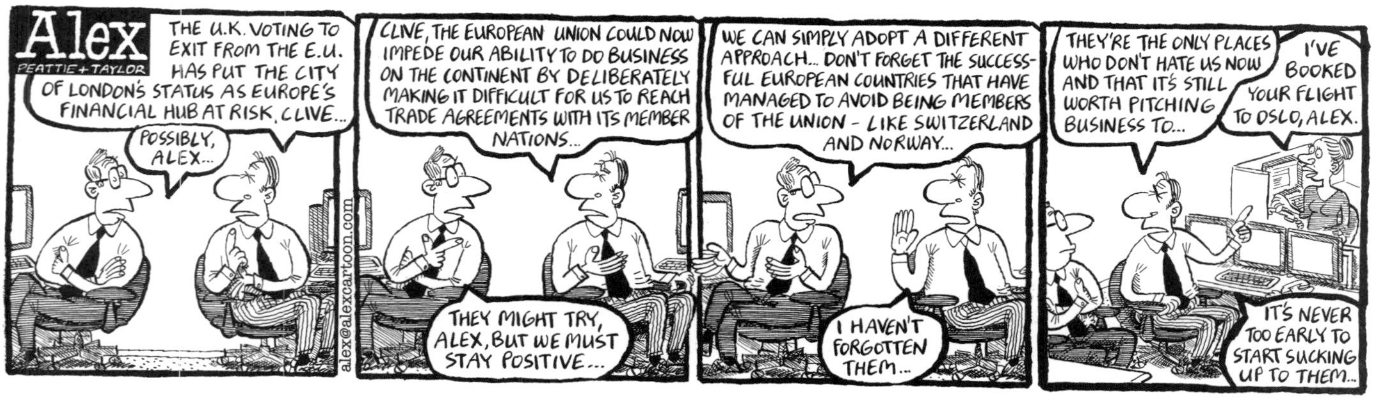
Alex
PEATTIE + TAYLOR
THE U.K. VOTING TO EXIT FROM THE E.U. HAS PUT THE CITY OF LONDON'S STATUS AS EUROPE'S FINANCIAL HUB AT RISK, CLIVE...
POSSIBLY, ALEX...
alex@alexcartoon.com
CLIVE, THE EUROPEAN UNION COULD NOW IMPEDE OUR ABILITY TO DO BUSINESS ON THE CONTINENT BY DELIBERATELY MAKING IT DIFFICULT FOR US TO REACH TRADE AGREEMENTS WITH ITS MEMBER NATIONS...
THEY MIGHT TRY, ALEX, BUT WE MUST STAY POSITIVE...
WE CAN SIMPLY ADOPT A DIFFERENT APPROACH... DON'T FORGET THE SUCCESSFUL EUROPEAN COUNTRIES THAT HAVE MANAGED TO AVOID BEING MEMBERS OF THE UNION - LIKE SWITZERLAND AND NORWAY...
I HAVEN'T FORGOTTEN THEM...
THEY'RE THE ONLY PLACES WHO DON'T HATE US NOW AND THAT IT'S STILL WORTH PITCHING BUSINESS TO...
I'VE BOOKED YOUR FLIGHT TO OSLO, ALEX.
IT'S NEVER TOO EARLY TO START SUCKING UP TO THEM...

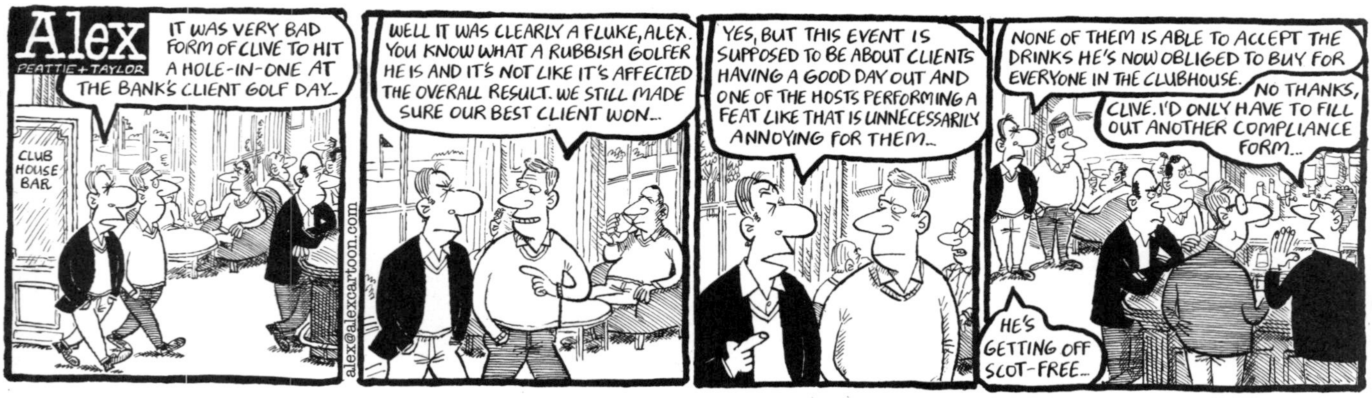
Alex
PEATTIE + TAYLOR
IT WAS VERY BAD FORM OF CLIVE TO HIT A HOLE-IN-ONE AT THE BANK'S CLIENT GOLF DAY...
CLUB HOUSE BAR
alex@alexcartoon.com
WELL IT WAS CLEARLY A FLUKE, ALEX. YOU KNOW WHAT A RUBBISH GOLFER HE IS AND IT'S NOT LIKE IT'S AFFECTED THE OVERALL RESULT. WE STILL MADE SURE OUR BEST CLIENT WON...
YES, BUT THIS EVENT IS SUPPOSED TO BE ABOUT CLIENTS HAVING A GOOD DAY OUT AND ONE OF THE HOSTS PERFORMING A FEAT LIKE THAT IS UNNECESSARILY ANNOYING FOR THEM...
NONE OF THEM IS ABLE TO ACCEPT THE DRINKS HE'S NOW OBLIGED TO BUY FOR EVERYONE IN THE CLUBHOUSE.
NO THANKS, CLIVE. I'D ONLY HAVE TO FILL OUT ANOTHER COMPLIANCE FORM...
HE'S GETTING OFF SCOT-FREE...

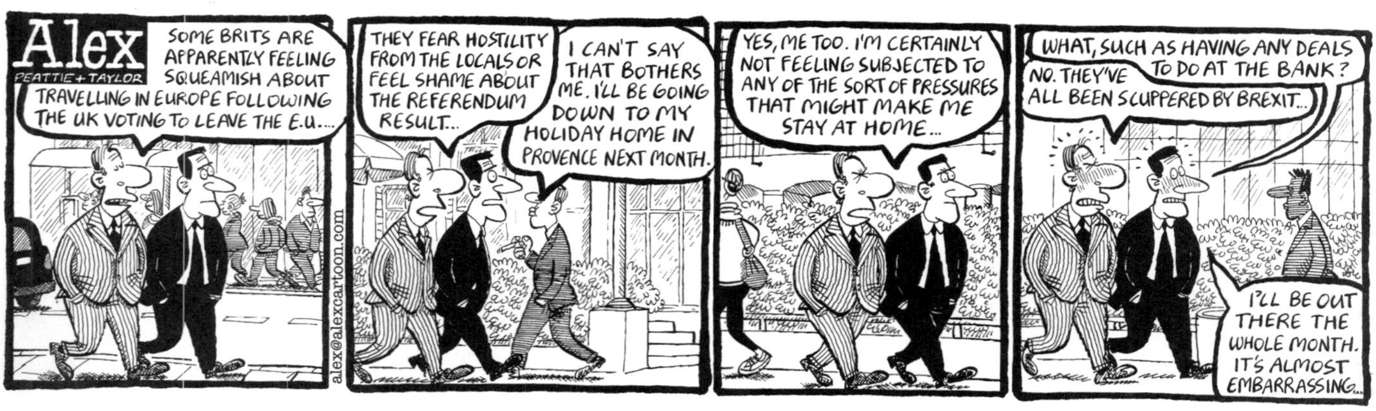
Alex
PEATTIE + TAYLOR
SOME BRITS ARE APPARENTLY FEELING SQUEAMISH ABOUT TRAVELLING IN EUROPE FOLLOWING THE UK VOTING TO LEAVE THE E.U....
alex@alexcartoon.com
THEY FEAR HOSTILITY FROM THE LOCALS OR FEEL SHAME ABOUT THE REFERENDUM RESULT...
I CAN'T SAY THAT BOTHERS ME. I'LL BE GOING DOWN TO MY HOLIDAY HOME IN PROVENCE NEXT MONTH.
YES, ME TOO. I'M CERTAINLY NOT FEELING SUBJECTED TO ANY OF THE SORT OF PRESSURES THAT MIGHT MAKE ME STAY AT HOME...
WHAT, SUCH AS HAVING ANY DEALS TO DO AT THE BANK?
NO. THEY'VE ALL BEEN SCUPPERED BY BREXIT...
I'LL BE OUT THERE THE WHOLE MONTH. IT'S ALMOST EMBARRASSING...

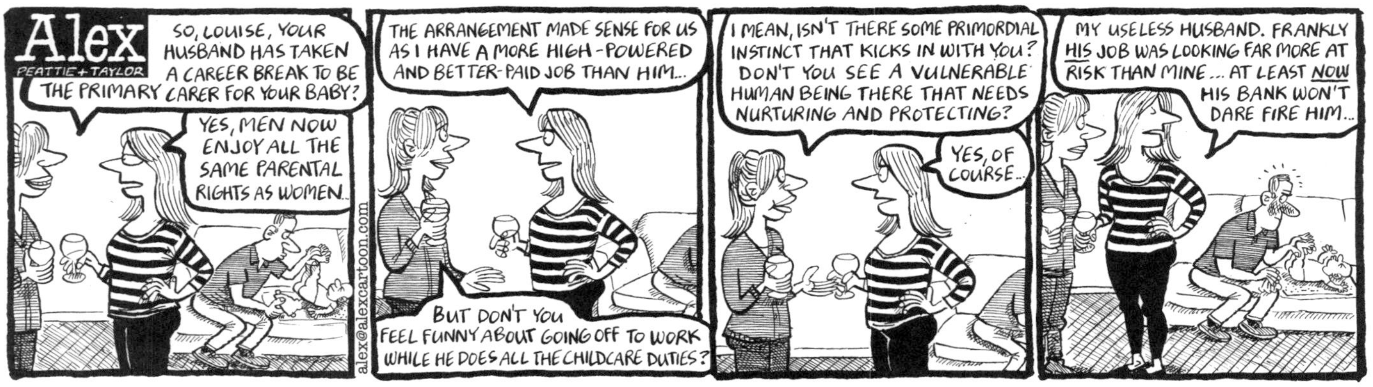
Alex
PEATTIE + TAYLOR
SO, LOUISE, YOUR HUSBAND HAS TAKEN A CAREER BREAK TO BE THE PRIMARY CARER FOR YOUR BABY?
YES, MEN NOW ENJOY ALL THE SAME PARENTAL RIGHTS AS WOMEN...
THE ARRANGEMENT MADE SENSE FOR US AS I HAVE A MORE HIGH-POWERED AND BETTER-PAID JOB THAN HIM...
BUT DON'T YOU FEEL FUNNY ABOUT GOING OFF TO WORK WHILE HE DOES ALL THE CHILDCARE DUTIES?
alex@alexcartoon.com
I MEAN, ISN'T THERE SOME PRIMORDIAL INSTINCT THAT KICKS IN WITH YOU? DON'T YOU SEE A VULNERABLE HUMAN BEING THERE THAT NEEDS NURTURING AND PROTECTING?
YES, OF COURSE...
MY USELESS HUSBAND. FRANKLY HIS JOB WAS LOOKING FAR MORE AT RISK THAN MINE... AT LEAST NOW HIS BANK WON'T DARE FIRE HIM...

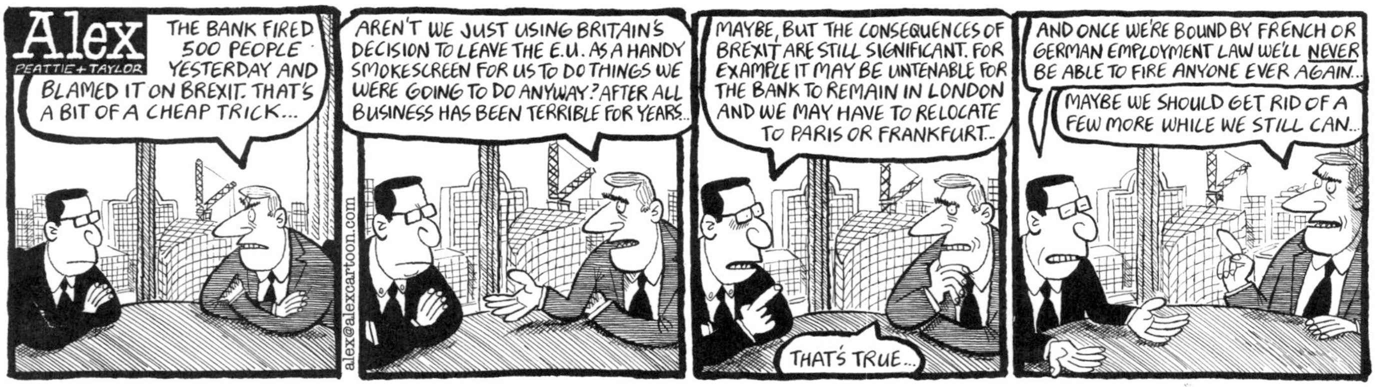
Alex
PEATTIE + TAYLOR
THE BANK FIRED 500 PEOPLE YESTERDAY AND BLAMED IT ON BREXIT. THAT'S A BIT OF A CHEAP TRICK...
AREN'T WE JUST USING BRITAIN'S DECISION TO LEAVE THE E.U. AS A HANDY SMOKESCREEN FOR US TO DO THINGS WE WERE GOING TO DO ANYWAY? AFTER ALL BUSINESS HAS BEEN TERRIBLE FOR YEARS...
alex@alexcartoon.com
MAYBE, BUT THE CONSEQUENCES OF BREXIT ARE STILL SIGNIFICANT. FOR EXAMPLE IT MAY BE UNTENABLE FOR THE BANK TO REMAIN IN LONDON AND WE MAY HAVE TO RELOCATE TO PARIS OR FRANKFURT...
THAT'S TRUE...
AND ONCE WE'RE BOUND BY FRENCH OR GERMAN EMPLOYMENT LAW WE'LL NEVER BE ABLE TO FIRE ANYONE EVER AGAIN...
MAYBE WE SHOULD GET RID OF A FEW MORE WHILE WE STILL CAN...

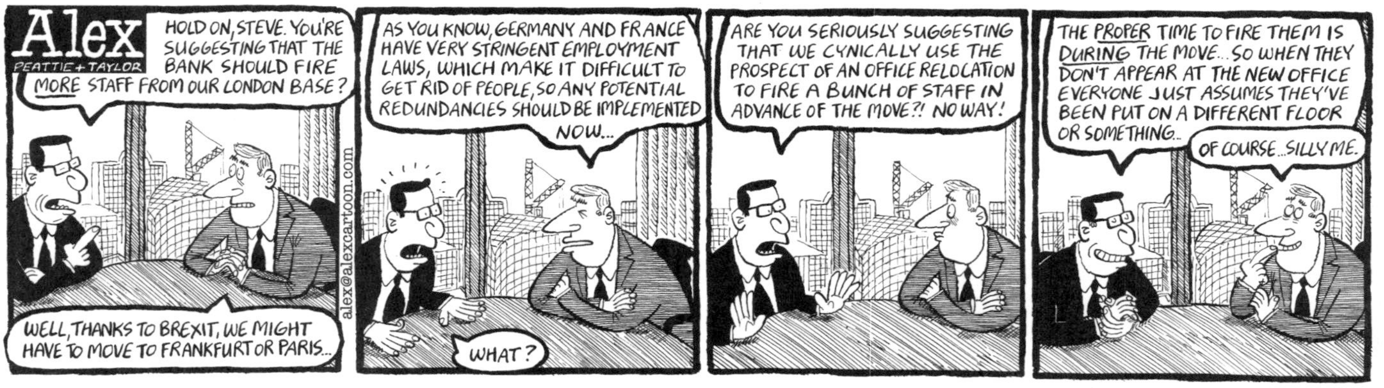
Alex
PEATTIE + TAYLOR
HOLD ON, STEVE. YOU'RE SUGGESTING THAT THE BANK SHOULD FIRE MORE STAFF FROM OUR LONDON BASE?
WELL, THANKS TO BREXIT, WE MIGHT HAVE TO MOVE TO FRANKFURT OR PARIS...
alex@alexcartoon.com
AS YOU KNOW, GERMANY AND FRANCE HAVE VERY STRINGENT EMPLOYMENT LAWS, WHICH MAKE IT DIFFICULT TO GET RID OF PEOPLE, SO ANY POTENTIAL REDUNDANCIES SHOULD BE IMPLEMENTED NOW...
WHAT?
ARE YOU SERIOUSLY SUGGESTING THAT WE CYNICALLY USE THE PROSPECT OF AN OFFICE RELOCATION TO FIRE A BUNCH OF STAFF IN ADVANCE OF THE MOVE?! NO WAY!
THE PROPER TIME TO FIRE THEM IS DURING THE MOVE... SO WHEN THEY DON'T APPEAR AT THE NEW OFFICE EVERYONE JUST ASSUMES THEY'VE BEEN PUT ON A DIFFERENT FLOOR OR SOMETHING...
OF COURSE... SILLY ME.

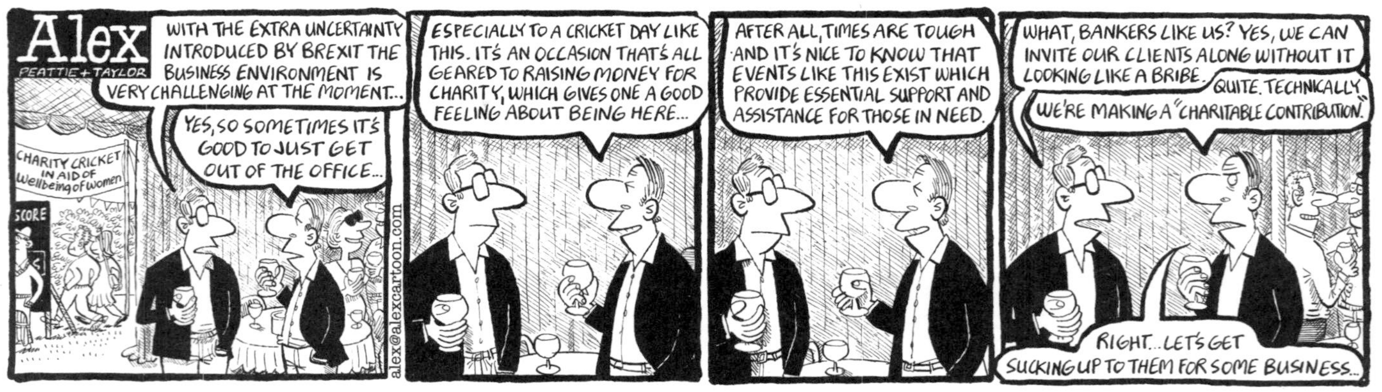
Alex
PEATTIE + TAYLOR
WITH THE EXTRA UNCERTAINTY INTRODUCED BY BREXIT THE BUSINESS ENVIRONMENT IS VERY CHALLENGING AT THE MOMENT...
YES, SO SOMETIMES IT'S GOOD TO JUST GET OUT OF THE OFFICE...
CHARITY CRICKET IN AID OF Wellbeing of Women
SCORE
alex@alexcartoon.com
ESPECIALLY TO A CRICKET DAY LIKE THIS. IT'S AN OCCASION THAT'S ALL GEARED TO RAISING MONEY FOR CHARITY, WHICH GIVES ONE A GOOD FEELING ABOUT BEING HERE...
AFTER ALL, TIMES ARE TOUGH AND IT'S NICE TO KNOW THAT EVENTS LIKE THIS EXIST WHICH PROVIDE ESSENTIAL SUPPORT AND ASSISTANCE FOR THOSE IN NEED.
WHAT, BANKERS LIKE US? YES, WE CAN INVITE OUR CLIENTS ALONG WITHOUT IT LOOKING LIKE A BRIBE.
QUITE. TECHNICALLY WE'RE MAKING A "CHARITABLE CONTRIBUTION."
RIGHT... LET'S GET SUCKING UP TO THEM FOR SOME BUSINESS...

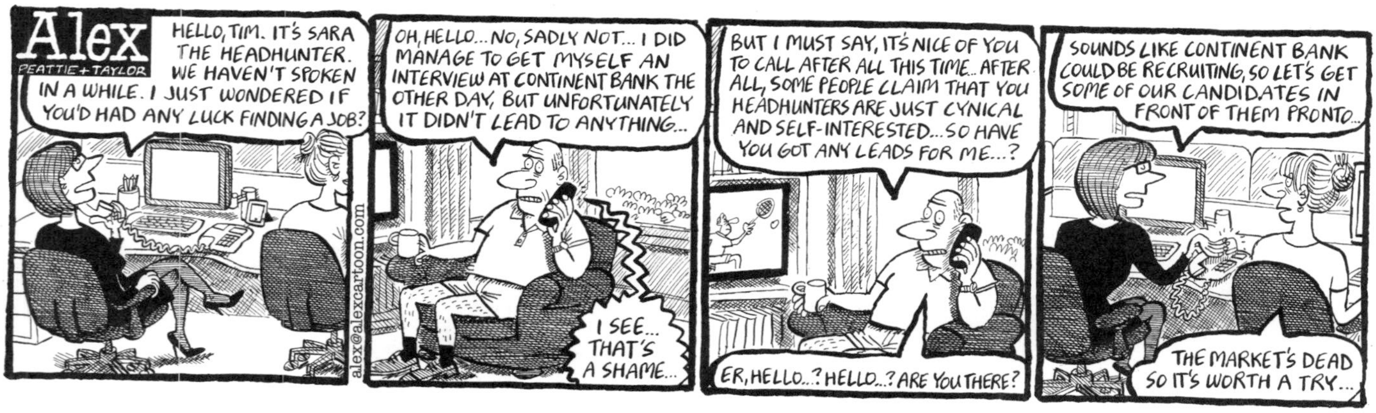
Alex
PEATTIE + TAYLOR
HELLO, TIM. IT'S SARA THE HEADHUNTER. WE HAVEN'T SPOKEN IN A WHILE. I JUST WONDERED IF YOU'D HAD ANY LUCK FINDING A JOB?
alex@alexcartoon.com
OH, HELLO... NO, SADLY NOT... I DID MANAGE TO GET MYSELF AN INTERVIEW AT CONTINENT BANK THE OTHER DAY, BUT UNFORTUNATELY IT DIDN'T LEAD TO ANYTHING...
I SEE... THAT'S A SHAME...
BUT I MUST SAY, IT'S NICE OF YOU TO CALL AFTER ALL THIS TIME... AFTER ALL, SOME PEOPLE CLAIM THAT YOU HEADHUNTERS ARE JUST CYNICAL AND SELF-INTERESTED... SO HAVE YOU GOT ANY LEADS FOR ME...?
ER, HELLO...? HELLO...? ARE YOU THERE?
SOUNDS LIKE CONTINENT BANK COULD BE RECRUITING, SO LET'S GET SOME OF OUR CANDIDATES IN FRONT OF THEM PRONTO...
THE MARKET'S DEAD SO IT'S WORTH A TRY...

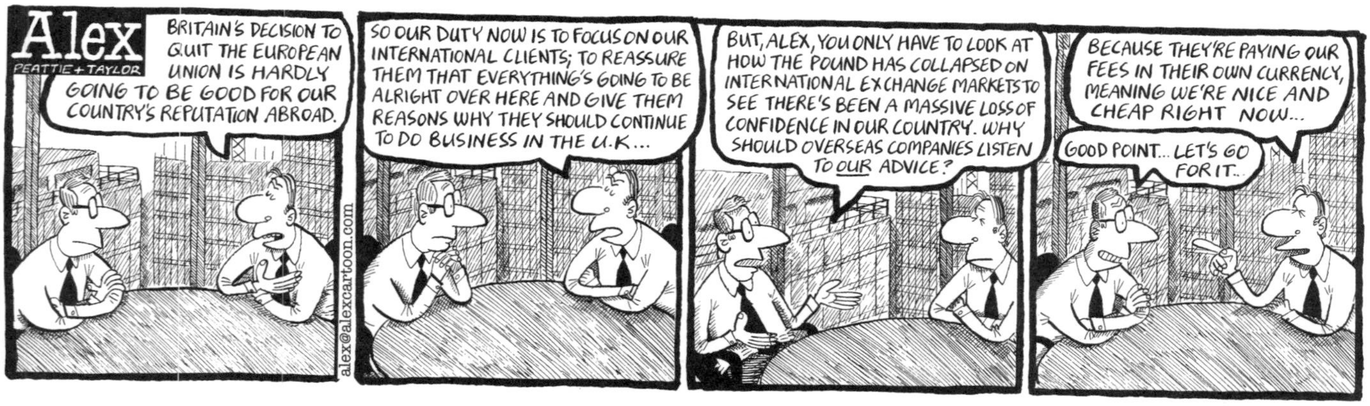
Alex
PEATTIE + TAYLOR
BRITAIN'S DECISION TO QUIT THE EUROPEAN UNION IS HARDLY GOING TO BE GOOD FOR OUR COUNTRY'S REPUTATION ABROAD.
alex@alexcartoon.com
SO OUR DUTY NOW IS TO FOCUS ON OUR INTERNATIONAL CLIENTS; TO REASSURE THEM THAT EVERYTHING'S GOING TO BE ALRIGHT OVER HERE AND GIVE THEM REASONS WHY THEY SHOULD CONTINUE TO DO BUSINESS IN THE U.K...
BUT, ALEX, YOU ONLY HAVE TO LOOK AT HOW THE POUND HAS COLLAPSED ON INTERNATIONAL EXCHANGE MARKETS TO SEE THERE'S BEEN A MASSIVE LOSS OF CONFIDENCE IN OUR COUNTRY. WHY SHOULD OVERSEAS COMPANIES LISTEN TO OUR ADVICE?
BECAUSE THEY'RE PAYING OUR FEES IN THEIR OWN CURRENCY, MEANING WE'RE NICE AND CHEAP RIGHT NOW...
GOOD POINT... LET'S GO FOR IT...

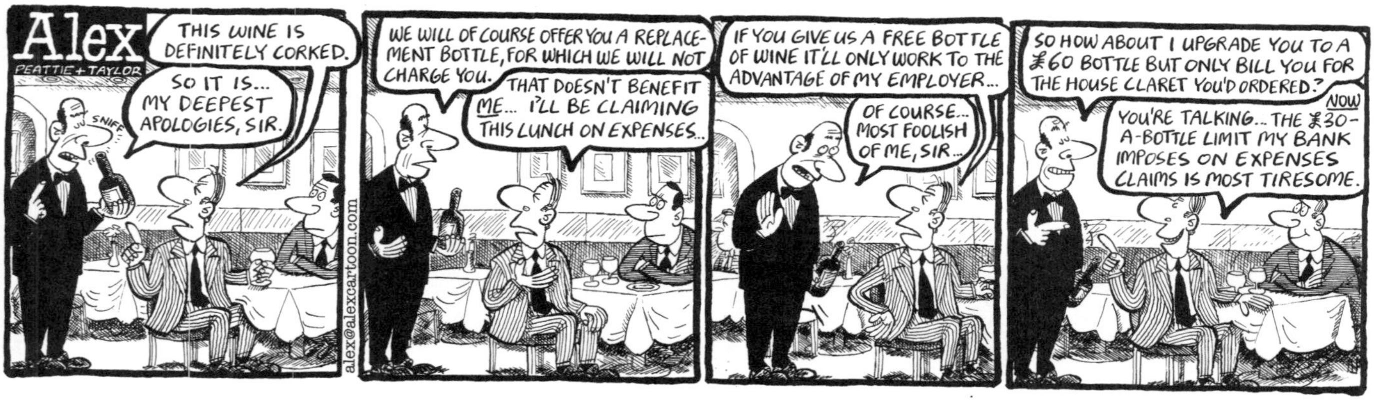
Alex
PEATTIE + TAYLOR
THIS WINE IS DEFINITELY CORKED.
SNIFF
SO IT IS... MY DEEPEST APOLOGIES, SIR.
alex@alexcartoon.com
WE WILL OF COURSE OFFER YOU A REPLACEMENT BOTTLE, FOR WHICH WE WILL NOT CHARGE YOU.
THAT DOESN'T BENEFIT ME... I'LL BE CLAIMING THIS LUNCH ON EXPENSES...
IF YOU GIVE US A FREE BOTTLE OF WINE IT'LL ONLY WORK TO THE ADVANTAGE OF MY EMPLOYER...
OF COURSE... MOST FOOLISH OF ME, SIR...
SO HOW ABOUT I UPGRADE YOU TO A £60 BOTTLE BUT ONLY BILL YOU FOR THE HOUSE CLARET YOU'D ORDERED?
NOW YOU'RE TALKING... THE £30-A-BOTTLE LIMIT MY BANK IMPOSES ON EXPENSES CLAIMS IS MOST TIRESOME.

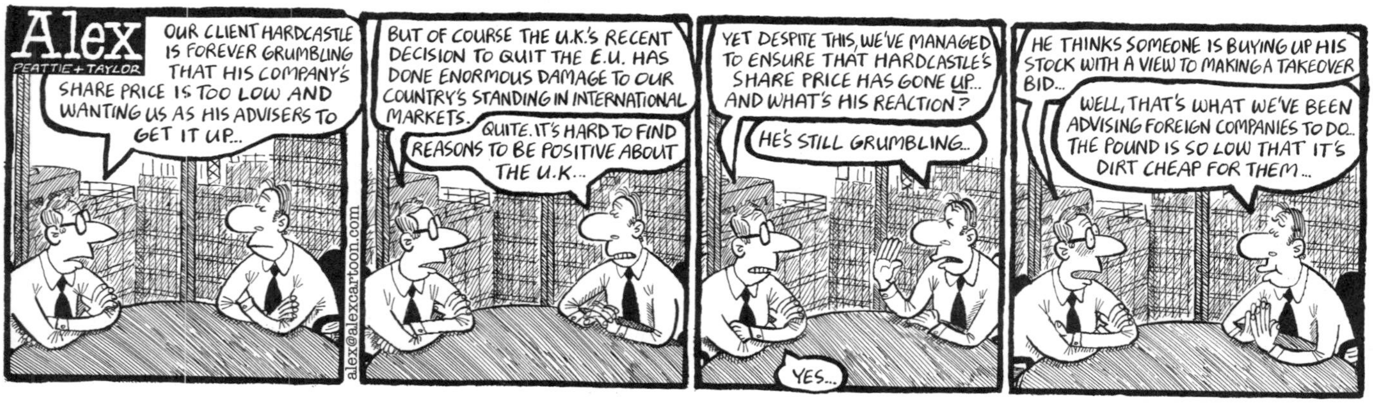
Alex
PEATTIE + TAYLOR
OUR CLIENT HARDCASTLE IS FOREVER GRUMBLING THAT HIS COMPANY'S SHARE PRICE IS TOO LOW AND WANTING US AS HIS ADVISERS TO GET IT UP...
alex@alexcartoon.com
BUT OF COURSE THE U.K.'S RECENT DECISION TO QUIT THE E.U. HAS DONE ENORMOUS DAMAGE TO OUR COUNTRY'S STANDING IN INTERNATIONAL MARKETS.
QUITE. IT'S HARD TO FIND REASONS TO BE POSITIVE ABOUT THE U.K...
YET DESPITE THIS, WE'VE MANAGED TO ENSURE THAT HARDCASTLE'S SHARE PRICE HAS GONE UP... AND WHAT'S HIS REACTION?
HE'S STILL GRUMBLING...
YES...
HE THINKS SOMEONE IS BUYING UP HIS STOCK WITH A VIEW TO MAKING A TAKEOVER BID...
WELL, THAT'S WHAT WE'VE BEEN ADVISING FOREIGN COMPANIES TO DO... THE POUND IS SO LOW THAT IT'S DIRT CHEAP FOR THEM...

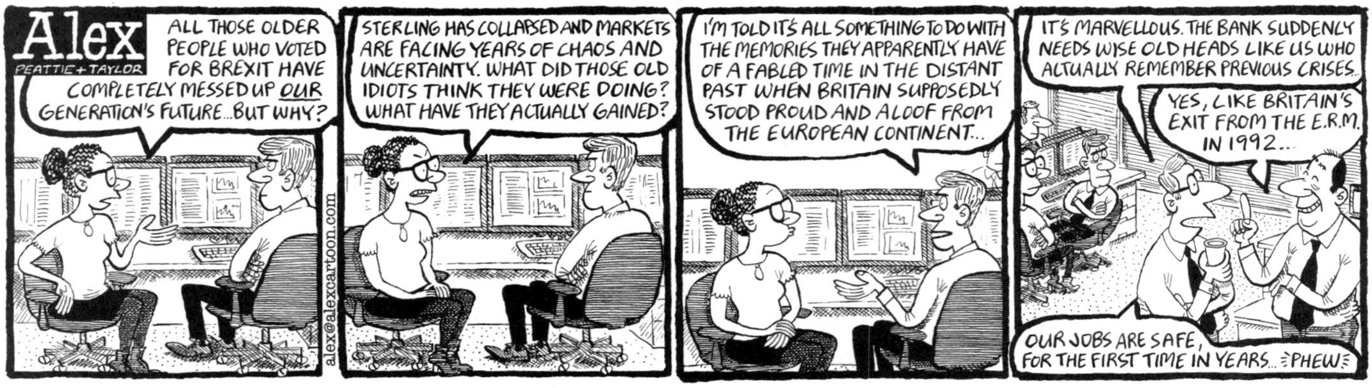
Alex
PEATTIE + TAYLOR
ALL THOSE OLDER PEOPLE WHO VOTED FOR BREXIT HAVE COMPLETELY MESSED UP OUR GENERATION'S FUTURE...BUT WHY?
STERLING HAS COLLAPSED AND MARKETS ARE FACING YEARS OF CHAOS AND UNCERTAINTY. WHAT DID THOSE OLD IDIOTS THINK THEY WERE DOING? WHAT HAVE THEY ACTUALLY GAINED?
I'M TOLD IT'S ALL SOMETHING TO DO WITH THE MEMORIES THEY APPARENTLY HAVE OF A FABLED TIME IN THE DISTANT PAST WHEN BRITAIN SUPPOSEDLY STOOD PROUD AND ALOOF FROM THE EUROPEAN CONTINENT...
IT'S MARVELLOUS. THE BANK SUDDENLY NEEDS WISE OLD HEADS LIKE US WHO ACTUALLY REMEMBER PREVIOUS CRISES...
YES, LIKE BRITAIN'S EXIT FROM THE E.R.M. IN 1992...
OUR JOBS ARE SAFE, FOR THE FIRST TIME IN YEARS... PHEW
alex@alexcartoon.com

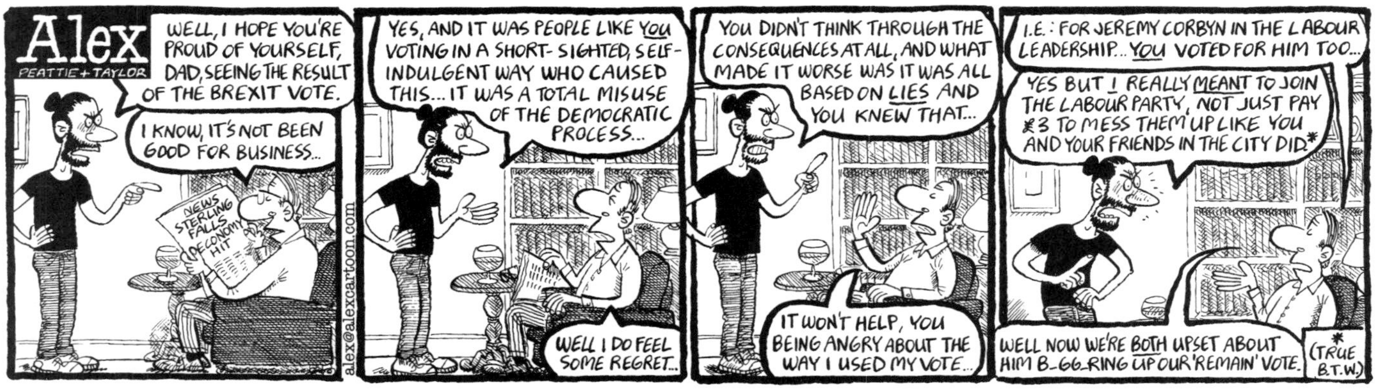
Alex
PEATTIE + TAYLOR
WELL, I HOPE YOU'RE PROUD OF YOURSELF, DAD, SEEING THE RESULT OF THE BREXIT VOTE.
I KNOW, IT'S NOT BEEN GOOD FOR BUSINESS...
NEWS
STERLING FALLS
ECONOMY HIT
YES, AND IT WAS PEOPLE LIKE YOU VOTING IN A SHORT-SIGHTED, SELF-INDULGENT WAY WHO CAUSED THIS... IT WAS A TOTAL MISUSE OF THE DEMOCRATIC PROCESS...
WELL I DO FEEL SOME REGRET...
YOU DIDN'T THINK THROUGH THE CONSEQUENCES AT ALL, AND WHAT MADE IT WORSE WAS IT WAS ALL BASED ON LIES AND YOU KNEW THAT...
IT WON'T HELP, YOU BEING ANGRY ABOUT THE WAY I USED MY VOTE...
I.E.: FOR JEREMY CORBYN IN THE LABOUR LEADERSHIP... YOU VOTED FOR HIM TOO...
YES BUT I REALLY MEANT TO JOIN THE LABOUR PARTY, NOT JUST PAY £3 TO MESS THEM UP LIKE YOU AND YOUR FRIENDS IN THE CITY DID*
WELL NOW WE'RE BOTH UPSET ABOUT HIM B_GG_RING UP OUR 'REMAIN' VOTE.
* (TRUE B.T.W.)
alex@alexcartoon.com

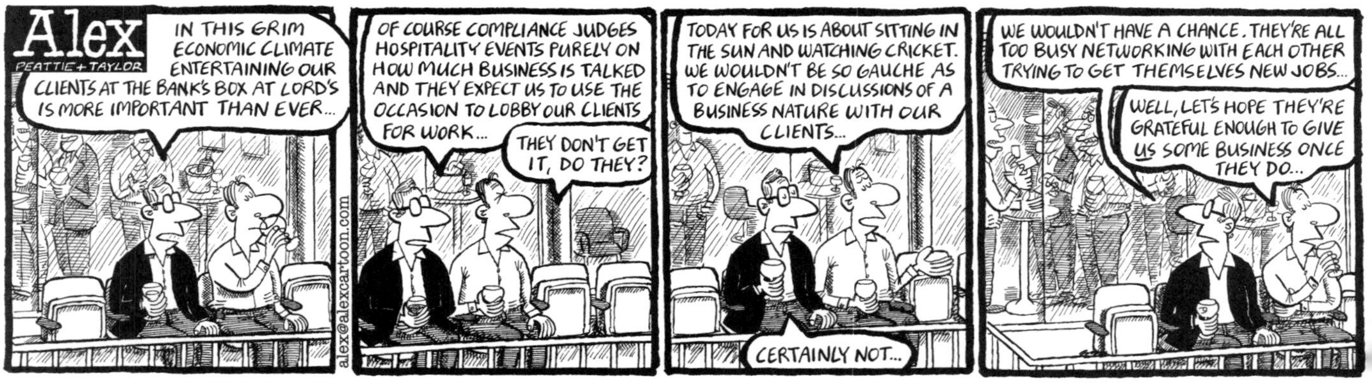
Alex
PEATTIE + TAYLOR
IN THIS GRIM ECONOMIC CLIMATE ENTERTAINING OUR CLIENTS AT THE BANK'S BOX AT LORD'S IS MORE IMPORTANT THAN EVER...
OF COURSE COMPLIANCE JUDGES HOSPITALITY EVENTS PURELY ON HOW MUCH BUSINESS IS TALKED AND THEY EXPECT US TO USE THE OCCASION TO LOBBY OUR CLIENTS FOR WORK...
THEY DON'T GET IT, DO THEY?
TODAY FOR US IS ABOUT SITTING IN THE SUN AND WATCHING CRICKET. WE WOULDN'T BE SO GAUCHE AS TO ENGAGE IN DISCUSSIONS OF A BUSINESS NATURE WITH OUR CLIENTS...
CERTAINLY NOT...
WE WOULDN'T HAVE A CHANCE. THEY'RE ALL TOO BUSY NETWORKING WITH EACH OTHER TRYING TO GET THEMSELVES NEW JOBS...
WELL, LET'S HOPE THEY'RE GRATEFUL ENOUGH TO GIVE US SOME BUSINESS ONCE THEY DO...
alex@alexcartoon.com

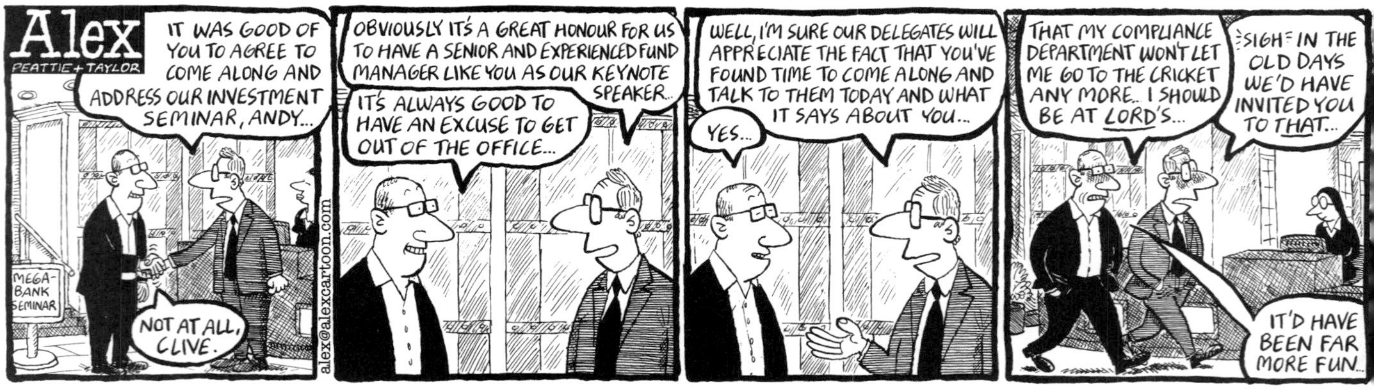
Alex
PEATTIE + TAYLOR
IT WAS GOOD OF YOU TO AGREE TO COME ALONG AND ADDRESS OUR INVESTMENT SEMINAR, ANDY...
MEGA-BANK SEMINAR
NOT AT ALL, CLIVE.
OBVIOUSLY IT'S A GREAT HONOUR FOR US TO HAVE A SENIOR AND EXPERIENCED FUND MANAGER LIKE YOU AS OUR KEYNOTE SPEAKER...
IT'S ALWAYS GOOD TO HAVE AN EXCUSE TO GET OUT OF THE OFFICE...
WELL, I'M SURE OUR DELEGATES WILL APPRECIATE THE FACT THAT YOU'VE FOUND TIME TO COME ALONG AND TALK TO THEM TODAY AND WHAT IT SAYS ABOUT YOU...
YES...
THAT MY COMPLIANCE DEPARTMENT WON'T LET ME GO TO THE CRICKET ANY MORE.. I SHOULD BE AT LORD'S...
SIGH IN THE OLD DAYS WE'D HAVE INVITED YOU TO THAT...
IT'D HAVE BEEN FAR MORE FUN...
alex@alexcartoon.com

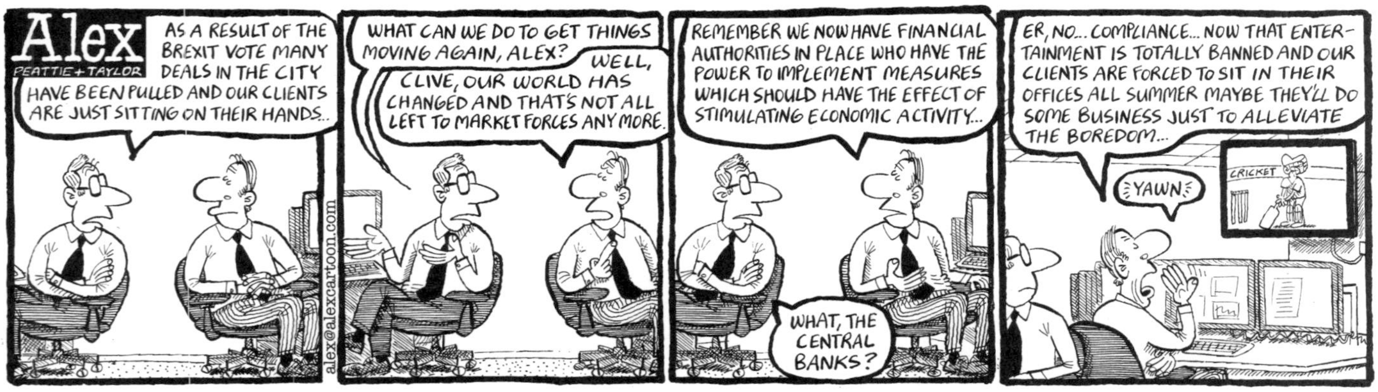
Alex
PEATTIE + TAYLOR
AS A RESULT OF THE BREXIT VOTE MANY DEALS IN THE CITY HAVE BEEN PULLED AND OUR CLIENTS ARE JUST SITTING ON THEIR HANDS...
alex@alexcartoon.com
WHAT CAN WE DO TO GET THINGS MOVING AGAIN, ALEX?
WELL, CLIVE, OUR WORLD HAS CHANGED AND THAT'S NOT ALL LEFT TO MARKET FORCES ANY MORE.
REMEMBER WE NOW HAVE FINANCIAL AUTHORITIES IN PLACE WHO HAVE THE POWER TO IMPLEMENT MEASURES WHICH SHOULD HAVE THE EFFECT OF STIMULATING ECONOMIC ACTIVITY...
WHAT, THE CENTRAL BANKS?
ER, NO... COMPLIANCE... NOW THAT ENTERTAINMENT IS TOTALLY BANNED AND OUR CLIENTS ARE FORCED TO SIT IN THEIR OFFICES ALL SUMMER MAYBE THEY'LL DO SOME BUSINESS JUST TO ALLEVIATE THE BOREDOM...
YAWN
CRICKET

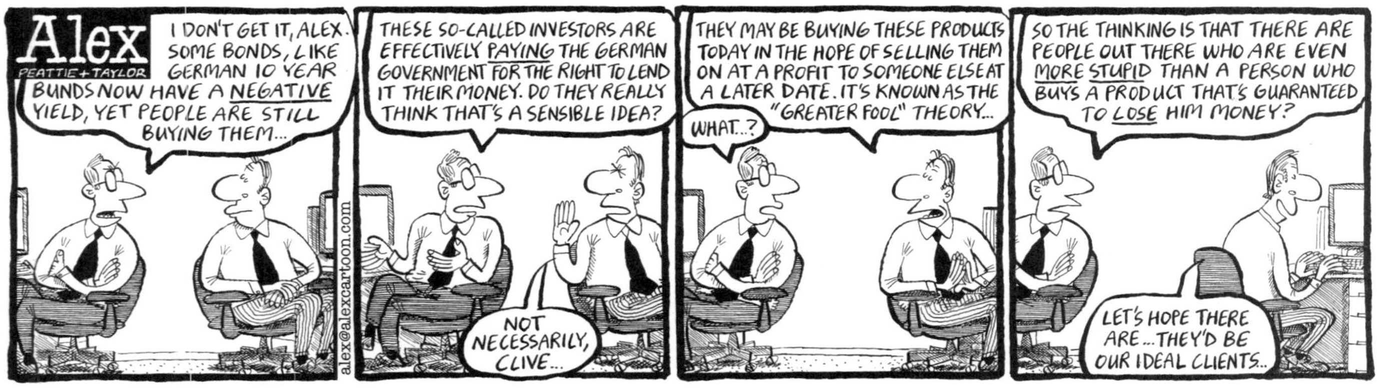
Alex
PEATTIE + TAYLOR
I DON'T GET IT, ALEX. SOME BONDS, LIKE GERMAN 10 YEAR BUNDS NOW HAVE A NEGATIVE YIELD, YET PEOPLE ARE STILL BUYING THEM...
alex@alexcartoon.com
THESE SO-CALLED INVESTORS ARE EFFECTIVELY PAYING THE GERMAN GOVERNMENT FOR THE RIGHT TO LEND IT THEIR MONEY. DO THEY REALLY THINK THAT'S A SENSIBLE IDEA?
NOT NECESSARILY, CLIVE...
THEY MAY BE BUYING THESE PRODUCTS TODAY IN THE HOPE OF SELLING THEM ON AT A PROFIT TO SOMEONE ELSE AT A LATER DATE. IT'S KNOWN AS THE "GREATER FOOL" THEORY...
WHAT...?
SO THE THINKING IS THAT THERE ARE PEOPLE OUT THERE WHO ARE EVEN MORE STUPID THAN A PERSON WHO BUYS A PRODUCT THAT'S GUARANTEED TO LOSE HIM MONEY?
LET'S HOPE THERE ARE... THEY'D BE OUR IDEAL CLIENTS...

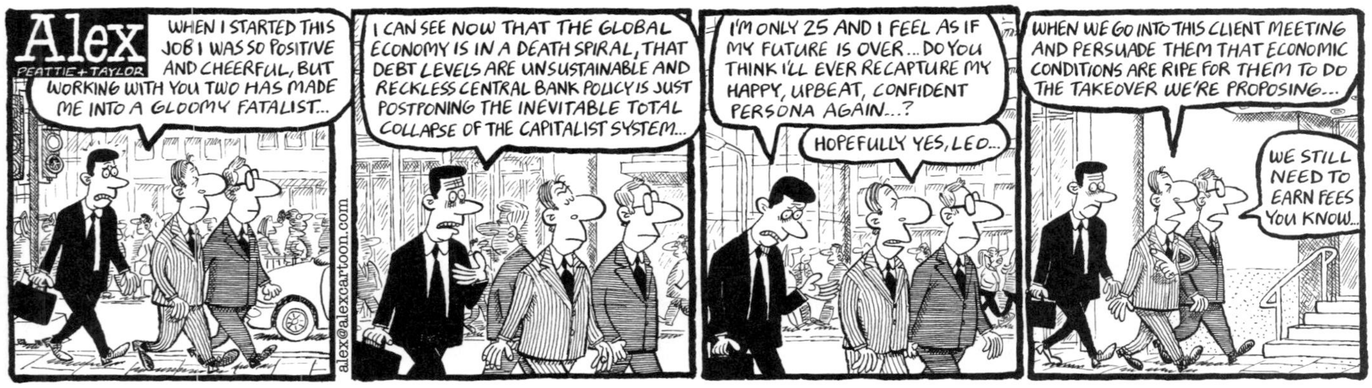
Alex
PEATTIE + TAYLOR
WHEN I STARTED THIS JOB I WAS SO POSITIVE AND CHEERFUL, BUT WORKING WITH YOU TWO HAS MADE ME INTO A GLOOMY FATALIST...
alex@alexcartoon.com
I CAN SEE NOW THAT THE GLOBAL ECONOMY IS IN A DEATH SPIRAL, THAT DEBT LEVELS ARE UNSUSTAINABLE AND RECKLESS CENTRAL BANK POLICY IS JUST POSTPONING THE INEVITABLE TOTAL COLLAPSE OF THE CAPITALIST SYSTEM...
I'M ONLY 25 AND I FEEL AS IF MY FUTURE IS OVER... DO YOU THINK I'LL EVER RECAPTURE MY HAPPY, UPBEAT, CONFIDENT PERSONA AGAIN...?
HOPEFULLY YES, LEO...
WHEN WE GO INTO THIS CLIENT MEETING AND PERSUADE THEM THAT ECONOMIC CONDITIONS ARE RIPE FOR THEM TO DO THE TAKEOVER WE'RE PROPOSING...
WE STILL NEED TO EARN FEES YOU KNOW...

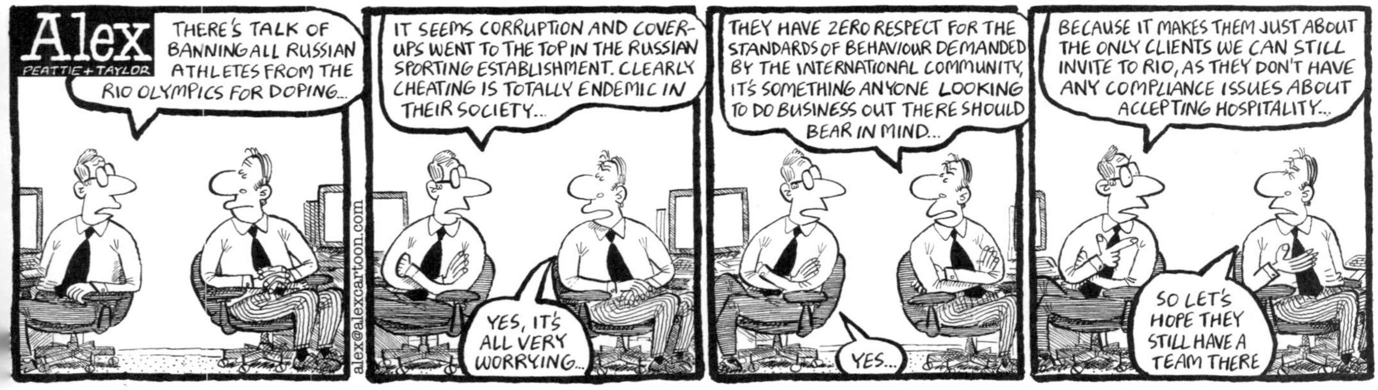
Alex
PEATTIE + TAYLOR
THERE'S TALK OF BANNING ALL RUSSIAN ATHLETES FROM THE RIO OLYMPICS FOR DOPING...
alex@alexcartoon.com
IT SEEMS CORRUPTION AND COVER-UPS WENT TO THE TOP IN THE RUSSIAN SPORTING ESTABLISHMENT. CLEARLY CHEATING IS TOTALLY ENDEMIC IN THEIR SOCIETY...
YES, IT'S ALL VERY WORRYING...
THEY HAVE ZERO RESPECT FOR THE STANDARDS OF BEHAVIOUR DEMANDED BY THE INTERNATIONAL COMMUNITY, IT'S SOMETHING ANYONE LOOKING TO DO BUSINESS OUT THERE SHOULD BEAR IN MIND...
YES...
BECAUSE IT MAKES THEM JUST ABOUT THE ONLY CLIENTS WE CAN STILL INVITE TO RIO, AS THEY DON'T HAVE ANY COMPLIANCE ISSUES ABOUT ACCEPTING HOSPITALITY...
SO LET'S HOPE THEY STILL HAVE A TEAM THERE

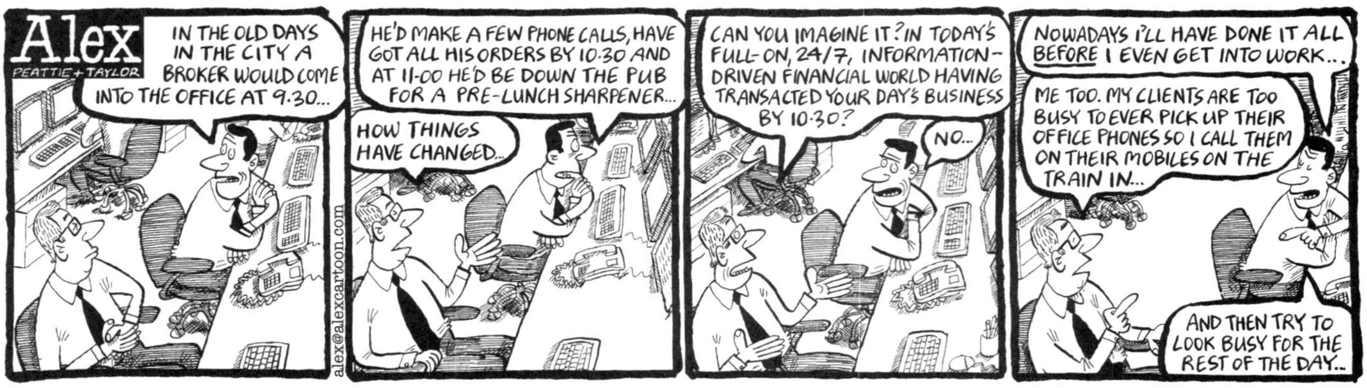
Alex
PEATTIE + TAYLOR
IN THE OLD DAYS IN THE CITY A BROKER WOULD COME INTO THE OFFICE AT 9.30...
HE'D MAKE A FEW PHONE CALLS, HAVE GOT ALL HIS ORDERS BY 10.30 AND AT 11-00 HE'D BE DOWN THE PUB FOR A PRE-LUNCH SHARPENER...
HOW THINGS HAVE CHANGED...
alex@alexcartoon.com
CAN YOU IMAGINE IT? IN TODAY'S FULL-ON, 24/7, INFORMATION-DRIVEN FINANCIAL WORLD HAVING TRANSACTED YOUR DAY'S BUSINESS BY 10.30?
NO...
NOWADAYS I'LL HAVE DONE IT ALL BEFORE I EVEN GET INTO WORK...
ME TOO. MY CLIENTS ARE TOO BUSY TO EVER PICK UP THEIR OFFICE PHONES SO I CALL THEM ON THEIR MOBILES ON THE TRAIN IN...
AND THEN TRY TO LOOK BUSY FOR THE REST OF THE DAY...

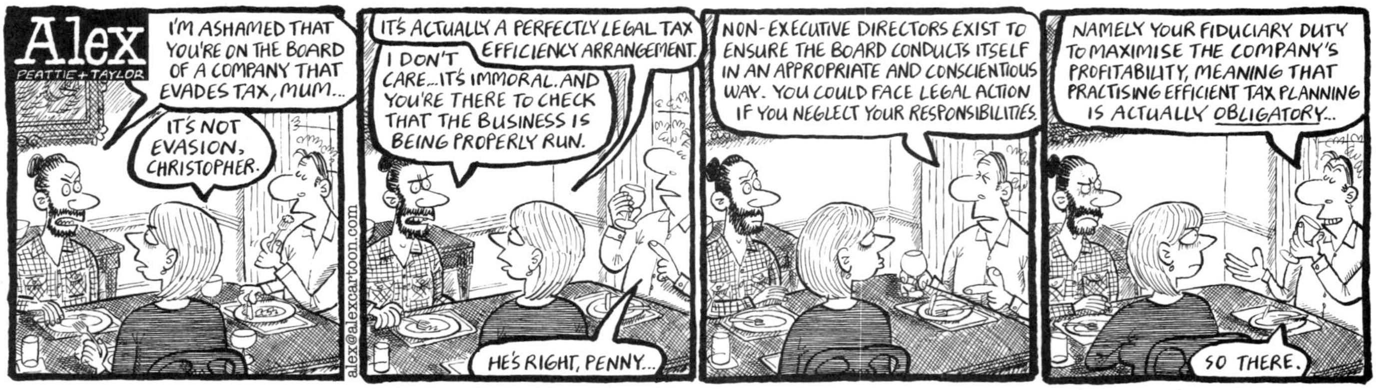
Alex
PEATTIE + TAYLOR
I'M ASHAMED THAT YOU'RE ON THE BOARD OF A COMPANY THAT EVADES TAX, MUM...
IT'S NOT EVASION, CHRISTOPHER.
alex@alexcartoon.com
IT'S ACTUALLY A PERFECTLY LEGAL TAX EFFICIENCY ARRANGEMENT.
I DON'T CARE... IT'S IMMORAL. AND YOU'RE THERE TO CHECK THAT THE BUSINESS IS BEING PROPERLY RUN.
HE'S RIGHT, PENNY...
NON-EXECUTIVE DIRECTORS EXIST TO ENSURE THE BOARD CONDUCTS ITSELF IN AN APPROPRIATE AND CONSCIENTIOUS WAY. YOU COULD FACE LEGAL ACTION IF YOU NEGLECT YOUR RESPONSIBILITIES.
NAMELY YOUR FIDUCIARY DUTY TO MAXIMISE THE COMPANY'S PROFITABILITY, MEANING THAT PRACTISING EFFICIENT TAX PLANNING IS ACTUALLY OBLIGATORY...
SO THERE.

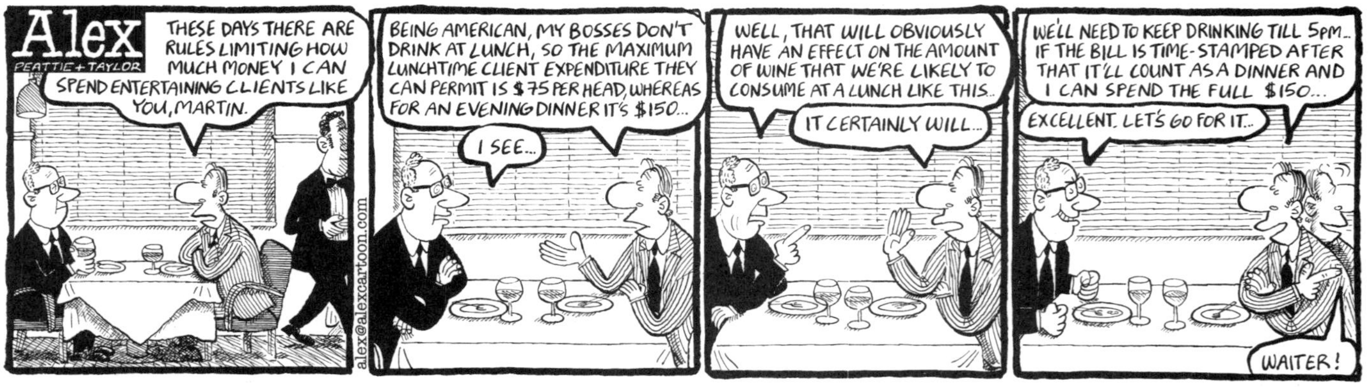
Alex
PEATTIE + TAYLOR
THESE DAYS THERE ARE RULES LIMITING HOW MUCH MONEY I CAN SPEND ENTERTAINING CLIENTS LIKE YOU, MARTIN.
alex@alexcartoon.com
BEING AMERICAN, MY BOSSES DON'T DRINK AT LUNCH, SO THE MAXIMUM LUNCHTIME CLIENT EXPENDITURE THEY CAN PERMIT IS $75 PER HEAD, WHEREAS FOR AN EVENING DINNER IT'S $150...
I SEE...
WELL, THAT WILL OBVIOUSLY HAVE AN EFFECT ON THE AMOUNT OF WINE THAT WE'RE LIKELY TO CONSUME AT A LUNCH LIKE THIS...
IT CERTAINLY WILL...
WE'LL NEED TO KEEP DRINKING TILL 5PM... IF THE BILL IS TIME-STAMPED AFTER THAT IT'LL COUNT AS A DINNER AND I CAN SPEND THE FULL $150...
EXCELLENT. LET'S GO FOR IT...
WAITER!

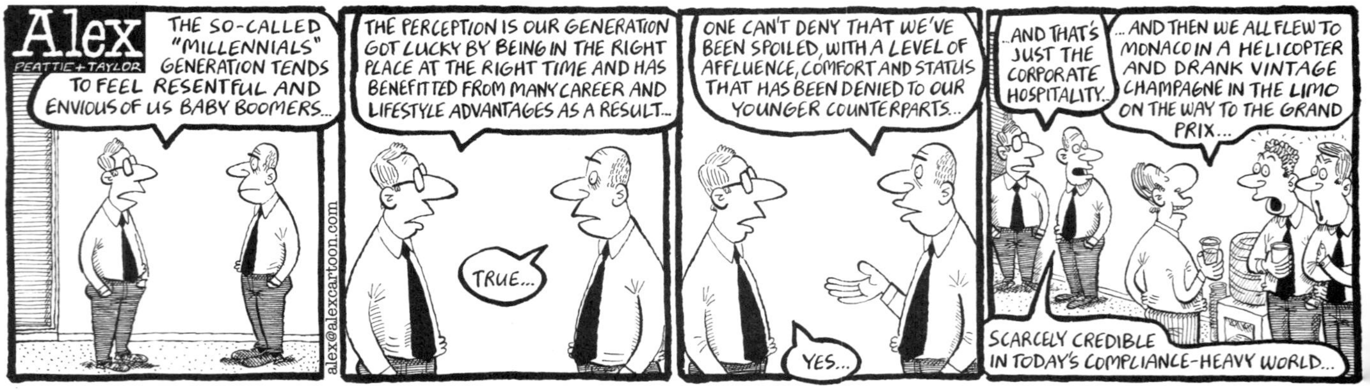
Alex
PEATTIE + TAYLOR
THE SO-CALLED "MILLENNIALS" GENERATION TENDS TO FEEL RESENTFUL AND ENVIOUS OF US BABY BOOMERS...
alex@alexcartoon.com
THE PERCEPTION IS OUR GENERATION GOT LUCKY BY BEING IN THE RIGHT PLACE AT THE RIGHT TIME AND HAS BENEFITTED FROM MANY CAREER AND LIFESTYLE ADVANTAGES AS A RESULT...
TRUE...
ONE CAN'T DENY THAT WE'VE BEEN SPOILED, WITH A LEVEL OF AFFLUENCE, COMFORT AND STATUS THAT HAS BEEN DENIED TO OUR YOUNGER COUNTERPARTS...
YES...
...AND THAT'S JUST THE CORPORATE HOSPITALITY...
...AND THEN WE ALL FLEW TO MONACO IN A HELICOPTER AND DRANK VINTAGE CHAMPAGNE IN THE LIMO ON THE WAY TO THE GRAND PRIX...
SCARCELY CREDIBLE IN TODAY'S COMPLIANCE-HEAVY WORLD...

ALEX WENT ON HOLIDAY. BUT CLIVE DIDN'T...

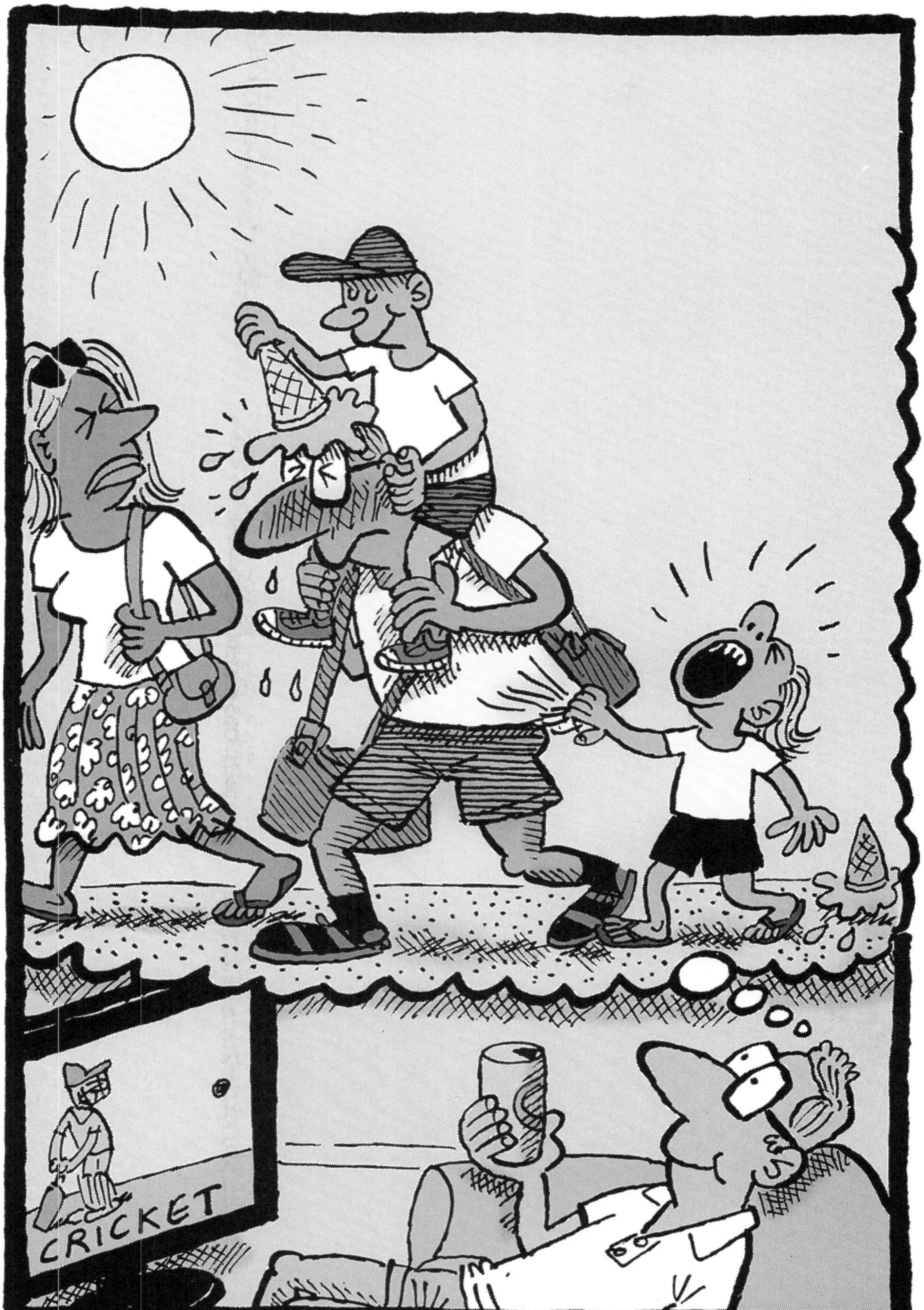
CRICKET

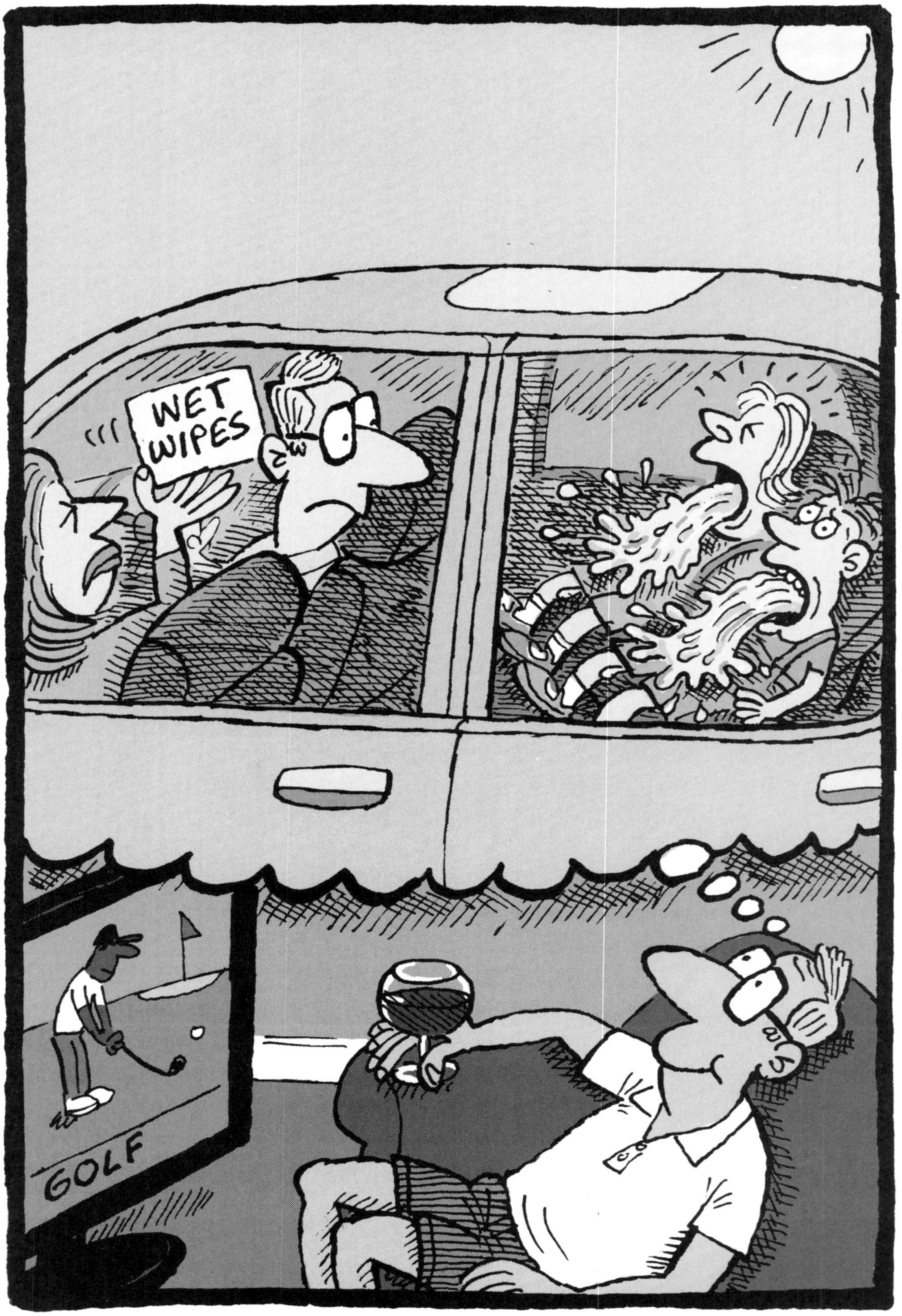
WET WIPES
GOLF

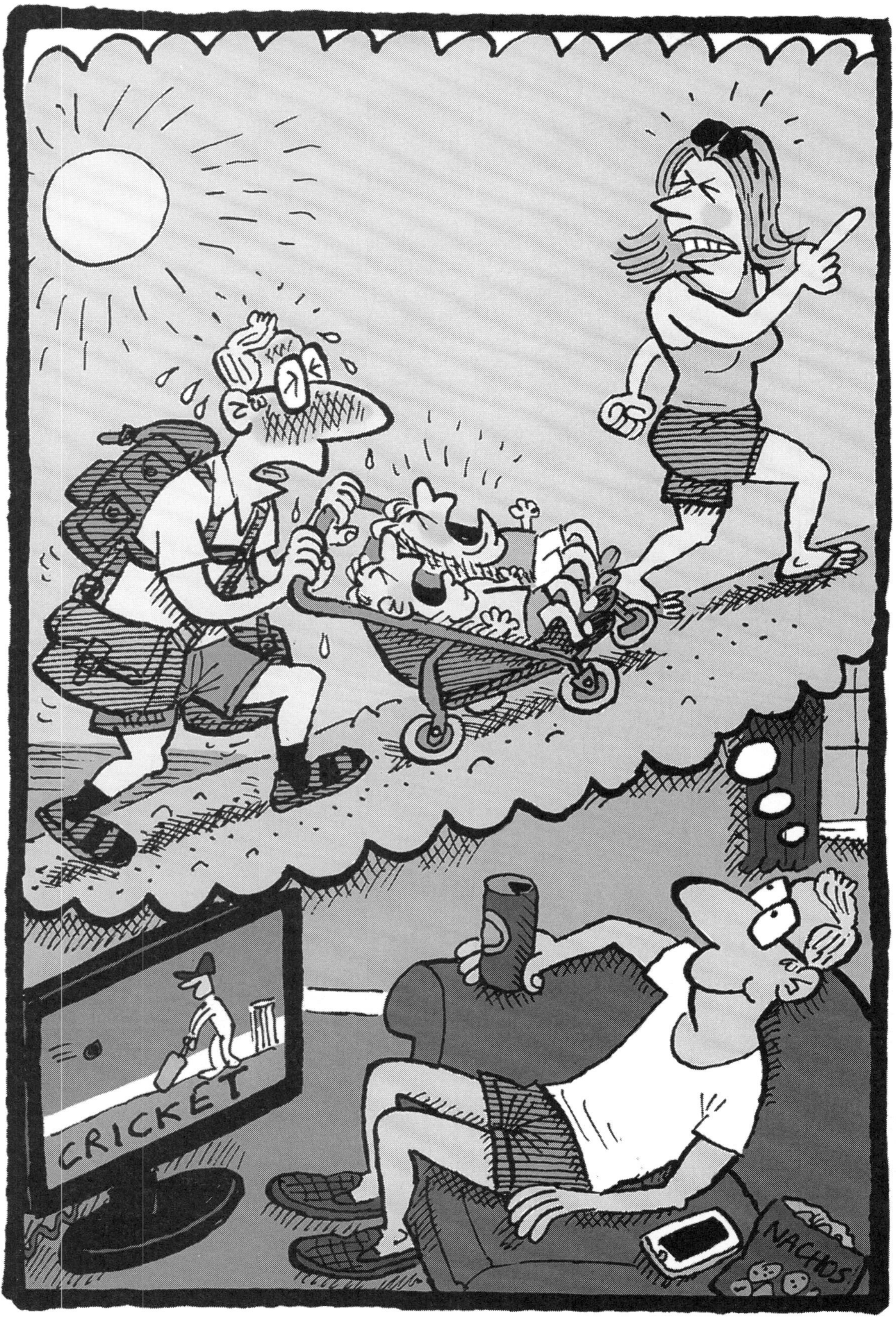
CRICKET
NACHOS!

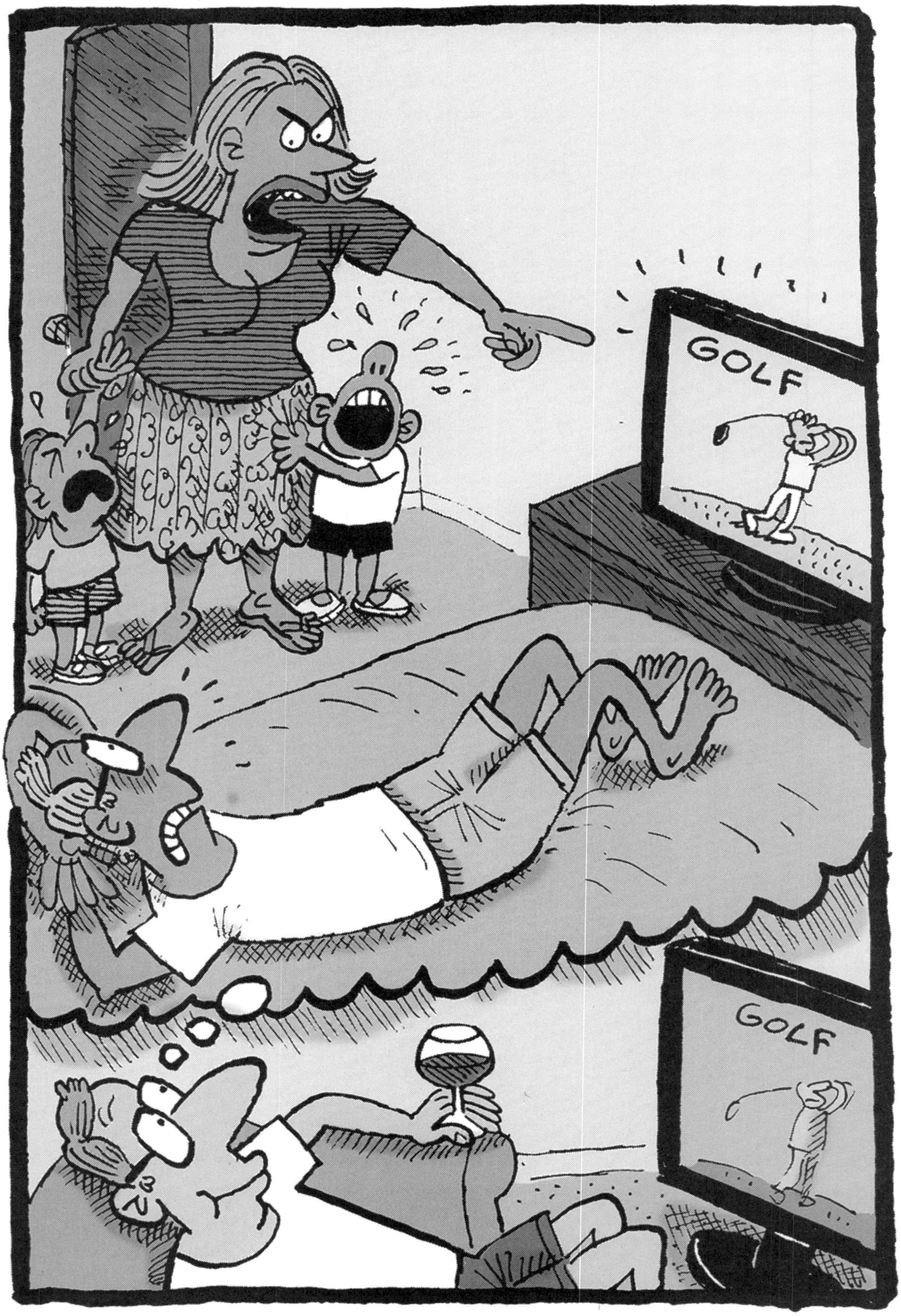
GOLF
GOLF

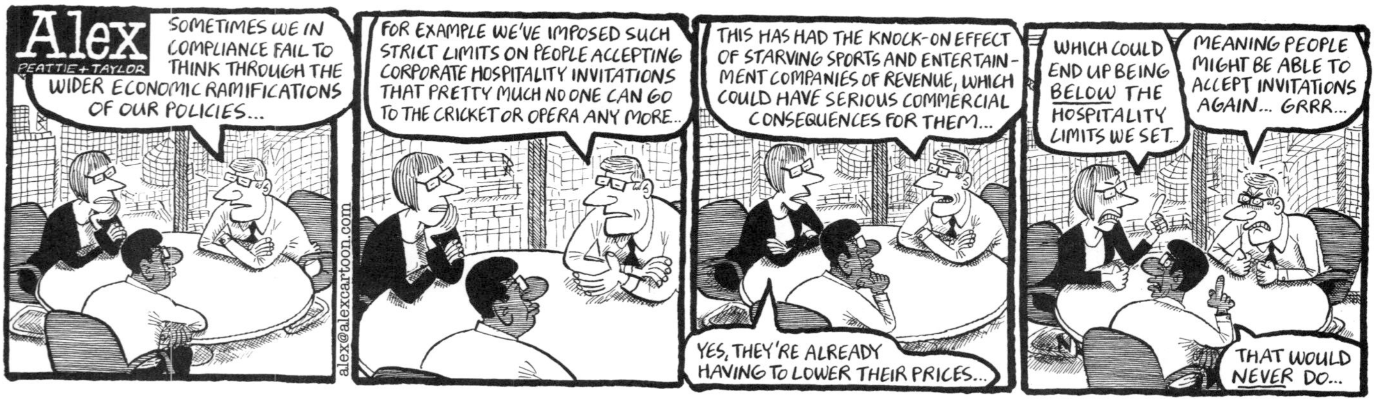
Alex
PEATTIE + TAYLOR
SOMETIMES WE IN COMPLIANCE FAIL TO THINK THROUGH THE WIDER ECONOMIC RAMIFICATIONS OF OUR POLICIES...
FOR EXAMPLE WE'VE IMPOSED SUCH STRICT LIMITS ON PEOPLE ACCEPTING CORPORATE HOSPITALITY INVITATIONS THAT PRETTY MUCH NO ONE CAN GO TO THE CRICKET OR OPERA ANY MORE...
alex@alexcartoon.com
THIS HAS HAD THE KNOCK-ON EFFECT OF STARVING SPORTS AND ENTERTAINMENT COMPANIES OF REVENUE, WHICH COULD HAVE SERIOUS COMMERCIAL CONSEQUENCES FOR THEM...
YES, THEY'RE ALREADY HAVING TO LOWER THEIR PRICES...
WHICH COULD END UP BEING BELOW THE HOSPITALITY LIMITS WE SET...
MEANING PEOPLE MIGHT BE ABLE TO ACCEPT INVITATIONS AGAIN... GRRR...
THAT WOULD NEVER DO...

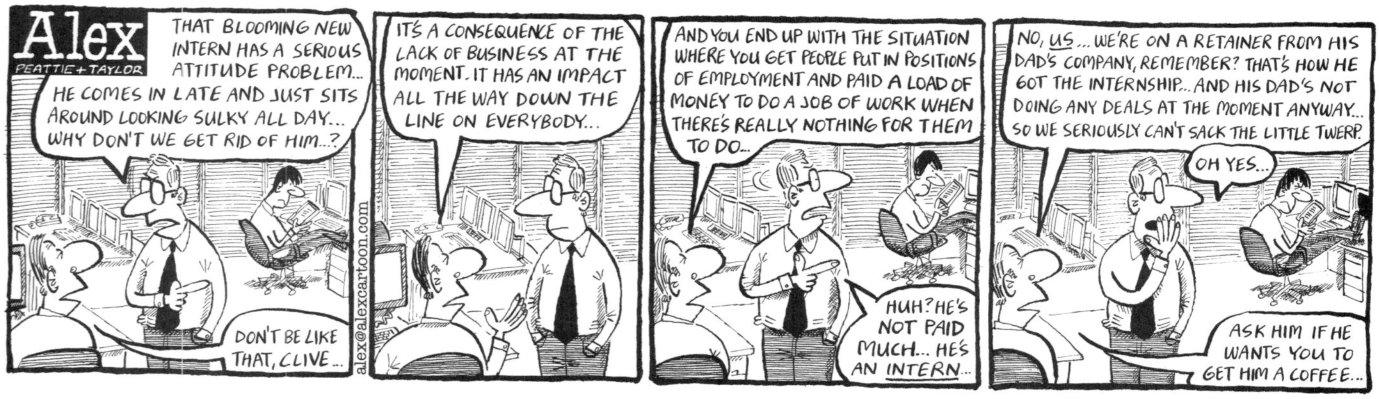
Alex
PEATTIE + TAYLOR
THAT BLOOMING NEW INTERN HAS A SERIOUS ATTITUDE PROBLEM...
HE COMES IN LATE AND JUST SITS AROUND LOOKING SULKY ALL DAY... WHY DON'T WE GET RID OF HIM...?
DON'T BE LIKE THAT, CLIVE...
IT'S A CONSEQUENCE OF THE LACK OF BUSINESS AT THE MOMENT. IT HAS AN IMPACT ALL THE WAY DOWN THE LINE ON EVERYBODY...
alex@alexcartoon.com
AND YOU END UP WITH THE SITUATION WHERE YOU GET PEOPLE PUT IN POSITIONS OF EMPLOYMENT AND PAID A LOAD OF MONEY TO DO A JOB OF WORK WHEN THERE'S REALLY NOTHING FOR THEM TO DO...
HUH? HE'S NOT PAID MUCH... HE'S AN INTERN...
NO, US... WE'RE ON A RETAINER FROM HIS DAD'S COMPANY, REMEMBER? THAT'S HOW HE GOT THE INTERNSHIP... AND HIS DAD'S NOT DOING ANY DEALS AT THE MOMENT ANYWAY... SO WE SERIOUSLY CAN'T SACK THE LITTLE TWERP.
OH YES...
ASK HIM IF HE WANTS YOU TO GET HIM A COFFEE...

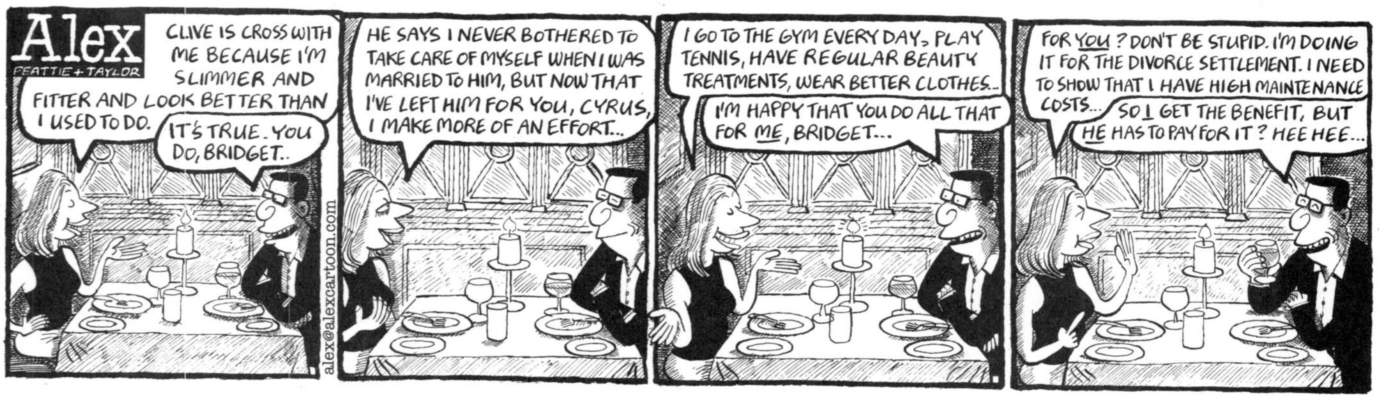
Alex
PEATTIE + TAYLOR
CLIVE IS CROSS WITH ME BECAUSE I'M SLIMMER AND FITTER AND LOOK BETTER THAN I USED TO DO.
IT'S TRUE. YOU DO, BRIDGET..
alex@alexcartoon.com
HE SAYS I NEVER BOTHERED TO TAKE CARE OF MYSELF WHEN I WAS MARRIED TO HIM, BUT NOW THAT I'VE LEFT HIM FOR YOU, CYRUS, I MAKE MORE OF AN EFFORT...
I GO TO THE GYM EVERY DAY, PLAY TENNIS, HAVE REGULAR BEAUTY TREATMENTS, WEAR BETTER CLOTHES...
I'M HAPPY THAT YOU DO ALL THAT FOR ME, BRIDGET...
FOR YOU? DON'T BE STUPID. I'M DOING IT FOR THE DIVORCE SETTLEMENT. I NEED TO SHOW THAT I HAVE HIGH MAINTENANCE COSTS...
SO I GET THE BENEFIT, BUT HE HAS TO PAY FOR IT? HEE HEE...

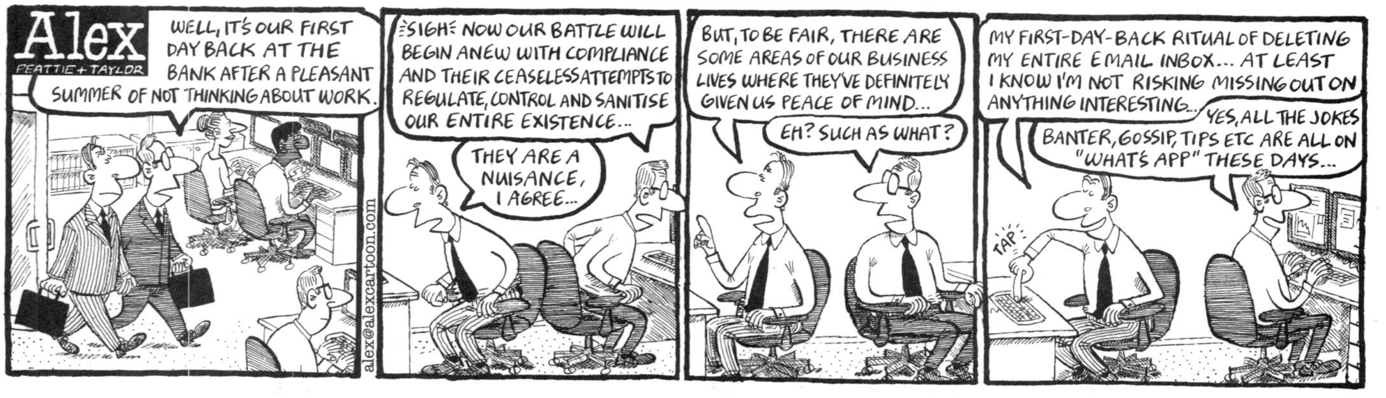
Alex
PEATTIE + TAYLOR
WELL, IT'S OUR FIRST DAY BACK AT THE BANK AFTER A PLEASANT SUMMER OF NOT THINKING ABOUT WORK.
alex@alexcartoon.com
SIGH NOW OUR BATTLE WILL BEGIN ANEW WITH COMPLIANCE AND THEIR CEASELESS ATTEMPTS TO REGULATE, CONTROL AND SANITISE OUR ENTIRE EXISTENCE...
THEY ARE A NUISANCE, I AGREE...
BUT, TO BE FAIR, THERE ARE SOME AREAS OF OUR BUSINESS LIVES WHERE THEY'VE DEFINITELY GIVEN US PEACE OF MIND...
EH? SUCH AS WHAT?
MY FIRST-DAY-BACK RITUAL OF DELETING MY ENTIRE EMAIL INBOX... AT LEAST I KNOW I'M NOT RISKING MISSING OUT ON ANYTHING INTERESTING...
YES, ALL THE JOKES BANTER, GOSSIP, TIPS ETC ARE ALL ON "WHAT'S APP" THESE DAYS...
TAP

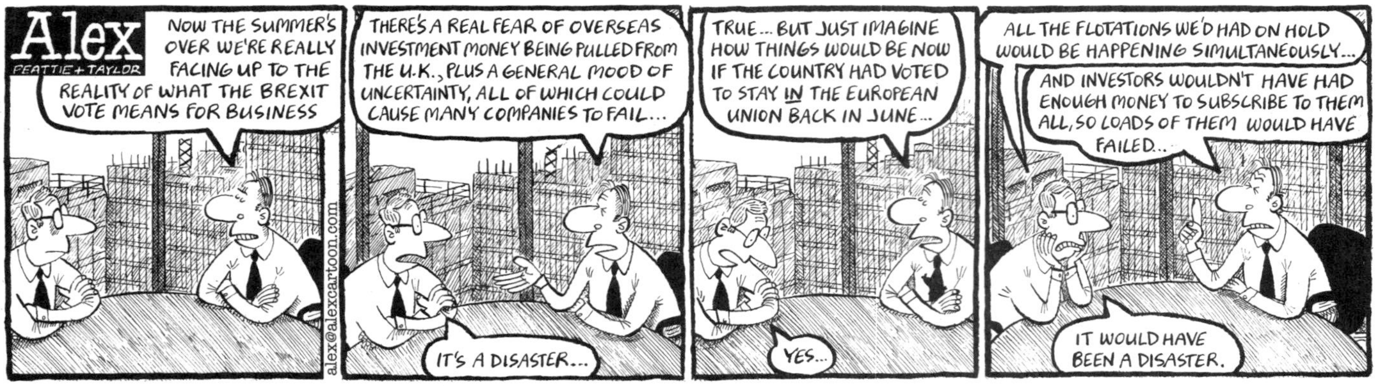
Alex
PEATTIE + TAYLOR
NOW THE SUMMER'S OVER WE'RE REALLY FACING UP TO THE REALITY OF WHAT THE BREXIT VOTE MEANS FOR BUSINESS
alex@alexcartoon.com
THERE'S A REAL FEAR OF OVERSEAS INVESTMENT MONEY BEING PULLED FROM THE U.K., PLUS A GENERAL MOOD OF UNCERTAINTY, ALL OF WHICH COULD CAUSE MANY COMPANIES TO FAIL...
IT'S A DISASTER...
TRUE... BUT JUST IMAGINE HOW THINGS WOULD BE NOW IF THE COUNTRY HAD VOTED TO STAY IN THE EUROPEAN UNION BACK IN JUNE...
YES...
ALL THE FLOTATIONS WE'D HAD ON HOLD WOULD BE HAPPENING SIMULTANEOUSLY...
AND INVESTORS WOULDN'T HAVE HAD ENOUGH MONEY TO SUBSCRIBE TO THEM ALL, SO LOADS OF THEM WOULD HAVE FAILED...
IT WOULD HAVE BEEN A DISASTER.

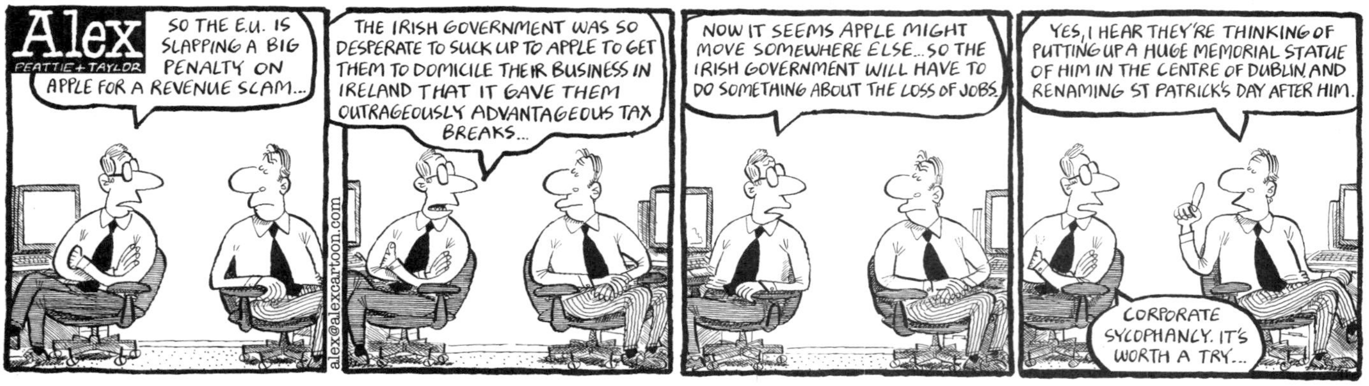
Alex
PEATTIE + TAYLOR
SO THE E.U. IS SLAPPING A BIG PENALTY ON APPLE FOR A REVENUE SCAM...
alex@alexcartoon.com
THE IRISH GOVERNMENT WAS SO DESPERATE TO SUCK UP TO APPLE TO GET THEM TO DOMICILE THEIR BUSINESS IN IRELAND THAT IT GAVE THEM OUTRAGEOUSLY ADVANTAGEOUS TAX BREAKS...
NOW IT SEEMS APPLE MIGHT MOVE SOMEWHERE ELSE... SO THE IRISH GOVERNMENT WILL HAVE TO DO SOMETHING ABOUT THE LOSS OF JOBS
YES, I HEAR THEY'RE THINKING OF PUTTING UP A HUGE MEMORIAL STATUE OF HIM IN THE CENTRE OF DUBLIN AND RENAMING ST PATRICK'S DAY AFTER HIM.
CORPORATE SYCOPHANCY. IT'S WORTH A TRY...

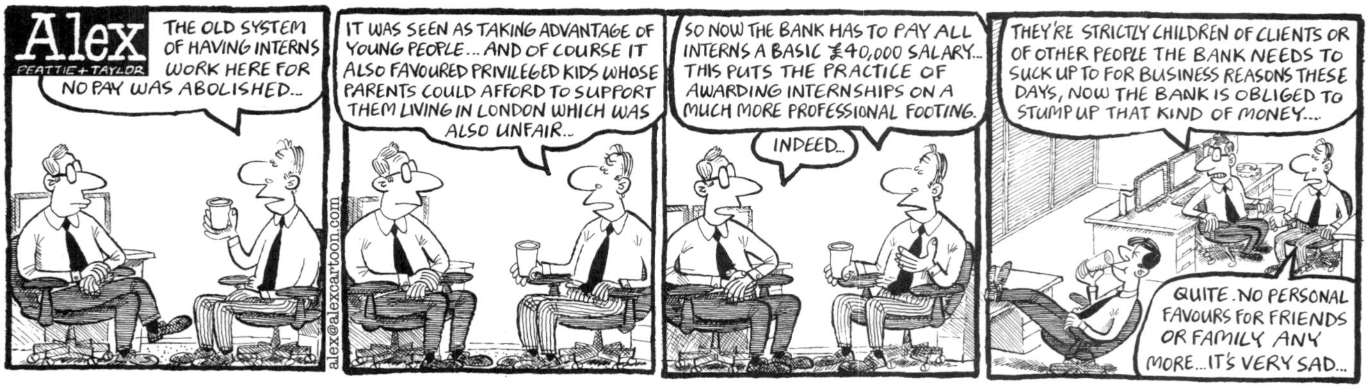
Alex
PEATTIE + TAYLOR
THE OLD SYSTEM OF HAVING INTERNS WORK HERE FOR NO PAY WAS ABOLISHED...
alex@alexcartoon.com
IT WAS SEEN AS TAKING ADVANTAGE OF YOUNG PEOPLE... AND OF COURSE IT ALSO FAVOURED PRIVILEGED KIDS WHOSE PARENTS COULD AFFORD TO SUPPORT THEM LIVING IN LONDON WHICH WAS ALSO UNFAIR...
SO NOW THE BANK HAS TO PAY ALL INTERNS A BASIC £40,000 SALARY... THIS PUTS THE PRACTICE OF AWARDING INTERNSHIPS ON A MUCH MORE PROFESSIONAL FOOTING.
INDEED...
THEY'RE STRICTLY CHILDREN OF CLIENTS OR OF OTHER PEOPLE THE BANK NEEDS TO SUCK UP TO FOR BUSINESS REASONS THESE DAYS, NOW THE BANK IS OBLIGED TO STUMP UP THAT KIND OF MONEY....
QUITE. NO PERSONAL FAVOURS FOR FRIENDS OR FAMILY ANY MORE... IT'S VERY SAD...

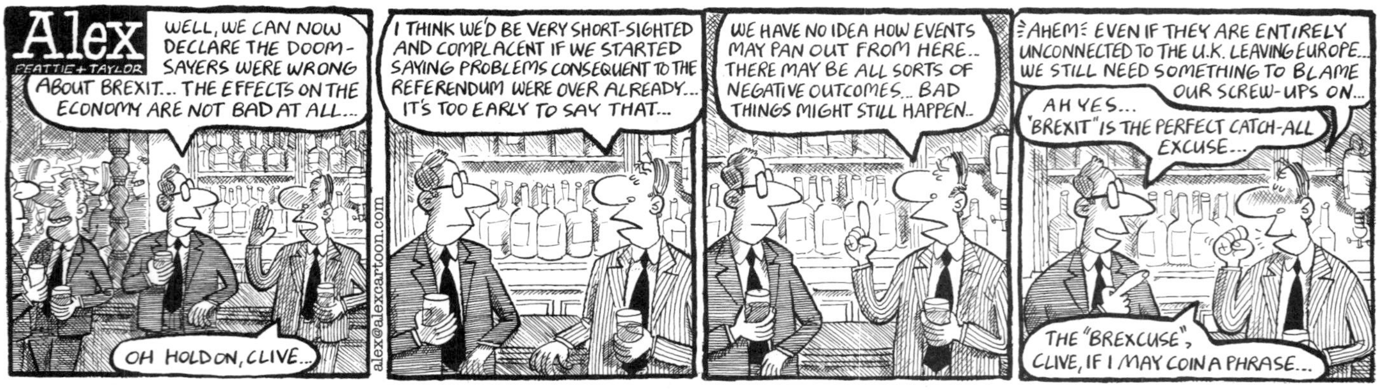
Alex
PEATTIE + TAYLOR
WELL, WE CAN NOW DECLARE THE DOOM-SAYERS WERE WRONG ABOUT BREXIT... THE EFFECTS ON THE ECONOMY ARE NOT BAD AT ALL...
OH HOLD ON, CLIVE...
alex@alexcartoon.com
I THINK WE'D BE VERY SHORT-SIGHTED AND COMPLACENT IF WE STARTED SAYING PROBLEMS CONSEQUENT TO THE REFERENDUM WERE OVER ALREADY... IT'S TOO EARLY TO SAY THAT...
WE HAVE NO IDEA HOW EVENTS MAY PAN OUT FROM HERE... THERE MAY BE ALL SORTS OF NEGATIVE OUTCOMES... BAD THINGS MIGHT STILL HAPPEN...
AHEM EVEN IF THEY ARE ENTIRELY UNCONNECTED TO THE U.K. LEAVING EUROPE... WE STILL NEED SOMETHING TO BLAME OUR SCREW-UPS ON...
AH YES... "BREXIT" IS THE PERFECT CATCH-ALL EXCUSE...
THE "BREXCUSE", CLIVE, IF I MAY COIN A PHRASE...

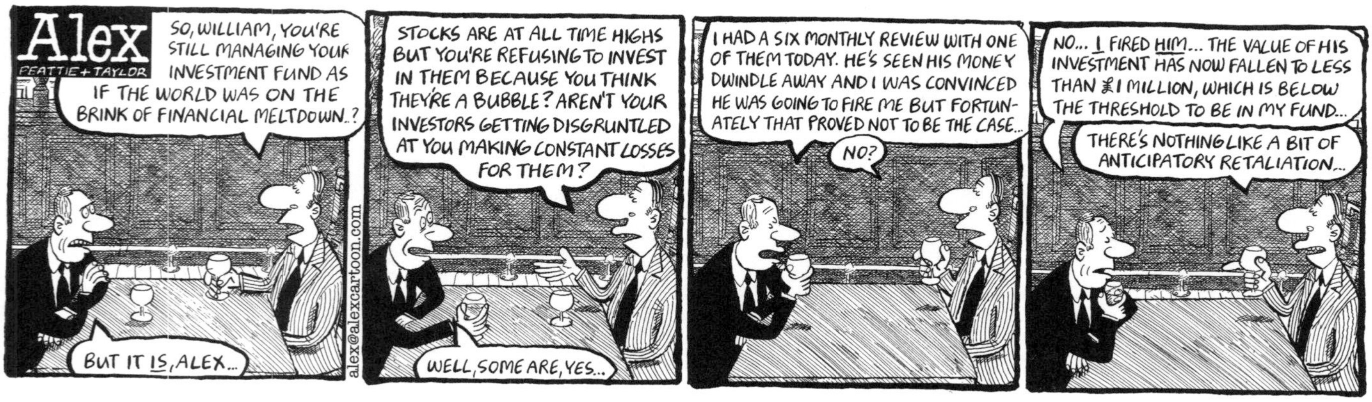
Alex
PEATTIE + TAYLOR
SO, WILLIAM, YOU'RE STILL MANAGING YOUR INVESTMENT FUND AS IF THE WORLD WAS ON THE BRINK OF FINANCIAL MELTDOWN..?
BUT IT IS, ALEX...
alex@alexcartoon.com
STOCKS ARE AT ALL TIME HIGHS BUT YOU'RE REFUSING TO INVEST IN THEM BECAUSE YOU THINK THEY'RE A BUBBLE? AREN'T YOUR INVESTORS GETTING DISGRUNTLED AT YOU MAKING CONSTANT LOSSES FOR THEM?
WELL, SOME ARE, YES...
I HAD A SIX MONTHLY REVIEW WITH ONE OF THEM TODAY. HE'S SEEN HIS MONEY DWINDLE AWAY AND I WAS CONVINCED HE WAS GOING TO FIRE ME BUT FORTUNATELY THAT PROVED NOT TO BE THE CASE...
NO?
NO... I FIRED HIM... THE VALUE OF HIS INVESTMENT HAS NOW FALLEN TO LESS THAN £1 MILLION, WHICH IS BELOW THE THRESHOLD TO BE IN MY FUND...
THERE'S NOTHING LIKE A BIT OF ANTICIPATORY RETALIATION...

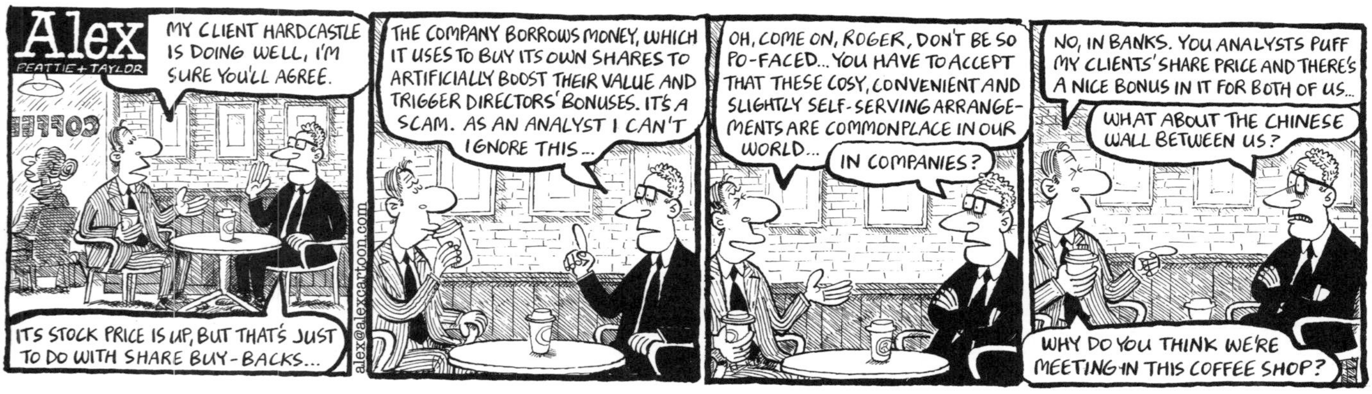
Alex
PEATTIE + TAYLOR
MY CLIENT HARDCASTLE IS DOING WELL, I'M SURE YOU'LL AGREE.
COFFEE
ITS STOCK PRICE IS UP, BUT THAT'S JUST TO DO WITH SHARE BUY-BACKS...
alex@alexcartoon.com
THE COMPANY BORROWS MONEY, WHICH IT USES TO BUY ITS OWN SHARES TO ARTIFICIALLY BOOST THEIR VALUE AND TRIGGER DIRECTORS' BONUSES. IT'S A SCAM. AS AN ANALYST I CAN'T IGNORE THIS...
OH, COME ON, ROGER, DON'T BE SO PO-FACED... YOU HAVE TO ACCEPT THAT THESE COSY, CONVENIENT AND SLIGHTLY SELF-SERVING ARRANGEMENTS ARE COMMONPLACE IN OUR WORLD...
IN COMPANIES?
NO, IN BANKS. YOU ANALYSTS PUFF MY CLIENTS' SHARE PRICE AND THERE'S A NICE BONUS IN IT FOR BOTH OF US...
WHAT ABOUT THE CHINESE WALL BETWEEN US?
WHY DO YOU THINK WE'RE MEETING IN THIS COFFEE SHOP?

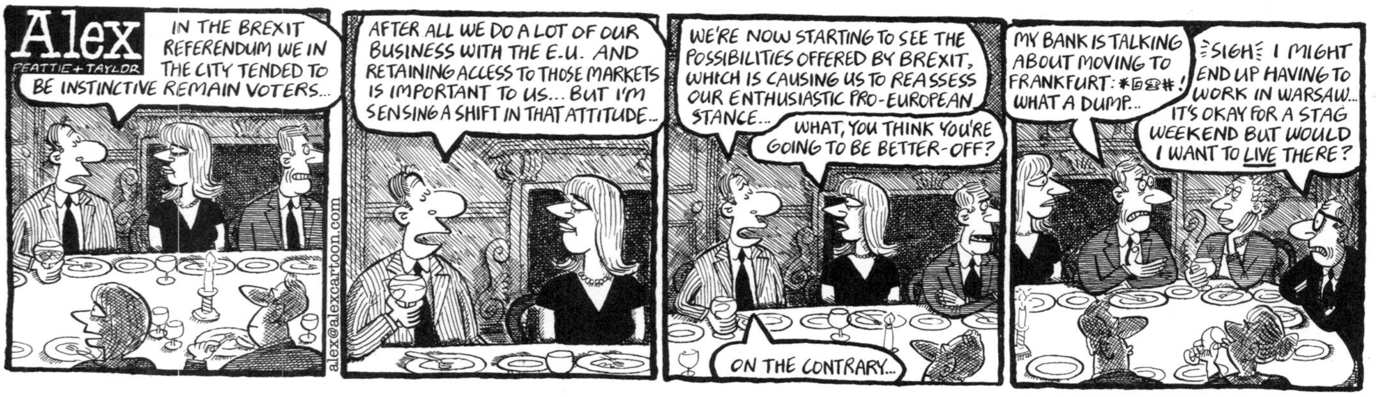
Alex
PEATTIE + TAYLOR
IN THE BREXIT REFERENDUM WE IN THE CITY TENDED TO BE INSTINCTIVE REMAIN VOTERS...
alex@alexcartoon.com
AFTER ALL WE DO A LOT OF OUR BUSINESS WITH THE E.U. AND RETAINING ACCESS TO THOSE MARKETS IS IMPORTANT TO US... BUT I'M SENSING A SHIFT IN THAT ATTITUDE...
WE'RE NOW STARTING TO SEE THE POSSIBILITIES OFFERED BY BREXIT, WHICH IS CAUSING US TO REASSESS OUR ENTHUSIASTIC PRO-EUROPEAN STANCE...
WHAT, YOU THINK YOU'RE GOING TO BE BETTER-OFF?
ON THE CONTRARY...
MY BANK IS TALKING ABOUT MOVING TO FRANKFURT:
WHAT A DUMP...
SIGH I MIGHT END UP HAVING TO WORK IN WARSAW... IT'S OKAY FOR A STAG WEEKEND BUT WOULD I WANT TO LIVE THERE?

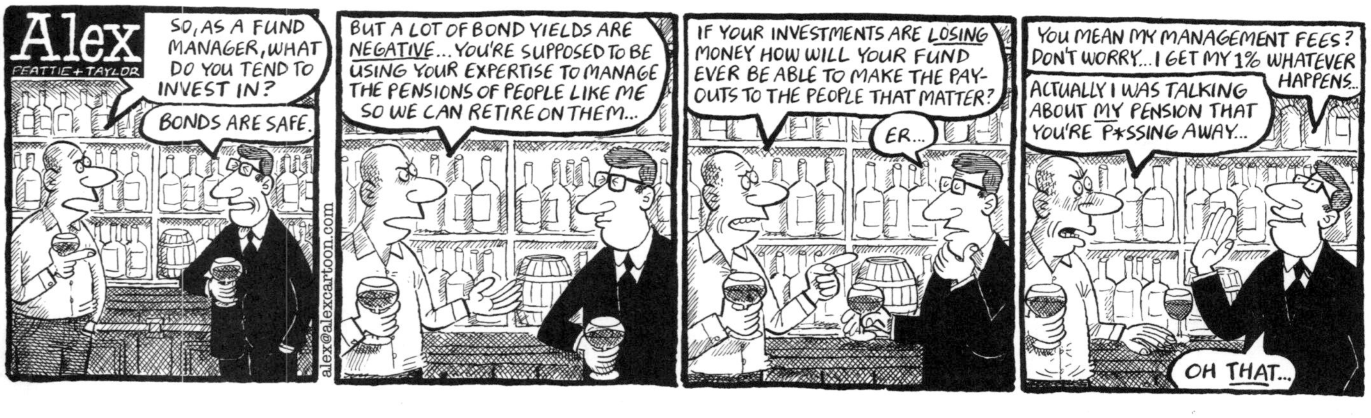
Alex
PEATTIE + TAYLOR
SO, AS A FUND MANAGER, WHAT DO YOU TEND TO INVEST IN?
BONDS ARE SAFE.
alex@alexcartoon.com
BUT A LOT OF BOND YIELDS ARE NEGATIVE... YOU'RE SUPPOSED TO BE USING YOUR EXPERTISE TO MANAGE THE PENSIONS OF PEOPLE LIKE ME SO WE CAN RETIRE ON THEM...
IF YOUR INVESTMENTS ARE LOSING MONEY HOW WILL YOUR FUND EVER BE ABLE TO MAKE THE PAY-OUTS TO THE PEOPLE THAT MATTER?
ER...
YOU MEAN MY MANAGEMENT FEES? DON'T WORRY... I GET MY 1% WHATEVER HAPPENS...
ACTUALLY I WAS TALKING ABOUT MY PENSION THAT YOU'RE P*SSING AWAY...
OH THAT...

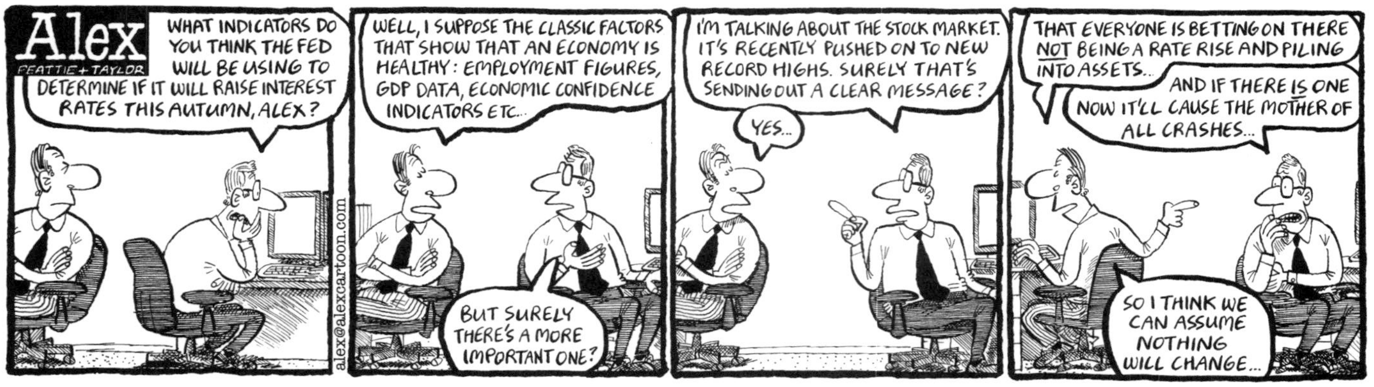
Alex
BEATTIE + TAYLOR
WHAT INDICATORS DO YOU THINK THE FED WILL BE USING TO DETERMINE IF IT WILL RAISE INTEREST RATES THIS AUTUMN, ALEX?
WELL, I SUPPOSE THE CLASSIC FACTORS THAT SHOW THAT AN ECONOMY IS HEALTHY: EMPLOYMENT FIGURES, GDP DATA, ECONOMIC CONFIDENCE INDICATORS ETC...
BUT SURELY THERE'S A MORE IMPORTANT ONE?
alex@alexcartoon.com
I'M TALKING ABOUT THE STOCK MARKET. IT'S RECENTLY PUSHED ON TO NEW RECORD HIGHS. SURELY THAT'S SENDING OUT A CLEAR MESSAGE?
YES...
THAT EVERYONE IS BETTING ON THERE NOT BEING A RATE RISE AND PILING INTO ASSETS...
AND IF THERE IS ONE NOW IT'LL CAUSE THE MOTHER OF ALL CRASHES...
SO I THINK WE CAN ASSUME NOTHING WILL CHANGE...

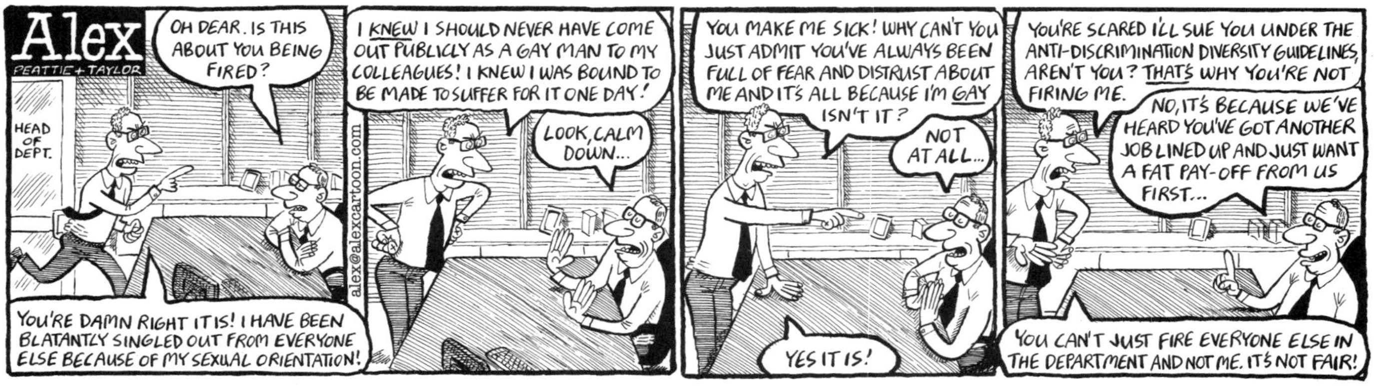
Alex
BEATTIE + TAYLOR
OH DEAR. IS THIS ABOUT YOU BEING FIRED?
HEAD OF DEPT.
YOU'RE DAMN RIGHT IT IS! I HAVE BEEN BLATANTLY SINGLED OUT FROM EVERYONE ELSE BECAUSE OF MY SEXUAL ORIENTATION!
I KNEW I SHOULD NEVER HAVE COME OUT PUBLICLY AS A GAY MAN TO MY COLLEAGUES! I KNEW I WAS BOUND TO BE MADE TO SUFFER FOR IT ONE DAY!
LOOK, CALM DOWN...
alex@alexcartoon.com
YOU MAKE ME SICK! WHY CAN'T YOU JUST ADMIT YOU'VE ALWAYS BEEN FULL OF FEAR AND DISTRUST ABOUT ME AND IT'S ALL BECAUSE I'M GAY ISN'T IT?
NOT AT ALL...
YES IT IS!
YOU'RE SCARED I'LL SUE YOU UNDER THE ANTI-DISCRIMINATION DIVERSITY GUIDELINES, AREN'T YOU? THAT'S WHY YOU'RE NOT FIRING ME.
NO, IT'S BECAUSE WE'VE HEARD YOU'VE GOT ANOTHER JOB LINED UP AND JUST WANT A FAT PAY-OFF FROM US FIRST...
YOU CAN'T JUST FIRE EVERYONE ELSE IN THE DEPARTMENT AND NOT ME. IT'S NOT FAIR!

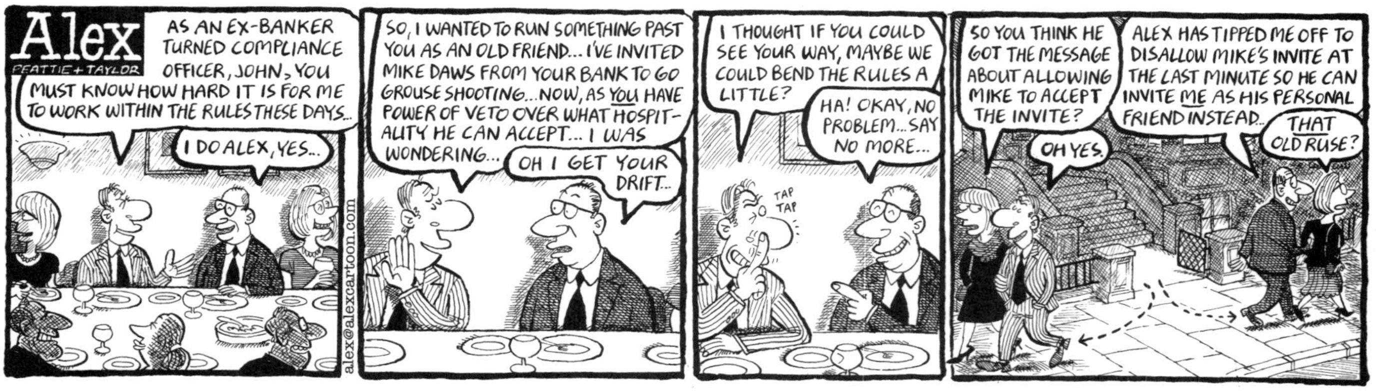
Alex
BEATTIE + TAYLOR
AS AN EX-BANKER TURNED COMPLIANCE OFFICER, JOHN, YOU MUST KNOW HOW HARD IT IS FOR ME TO WORK WITHIN THE RULES THESE DAYS...
I DO ALEX, YES...
SO, I WANTED TO RUN SOMETHING PAST YOU AS AN OLD FRIEND... I'VE INVITED MIKE DAWS FROM YOUR BANK TO GO GROUSE SHOOTING... NOW, AS YOU HAVE POWER OF VETO OVER WHAT HOSPITALITY HE CAN ACCEPT... I WAS WONDERING...
OH I GET YOUR DRIFT...
alex@alexcartoon.com
I THOUGHT IF YOU COULD SEE YOUR WAY, MAYBE WE COULD BEND THE RULES A LITTLE?
HA! OKAY, NO PROBLEM... SAY NO MORE...
TAP TAP
SO YOU THINK HE GOT THE MESSAGE ABOUT ALLOWING MIKE TO ACCEPT THE INVITE?
OH YES.
ALEX HAS TIPPED ME OFF TO DISALLOW MIKE'S INVITE AT THE LAST MINUTE SO HE CAN INVITE ME AS HIS PERSONAL FRIEND INSTEAD...
THAT OLD RUSE?

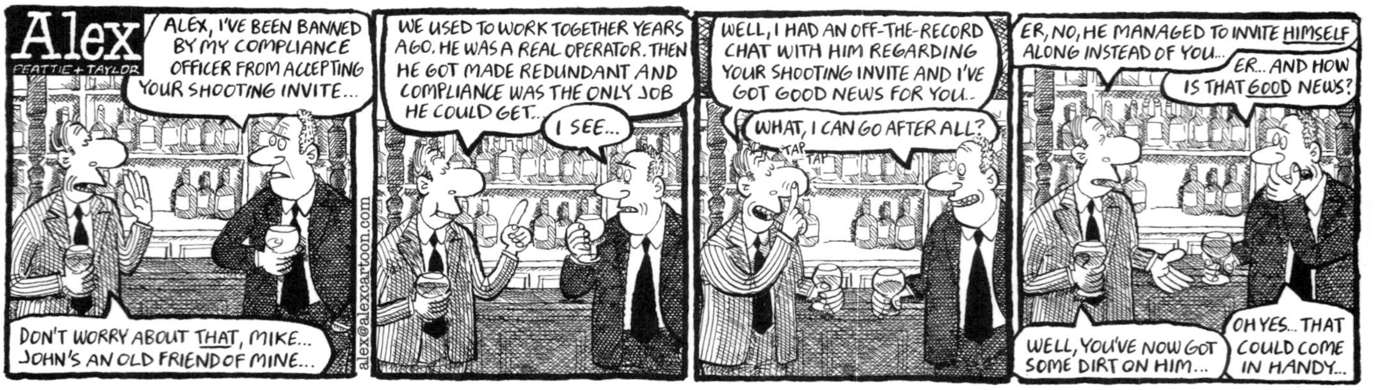
Alex
BEATTIE + TAYLOR
ALEX, I'VE BEEN BANNED BY MY COMPLIANCE OFFICER FROM ACCEPTING YOUR SHOOTING INVITE...
DON'T WORRY ABOUT THAT, MIKE... JOHN'S AN OLD FRIEND OF MINE...
WE USED TO WORK TOGETHER YEARS AGO. HE WAS A REAL OPERATOR. THEN HE GOT MADE REDUNDANT AND COMPLIANCE WAS THE ONLY JOB HE COULD GET...
I SEE...
alex@alexcartoon.com
WELL, I HAD AN OFF-THE-RECORD CHAT WITH HIM REGARDING YOUR SHOOTING INVITE AND I'VE GOT GOOD NEWS FOR YOU...
WHAT, I CAN GO AFTER ALL?
TAP TAP
ER, NO, HE MANAGED TO INVITE HIMSELF ALONG INSTEAD OF YOU...
ER... AND HOW IS THAT GOOD NEWS?
WELL, YOU'VE NOW GOT SOME DIRT ON HIM...
OH YES... THAT COULD COME IN HANDY...

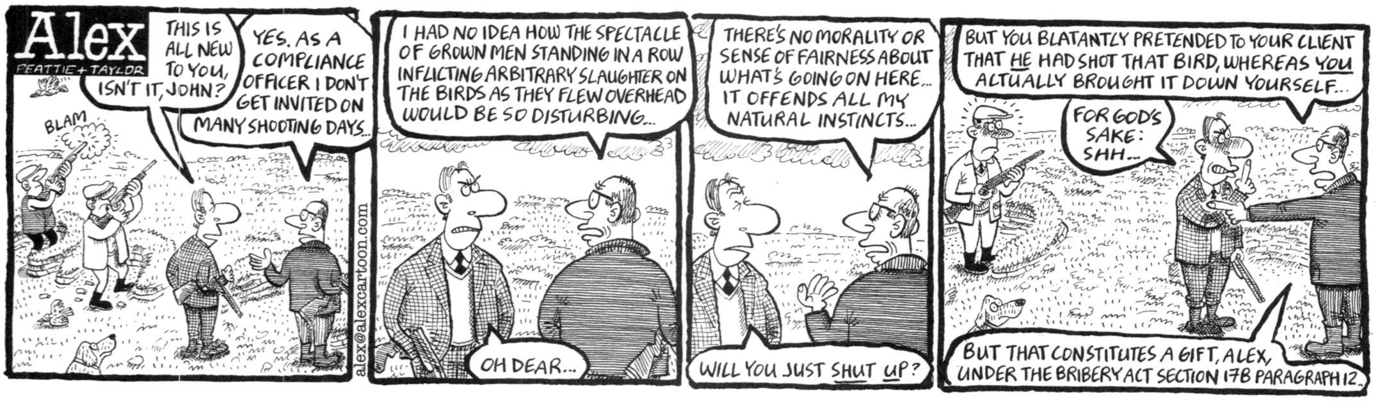
Alex
PEATTIE + TAYLOR
THIS IS ALL NEW TO YOU, ISN'T IT, JOHN?
YES. AS A COMPLIANCE OFFICER I DON'T GET INVITED ON MANY SHOOTING DAYS...
BLAM
alex@alexcartoon.com
I HAD NO IDEA HOW THE SPECTACLE OF GROWN MEN STANDING IN A ROW INFLICTING ARBITRARY SLAUGHTER ON THE BIRDS AS THEY FLEW OVERHEAD WOULD BE SO DISTURBING...
OH DEAR...
THERE'S NO MORALITY OR SENSE OF FAIRNESS ABOUT WHAT'S GOING ON HERE... IT OFFENDS ALL MY NATURAL INSTINCTS...
WILL YOU JUST SHUT UP?
BUT YOU BLATANTLY PRETENDED TO YOUR CLIENT THAT HE HAD SHOT THAT BIRD, WHEREAS YOU ACTUALLY BROUGHT IT DOWN YOURSELF...
FOR GOD'S SAKE: SHH...
BUT THAT CONSTITUTES A GIFT, ALEX, UNDER THE BRIBERY ACT SECTION 17B PARAGRAPH 12...

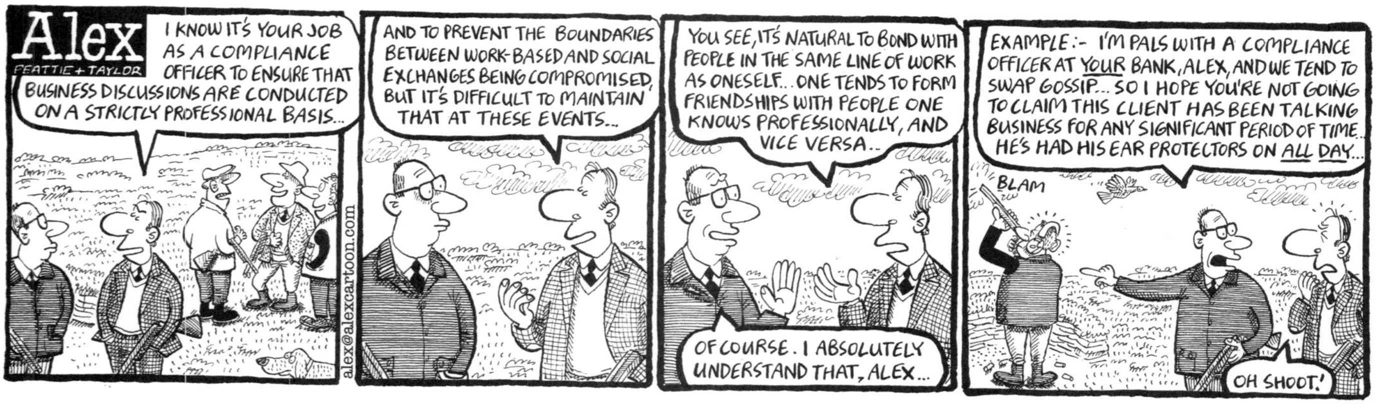
Alex
PEATTIE + TAYLOR
I KNOW IT'S YOUR JOB AS A COMPLIANCE OFFICER TO ENSURE THAT BUSINESS DISCUSSIONS ARE CONDUCTED ON A STRICTLY PROFESSIONAL BASIS...
alex@alexcartoon.com
AND TO PREVENT THE BOUNDARIES BETWEEN WORK-BASED AND SOCIAL EXCHANGES BEING COMPROMISED, BUT IT'S DIFFICULT TO MAINTAIN THAT AT THESE EVENTS...
YOU SEE, IT'S NATURAL TO BOND WITH PEOPLE IN THE SAME LINE OF WORK AS ONESELF... ONE TENDS TO FORM FRIENDSHIPS WITH PEOPLE ONE KNOWS PROFESSIONALLY, AND VICE VERSA...
OF COURSE. I ABSOLUTELY UNDERSTAND THAT, ALEX...
EXAMPLE:- I'M PALS WITH A COMPLIANCE OFFICER AT YOUR BANK, ALEX, AND WE TEND TO SWAP GOSSIP... SO I HOPE YOU'RE NOT GOING TO CLAIM THIS CLIENT HAS BEEN TALKING BUSINESS FOR ANY SIGNIFICANT PERIOD OF TIME. HE'S HAD HIS EAR PROTECTORS ON ALL DAY...
BLAM
OH SHOOT!

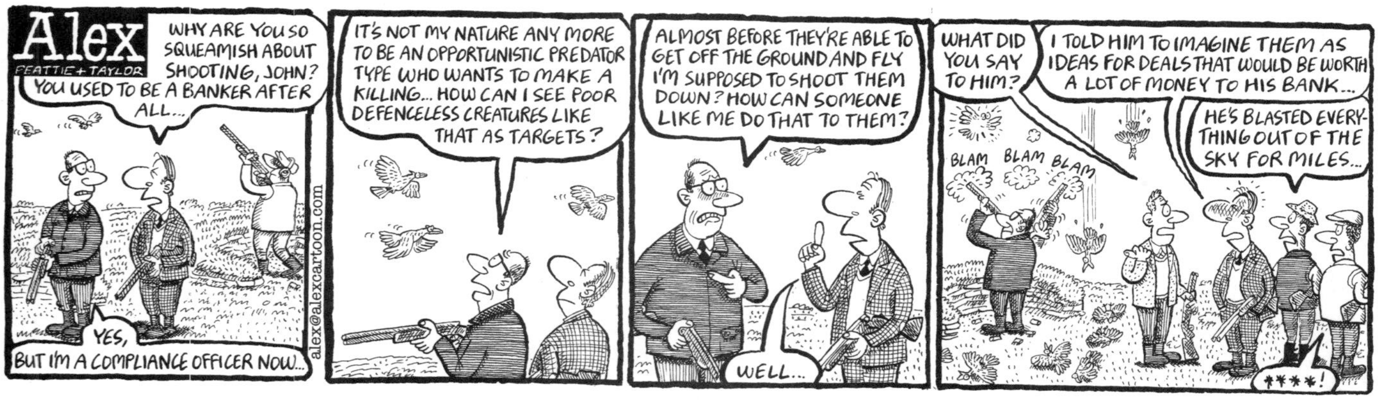
Alex
PEATTIE + TAYLOR
WHY ARE YOU SO SQUEAMISH ABOUT SHOOTING, JOHN? YOU USED TO BE A BANKER AFTER ALL...
YES, BUT I'M A COMPLIANCE OFFICER NOW...
alex@alexcartoon.com
IT'S NOT MY NATURE ANY MORE TO BE AN OPPORTUNISTIC PREDATOR TYPE WHO WANTS TO MAKE A KILLING... HOW CAN I SEE POOR DEFENCELESS CREATURES LIKE THAT AS TARGETS?
ALMOST BEFORE THEY'RE ABLE TO GET OFF THE GROUND AND FLY I'M SUPPOSED TO SHOOT THEM DOWN? HOW CAN SOMEONE LIKE ME DO THAT TO THEM?
WELL...
WHAT DID YOU SAY TO HIM?
I TOLD HIM TO IMAGINE THEM AS IDEAS FOR DEALS THAT WOULD BE WORTH A LOT OF MONEY TO HIS BANK...
HE'S BLASTED EVERYTHING OUT OF THE SKY FOR MILES...
BLAM BLAM BLAM
****!

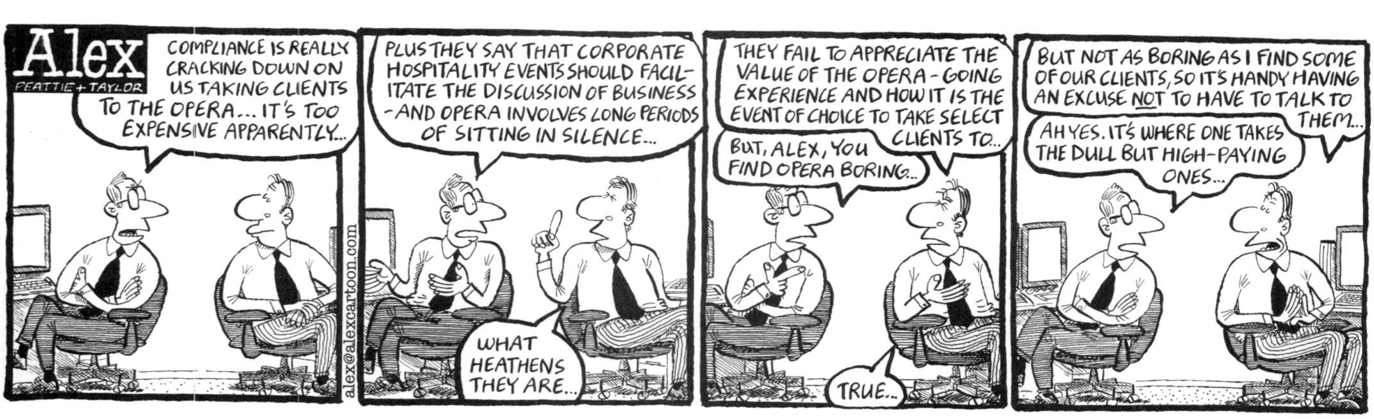
Alex
PEATTIE + TAYLOR
COMPLIANCE IS REALLY CRACKING DOWN ON US TAKING CLIENTS TO THE OPERA... IT'S TOO EXPENSIVE APPARENTLY...
alex@alexcartoon.com
PLUS THEY SAY THAT CORPORATE HOSPITALITY EVENTS SHOULD FACILITATE THE DISCUSSION OF BUSINESS - AND OPERA INVOLVES LONG PERIODS OF SITTING IN SILENCE...
WHAT HEATHENS THEY ARE...
THEY FAIL TO APPRECIATE THE VALUE OF THE OPERA-GOING EXPERIENCE AND HOW IT IS THE EVENT OF CHOICE TO TAKE SELECT CLIENTS TO...
BUT, ALEX, YOU FIND OPERA BORING...
TRUE...
BUT NOT AS BORING AS I FIND SOME OF OUR CLIENTS, SO IT'S HANDY HAVING AN EXCUSE NOT TO HAVE TO TALK TO THEM...
AH YES. IT'S WHERE ONE TAKES THE DULL BUT HIGH-PAYING ONES...

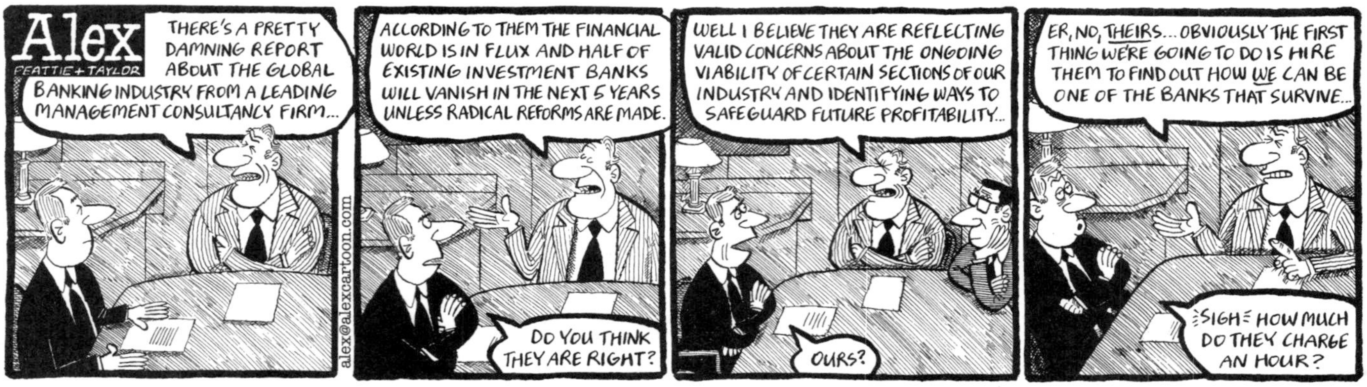
Alex
PEATTIE + TAYLOR
THERE'S A PRETTY DAMNING REPORT ABOUT THE GLOBAL BANKING INDUSTRY FROM A LEADING MANAGEMENT CONSULTANCY FIRM...
alex@alexcartoon.com
ACCORDING TO THEM THE FINANCIAL WORLD IS IN FLUX AND HALF OF EXISTING INVESTMENT BANKS WILL VANISH IN THE NEXT 5 YEARS UNLESS RADICAL REFORMS ARE MADE.
DO YOU THINK THEY ARE RIGHT?
WELL I BELIEVE THEY ARE REFLECTING VALID CONCERNS ABOUT THE ONGOING VIABILITY OF CERTAIN SECTIONS OF OUR INDUSTRY AND IDENTIFYING WAYS TO SAFEGUARD FUTURE PROFITABILITY...
OURS?
ER, NO, THEIRS... OBVIOUSLY THE FIRST THING WE'RE GOING TO DO IS HIRE THEM TO FIND OUT HOW WE CAN BE ONE OF THE BANKS THAT SURVIVE...
SIGH HOW MUCH DO THEY CHARGE AN HOUR?

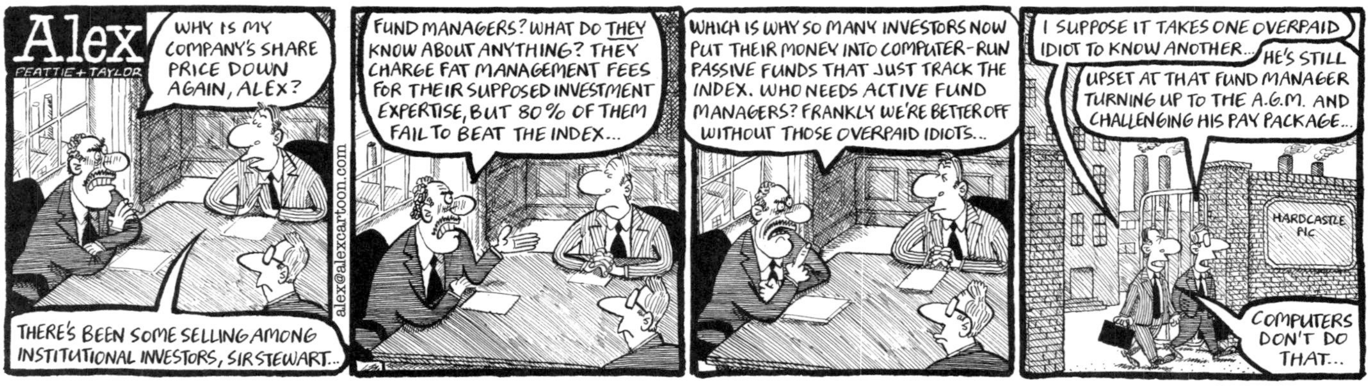
Alex
PEATTIE + TAYLOR
WHY IS MY COMPANY'S SHARE PRICE DOWN AGAIN, ALEX?
THERE'S BEEN SOME SELLING AMONG INSTITUTIONAL INVESTORS, SIR STEWART...
alex@alexcartoon.com
FUND MANAGERS? WHAT DO THEY KNOW ABOUT ANYTHING? THEY CHARGE FAT MANAGEMENT FEES FOR THEIR SUPPOSED INVESTMENT EXPERTISE, BUT 80% OF THEM FAIL TO BEAT THE INDEX...
WHICH IS WHY SO MANY INVESTORS NOW PUT THEIR MONEY INTO COMPUTER-RUN PASSIVE FUNDS THAT JUST TRACK THE INDEX. WHO NEEDS ACTIVE FUND MANAGERS? FRANKLY WE'RE BETTER OFF WITHOUT THOSE OVERPAID IDIOTS...
I SUPPOSE IT TAKES ONE OVERPAID IDIOT TO KNOW ANOTHER...
HE'S STILL UPSET AT THAT FUND MANAGER TURNING UP TO THE A.G.M. AND CHALLENGING HIS PAY PACKAGE...
HARDCASTLE PLC
COMPUTERS DON'T DO THAT...

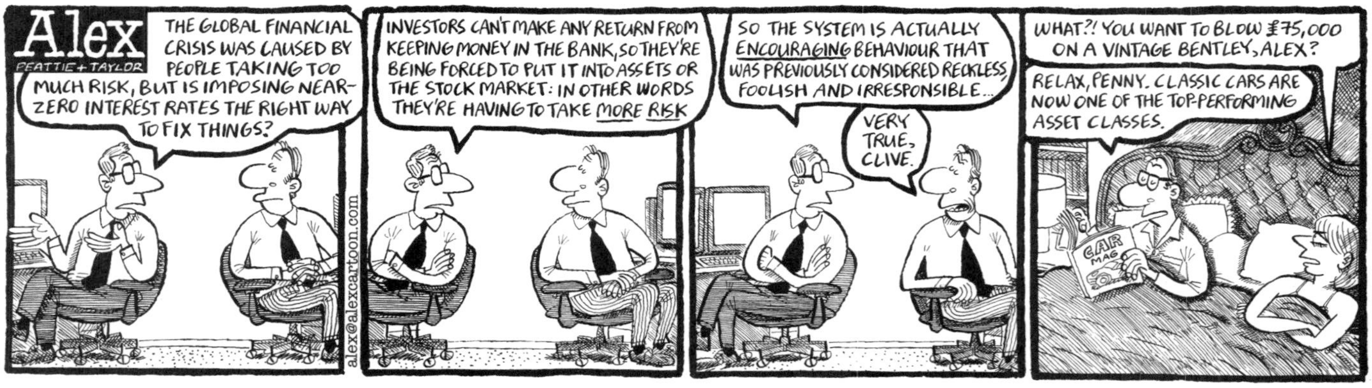
Alex
PEATTIE + TAYLOR
THE GLOBAL FINANCIAL CRISIS WAS CAUSED BY PEOPLE TAKING TOO MUCH RISK, BUT IS IMPOSING NEAR-ZERO INTEREST RATES THE RIGHT WAY TO FIX THINGS?
alex@alexcartoon.com
INVESTORS CAN'T MAKE ANY RETURN FROM KEEPING MONEY IN THE BANK, SO THEY'RE BEING FORCED TO PUT IT INTO ASSETS OR THE STOCK MARKET: IN OTHER WORDS THEY'RE HAVING TO TAKE MORE RISK
SO THE SYSTEM IS ACTUALLY ENCOURAGING BEHAVIOUR THAT WAS PREVIOUSLY CONSIDERED RECKLESS, FOOLISH AND IRRESPONSIBLE...
VERY TRUE, CLIVE.
WHAT?! YOU WANT TO BLOW £75,000 ON A VINTAGE BENTLEY, ALEX?
RELAX, PENNY. CLASSIC CARS ARE NOW ONE OF THE TOP-PERFORMING ASSET CLASSES.
CAR MAG

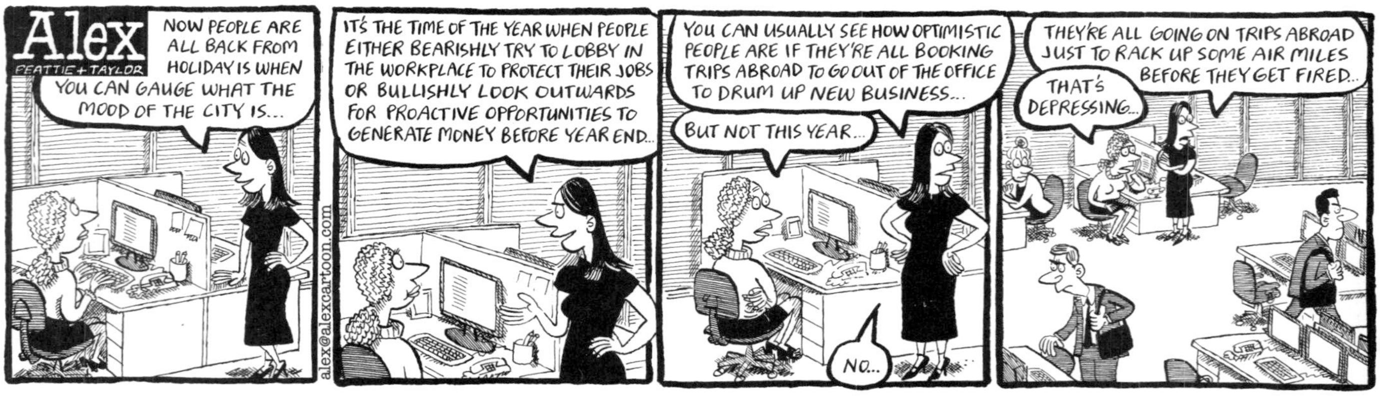
Alex
PEATTIE + TAYLOR
NOW PEOPLE ARE ALL BACK FROM HOLIDAY IS WHEN YOU CAN GAUGE WHAT THE MOOD OF THE CITY IS...
alex@alexcartoon.com
IT'S THE TIME OF THE YEAR WHEN PEOPLE EITHER BEARISHLY TRY TO LOBBY IN THE WORKPLACE TO PROTECT THEIR JOBS OR BULLISHLY LOOK OUTWARDS FOR PROACTIVE OPPORTUNITIES TO GENERATE MONEY BEFORE YEAR END...
YOU CAN USUALLY SEE HOW OPTIMISTIC PEOPLE ARE IF THEY'RE ALL BOOKING TRIPS ABROAD TO GO OUT OF THE OFFICE TO DRUM UP NEW BUSINESS...
BUT NOT THIS YEAR...
NO...
THEY'RE ALL GOING ON TRIPS ABROAD JUST TO RACK UP SOME AIR MILES BEFORE THEY GET FIRED...
THAT'S DEPRESSING...

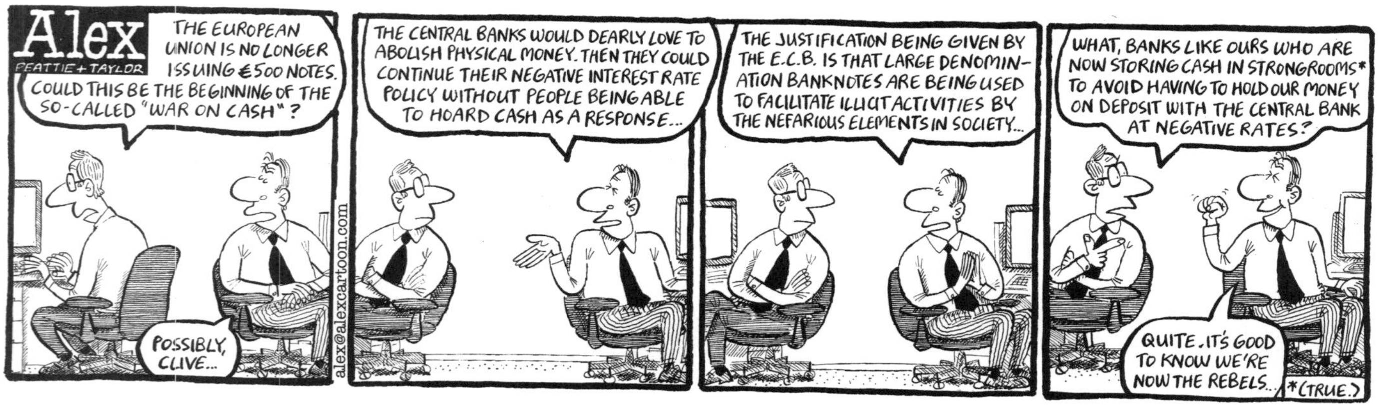
Alex
PEATTIE + TAYLOR
THE EUROPEAN UNION IS NO LONGER ISSUING €500 NOTES. COULD THIS BE THE BEGINNING OF THE SO-CALLED "WAR ON CASH"?
POSSIBLY, CLIVE...
alex@alexcartoon.com
THE CENTRAL BANKS WOULD DEARLY LOVE TO ABOLISH PHYSICAL MONEY. THEN THEY COULD CONTINUE THEIR NEGATIVE INTEREST RATE POLICY WITHOUT PEOPLE BEING ABLE TO HOARD CASH AS A RESPONSE...
THE JUSTIFICATION BEING GIVEN BY THE E.C.B. IS THAT LARGE DENOMINATION BANKNOTES ARE BEING USED TO FACILITATE ILLICIT ACTIVITIES BY THE NEFARIOUS ELEMENTS IN SOCIETY...
WHAT, BANKS LIKE OURS WHO ARE NOW STORING CASH IN STRONGROOMS* TO AVOID HAVING TO HOLD OUR MONEY ON DEPOSIT WITH THE CENTRAL BANK AT NEGATIVE RATES?
QUITE. IT'S GOOD TO KNOW WE'RE NOW THE REBELS...
*(TRUE.)

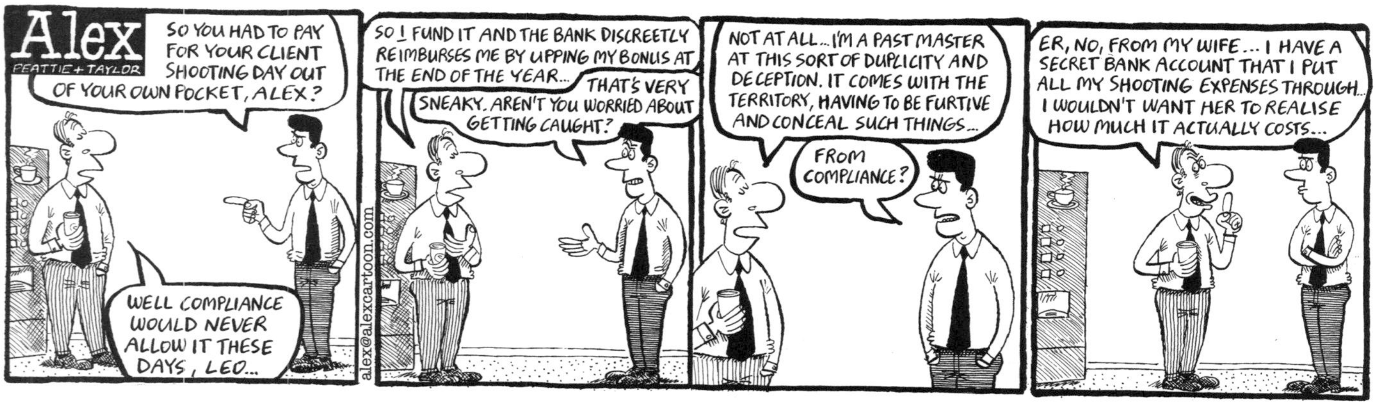
Alex
PEATTIE + TAYLOR
SO YOU HAD TO PAY FOR YOUR CLIENT SHOOTING DAY OUT OF YOUR OWN POCKET, ALEX?
WELL COMPLIANCE WOULD NEVER ALLOW IT THESE DAYS, LEO...
alex@alexcartoon.com
SO I FUND IT AND THE BANK DISCREETLY REIMBURSES ME BY UPPING MY BONUS AT THE END OF THE YEAR...
THAT'S VERY SNEAKY. AREN'T YOU WORRIED ABOUT GETTING CAUGHT?
NOT AT ALL... I'M A PAST MASTER AT THIS SORT OF DUPLICITY AND DECEPTION. IT COMES WITH THE TERRITORY, HAVING TO BE FURTIVE AND CONCEAL SUCH THINGS...
FROM COMPLIANCE?
ER, NO, FROM MY WIFE... I HAVE A SECRET BANK ACCOUNT THAT I PUT ALL MY SHOOTING EXPENSES THROUGH... I WOULDN'T WANT HER TO REALISE HOW MUCH IT ACTUALLY COSTS...

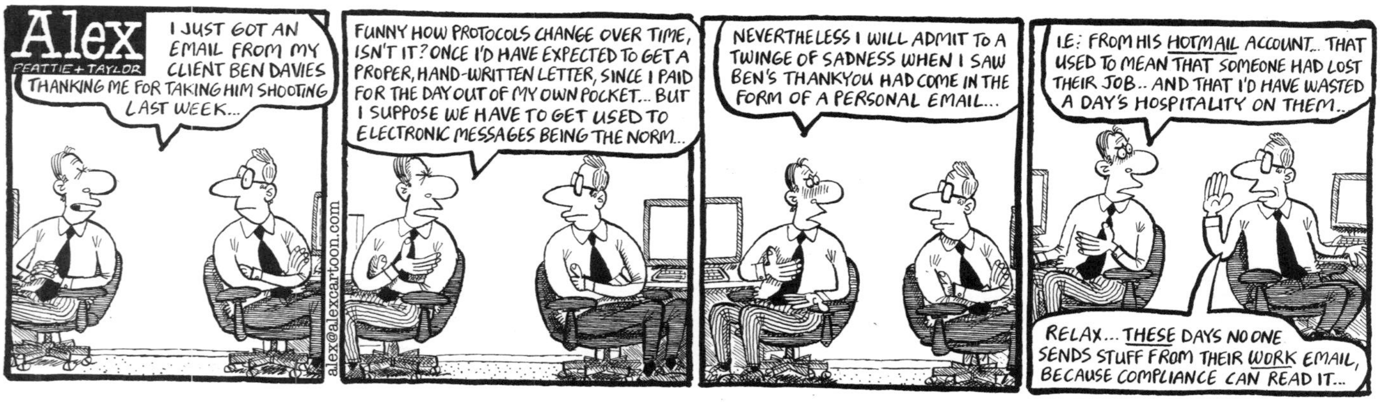
Alex
PEATTIE + TAYLOR
I JUST GOT AN EMAIL FROM MY CLIENT BEN DAVIES THANKING ME FOR TAKING HIM SHOOTING LAST WEEK...
alex@alexcartoon.com
FUNNY HOW PROTOCOLS CHANGE OVER TIME, ISN'T IT? ONCE I'D HAVE EXPECTED TO GET A PROPER, HAND-WRITTEN LETTER, SINCE I PAID FOR THE DAY OUT OF MY OWN POCKET... BUT I SUPPOSE WE HAVE TO GET USED TO ELECTRONIC MESSAGES BEING THE NORM...
NEVERTHELESS I WILL ADMIT TO A TWINGE OF SADNESS WHEN I SAW BEN'S THANKYOU HAD COME IN THE FORM OF A PERSONAL EMAIL...
I.E. FROM HIS HOTMAIL ACCOUNT... THAT USED TO MEAN THAT SOMEONE HAD LOST THEIR JOB.. AND THAT I'D HAVE WASTED A DAY'S HOSPITALITY ON THEM...
RELAX... THESE DAYS NO ONE SENDS STUFF FROM THEIR WORK EMAIL, BECAUSE COMPLIANCE CAN READ IT...

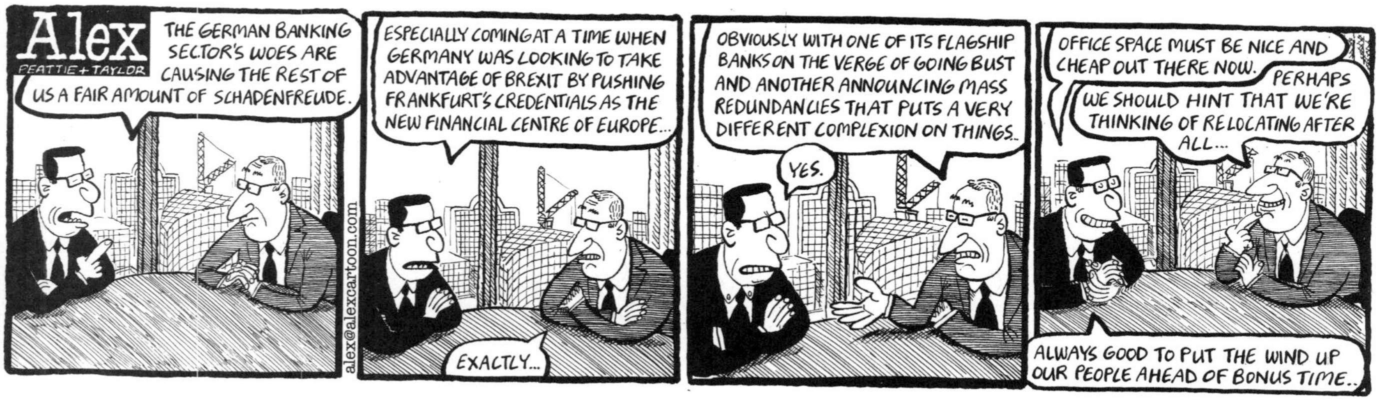
Alex
PEATTIE + TAYLOR
THE GERMAN BANKING SECTOR'S WOES ARE CAUSING THE REST OF US A FAIR AMOUNT OF SCHADENFREUDE.
alex@alexcartoon.com
ESPECIALLY COMING AT A TIME WHEN GERMANY WAS LOOKING TO TAKE ADVANTAGE OF BREXIT BY PUSHING FRANKFURT'S CREDENTIALS AS THE NEW FINANCIAL CENTRE OF EUROPE...
EXACTLY...
OBVIOUSLY WITH ONE OF ITS FLAGSHIP BANKS ON THE VERGE OF GOING BUST AND ANOTHER ANNOUNCING MASS REDUNDANCIES THAT PUTS A VERY DIFFERENT COMPLEXION ON THINGS..
YES.
OFFICE SPACE MUST BE NICE AND CHEAP OUT THERE NOW.
PERHAPS WE SHOULD HINT THAT WE'RE THINKING OF RELOCATING AFTER ALL...
ALWAYS GOOD TO PUT THE WIND UP OUR PEOPLE AHEAD OF BONUS TIME...

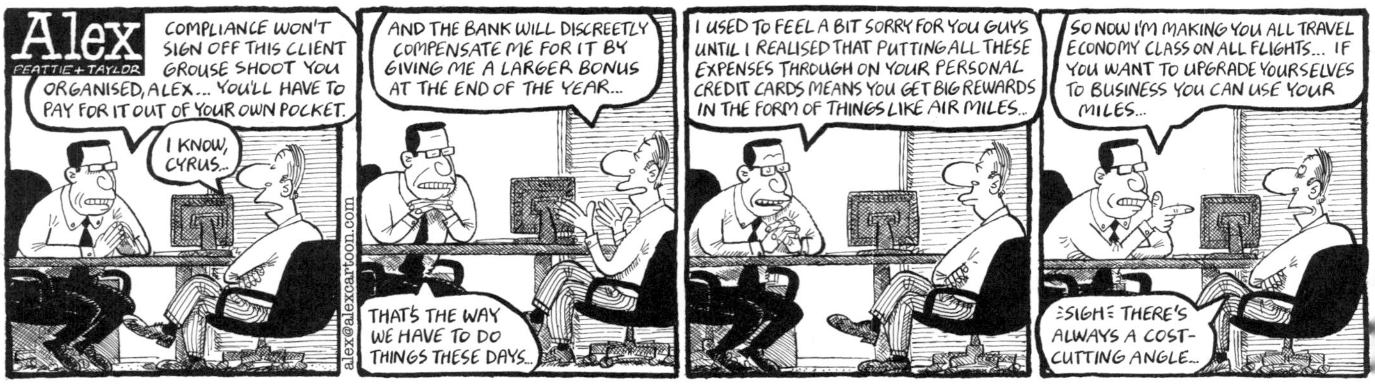
Alex
PEATTIE + TAYLOR
COMPLIANCE WON'T SIGN OFF THIS CLIENT GROUSE SHOOT YOU ORGANISED, ALEX... YOU'LL HAVE TO PAY FOR IT OUT OF YOUR OWN POCKET.
I KNOW, CYRUS...
alex@alexcartoon.com
AND THE BANK WILL DISCREETLY COMPENSATE ME FOR IT BY GIVING ME A LARGER BONUS AT THE END OF THE YEAR...
THAT'S THE WAY WE HAVE TO DO THINGS THESE DAYS...
I USED TO FEEL A BIT SORRY FOR YOU GUYS UNTIL I REALISED THAT PUTTING ALL THESE EXPENSES THROUGH ON YOUR PERSONAL CREDIT CARDS MEANS YOU GET BIG REWARDS IN THE FORM OF THINGS LIKE AIR MILES...
SO NOW I'M MAKING YOU ALL TRAVEL ECONOMY CLASS ON ALL FLIGHTS... IF YOU WANT TO UPGRADE YOURSELVES TO BUSINESS YOU CAN USE YOUR MILES...
SIGH THERE'S ALWAYS A COST-CUTTING ANGLE...

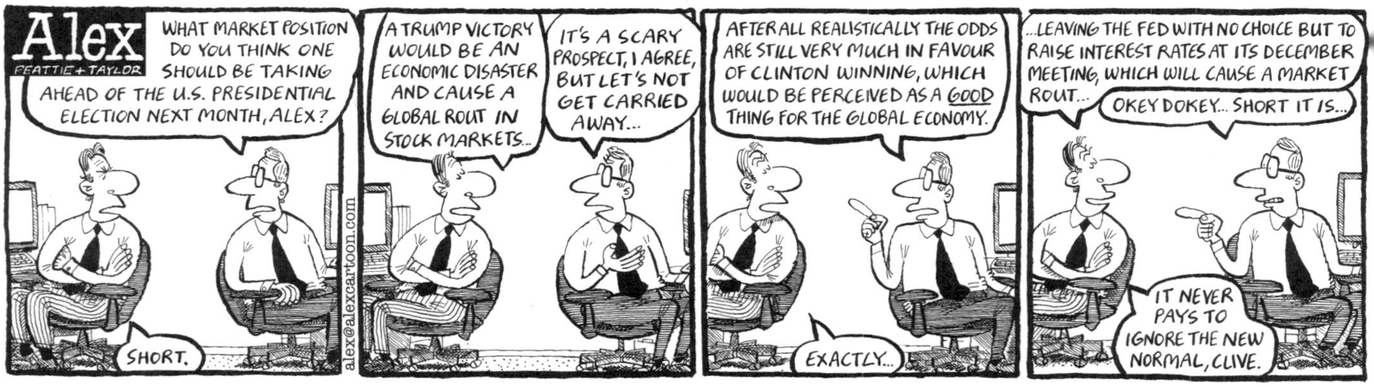
Alex
PEATTIE + TAYLOR
WHAT MARKET POSITION DO YOU THINK ONE SHOULD BE TAKING AHEAD OF THE U.S. PRESIDENTIAL ELECTION NEXT MONTH, ALEX?
SHORT.
alex@alexcartoon.com
A TRUMP VICTORY WOULD BE AN ECONOMIC DISASTER AND CAUSE A GLOBAL ROUT IN STOCK MARKETS...
IT'S A SCARY PROSPECT, I AGREE, BUT LET'S NOT GET CARRIED AWAY...
AFTER ALL REALISTICALLY THE ODDS ARE STILL VERY MUCH IN FAVOUR OF CLINTON WINNING, WHICH WOULD BE PERCEIVED AS A GOOD THING FOR THE GLOBAL ECONOMY.
EXACTLY...
...LEAVING THE FED WITH NO CHOICE BUT TO RAISE INTEREST RATES AT ITS DECEMBER MEETING, WHICH WILL CAUSE A MARKET ROUT...
OKEY DOKEY... SHORT IT IS...
IT NEVER PAYS TO IGNORE THE NEW NORMAL, CLIVE.

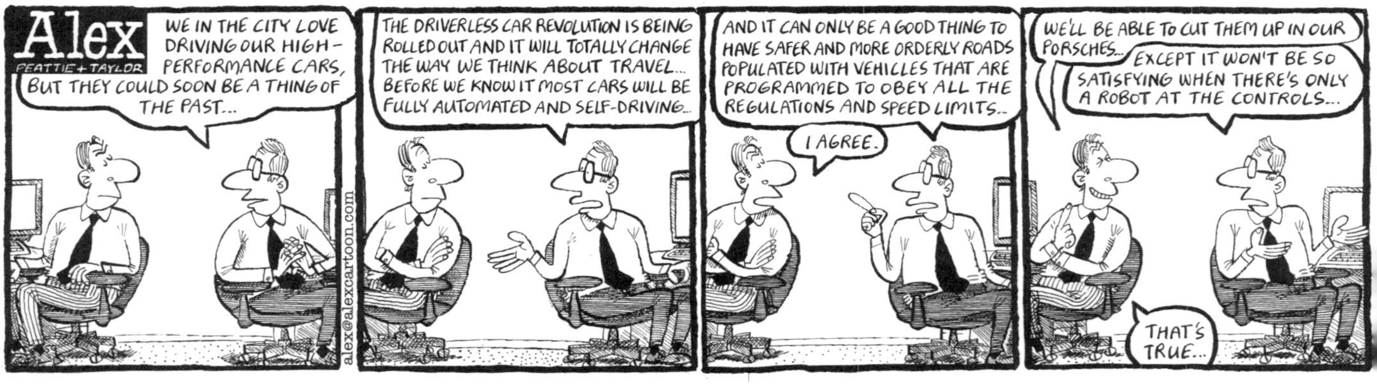
Alex
PEATTIE + TAYLOR
WE IN THE CITY LOVE DRIVING OUR HIGH-PERFORMANCE CARS, BUT THEY COULD SOON BE A THING OF THE PAST...
alex@alexcartoon.com
THE DRIVERLESS CAR REVOLUTION IS BEING ROLLED OUT AND IT WILL TOTALLY CHANGE THE WAY WE THINK ABOUT TRAVEL... BEFORE WE KNOW IT MOST CARS WILL BE FULLY AUTOMATED AND SELF-DRIVING...
AND IT CAN ONLY BE A GOOD THING TO HAVE SAFER AND MORE ORDERLY ROADS POPULATED WITH VEHICLES THAT ARE PROGRAMMED TO OBEY ALL THE REGULATIONS AND SPEED LIMITS...
I AGREE.
WE'LL BE ABLE TO CUT THEM UP IN OUR PORSCHES...
EXCEPT IT WON'T BE SO SATISFYING WHEN THERE'S ONLY A ROBOT AT THE CONTROLS...
THAT'S TRUE...

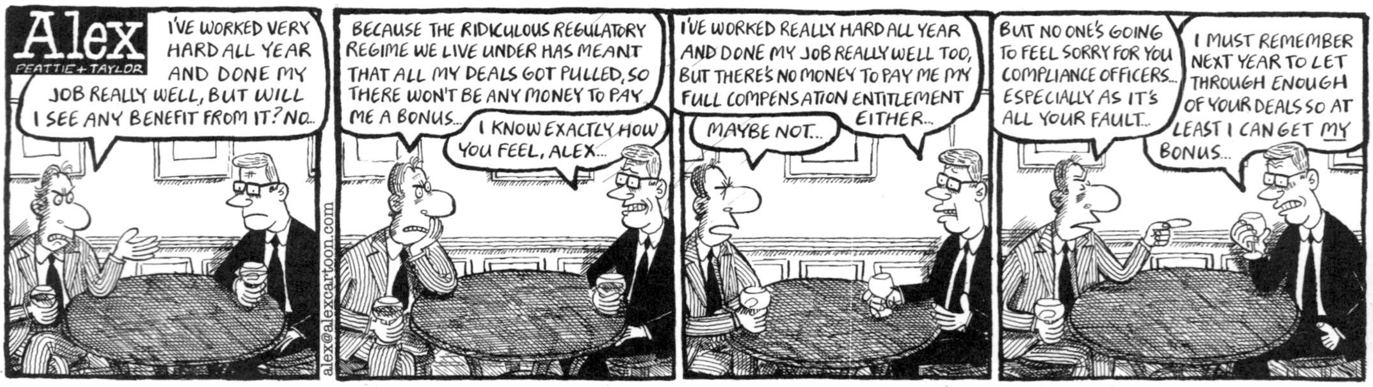
Alex
PEATTIE + TAYLOR
I'VE WORKED VERY HARD ALL YEAR AND DONE MY JOB REALLY WELL, BUT WILL I SEE ANY BENEFIT FROM IT? NO...
alex@alexcartoon.com
BECAUSE THE RIDICULOUS REGULATORY REGIME WE LIVE UNDER HAS MEANT THAT ALL MY DEALS GOT PULLED, SO THERE WON'T BE ANY MONEY TO PAY ME A BONUS...
I KNOW EXACTLY HOW YOU FEEL, ALEX...
I'VE WORKED REALLY HARD ALL YEAR AND DONE MY JOB REALLY WELL TOO, BUT THERE'S NO MONEY TO PAY ME MY FULL COMPENSATION ENTITLEMENT EITHER...
MAYBE NOT...
BUT NO ONE'S GOING TO FEEL SORRY FOR YOU COMPLIANCE OFFICERS... ESPECIALLY AS IT'S ALL YOUR FAULT...
I MUST REMEMBER NEXT YEAR TO LET THROUGH ENOUGH OF YOUR DEALS SO AT LEAST I CAN GET MY BONUS...

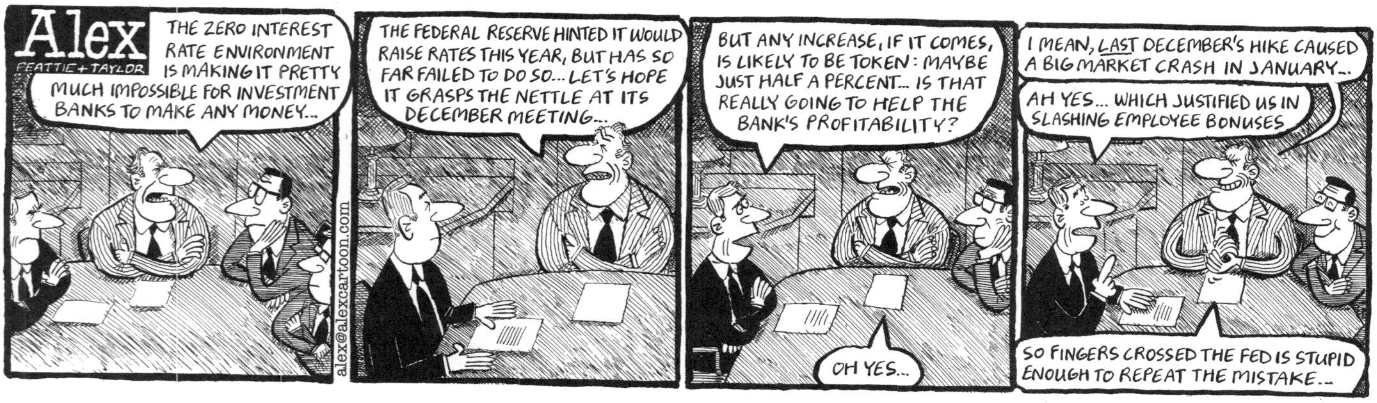
Alex
PEATTIE + TAYLOR
THE ZERO INTEREST RATE ENVIRONMENT IS MAKING IT PRETTY MUCH IMPOSSIBLE FOR INVESTMENT BANKS TO MAKE ANY MONEY...
alex@alexcartoon.com
THE FEDERAL RESERVE HINTED IT WOULD RAISE RATES THIS YEAR, BUT HAS SO FAR FAILED TO DO SO... LET'S HOPE IT GRASPS THE NETTLE AT ITS DECEMBER MEETING...
BUT ANY INCREASE, IF IT COMES, IS LIKELY TO BE TOKEN: MAYBE JUST HALF A PERCENT... IS THAT REALLY GOING TO HELP THE BANK'S PROFITABILITY?
OH YES...
I MEAN, LAST DECEMBER'S HIKE CAUSED A BIG MARKET CRASH IN JANUARY...
AH YES... WHICH JUSTIFIED US IN SLASHING EMPLOYEE BONUSES
SO FINGERS CROSSED THE FED IS STUPID ENOUGH TO REPEAT THE MISTAKE...

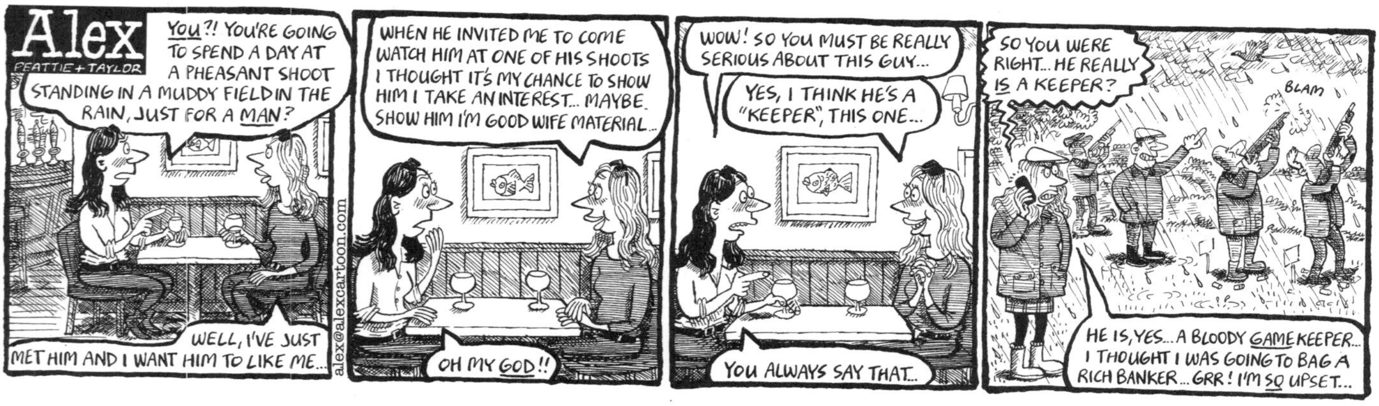
Alex
PEATTIE + TAYLOR
YOU?! YOU'RE GOING TO SPEND A DAY AT A PHEASANT SHOOT STANDING IN A MUDDY FIELD IN THE RAIN, JUST FOR A MAN?
WELL, I'VE JUST MET HIM AND I WANT HIM TO LIKE ME...
alex@alexcartoon.com
WHEN HE INVITED ME TO COME WATCH HIM AT ONE OF HIS SHOOTS I THOUGHT IT'S MY CHANCE TO SHOW HIM I TAKE AN INTEREST... MAYBE SHOW HIM I'M GOOD WIFE MATERIAL...
OH MY GOD!!
WOW! SO YOU MUST BE REALLY SERIOUS ABOUT THIS GUY...
YES, I THINK HE'S A "KEEPER", THIS ONE...
YOU ALWAYS SAY THAT...
SO YOU WERE RIGHT... HE REALLY IS A KEEPER?
BLAM
HE IS, YES... A BLOODY GAMEKEEPER... I THOUGHT I WAS GOING TO BAG A RICH BANKER... GRR! I'M SO UPSET...

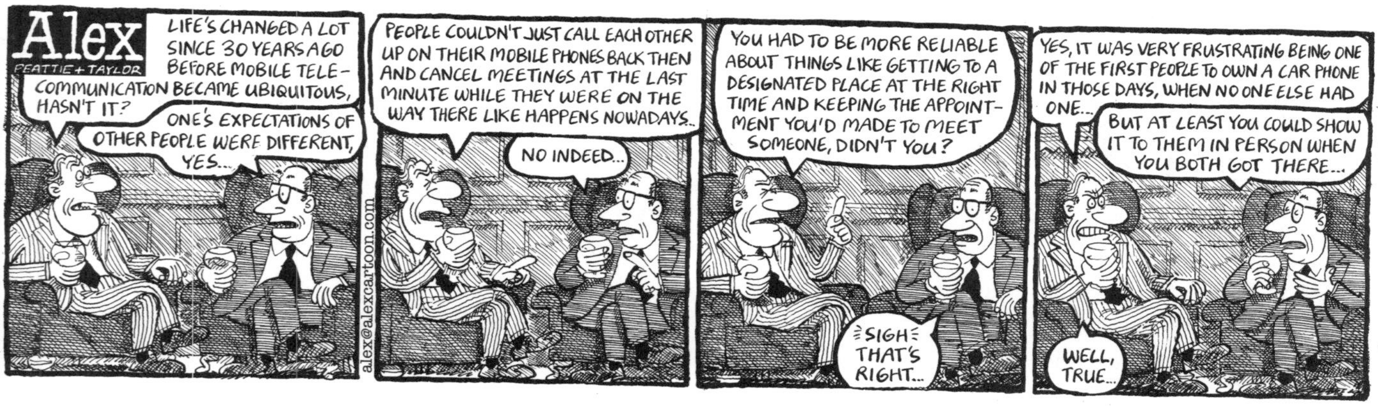
Alex
PEATTIE + TAYLOR
LIFE'S CHANGED A LOT SINCE 30 YEARS AGO BEFORE MOBILE TELE-COMMUNICATION BECAME UBIQUITOUS, HASN'T IT?
ONE'S EXPECTATIONS OF OTHER PEOPLE WERE DIFFERENT, YES...
alex@alexcartoon.com
PEOPLE COULDN'T JUST CALL EACH OTHER UP ON THEIR MOBILE PHONES BACK THEN AND CANCEL MEETINGS AT THE LAST MINUTE WHILE THEY WERE ON THE WAY THERE LIKE HAPPENS NOWADAYS...
NO INDEED...
YOU HAD TO BE MORE RELIABLE ABOUT THINGS LIKE GETTING TO A DESIGNATED PLACE AT THE RIGHT TIME AND KEEPING THE APPOINT-MENT YOU'D MADE TO MEET SOMEONE, DIDN'T YOU?
SIGH THAT'S RIGHT...
YES, IT WAS VERY FRUSTRATING BEING ONE OF THE FIRST PEOPLE TO OWN A CAR PHONE IN THOSE DAYS, WHEN NO ONE ELSE HAD ONE...
BUT AT LEAST YOU COULD SHOW IT TO THEM IN PERSON WHEN YOU BOTH GOT THERE...
WELL, TRUE...

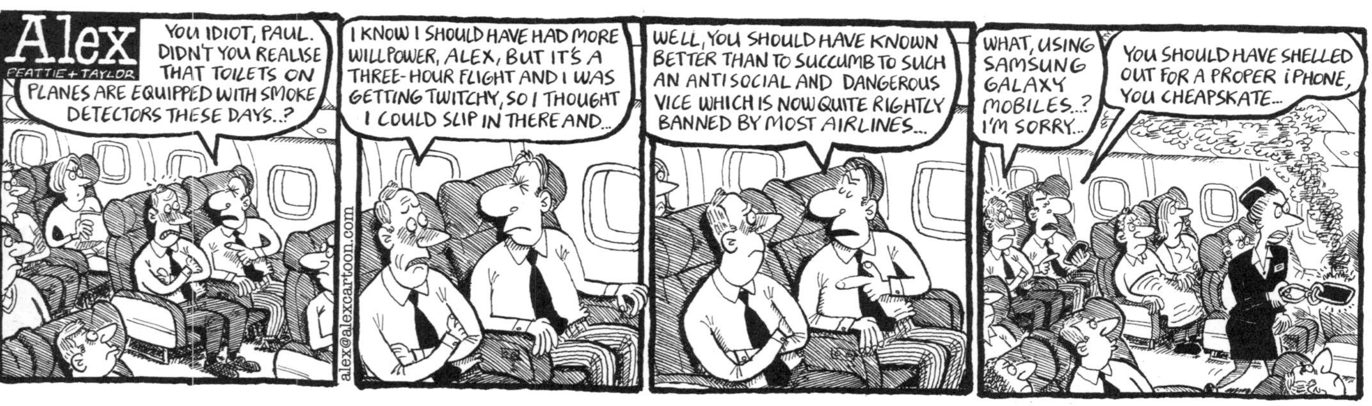
Alex
PEATTIE + TAYLOR
YOU IDIOT, PAUL. DIDN'T YOU REALISE THAT TOILETS ON PLANES ARE EQUIPPED WITH SMOKE DETECTORS THESE DAYS..?
alex@alexcartoon.com
I KNOW I SHOULD HAVE HAD MORE WILLPOWER, ALEX, BUT IT'S A THREE-HOUR FLIGHT AND I WAS GETTING TWITCHY, SO I THOUGHT I COULD SLIP IN THERE AND...
WELL, YOU SHOULD HAVE KNOWN BETTER THAN TO SUCCUMB TO SUCH AN ANTI SOCIAL AND DANGEROUS VICE WHICH IS NOW QUITE RIGHTLY BANNED BY MOST AIRLINES...
WHAT, USING SAMSUNG GALAXY MOBILES..? I'M SORRY...
YOU SHOULD HAVE SHELLED OUT FOR A PROPER iPHONE, YOU CHEAPSKATE...

Also available from Masterley Publishing

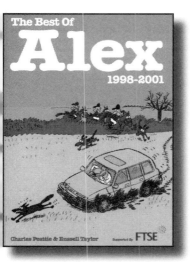

The Best Of
Alex
1998-2001
Charles Peattie & Russell Taylor
FTSE

The Best of Alex 1998 - 2001
Boom to bust via the dotcom bubble.

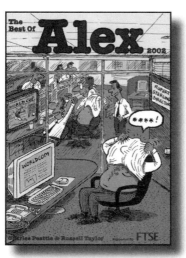

The Best Of
Alex
2002
WORLDCOM
****!
Charles Peattie & Russell Taylor
FTSE

The Best of Alex 2002
Scandals rock the corporate world.

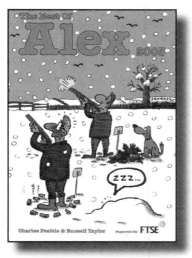

The Best Of
Alex
2003
ZZZ...
Charles Peattie & Russell Taylor
FTSE

The Best of Alex 2003
Alex gets made redundant.

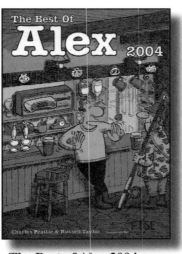

The Best Of
Alex
2004
Charles Peattie & Russell Taylor

The Best of Alex 2004
And gets his job back.

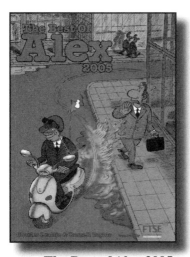

The Best Of
Alex
2005
FTSE

The Best of Alex 2005
Alex has problems with the French.

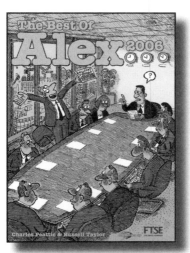

The Best Of
Alex
2006
?
Charles Peattie & Russell Taylor
FTSE

The Best of Alex 2006
Alex gets a new American boss.

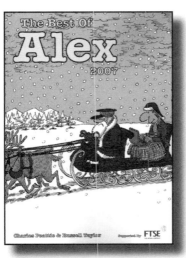

The Best Of
Alex
2007
Charles Peattie & Russell Taylor
FTSE

The Best of Alex 2007
Alex restructures Christmas.

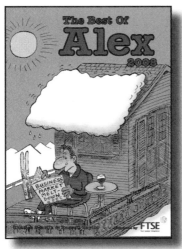

The Best Of
Alex
2008
BUSINESS
MARKET MELT-DOWN
FTSE

The Best of Alex 2008
The credit crunch bites

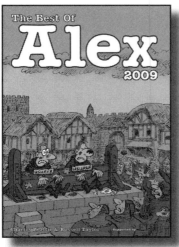

The Best Of
Alex
2009
Charles Peattie & Russell Taylor

The Best of Alex 2009
Global capitalism self-destructs.

The Best Of
Alex
2010
POST CARDS
TWITTER
FACE BOOK
Charles Peattie & Russell Taylor
FTSE

The Best of Alex 2010
Somehow the City lurches on.

The Best Of
Alex 2011
GOLD
Charles Peattie & Russell Taylor

The Best of Alex 2011
The financial crisis continues.

The Best Of
Alex 2012
OLYMPICS COVERAGE
Charles Peattie & Russell Taylor

The Best of Alex 2012
The Olympics come to London.

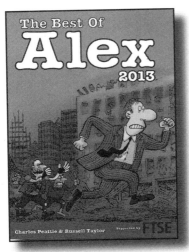

The Best Of
Alex
2013
Charles Peattie & Russell Taylor
FTSE

The Best of Alex 2013
It's a wonderful crisis.

The Best Of
Alex
2014
CLICK
Charles Peattie & Russell Taylor
FTSE

The Best of Alex 2014
The 'New Normal' takes hold.

The Best Of
Alex 2015
COMPLIANCE DECLARATION
Charles Peattie & Russell Taylor
FTSE

The Best of Alex 2015
Compliance rules the roost.

Celeb
The Original Gary Bloke From
PRIVATE EYE
Charles Peattie and Mark Warren

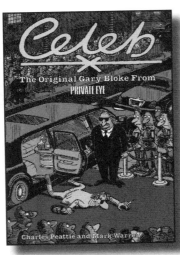

Celeb
Wrinkly rock star Gary Bloke.

Cartoon originals and prints
All our cartoon originals are for sale. They measure 4 x 14 inches. Prints are also available.
All originals and prints are signed by the creators.

For further details on prices and delivery charges for books, cartoons or merchandise:
Tel: +44 (0)1491 871 894
Email: alex@alexcartoon.com
Web: www.alexcartoon.com
Twitter: @alexmasterley